STUDYING THE NOVICE PROGRAMMER

Edited by

ELLIOT SOLOWAY
JAMES C. SPOHRER

University of Michigan

Psychology Press
Taylor & Francis Group

New York   London

First Published by
Lawrence Erlbaum Associates, Inc., Publishers
365 Broadway
Hillsdale, New Jersey 07642

Transferred to Digital Printing 2009 by Psychology Press
270 Madison Ave, New York NY 10016
27 Church Road, Hove, East Sussex, BN3 2FA

Library of Congress Cataloging-in-Publication Data

Studying the novice programmer / edited by Elliot Soloway, James C.
    Spohrer.
        p.   cm.
    Bibliography: p.
    Includes indexes.
    ISBN 0-8058-0002-6
    ISBN 0-8058-0003-4 (pbk)
        1. Microcomputers — Programming — Psychological aspects.
    I. Soloway, Elliot.   II. Spohrer, James C.
        QA76.6.S882   1988   88–24586
    005.26'019 — dc19   CIP

Publisher's Note
The publisher has gone to great lengths to ensure the quality of this reprint
but points out that some imperfections in the original may be apparent.

CONTENTS

SECTION I:
EARLY WORK

It is quite appropriate to begin a book on novice programmers with two papers by Seymour Papert. Papert, more than any other, challenged educators of the early 70's to begin thinking creatively about the potential of computers in the classroom. Two of his main messages to educators were:

1. Have children use computers to do more than just add numbers; make computers that children can use to do interesting things.
2. Do not focus on teaching programming as a job skill. Instead, use computers and programming as a vehicle for teaching thinking.

The two papers in this section deal with these two issues.

In "Twenty Things To Do With A Computer", Papert and Solomon attempt to stretch the imaginations of educators by presenting exciting ways for children to use computers. Instead of routine numeric calculations, the authors present projects like controlling real and simulated robots with sensors and effectors that can draw pictures and move around a room; other projects include generating music, poetry, animations, and videogames. Reading this paper that was written 15 years ago will certainly leave the reader with many questions. For instance, fifteen years later, how do we measure up? Are students provided the opportunity to work on projects as varied as these, or are they still mainly learning how to use the computer to write programs that perform simple numeric calculations? What new projects could we add to the list today, given advances like low cost text-to-speech systems? Has the availability of application software for composing music, drawing pictures, making posters, designing toys, etc. had an effect on the type of computer courses being offered to students?

In the second paper, "Teaching Children Thinking", Papert argues that computation is the richest known source for providing children better things to do and better ways to think about themselves doing those things. By providing children with interesting things to do and helping them to think about what they are doing, Papert believes children will become skilled thinkers. Computers and programming are important both because they provide so many opportunities for intrinsically motivating activities, and also because writing programs can concretize and elucidate algorithmic ways of thinking. Building models, developing formal systems to elucidate seemingly complex patterns and behaviors, as well as creating and controlling environments are all things that children can be taught to do with the aid of computers. Case histories of children using computers at school illustrate how the children learn about thinking skills through programming projects.

1

TWENTY THINGS TO DO WITH A COMPUTER

SEYMOUR PAPERT
CYNTHIA SOLOMON
Artificial Intelligence Laboratory
Massachusetts Institute of Technology

When people talk about computers in education they do not all have the same image in mind. Some think of using the computer to program the kid; others think of using the kid to program the computer. But most of them have at least this in common; the transaction between the computer and the kid will be some kind of "conversation" or "questions and answers" in words or numbers.

In the real world, computers are used in many different ways. Some are programmed to fly airplanes — not to *tell* a human pilot what to do, but to pull the levers with their own electro-mechanical effectors and to read the altitudes, airspeeds and what-not with their own electronic sensing devices. Computers are programmed to generate music or to condition dogs by ringing bells and delivering meat powder while the modern-day Pavlov is happily asleep. Some computers are programmed to control lathes and milling machines in industrial plants; others generate pictures for animated film cartoons.

Why then should computers in schools be confined to computing the sum of the squares of the first twenty-odd numbers and similar so-called problem-solving uses? Why not use them to produce some action? There is no better reason than the intellectual timidity of the computers-in-education community, which seems remarkably reluctant to use the computers for any purpose that fails to look very much like something that has been taught in schools for the past centuries. This is all the more remarkable since the computerists are custodians of a momentous intellectual and technological revolution. Concepts from the sciences of computation — "cybernetics," "information theory," "artificial intelligence" and all its other names — have deeply affected thinking in biology, psychology and even the philosophy of mathematics. Machines from its engineering branches are changing our way of life. How strange, then, that "computers in education" should so often reduce to "using bright new gadgets to teach the same old stuff in thinly disguised versions of the same old way."

Our purpose here, however, is not to complain of what other people have not done, but to tell of some exciting things you can do with the computer you have now or with the one you will be incited to get by the pages that follow. More than half the suggestions we are about to make have been implemented and tested in our elementary school teaching program. This does not imply that they are not of equal or greater value at other levels of education; on the contrary, we are convinced that they give a glimpse of the proper way to introduce *everyone*—whatever age and whatever level of academic performance—to programming, to more general knowledge of computation and, indeed (we say courageously steeling ourselves for the onslaught), to mathematics, to physics and to all formal subjects including linguistics and music.

Each section of this article describes something one can do with a computer. Most of these "things to do" assume that your computer can spin motors, activate electromagnets, switch lights, read the state of light-sensitive cells and so on. The amazing fact is that it is very easy to make your computer do all these things! The last section of this article says something about how to make it do so if it doesn't already. While reading the article you need not (and should not, it is a distraction) think about how the commands we describe will produce their effects. As you read on you will be learning a computer language called LOGO. In order to use a computer language, you do not need to know how the computer works—no more than you would need to know how a human brain works in order to give a person instructions. In both cases you need only know how to describe what you want in an appropriate language.

MAKE A TURTLE

Figure 1 shows one of our turtles—so named in honor of a famous species of cybernetic animal made by Grey Walter, an English neurophysiologist. Grey Walter's turtle had life-like behavior patterns built into its wiring diagram. Ours have no behavior except the ability to obey a few simple commands from a computer to which they are attached by a wire that plugs into a control-box that connects to a telephone line that speaks to the computer, which thinks it is talking to a teletype so that no special system programming is necessary to make the computer talk to the turtle. (If you'd

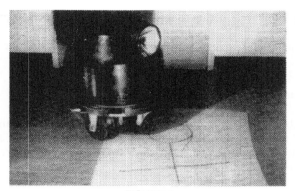

FIGURE 1

like to make a fancier turtle, you might use a radio link. But we'd like turtles to be cheap enough for every kid to play with one.)

The turtle can send signals back to the computer. These signals appear to the computer just like the signals from a teletype — so, again, no special system programming is necessary to make a turtle talk to a computer. Where do the signals come from? They are generated by sense organs attached to the turtle. Our turtles do not have a fixed set of sense organs. Rather, they have inlets into which one can plug wires to attach any sense organs one is clever enough to make. Touch sensors, light-sensitive cells and sound detectors are obvious examples that require very little cleverness. Accelerometers and tilt detectors lead to more sophisticated fun.

Turtles can have effector organs as well. The activities described here use only a simple one — a pen located at the turtle's center, which can be lowered to leave a trace of the turtle's path, thus turning it into a remarkable geometric instrument.

PROGRAM THE TURTLE TO DRAW A MAN

A bad way to use a turtle is to know just which character symbols will cause the turtle's motors to move. A better way is to design a good language. This means deciding on a set of intelligible commands and building these into the computer language. For example, we can type LEFT 90 on the console keyboard and thereby cause the turtle to rotate 90° about its central axis in the left (i.e., counter-clockwise) direction. Obviously this is better than having to figure, every time one wants to use the turtle, the number of steps of the stepping motors one needs to produce the desired movement and writing a complicated instruction to send out control characters to produce these steps.

The following diagram explains the main commands in our turtle language.

Turtle Language

At any time the turtle is at a particular *place* and facing in a particular *direction*. The place and direction together are the turtle's geometric *state*. The picture shows the turtle in a field, used here only to give the reader a frame of reference:

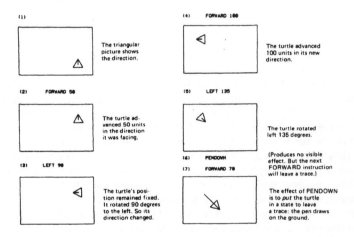

To make the computer do anything more complicated you have to write a program. For example (using our language, LOGO, in a way that should be self-explanatory), one might type into the computer the following definition:

TO says that a definition follows.

```
TO   DRAW :DISTANCE
1    FORWARD :DISTANCE
2    BACK :DISTANCE
END
```

DRAW is the command being defined.

:DISTANCE says that the command will have an input and that in the definition its name will be "DISTANCE."

Now if we type the command DRAW 100 the computer will say to itself, "How do I DRAW?" Well, the definition says, "TO DRAW 100, first go forward 100 units, then go back 100 units and that's all." So if the turtle is in PENDOWN state it will draw a line and come back to its starting position. Now, using DRAW as a sub-procedure, let's give the computer a new command VEE, by typing the following definition:

```
TO  VEE :SIZE
1    LEFT 50
2    DRAW :SIZE
3    RIGHT 100
4    DRAW :SIZE
5    LEFT 50
END
```

A defined command can be used in defining new commands just as if it were a primitive LOGO term like FORWARD or LEFT.

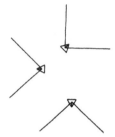

The command VEE 100 will now cause the turtle to draw V's as shown in the figures. The starting and finishing positions of the turtle are shown by the usual triangle.

Now

```
TO  MAN :SIZE
1    VEE :SIZE
2    RIGHT 180
3    FORWARD :SIZE
4    VEE :SIZE
5    FORWARD :SIZE/2
```

We now use the previously defined command in making our new command. In other words DRAW is a sub-procedure of VEE; VEE is a sub-procedure of MAN.

MAN 100 will draw

MAN 20 will draw

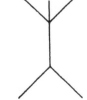

Here are some other drawings the fifth grade kids made the turtle draw.

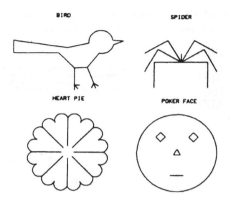

TURTLE BIOLOGY

To make the turtle more like a living creature we must give it behavior patterns. This involves using sense organs. A well-conceived turtle should be very flexible in this respect: instead of fixed sense organs like real animals, it should have a number of sockets (we find that eight is good) into which you can plug any on-off device such as a micro-switch, or light detector or whatever you think up. Such devices are easy and cheap to make.

Let's give the turtle a ridiculously simple piece of behavior based on using four touch sensors which we shall call FRONTTOUCH, BACKTOUCH, LEFT-TOUCH and RIGHTTOUCH. The behavior consists of going straight ahead until it touches the wall, turning back and so on. (The "and so on" illustrates the need for "loops" or "recursion" in the procedure we are about to write. To prepare yourself for the concept, consider the plight of a person who never fails to keep a promise and who has been tricked into saying, "I promise to repeat what I have just said.")

```
TO   MARCH
1    TEST FRONTTOUCH
2    IFTRUE RIGHT 180
3    FORWARD 1
4    MARCH
END
```

The TEST will be "TRUE" if FRONTTOUCH is "TRUE"; i.e., if the front touch sensor is activated.

IFTRUE depends on the TEST. The turtle does an about face if the front touch sensor is touching the wall.

In any case the turtle takes a little step forward.

MARCH is the name of this procedure. It is also used as a command in the procedure. This is recursion. When the computer gets this, it starts to carry out the directions on how to MARCH. So, it starts again at line 1.

The next definition explains this idea in a way that might be clearer for people who are used to another style of programming. It also illustrates some flexibility in LOGO by showing other LOGO idioms to express the same idea:

```
TO  MARCH
1    IF FRONTTOUCH RIGHT 180
2    FORWARD 1
3    GO 1
END
```

This is equivalent to lines 1 and 2 above.

"GO 1" instructs the computer to go to line 1.

A more interesting behavior is to go to the wall and circumnavigate the room. Getting the turtle to find the wall is easy: just as in MARCH. To make it follow the wall we use the important concept of *feedback*. The idea is this. Imagine yourself walking next to a wall on your left *with your eyes closed*. Every now and then you put out your left hand. If it does not touch the wall, you say to yourself, "I'm wandering into space, better turn left a little." If you do feel the wall you say (slightly perversely), "Maybe I'm getting too close, better turn right a little." The result is that you will follow the wall perhaps in a slightly wavy line.

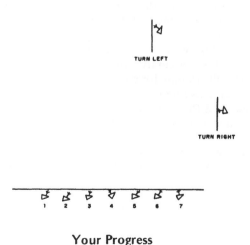

TURN LEFT

TURN RIGHT

Your Progress

Interestingly, this procedure would make you circumnavigate a house walking on the outside. Watch what happens at the corner:

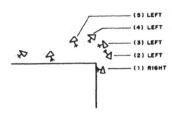

To circumnavigate the room from the inside one could use FRONTTOUCH to know when to turn. A small extension of the procedure could enable the turtle to find a door and escape from the room, or to explore a maze.

Using light sensors one can imitate a moth's flight to the candle, and cause turtles to pursue one another or to engage in dances or fights.

MAKE A DISPLAY TURTLE

In our fifth-grade class a turtle that walks on the floor is called a "turtle turtle." Another kind is called a "display turtle." This kind exists on a "scope" (i.e., cathode ray tube; a TV-like screen) as a picture just like the triangle we have used to illustrate the same commands, leaving a line of light as a trace when given the command PENDOWN. The disadvantage of the display turtle is that it cannot move physically about the world, touching, pushing and playing, but it has advantages for some purposes. One is that it is very fast and accurate. Another is that one can command it to draw a line which will last only for a stated length of time — say, a tenth of a second. Thus it can make moving pictures.

In LOGO the command PEN :NUMBER causes all lines to appear for :NUMBER tenths of a second. Thus PEN 10 makes all lines last a second before vanishing.

The command FLY will cause a bird to move across the screen if the following procedure has been written, as well as the procedure BIRD, which draws a bird.

```
TO  FLY
10  PEN 2
20  BIRD
30  FORWARD 5
40  WAIT 2
50  FLY
END
```

This procedure draws a bird. The picture of the bird will last 0.2 seconds.

It waits 0.2 seconds. By this time the bird has vanished.

This causes the whole action to repeat as the machine gives itself the command FLY.

PLAY SPACEWAR

Spacewar is a famous computer game invented at Massachusetts Institute of Technology in the days when display programming was new and unusual. Two people play it. On the "scope" appear two spaceships, together with background frills such as stars, the sun, etc. There are two players; each controls a spaceship and may cause it to turn, go forward or shoot out a stream of rockets. Whoever destroys the other ship wins. The excitement of the game is increased by such dangers as getting caught by the sun's gravity and vanishing in a brilliant explosion.

When our fifth grade class visited M.I.T., they were caught up by the fun of playing the game. (It really is orders of magnitude better than non-computerized pin-tables.) Unlike most people, our children could go back to school the next day and get caught up by the even greater fun of programming their own versions of spacewar.

DIFFERENTIAL GEOMETRY

The "turtle language" provides a very remarkable formal system for describing many geometric objects; we think it is vastly superior to Cartesian coordinates as an introductory path into geometry. To see this let's study a very simple procedure, known in our fifth grade class as POLY. In its simplest form POLY has two inputs called "STEP" and "ANGLE." In LOGO it is written:

```
TO   POLY :STEP :ANGLE
1    FORWARD :STEP
2    LEFT :ANGLE
3    POLY :STEP :ANGLE
END
```

The following pictures show the effect of invoking this procedure with different inputs (the first input is the side size; the second is the angle).

DRAW SPIRALS

To change the procedure called POLY so as to draw spirals we make a very small addition to line 3. We can also change the name—but this is, of course, unnecessary.

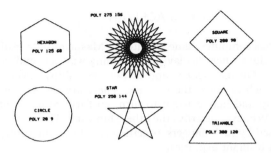

```
TO   POLY :STEP :ANGLE
1    FORWARD :STEP
2    LEFT :ANGLE
3    POLY :STEP :ANGLE
END

TO   POLYSPI :STEP :ANGLE
1    FORWARD :STEP
2    LEFT :ANGLE
3    POLYSPI :STEP+5 :ANGLE
END
```

HAVE A HEART (AND LEARN TO DEBUG)

Making a procedure to draw a heart required the following steps.

Step 1:

Find something like a heart that we know how to make. Idea: a triangle.

```
TO   TRI :SIZE
1    FORWARD :SIZE
2    RIGHT 120
3    FORWARD :SIZE
4    RIGHT 120
5    FORWARD :SIZE
END
```

Step 2:   Make a plan to modify TRI. Idea: Make a procedure TO TOP.

```
TO  TOP :SIZE
1    SEG :SIZE/2
2    RIGHT 180
3    SEG :SIZE/2
END
```

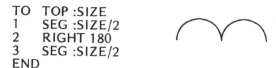

Then replace line 1 in TRI by 1 TOP :SIZE. This is easy but the result is:

HEART WITH BUG

Step 3:   Debug. Trying out this idea produced a bug. Why? Because replacing "FORWARD" by "TOP" in line 1 of TRI has side effects we did not anticipate! (And is therefore typical of almost all good ideas in almost all good projects.) To remedy this we must change line 2 as well; and while we are about it, let's change the name to "HEART1."

```
TO  HEART1 :SIZE
1    TOP :SIZE
2    RIGHT 30
3    FORWARD :SIZE
4    RIGHT 120
5    FORWARD :SIZE
END
```

Step 4:   Consider: is this a good enough abstract model of a heart. No. Let's curve its sides. After a little debugging we get:

```
TO  HEART2 :SIZE
1    TOP :SIZE
2    SEG 2*:SIZE 60
3    RIGHT 60
4    SEG 2*:SIZE 60
END
```

MINITHEOREM: A heart can be made of four circular segments.

GROWFLOWERS

A computer program to draw this flower uses the geometric observation
that petals can be decomposed (rather surprisingly!) as two quarter circles.
So let's asume we have a procedure called TO QCIRCLE whose effect is
shown by the examples. Some of them show initial and final positions of the
turtle, some do not.

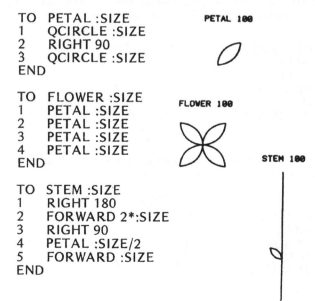

QCIRCLE 50

QCIRCLE 100

Now let's see how to make a petal.

```
TO  PETAL :SIZE              PETAL 100
1   QCIRCLE :SIZE
2   RIGHT 90
3   QCIRCLE :SIZE
END

TO  FLOWER :SIZE            FLOWER 100
1   PETAL :SIZE
2   PETAL :SIZE
3   PETAL :SIZE
4   PETAL :SIZE
END                                    STEM 100

TO  STEM :SIZE
1   RIGHT 180
2   FORWARD 2*:SIZE
3   RIGHT 90
4   PETAL :SIZE/2
5   FORWARD :SIZE
END
```

```
TO   PLANT :SIZE
1    PENDOWN
2    FLOWER :SIZE
3    STEM :SIZE
4    PENUP            PLANT 100
END
```

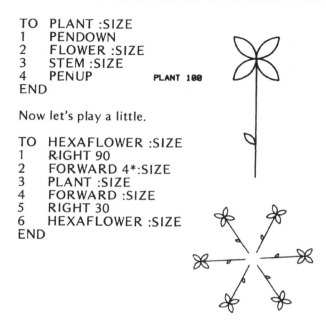

Now let's play a little.

```
TO   HEXAFLOWER :SIZE
1    RIGHT 90
2    FORWARD 4*:SIZE
3    PLANT :SIZE
4    FORWARD :SIZE
5    RIGHT 30
6    HEXAFLOWER :SIZE
END
```

MAKE A MOVIE

We describe how to make a very simple movie, in which the whole plot consists of a flower growing.

A flower can be drawn as well by the physical turtle described in idea number 1 as by a display turtle. Movies need a display turtle. The following commands in LOGO allow us to take advantage of a special feature of CRT drawings — their ability to vanish! We recall that the command PENDOWN causes the turtle to leave a trace. The commands PEN 50 (or PEN 10, etc.) cause a trace that will stay for 50-tenths of a second (or 10-tenths of a second, etc.) and then vanish. The command WIPE causes everything to vanish instantly.

Now let's try making successive frames of our little movie. First we do it by direct commands, rather than writing a new procedure.

```
PENDOWN
PLANT      5
WIPE
PLANT      10
WIPE
PLANT      30 etc.
```

This can be automated slightly by

PEN   50
PLANT   10
PLANT   20
PLANT   30
    .
    ..
    .

PEN 50 causes the picture to vanish after 5 seconds. So WIPE is not needed.

We give the commands PLANT 10, PLANT 20, PLANT 30 immediately after the previous picture vanishes.

To automate the process further we build a procedure around the central action command:

PLANT :SIZE
WAIT 5

A pause of half a second occurs, so that the next round does not rush in before the previous plant is seen. PEN 50 would be chosen to match WAIT 5.

Now make some more exciting movies!

A superprocedure to issue these commands will be called MOVIE. It will make successive frames appear at half-second intervals.

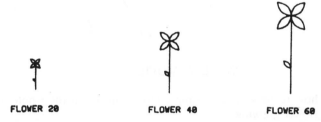

FLOWER 20   FLOWER 40   FLOWER 60

To command itself recursively at any given time, it must know the appropriate input for PLANT. It also needs to know its frame number so as to know when to stop. We notice that remembering the frame number eliminated the need to remember separately the input to PLANT—this is merely the frame number multiplied by 10. So the little movie program is:

```
TO  MOVIE :THISFRAME :ENDFRAME
1    IF :THISFRAME = :ENDFRAME STOP
2    PLANT :THISFRAME*10
3    MOVIE :THISFRAME+1 :ENDFRAME
END
```

The meaning of these inputs is explained below.

We think of a movie as a process. As it goes on we need to know two things: where we are and where we are going. The two inputs are set up for this. The first is :THISFRAME. It starts at 1 and increases by 1 on each round. It is the frame number. The second input remains constant during the showing of the movie.

How to Think about the Inputs

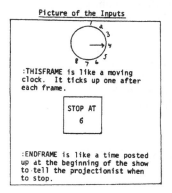

Picture of the Inputs

:THISFRAME is like a moving clock. It ticks up one after each frame.

STOP AT
6

:ENDFRAME is like a time posted up at the beginning of the show to tell the projectionist when to stop.

MAKE A MUSIC BOX AND PROGRAM A TUNE

A music box is a device for making sound under control of a computer. Our style of music box "listens in" to the signals sent by a computer to a teletype. Just as the teletype "decodes" them as instructions to print particular characters, and the turtle decodes them as movements, the music box decodes them as instructions to emit particular sounds. It is only a slight technical frill to give the music box several "voices" that will play simultaneously.

One (very bad) way to make the computer play "Frere Jacques" would be to write the following LOGO procedure:

```
TO  FJ
1    PRINT "AAA!CCC!EEE!AAA!AAA!CCC!EEE!
     AAA!EEE!FFF!HHHHHHHH!EEE!FFF!
     HHHHHHH! . . . "
END
```

A better approach is to program the computer to accept descriptions of music in a good notation. An example is the following, which is one of several we are trying experimentally. (This notation and many of the ideas about the musical aspect of our work is due to Terry Winograd[1] and Jeanne Bamberger.[2])

Our music box can play a five-octave range of notes, with as many as four at a time. One octave is chosen as the base, and its twelve chromatic tones are numbered 1 through 12. Notes in the next octave up can be indicated

---

[1] Assistant professor, Department of Electrical Engineering, M.I.T.
[2] Research associate, Department of Electrical Engineering, M.I.T.

either by continuing beyond 12 or by using the sign "★" Thus 1★ represent the same note. A star preceding a number means "down an octave." The LOGO command SING takes a sequence of notes as input and plays them in order. Thus SING "1 3 5 6 8 10 12 1★" will cause a major scale to be played.

To add rhythm to the tune we use a LOGO operation MUSIC, which takes two inputs—one a sequence of notes, the other a sequence of durations—and combines them in the obvious way.

Now we use LOGO (following Terry Winograd) to write a better "Frere Jacques" procedure.

```
TO  FRERE1
1   SING MUSIC OF "1 3 5 1" "2 2 2 2"
END

TO  FRERE2
1   SING MUSIC "5 6 8" "2 2 4"
END

TO  FRERE3
1   SING MUSIC "8 10 8 6 5 1" "1 1 1 1 2 2"
END

TO  FRERE4
1   SING MUSIC "1★ 8 1" AND "2 2 4"
END

TO  FREREJACQUES
1   FRERE1
2   FRERE1
3   FRERE2
4   FRERE2
5   FRERE3
6   FRERE3
7   FRERE4
8   FRERE4
9   FREREJACQUES
END
```

PLAY WITH SEMI-RANDOM MUSICAL EFFECTS AND THEN TRY SERIOUS COMPOSING

Following Winograd again, we write a procedure, called RANDOMSONG, that will select randomly from a given set of tones. Trying it with different inputs produces very different musical effects. Thus RANDOMSONG "2 4 7 9 11" is described as "oriental," while RANDOMSONG "1 3 5 6 9 11" is described as "spooky."

Then you can try making some effects of your own. And after a while, you may like to write a piece of music with real structure.

Many people would like to try their hand at musical composition, but cannot play well enough to hear their ideas. If you are one of them, this is your chance. The music box is an obedient orchestra that will play precisely whatever you can describe to it.

COMPUTERIZE AN ERECTOR SET CRANE AND BUILD A TOWER OF BLOCKS

A turtle is driven by two motors. Detached from the rest of the turtle the motors can pull strings that can work any mechanism; for example, a crane built of erector set parts.

To pick up objects make a grab—or use an electro-magnet. Make a pile of iron discs, one on top of the other. Program the computer and crane and magnet to play Tower of Hanoi.

MAKE A SUPER LIGHT SHOW

The school computer should have a large number of output ports to allow the computer to switch lights on and off, start tape recorders, actuate slide projectors and start and stop all manner of little machines. There should also be input ports to allow signals to be sent to the computer. We leave to your imagination the possibilities that this opens of making "interactive environments" for the next school festivity or even more solemn purposes.

In a similar spirit, but with a little more work, make an array of light bulbs to display the news of the day like they do it in Times Square. Or generate funny cartoons on the light bulb array. Or put up the scores at ball games and track events.

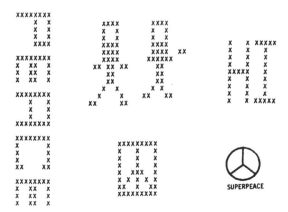

WRITE CONCRETE POETRY

Perhaps we have carried too far our reaction against using computers to write symbols on teletype paper. Here are some examples of teletype output from procedures simple enough for the first weeks of a fifth grade course. We use teletype pictures as an initiation project to learn the very basic principles of using the computer, the terminal, the procedure definition idiom, the ritual for editing procedures and so on. Writing a random sentence generator made a girl exclaim, "So that's why we call words 'nouns' and 'verbs.' " What she meant was: for the first time I see a use for classifying words.

```
THE FUNNY PROF TALKED WHILE THAT
    COOL KID KISSED . . .
SOME FUNNY PROF WALKED BUT A
    BEAUTIFUL KID CLAPPED . . .
A WILD DONKEY KISSED WHILE THE FUNNY
    PROF CLAPPED . . .
SOME GROSS PROF WALKED ALTHOUGH
    SOME COOL KID HUMMED . . .
```

?HAIKU

```
ALL GREEN IN THE TWIGS
I GLIMPSE FAINT BIRDS IN THE COLD
WHIZZ THE SUN HAS CRACKED

ALL CURVED IN THE PEAKS
I SEE CLEAR PEAKS IN THE DUSK
WHIZZ THE FLOWER HAS CRACKED

ALL CURVED IN THE PEAKS
I GLIMPSE DARK TREES IN THE DAWN
WHIRR THE STORM HAS CRACKED
```

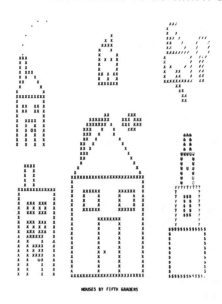

HOUSES BY FIFTH GRADERS

TRY C.A.I. AND PSYCHOLOGY

A slight extension of the sentence generator idea leads to generating mathematical sentences that are *true* (as well as grammatical), though somewhat boring. For example:

```
TO  RANDOMSUM
1   MAKE
        NAME "NUMBER1"
        THING RANDOM
2   MAKE
        NAME "NUMBER2"
        THING RANDOM
3   MAKE
        NAME "SUM"
        THING :NUMBER1 + NUMBER2
4   TYPE (SENTENCE :NUMBER1 "+" :NUMBER2
    "=" :SUM)
5   RANDOMSUM
END
```

The effect is something like

$$7 + 4 = 11$$
$$3 + 2 = \ \ 5$$
$$9 + 6 = 15$$

and so on.

A slight modification will cause the computer to print something like 7 + 4 = ? and wait for a human victim to type something in order to insult him if he fails to give the appropriate answer. For example:

```
7 + 4 = ?                        (Computer)
ELEVEN                           (Victim)
IDIOT, THE ANSWER IS 11          (Computer)
```

Even when the procedure has been modified to accept "ELEVEN" we can still tease the victim:

```
7 + 4 = ?
ELEVEN
DON'T THINK YOU ARE SMART, YOU TOOK
MORE THAN 2 SECONDS.
```

By taking the timing idea more seriously, one can do endless experiments to find out such facts as which multiplications are hardest (for example: 1×1 is very easy, but one might disagree about whether 7×9 is easier than 8×6). Or if one gets bored with teaching arithmetic, one can teach children how to estimate lengths of time, to recognize rhythmic patterns and so on endlessly.

The conclusion from all this is that we have at last discovered the true role of CAI in education. Writing CAI programs is one of the twenty best projects for the first semester of a fifth grade computer science course!

In a similar spirit, it is fun to do "optical illusion" experiments with the display turtle.

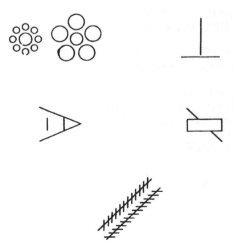

PHYSICS IN THE FINGERTIPS

We begin by inviting the reader to carry out the illustrated experiments — or to recall doing something similar.

One of the goals of this unit of study will be to understand how people do this and particularly to understand what properties of a human being determine what objects he can and what objects he cannot balance.

A "formal physical" model of the stick balancing situation is provided by the apparatus illustrated next:

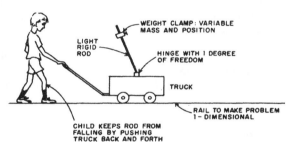

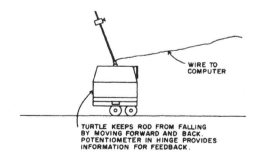

A computer-controlled version replaces the track and the child by a turtle with the angle sensor plugged into its sensor socket. A simple-minded procedure will do a fair amount of balancing (provided that the turtle is fast!):

```
TO  BALANCE
1   TEST ANGLE > 10
2   IFTRUE FORWARD 8
3   TEST ANGLE < -10
4   IFTRUE BACK 8
5   WAIT 1
6   BALANCE
END
```

This procedure is written as part of a project plan that begins by saying: neglect all complications; try something. Complications that have been neglected include:

1. The end of the line bug.
2. The overshoot bug.
   (Perhaps in lines 2 and 4 the value 8 is too much or too little.)
3. *The Wobbly Bug*
   The TEST in the procedure might catch the rod over to the left while it is in rapid motion towards the right. When this happens, we should leave well enough alone!

One by one these bugs, and others, can be eliminated. It is not hard to build a program and choose constants so that with a given setting of the movable weight, balance will be maintained for long periods of time.

Feeding Energy

Again we begin with some fingertip physics by considering some toys:

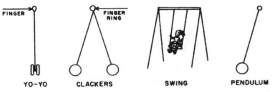

All these systems will run down unless supplied with energy. How is the energy fed in? A good starting system is the clock pendulum on a rigid rod.

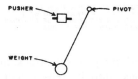

A linear actuator or one of the rotating joints can be used as a "pusher." A simple experiment will show the need for a good phase relationship. When this is understood, proceed to the flexible string and finally the interesting case of the swing in which the source of energy is carried by the pendulum.

A mechanical YO-YO player provides a different setting for similar principles and is an impressive example of a "skill" that can really be achieved quite easily by machines. Moreover, it opens up a huge vista of challenging problems. Causing the YO-YO to SLEEP is a feasible, hard project in our context. The more elaborate tricks like WALKING-THE-DOG or ROUND-THE-WORLD would probably succumb, but would need a lot of work and ingenuity.

EXPLAIN YOURSELF

Building machines to balance sticks did not actually answer the original question about why people can balance broomsticks but not toothbrushes. What property of people determines how long (or short) a stick one can balance? The answer is *reaction time*! Now go back to the balancing machines to give them reaction times similar to those of people (which you will find out by carrying idea number 16 a little further). How good a model can you make of a person? Does this explain you—or at least explain one of your characteristics? Could similar models explain other human characteristics?

PUPPETS

The computer controls enough motors to pull enough strings to manipulate the desired number of marionettes. Like many of these projects, this one has a great educational property: some effect can be obtained by extremely simple means; extra effort will produce more exciting effects; and to emulate a skilled human puppeteer will require a very thorough understanding of the geometric and dynamic principles of movement.

RECURSION LINE

Think up twenty more things to do.

EPILOG: HOW TO MAKE THOSE THINGS HAPPEN

Most of the devices we have mentioned are extremely simple and much cheaper than teletypes. The hardest problem has been getting the computer to communicate with the device. The approach we have developed centers around the concept of a "universal controller." This we define as a black box which looks to the computer like a teletype. So, to use it you would program the computer to print a piece of text which might read "!!(!!(!!(!!(!!(" knowing that the controller will turn "!" and "(" into turtle signals whose effect will be to cause forward and left steps, respectively. Thus any programming language, running on any operating system (including commerical time-sharing services) can be used to control a turtle.

In our image of a school computation laboratory, an important role is played by numerous "controller ports" which allow any student to plug any device into the computer. The ports are protected by fuses and suitable interfaces so that little harm will be done if anyone carelessly puts the main voltage into a computer output port. The laboratory will have a supply of motors, solenoids, relays, sense devices of various kinds, etc. Using them, the students will be able to invent and build an endless variety of cybernetic systems.

This is not the place to discuss strictly practical problems like where to buy good motors. We do, however, expect that very soon someone will supply a full range of suitable things. In any case we would be happy to provide advice and information.

ON THE COST OF COMPUTATION IN SCHOOLS

A final word about the cost of doing all this. Turtles, music boxes, computer-controlled motors and the like are less expensive than teletypes. Displays are slightly more expensive but are becoming rapidly cheaper. If computers are being used in a school, there is no good economic argument for accepting the narrowness of the pure teletype terminal.

Some school administrators and town politicians still consider the cost of using computers at all as too high. If you are engaged in battles on this point, write to LOGO Information[3] to be briefed on the latest ideas and

---

[3] LOGO Information, Artificial Intelligence Laboratory, Massachusetts Institute of Technology, Cambridge, Massachusetts 02139.

prices of equipment. At the moment a good estimate of what computation ought to cost is $30 per student per year, for one hour per student per week of terminal time. This is based on the assumption that several hundred students will be involved. The price could be halved within a year if several hundred schools would commit themselves to installing identical systems. *Only inertia and prejudice, not economics or lack of good educational ideas, stand in the way of providing every child in the world with the kind of experience of which we have tried to give you some glimpses.* If every child were to be given access to a computer, computers would be cheap enough for every child to be given access to a computer.

ACKNOWLEDGMENT

This work was supported by the National Science Foundation under grant No. GJ-1049 and conducted at the Artificial Intelligence Laboratory, a Massachusetts Institute of Technology research program supported in part by the Advanced Research Projects Agency of the Department of Defense and monitored by the Office of Naval Research under contract No. N00014-70-A-0362-0002.

This article has been reprinted by permission of Educational Technology Publications.

2
TEACHING CHILDREN THINKING[1]

SEYMOUR PAPERT
The Artificial Intelligence Laboratory
Massachusetts Institute of Technology

INTRODUCTION

This paper is dedicated to the hope that someone with power to act will one day see that contemporary research on education is like the following experiment by a nineteenth century engineer who worked to demonstrate that engines were better than horses. This he did by hitching a ⅛ HP motor in parallel with his team of four strong stallions. After a year of statistical research he announced a significant difference. However, it was generally thought that there was a Hawthorne effect on the horses . . . the purring of the motor made them pull harder.

The phrase 'technology and education' usually means inventing new gadgets to teach the same old stuff in a thinly disguised version of the same old way. Moreover, if the gadgets are computers, the same old teaching becomes incredibly more expensive and biased towards its dullest parts, namely the kind of rote learning in which measurable results can be obtained by treating the children like pigeons in a Skinner box.

The purpose of this essay is to present a grander vision of an educational system in which technology is used not in the form of machines for processing children but as something the child himself will learn to manipulate, to extend, to apply to projects, thereby gaining a greater and more articulate mastery of the world, a sense of the power of applied knowledge and a self-confidently realistic image of himself as an intellectual

---

[1]This is the major part of a paper delivered to the IFIP Conference on Computer Education in Amsterdam, August 1970, and is published with kind permission of the author.

agent. Stated more simply, I believe with Dewey, Montessori and Piaget that children learn by doing and by thinking about what they do. And so the fundamental ingredients of educational innovation must be better things to do and better ways to think about oneself doing these things.

I claim that computation is by far the richest known source of these ingredients. We can give children unprecedented power to invent and carry out exciting projects by providing them with access to computers, with a suitably clear and intelligible programming language and with peripheral devices capable of producing on-line real-time action.

Examples are: spectacular displays on a colour scope, battles between computer controlled 'turtles', conversational programs, game-playing heuristic programs, etc. Programmers can extend the list indefinitely.

Thus in its embodiment as the physical computer, computation opens a vast universe of things to do. But the real magic comes when this is combined with the conceptual power of theoretical ideas associated with computation.

Computation has had a profound impact by concretizing and elucidating many previously subtle concepts in psychology, linguistics, biology, and the foundations of logic and mathematics. I shall try to show how this elucidation can be projected back to the initial teaching of these concepts. By so doing much of what has been most perplexing to children is turned to transparent simplicity; much of what seemed most abstract and distant from the real world turns into concrete instruments familiarly employed to achieve personal goals.

Mathematics is the most extreme example. Most children never see the point of the formal use of language. They certainly never have the experience of inventing original formalisms adapted to a particular task. Yet anyone who works with a computer does this all the time. We find that terminology and concepts properly designed to articulate this process are avidly seized by the children who really want to make the computer do things. And soon the children have become highly sophisticated and articulate in the art of setting up models and developing formal systems.

The most important (and surely controversial) component of this impact is on the child's ability to articulate the working of his own mind and particularly the interaction between himself and reality in the course of learning and thinking. This is the central theme of this paper, and I shall step back at this point to place it in the perspective of some general ideas about education. We shall return later to the use of computers.

THE DON'T-THINK-ABOUT-THINKING PARADOX

It is usually considered good practice to give people instruction in their occupational activities. Now, the occupational activities of children are learning, thinking, playing and the like. Yet, we tell them nothing about those things. Instead, we tell them about numbers, grammar and the French Revolution; somehow hoping that from this disorder the really important things will emerge all by themselves. And they sometimes do. But the alienation-dropout-drug complex is certainly not less frequent.

In this respect it is not a relevant innovation to teach children also about sets and linguistic productions and Eskimos. The paradox remains: why don't we teach them to think, to learn, to play? The excuses people give are as paradoxical as the fact itself. Basically there are two. Some people say: we know very little about cognitive psychology; we surely do not want to teach such half-baked theories in our school! And some people say: making the children self-conscious about learning will surely impede their learning. Asked for evidence they usually tell stories like the one about a millipede who was asked which foot he moved first when he walked. Apparently the attempt to verbalize the previously unconscious action prevented the poor beast from ever walking again.

The paradox is not in the flimsiness of the evidence for these excuses. There is nothing remarkable in that: all established doctrine about education has similarly folksy foundations. The deep paradox resides in the curious assumption that our choice is this: *either* teach the children half-baked cognitive theory *or* leave them in their original state of cognitive innocence. Nonsense. The child does not wait with a virginally empty mind until we are ready to stuff it with a statistically validated curriculum. He is constantly engaged in inventing theories about everything, including himself, schools and teachers. So the real choice is: *either* give the child the best ideas we can muster about cognitive processes *or* leave him at the mercy of the theories he invents or picks up in the gutter. The question is: who can do better, the child or us?

Let's begin by looking more closely at how well the child does.

THE POP-ED CULTURE

One reads in Piaget's books about children reinventing a kind of Democritean atomic theory to reconcile the disappearance of the dissolving sugar with their belief in the conservation of matter. They believe that vision is made possible by streams of particles sent out like machine gun bullets from the eyes and even, at a younger age, that the trees make the wind by flapping their branches. It is criminal to react (as some do) to Piaget's findings by proposing to teach the children 'the truth'. For they surely gain more in their intellectual growth by the act of inventing a theory than they can possibly lose by believing, for a while, whatever theory they invent. Since they are not in the business of making the weather, there is no reason for concern about their meteorological unorthodoxy. But they are in the business of making minds — notably their own — and we should consequently pay attention to their opinons about how minds work and grow.

There exists amongst children, and in the culture at large, a set of popular ideas about education and the mind. These seem to be sufficiently widespread, uniform and dangerous to deserve a name, and I propose *The Pop-Ed Culture*. The following examples of Pop-Ed are taken from real children. My samples are too small for me to guess at their prevalence. But I am sure very similar trends must exist very widely and that identifying and finding methods to neutralize the effects of Pop-Ed culture will become one of the central themes of research on education. Examples of Pop-Ed thinking are:

(a) BLANK-MIND THEORIES   Asked how one sets about thinking a child said: 'make your mind a blank and wait for an idea to come.' This is related to the common prescription for memorizing: 'keep your mind a blank and say it over and over'. There is a high correlation, in my small sample, between expessing something of this sort and complaining of inability to remember poetry!

(b) GETTING-IT THEORIES   Many children who have trouble understanding mathematics also have a hopelessly deficient model of what mathemathical understanding is like. Particularly bad are models which expect understanding to come in a flash, all at once, ready made. This binary model is expressed by the fact that the child will admit the existence of only two states of knowledge often expressed by 'I get it' and 'I don't get it'. They lack — and even resist — a model of understanding something through a process of additions, refinements, debugging and so on. These children's way of thinking about learning is clearly disastrously antithetical to learning any concept that cannot be acquired in one bite.

(c) FACULTY THEORIES   Most children seem to have, and extensively use, an elaborate classification of mental abilities: 'he's a brain', 'he's a retard', 'he's dumb', 'I'm not mathematical-minded'. The disastrous consequence is the habit of reacting to failure by *classifying* the problem as too hard, or oneself as not having the required aptitude, rather than by *diagnosing the specific deficiency* of knowledge or skill.

COMPUTER SCIENCE AS A SCHOOL SUBJECT

Talking to children about all these bad theories is almost certainly inadequate as an effective antidote. In common with all the greatest thinkers in the philosophy of education I believe that the child's intellectual growth must be rooted in his experience. So I propose creating an environment in which the child will become highly involved in experiences of a kind to provide rich soil for the growth of intuitions and concepts for dealing with thinking, learning, playing, and so on. An example of such an experience is writing simple heuristic programs that play games of strategy or try to outguess a child playing tag with a computer controlled 'turtle'.

Another, related example, which appeals enormously to some children with whom we have worked is writing teaching programs. These are like traditional CAI programs but conceived, written, developed and even tested (on other children) by the children themselves.

(Incidentally, this is surely the proper use for the concept of drill-and-practice programs. Writing such programs is an ideal project for the second term of an elementary school course of the sort I shall describe in a moment. It is said that the best way to learn something is to teach it. Perhaps writing a teaching program is better still in its insistence on forcing one to consider all possible misunderstandings and mistakes. I have seen children for whom *doing* arithmetic would have been utterly boring and alienated become passionately involved in writing programs to teach arithmetic and in the pros and cons of criticisms of one another's programs like: 'Don't just tell him the right answer if he's wrong, give him useful advice.' And discussing 'what kind of advice is useful' leads deep into understanding both the concept being taught and the processes of teaching and learning.)

Can children do all this? In a moment I shall show some elements of a programming language called LOGO, which we have used to teach children of most ages and levels of academic performance how to use the computer. The language is always used 'on-line', that is to say the user sits at a console, gives instructions to the machine and immediately gets a reaction. People who know languages can think of it as 'baby LISP', though this is misleading in that LOGO is a full-fledged universal language. Its babyish feature is the existence of self-contained sub-sets that can be used to achieve some results after ten minutes of instruction. Our most extensive teaching experiment was with a class of seventh grade children (twelve year olds) chosen near the average in previous academic record. Within three months these children could write programs to play games like the simple form of NIM in which players take 1, 2, or 3 matches from a pile; soon after that they worked on programs to generate random sentences—like what is sometimes called concrete poetry—and went on from there to make conversational and teaching programs. So the empirical evidence is very strong that we can do it, and next year we shall be conducting a more extensive experiment with fifth grade children. The next sections will show some of the elementary exercises we shall use in the first weeks of the course. They will also indicate another important aspect of having children do their work with a computer: the possibility of working on projects with enough duration for the child to become personally—intellectually and emotionally—involved. The final section will indicate a facet of how more advanced projects are handled and how we see the effects of the kind of sophistication developed by the children.

YOU CAN TAKE THE CHILD TO EUCLID
BUT YOU CAN'T MAKE HIM THINK

Let's go back to Dewey for a moment. Intellectual growth, he often told us, must be rooted in the child's experience. But surely one of the fundamental problems of the school is how to extend or use the child's experience. It must be understood that 'experience' does not mean more busy work: two children who are made to measure the areas to two triangles do not necessarily undergo the same experience. One might have been highly *involved* (e.g. anticipating the outcome, being surprised, guessing at a general law) while the other was quite *alienated* (the opposite). What can be done to involve the mathematically alienated child? It is absurd to think this can be done by using the geometry to survey the school grounds instead of doing it on paper. Most children will enjoy running about in the bright sun. But most alienated children will remain alienated. One reason I want to emphasize here is that surveying the school grounds is not a good research project on which one can work for a long enough time to accumulate results and become involved in their development. There is a simple trick, which the child sees or does not see. If he sees it he succeeds in measuring the grounds and goes back to class the next day to work on something quite different.

Contrast this situation with a different context in which a child might learn geometry. The child uses a time-shared computer equipped with a CRT. He programs on-line in a version of the programming language LOGO, which will be described in more detail below.

On the tube is a cursor point with an arrow indicating a direction. The instruction

    FORWARD 100

causes the point to move in the direction of the arrow through 100 units of distance. The instruction

    LEFT 90

causes the arrow to rotate 90°

The child knows enough from previous experience to write the following almost self-explanatory program:

```
TO CIRCLE
FORWARD 1
LEFT 1
CIRCLE
END
```

The word 'TO' indicates that a new procedure is to be defined, and it will be called 'CIRCLE'. Typing

```
CIRCLE
```

will now cause the steps in the procedure to be executed one at a time.

Thus:

1st Step: FORWARD 1	The point creeps ahead 1 unit.
2nd Step: LEFT 1	The arrow rotates 1°.
3rd Step: CIRCLE	This is a recursive call; naturally it has the same effect as the command CIRCLE typed by the child. That is to say, it initiates the same process:
1st Step: FORWARD 1	The point creeps on, but in the new, slighty different direction.
2nd Step: LEFT 1	The arrow now makes an angle of 2° with its initial direction.
3rd Step: CIRCLE	This initiates the same process all over again. And so on, forever.

It is left as a problem for the reader to discover why this point will describe a circle rather than, say, a spiral. He will find that it involves some real geometry of a sort he may not yet have encountered. The more immediately relevant point is that the child's work has resulted in a certain happening, namely a circle has appeared. It occurs to the child to make the circle roll!

How can this be done? A plan is easy to make:
   Let the point go round the circle once.
   Then FORWARD 1
   Then repeat.
But there is a serious problem! The program as written causes the point to go round and round forever. To make it go just once round we need to give the procedure an *input* (in more usual jargon: a variable).

This *input* will be used by the procedure to remember how far round it has gone. Let's call it 'DEGREES' and let it represent the number of degrees still to go, so it starts off being 360 and ends up 0. The way this is written in LOGO is:

TO CIRCLE: DEGREES   :DEGREES means: the thing whose name is
                             'DEGREES'.
IF: DEGREES = 0 STOP
FORWARD 1
LEFT 1
CIRCLE: DEGREES − 1   Each time round the number of degrees remaining
                             is reduced by 1.

Now we can use this as a sub-procedure for ROLL:

    TO ROLL
    CIRCLE 360
    FORWARD 10
    ROLL
    END

Or, to make it roll a fixed distance:

    TO ROLL :DISTANCE
    IF :DISTANCE = 0 STOP
    CIRCLE 360
    FORWARD 10
    ROLL :DISTANCE − 1
    END

Or we can make the circle roll around a circle:

    TO FUNNY ROLL
    CIRCLE 360
    FORWARD 10
    LEFT 10
    FUNNY ROLL

These examples will, if worked on with a good dose of imagination, indicate the sense in which there are endless possibilities of creating even more, but gradually more, complex and occasionally spectacularly beautiful effects. Even an adult can get caught up in it! Not every child will. But if he does, the result is very likely to be a true extension of his experience in Dewey's sense. And evidence is accumulating for the thesis that there is scarcely any child who cannot be involved in some computational project.

CASE HISTORIES FROM THE MUZZEY JUNIOR HIGH SCHOOL EXPERIMENT

The following piece is extracted verbatim from a report on the seventh grade teaching experiment performed at Muzzey Junior High School at Lexington.

Problem vs. Project

The most exciting single aspect of the experiment was that most of the children acquired the ability and motivation to work on *projects* that extend in time over several days, or even weeks. This is in marked contrast with the style of work in most mathematics classes where the children work on problems of much shorter duration and more rigidly defined by the teacher. Our goal is to achieve a work style similar to that of the better art classes, where a child might work over a period of several weeks on making an object; a soap carving for example.

The similarity has several dimensions. The first is that the duration of the process is long enough for the child to become *involved,* to try several ideas, to have the experience of putting something of oneself in the final result, to compare one's work with that of other children, to discuss, to criticise and to be criticised on some other basis than 'right or wrong'. The point about criticism is related to a sense of creativity that is important in many ways which we shall talk about later — including, particularly, its role in helping the child develop a healthy self-image as an active intellectual agent.

Let's take an example. A continuing project over the last third of the year was working on various kinds of 'language generating' programs. The children studied a program (given as a model) which generated two word sentences like:

CATS RUN
DOGS SHOUT
CHILDREN BITE
DOGS RUN
CATS RUN
.
.
.

The assignment was to study the model and go on to make more interesting programs. The sample printout that follows brought great joy to its creator who had worked hard on mastering the mathematical concepts needed for the program, on choosing sets of words to create an interesting effect and on converting her exceedingly vague (and unloved) knowledge about grammar into a useful, practical form.

INSANE RETARD MAKES BECAUSE SWEET SNOOPY SCREAMS
SEXY WOLF LOVES THATS WHY THE SEXY LADY HATES UGLY
MAN LOVES BECAUSE UGLY DOG HATES
MAD WOLF HATES BECAUSE INSANE WOLF SKIPS SEXY RETARD
SCREAMS THATS WHY THE SEXY RETARD HATES THIN SNOOPY
RUNS BECAUSE FAT WOLF HOPS
SWEET FOGINY SKIPS A FAT LADY RUNS

The next class assignment was to generate mathematical sentences which were later used in 'teaching programs.' For example:

8*BOX + 6 = 48
WHAT IS BOX?

Finally, in the last weeks, someone in the class said she wanted to make a French sentence generator . . . for which she spurned advice and went to work. In the course of time other children liked the idea and followed suit — evoking from the first girl prideful complaints like 'why do they all have to take my idea?' The interesting feature was that although they took her idea, they imprinted it strongly with their own personalities, as shown by the following case studies:

K.M.   The girl who initiated the project. Thoughtful, serious about matters that are important to her, often disruptive in class. Her approach to the French project was to begin by writing procedures to conjugate all the regular verbs and some irregular ones. The end of the school year fell before she had made a whole sentence generator. But she did make a program with competence at conjugating — e.g. given VOUS and FINIR as inputs it would reply: VOUS FINISSEZ.

M.R.   A gay, exuberant girl, who made the 'SEXY COMPUTER' program quoted above. Only half seriously she declared her intention of making the first operational French sentence generator. In a sense she did — but with cavalier disregard for the Academy's rules of spelling and grammar!

J.C.   A clear mind with a balanced sense of proportion. Deliberately decided to avoid the trap of getting so involved with conjugation that no sentence would ever be generated.

Too serious to allow his program to make mistakes. Found a compromise: he would make a program that knew only the third person — but was still non-trivial because it did know the difference between singular and plural as well as the genders: thus it would say.

LE BON CHIEN MANGE
but
LES BONNES FILLES MANGENT.

A Detail from a Child's Mathematical Research Project

The fine texture of the work on projects of this sort can only be shown by case studies. The following vignette needs very little reference to LOGO — thus illustrating how the projects are more than programming.

J is the author of the last French program mentioned. A little earlier he is working on generating equations as part of a project to make 'a program to teach 8th grade algebra.' He has perfected a program to generate equations with coefficients in the range of 0–9 using a 'random' number generator. His present problem is to obtain larger coefficients.

First solution: Almost everyone tries this: get bigger numbers by adding smaller ones obtained from the old procedure. Amongst other considerations, this looks like a good technique that has often paid well: use old functions to define new ones.

Consequences: J chooses his equation generator but soon finds some annoying features:

The new coefficients are in the range 0–18, which is unnatural and not very big.

There is a preference for some numbers e.g. 9 comes up ten times as often as 18!

Comment: The first problem can be alleviated by adding more numbers. One can even add a random number of random numbers.

But this aggravates the second problem. J understands this qualitatively but does not see a way out. It is interesting that children and adults often have a resistance to making numbers by 'non-numerical' operations.

In this case the solution is to concatenate the single digit random numbers instead of adding them. LOGO has a simple way to express this and J is quite accustomed to making non-numerical strings by concatenation. In fact this is how he makes the equation! *Nevertheless* he resists.

The problem is discussed in a class meeting and after some prompting everyone suddenly 'discovers' the solution.

New Solution: J changes his program, now making numbers up to 99 by concatenation; he does some crude check of uniformity of distribution and tries his program.

Disaster: For a while it seems to go well. But in the course of playing with the 'teaching program' a user types 5 and is surprised to get a reply like:

You knucklehead; You took 11 seconds and your answer is wrong. The answer is 05. Here is some advice . . . etc.

Comment: Poor J will get the sympathy of every mathematician who must at some stage have tried to generalize a result by extending the domain of an innocent looking function only to find that the extended function violates some obscure but essential condition. He is also in the heart of the problem of representation. Is '05' a good representation? Yes, no . . . have your choice, but face the consequences and be consistent. J's problem is that his procedures accept '05' for arithmetic operations but not for the test of identity!

Solution: Change the identity test or peel off the leading zero. J chose the latter. His program worked for a while and was used, in ways that we shall see, to great effect.

New step: Later J was urged to allow negative numbers. He found a good way: use the one digit random number: generator to make a binary decision: If less than 5, positive; Otherwise, negative.

That Problem Again: J had a program working perfectly with negatives. Then one day decided to make it more symmetrical by using $+5$ and -5 for positive and negative. This brought him back to the old problems raised by differences between the machine's representation and the human user's. At this point the year ended with J's program not quite as effective as it had been at its peak.

ACKNOWLEDGMENTS

This paper is deeply influenced by Cynthia Solomon and Marvin Minsky.

This work was supported by NSF CJ-1049 and earlier NSF grants, and ONR Contract number NONR-4102(02).

This article has been reprinted by permission of the Association of Teachers of Mathematics.

FURTHER READING

1. S. Papert and C. Solomon, 'Twenty things to do with a computer', *Educational Technology,* March, 1971.

2. S. Papert, 'Teaching children to be mathematicians vs. teaching about mathematics', to appear in *International Journal of Mathematical Education in Science and Technology.*

3. *LOGO memos,* a continuing series of papers published by the Artificial Intelligence Laboratory, M.I.T., Cambridge, MA, U.S.A.

SECTION II:
TRANSFER

Why should programming be taught in the schools? The two most commonly heard answers to this question are: (1) computers are the future, so students should become familiar with them to enhance their job skills and to make them informed citizens in a technological society, and (2) learning to program is a cognitively demanding activity that can open the door to new ways of exploring powerful ideas and thereby help students develop "good habits of mind" that will make them more creative and effective problem-solvers. This second answer to the question of why programming should be taught in the schools deals with the problem of *transfer:* how to make knowledge and skills learned in one context available in unforeseeable ways in some other context.

In this section, we present four papers that address the problem of do programming skills and concepts transfer and thereby enhance students' problem solving abilities. Most studies of transfer have at their core a common empirical approach: start with two groups of subjects (control and experimental) that score the same on a pre-test of certain abilities, next administer training of a certain type in a particular skill (i.e., programming) to the experimental group, but not the control group, and finally look for improved post-test scores in the experimental group. However, despite the core similarity and seeming simplicity of transfer experiments, the space of experimental variations is very large, and potentially uncontrollable factors can make any results difficult to interpret. We have chosen the papers in this section not only because of the significance of their findings, but also because they illustrate important experimental design variations and raise important methodological issues.

One source of variation in transfer studies concerns the issue of how and what instruction is delivered. For instance, Howe used the computer in two ways to encourage students to discover mathematics concepts: as a tool for eliminating tedious aspects of certain exploratory activities, and as a "kit of parts" for building new exploration tools on their own. This approach to instruction is particularly appropriate when a specific target domain for transfer, such as understanding mathematical concepts, has been selected. In more standard programming courses, Linn and Dalbey point out that at exemplary schools design skills and problem solving skills are explicitly emphasized, whereas at less exemplary schools instruction is more strictly focussed on simply mastering an understanding of the specific language constructs.

Another source of variation in transfer studies concerns the issue of where you look for transfer — what skills may be enhanced by programming instruction. In the paper by Howe and his colleagues, the target domain for transfer was chosen specifically to be mathematics, whereas in both the Kurland paper and Mayer paper, "far" transfer tasks evaluating general reasoning skills as well as "near" transfer tasks evaluating skills closely analogous to programming were examined. Both Kurland and Mayer found evidence of transfer in the "near" transfer tasks, but the results for "far" transfer were disappointing. Kurland and her colleagues suggest that one reason for the failure to find "far" transfer could be that students, even after two years of courses, have not attained a very high skill level in programming. In the paper by Linn and Dalbey, the issue of where to look for transfer was replaced by the issue of what skill level do students attain and what factors are important predictors of higher achievement. Their investigations showed that only in exemplary classrooms were students able to move very far along the chain of cognitive accomplishments from knowledge of single language features, to design skills, and finally to general problem-solving skills.

The papers in this section raise many other issues relating to the transfer of programming skills that should be of interest to educators and researchers alike. Finally, the paper by Kessler and Anderson in the section on learning programming concepts bears on the more specific topic of intra-programming transfer, that is transfer between specific programming skills.

3
TEACHING MATHEMATICS THROUGH PROGRAMMING IN THE CLASSROOM

J. A. M. HOWE
P. M. ROSS
K. R. JOHNSON
F. PLANE
R. INGLIS
Department of Artificial Intelligence,
University of Edinburgh, Scotland

An experiment in teaching mathematics to nearly 90 secondary school children, with the aid of microcomputers, has been running in an Edinburgh classrom since August 1980. The 6 TERAK microcomputers are being used in a way that is unconventional in CAL terms; they are being used by the children themselves to experiment with mathematical processes, in a new version of the LOGO language specially written for this investigation. Using these microcomputers in such a way allows the children to develop useful planning and 'debugging' talents, as well as helping them towards an understanding of the structure implicit in particular mathematical topics.

This paper describes the early stages of the investigation, and argues in favour of using microcomputers in schools to provide pupils with constructive general-purpose modeling tools. In addition to the more conventional type of CAI program that is directed towards a particular topic in a particular subject. The description of the investigation falls naturally into three parts: details of the version of LOGO being used, a short account of the background to the whole project and an explanation of how it fits, in practice, into the childrens' normal mathematics lessons.

INTRODUCTION

The essential principle underlying the teaching of programming in a mathematics class is that the pupils can use the computer as a mathematical "laboratory" in which to experiment. Devising a program to experiment with a mathematical concept, in effect "telling the machine how to do it", not only involves the child in the discipline of stating his thoughts in a precise (programming) language, but also involves him in the cycle of modifying his ideas as a result of seeing what the computer does with his descriptions, and this is potentially a formative experience in developing problem-solving skills.

Feurzeig *et al.*[2], the original proponents of the idea of teaching programming in mathematics classes, claimed (amongst other things) that doing so would provide pupils with an excellent environment for mathematical exploration and a context for getting to understand the general ideas necessary for problem-solving. Research during the past decade has gone some way towards justifying this. For example, there have been encouraging results from studies by Statz[5] on whether learning to program improves problem-solving and from Howe *et al.*[4] on the links between programming and mathematical ability.

Of course, there are vital prerequisites for the success of the idea: reliable computer hardware with good graphics, and powerful and easily usable software, so that the effort of using the computer does not obscure the general aims. The chosen programming language must be powerful, flexible and relatively "characterless"; that is it must not make certain kinds of operation easy and others hard, which would tend to impose certain kinds of approach to problems. It must also embody a simple and believable model of how the computer works, and give meaningful error messages expressed in terms of that model. To give a counter example, some versions of BASIC have opted to provide graphics commands compatible with the SIGGRAPH specifications, which require the idea of mappings from "windows" to "viewports" and from "viewports" to the screen, a notion much too bewildering for a tyro. Until recently, the hardware requirements have only been available on time-sharing mainframe systems, and so the approach has been impractical except in educational research laboratories. Now, microcomputers are powerful enough, and almost cheap enough, for the idea to be feasible in a school mathematics class room. The software requirements have been available, on certain large machines, for about ten years in the form of the LOGO language. It is not (yet) commercially available on any microcomputer, and so we have written a new version for the TERAK machine, a particularly versatile microcomputer.

Our current investigation is attempting to study some of the difficulties of integrating programming work into mathematics classes for half of the first year group in a secondary school (the other half being a control group). For instance, merely learning to use a computer will take up a part of the mathematics timetable—does the constraint of the syllabus allow enough time for worthwhile kinds of experimentation? This project is the natural continuation of a 2-yr study conducted within the Department of Artificial Intelligence. However, before describing the results of that study and the early stages of the present one, we shall first describe the version of the LOGO language that we are using.

ABOUT LOGO

Operational Aspects

LOGO is an interactive, graphics-handling, list-processing language, originally based on another called LISP. Its most publicised feature is an orientable graphics cursor, called the "turtle", which can be controlled by body-centred commands such as FORWARD <a distance> or LEFT <an angle>. The turtle can also be controlled by Cartesian commands. However, there are other general characteristics of LOGO that are less remarked upon but are much more important. One is that the language is genuinely extensible, another is the list-handling features.

To the experienced user the TERAK version of LOGO is a collection of about a hundred procedures that he can employ for such tasks as drawing on the screen, manipulating numbers and printing out text. (It is worth noting that only twenty of the hundred have anything to do with "turtle geometry"). In particular a certain few of them give the user the power to extend the language by defining new procedures, in terms of the existing set, that are syntactically indistinguishable from the existing set and can have the same syntactic possibilities. The mechanism for doing this is a simple screen editor, and the definition of a new procedure is superficially similar to a program in BASIC. The only requirement is that everything in the definition is known to the system *at the time the procedure is run*. This means that procedures can call each other, and be recursive. For example, the factorial function when defined in LOGO might look like this (with comments in lower case):

FACTORIAL 'N   N is the name of the input for the purposes of the definition.
10 RESULT (IF ZEROQ :N THEN 1 ELSE
MULTIPLY :N   (FACTORIAL SUBTRACT :N 1))
:N is the value of the input.

This procedure can then be used anywhere, e.g. PRINT FACTORIAL 7 will print 5040. This is shorter and much more readable and comprehensible than what many versions of BASIC will allow:

50 N = 7
60 GOSUB 1000
70 PRINT X
....
1000 X = 1
1010 FOR J = 1, N
1020 X = X * J
1030 NEXT J
1040 RETURN

In our microcomputer version of LOGO, there is enough space to have about twenty average-sized procedures co-existing with the initial set.

Clearly there are many mathematical topics with which one might experiment whose concepts are rather distant from those dealt with by the hundred built-in procedures. If one were restricted to using only those, the system's usefulness would be very limited. However, the normal way of using the system is to build and use an additional set of procedures that are appropriate to the topic. For example, in set theory one might extend the language by building two procedures called UNION and INTERSECTION, that manipulate representations of sets appropriately, and then use these to verify or predict relations such as the distributive law. Of course, building the language extension must happen before one can use it, and this step may be too difficult or disproportionately time-consuming for a schoolchild. Because of this there is, besides a long-term procedure filing system, a mechanism by which a teacher (or whoever) can create a new system that incorporates any particular set of language extending procedures. When the pupil starts the new system, the extension is there waiting to be used.

The LOGO system, as described so far, would still not be particularly adaptable or useful were it not for the list-handling procedures. The built-in procedures each manipulate one or more of three data types: words, which are just text strings without spaces, numbers (including decimal parts if needed), and lists. A list is an ordered set of numbers, words or lists. Because lists can contain lists, and can be expanded or contracted at will, they can represent almost any kind of structure. Common examples include sentences, co-ordinates, general sets, tree structures, networks and symbolic descriptions of geometric figures.

Educational Aspects

It should be clear from the foregoing descriptions that LOGO can be used in two distinctly different ways. In the more conventional of the two, the child is provided with one or more procedures and merely runs them in order to see a concept demonstrated in an unusual or graphic manner. As an example of this, we shall describe the procedures that we have used to introduce children to the topic of bar charts.

The first is called TYPIST. It is used with a worksheet that introduces simple experiments with letter frequencies. Essentially it is useful for taking the tedious bit out of an otherwise useful and instructive activity. When run, it clears the screen, draws a line across it halfway up, and sets up a bar for each letter of the alphabet at the bottom. When the user types, the letters appear in the top half and the appropriate bars grow at the bottom. The letters are in the graphics display, so that the pupil can have a copy of the whole display on the printer.

The second is a procedure called CHOOSY, with one numeric input. It selects a random digit the given number of times, and grows a bar chart on the screen which shows how many times each digit has been chosen so far. We have used it to make some points about randomness. Both CHOOSY and TYPIST are merely simple games, useful because they present an idea in a powerful and unusual way. (Each is about 25 lines long.)

In addition to these, the pupil can experiment with random walks and random numbers by using procedures built permanantly into LOGO. For example, the command.

REPEAT 100 (FORWARD 5 AND RIGHT PICK 360)

will draw a random walk of constant step size. A pupil of about 14 or more could easily experiment with this idea — by making the step size vary as well, for instance, or restricting the random angle to multiples of 10. Questions they might ask are "does a constant step size make it more likely for the walk to leave the screen?"; "does a restricted choice of angle make the turtle stay on the screen, and if so, what are the restrictions?"; "does the turtle always return to the centre in a 2-D walk, or only in a 1-D walk?". Of course, it is possible that a pupil might never think of such experiments — it seems sensible to seed the imagination by asking one or two questions on a worksheet that can be solved without too much (or too little!) effort, and suggesting one or two open-ended projects.

A procedure such as TYPIST could equally well be written in BASIC, since only the author of the package needs to know what is happening inside it. This "black box" approach is relatively undemanding of the user, as opposed to the "glass box" or "kit of parts" approach. In this latter style, the user is given, or has to build, a language extension that contains the "atomic elements" for the topic under study. If the learner has to build his own "kit of parts" out of the existing set, such a UNION and INTERSECTION in set theory, then his noetic task is essentially one of clarifying and extending his existing understanding of the topic, since he has to translate the processes into procedures, and the objects into a representation suitable for the computer. As Howe[3] points out, this places considerable cognitive demands on him. Not only does he need to be at least partially familiar with the mathematics aspects, he also needs to know what computing procedures are available to him and to have some sense of what their potentialities are, besides having a vocabulary of computing constructs. For example, when constructing a drawing that includes circular arcs, he may need to know:

(i) that procedures ARCL and ARCR, that draw leftward and rightward arcs, exist;

(ii) that they each take a radius as first input, and an angle through which to turn as the second;

(iii) that the angle of turning is necessarily the same as the angle subtended by the arc at the centre;

(iv) that neither input need be an integer;

(v) that the procedures do certain sensible things if either or both of the inputs are negative.

A sensible alternative is to provide the learner with a prewritten "kit of parts", but this does not remove the load, merely lessens it. He still has to become familiar with what the component procedures do and how they may be written using these components. We shall describe two examples of how this might work out in practice in a mathematics class. They are taken from the first- and second-year syllabuses, and concern the topics of number bases and of geometric transformations.

Example 1. Number Bases

In this topic we have chosen to provide a set of LOGO procedures that allow a user to perform calculations in any number base, and to convert numbers from one base to another. The choice of representation is, as always, of paramount importance — in this case, the representation should

(a) make it clear which base a number is in (EVERY time it is seen)

(b) make the idea of columns (or digits) clear

(c) be usable in ANY base. In particular, this means avoiding the artificial conventions for digits, such as the common one of using A–F for hexadecimal digits.

(d) be very readable!

The one we chose is a list, essentially a list of the digits together with a final element which is itself a list and contains the base as a number in base 10. For example, 31 (decimal) would be represented as

    [3 1 [10]]

in base 10, and in base 16 as

    [1 15 [16]]   (meaning $1 \times 16 + 15$)

and -256 (decimal) would be written in base 16 as

    [$-$100 [16]]

This notation has the advantage of being recognisably different from the normal, so that any integer is definitely in base 10.

There are six procedures in the set, and the base in use at a given time is determined by a global variable called BASE. The procedures are

(a) CONVERT. This takes a number or list, and turns it into a list expressing that number in the given base. Thus, if BASE is 7,
> PRINT CONVERT 16 will print [2 2 [7]]
> PRINT CONVERT [3 3 [8]] will print [3 6 [7]]

(b) DEC. This turns a list into a decimal number, so that
> PRINT DEC [3 6 [7]] will print 27.

(c) SUM. This takes two arguments, each either lists or decimal numbers, and returns their sum in the current base.

(d) PRODUCT. This is similar to SUM.

(e) DIFFERENCE. This is similar to SUM.

(f) QUOTIENT. This is similar to SUM.

Because the procedures will accept numbers either as normal decimals or in the list notation, it is easy to make the point that a number is the same whatever notation it happens to be expressed in. Doing simple sums makes the idea of columns and the idea of carrying fairly clear, e.g.

> PRINT SUM [1 5 [8]][1 4 [8]]
> prints the 'number; [3 1 [8]]

and this can be verified by using DEC to turn these back into decimal numbers and doing a normal addition.

It is worth noting that, written in LOGO, the procedures CONVERT and DEC are about 6 lines long, and the other four are each 3 lines long. A pupil who used these to become familiar with the idea of number bases could then look inside these procedures to see how they are implemented, thus learning the simple algorithm by which a number can be converted from one base to another. (If such an algorithm is too complex or not clearly expressible in LOGO, there is a mechanism by which a teacher can prevent pupils from ever seeing inside a procedure.) These procedures could be used at various levels in secondary school maths. Clearly they can be used in S1 and S2, but a pupil in S3 or S4 could use them to study the question of whether the idea of a fractional or negative base is at all sensible—this might involve rewriting the CONVERT algorithm, as the provided one might not be general enough.

The above procedures, written in LOGO, look like this (comments are given in lower case):

```
CONVERT 'I
10 IF LISTQ :I THEN MAKE 'I DEC :I
```
If the input is a list, use DEC to turn it into a number.

```
20 NEW 'L AND MAKE 'L [ ]
```
L will hold the final result.
```
30 NEW 'NEG AND MAKE 'NEG 'FALSE
```
NEG holds the sign temporarily.

```
40 IF (LESSQ :I 0) THEN MAKE 'NEG 'TRUE
   AND MAKE 'I SBT 0 :I
50 WHILE (GREATERQ :I (SUBTRACT :BASE 1))
   MAKE 'L PUTFIRST (REMAINDER :I :BASE) :L
   AND
   MAKE 'I (SHARE :I :BASE)
```
SHARE = integer division.
```
60 MAKE 'L PUTFIRST :I :L
```
Insert remaining digit.
```
70 IF :NEG THEN MAKE 'L PUTFIRST '−:L
```
Insert sign if negative.
```
80 RESULT JOIN :L < <:BASE> >
```
Attach list giving base.

```
DEC 'L
10 NEW 'B AND MAKE 'B :L{COUNT :L}{1}
```
B = base of input.
```
20 NEW 'I AND MAKE 'I 0
```
I will hold final result.
```
30 NEW 'NEG AND MAKE 'NEG 'FALSE
```
NEG holds the sign temporarily.

```
40 IF (EQUALQ :L{1}'−) THEN
   MAKE 'NEG 'TRUE AND MAKE 'L REST :L
```
Prune off any sign.
```
50 WHILE (GREATERQ COUNT :L 1)
   MAKE 'I (ADD (MULTIPLY :I :B) :L{1})
   AND MAKE 'L REST :L
```
Assemble no. from digits.
```
60 RESULT IF :NEG THEN SUBTRACT 0 :I ELSE :I
```

```
SUM 'A 'B
10 IF LISTQ :A THEN MAKE 'A DEC :A
```
Make first input a number.
```
20 IF LISTQ :B THEN MAKE 'B DEC :B
```
Make second input a number.
```
30 RESULT CONVERT (ADD :A :B)
```
Convert their sum!

The other procedures are nearly identical to SUM.

Example 2. Geometric Transformations

In this topic we have written a set of procedures that will allow a child to experiment with linear and rotational transformations and reflections. The set is a nice example of the toolkit idea—it consists of the following:

(a) two procedures called AHEAD and TURN, which can be used to create geometric patterns e.g. one might define TRIANGLE as

TRIANGLE 'SIDE

10 REPEAT 3 (AHEAD :SIDE AND TURN 120)

These are used instead of FORWARD etc., so that drawings can be rescaled by changing a global variable called SCALE. The definition of AHEAD shows how this is done:

AHEAD 'N

10 FORWARD (MULTIPLY :N :SCALE)

If the value of SCALE is 2, the figure drawn by TRIANGLE 20 will be twice as large as when the value of SCALE is 1.

(b) a procedure called AXES which draws co-ordinate axes with the origin in the centre of the screen (and labels them).

(c) a procedure called DRAW, that takes two inputs. The first is the name of a procedure defined by the user using AHEAD and TURN, and the second is a list giving X and Y co-ordinates relative to the displayed axes. The command DRAW 'TRIANGLE [50 10] would draw the triangle at the current SCALE starting at $X = 50$, $Y = 10$.

(d) REFLECT, which takes one number. It draws the reflection of the shape most recently DRAWN, in a mirror inclined at the given angle to the X-axis. It also draws a dotted line to represent the mirror.

(e) ROTATE, which rotates the turtle about the origin by the given number of degrees. Hence,

DRAW TRIANGLE [50 10] followed by

ROTATE 90 AND TRIANGLE

will draw the triangle rotated through 90 degrees about the origin, therefore starting at $X = -10$, $Y = 50$.

With this set, it is possible to experiment with compounding sequences of rotations and reflections, such as trying to find how to reflect any shape in the origin. The shapes do NOT have to be closed shapes! The set is introduced to S1 pupils in the course of several worksheets, again leading towards potentially interesting experiments. A pupil higher up the school might choose instead to reproduce how, for example, REFLECT works, learning some ideas in trigonometry in the process.

We use worksheets together with the language extension for any topic, so that learner can assimilate the knowledge gradually and in a structured way. The worksheets contain information and exercises, and "seeds"—suggestions for open-ended experimentation. They have a further important function, not explicit, which is to introduce the learner to the parallels between the computer representation and the mathematical one—for instance, the list representation in the number bases example. The choice of representation in LOGO is a very important one, with major repercussions. In particular it sets limits on what the user can do at his level of competence, and these limits may be too narrow to allow him to draw adequate mathematical parallels. An interesting example of this is given by du Boulay[1], in a study that attempted to use LOGO to re-teach mathematics to a group of primary school teacher trainees who had self-confessed "blocks" about mathematics. When studying the topic of fractions, his volunteers started by trying to represent fractions as pie-charts. However, they were thwarted by the technical difficulties of constructing drawings of pie-charts, and so never got to grips with ideas about fractions. Even when they were given procedures that did the drawings, the task of interpreting the drawings proved too hard, especially in the potentially interesting cases of combining fractions with unequal denominators and of vulgar fractions. The unfortunate general conclusion that may be drawn from this is that only in those cases in which the choice of representation is simple and obvious can the learner be allowed to indulge in unprompted experimentation. The pedagogical and time penalties may otherwise be too great.

It might be suggested that, since worksheets and prewritten procedures steer the user towards particular discoveries, experimentation in this LOGO "mathematics laboratory" raises questions similar to those that used to be asked about work in physics laboratories. Why have pupils "discover" things when it is quicker to tell them or show them the "discovery" process? Clearly one answer is that there is a tremendous psychological advantage in the user doing it himself, even if fairly unproductively. There are also very important differences between the two kinds of laboratory: physics experiments are aimed at the discovery of a (finite) number of laws, whereas mathematical ones are aimed at the discovery of an infinite number of patterns — discoveries can be genuinely personal! There is also as much to learn from designing the apparatus as from using it, something rarely true in physics at a school level.

BACKGROUND TO THE PRESENT STUDY

The evidence from a two-year evaluation study within the department suggests that this approach to mathematics can benefit the less able child. Our pupils were 11–13 year old boys from a local school, divided into two groups of 11 each. The experimental group, of lower initial ability compared to the others, came to our LOGO classroom during normal school hours, and the control group followed a normal timetable. The boys' performance on various tests was recorded at several stages during the two years.

In this study, the experimental group spent the first year learning computing concepts and techniques. The worksheets introduced the boys to computational ideas such as procedures, variables and recursion; problem-solving tactics like decomposition, and the use of debugging skills such as using a trace facility. In the second year, the emphasis shifted to using programming to explore school mathematics topics in arithmetic, geometry and algebra. From the results of the study[4], we concluded that the experimental group's ability to do maths and their understanding of maths had improved relative to the performance of the control group. In particular an item analysis suggested that their grasp of algebraic topics was marginally better than that of the control group. Moreover, the class teachers were of the opinion that the experimental group pupils "could argue sensibly about mathematical issues" and "explain mathematical difficulties clearly", but rated the control group poorly for this. Although these results were encouraging, there are many uncontrollable factors that could account for them. For example, the experimental group might have benefited by the closer personal attention they received, or the extra time they spent on mathematics. The results might also be explained by a Hawthorne effect. For these reasons we moved the work into a school classroom, where the pupils could be taught by their normal class teachers as part of the normal timetable.

THE PRESENT STUDY

In the state secondary school in question, mathematics classes in the first year are of mixed ability. We have installed 6 microcomputers and 2 printers in one room, and 3 of the 6 first-year classes come to it for their normal maths lessons. The other three classes act as a control group, and never see the computers. The class teachers, each of whom had an initial course on programming in LOGO, are now solely responsible for the teaching; our own role is now one of observers, responsible for producing teaching materials and maintaining the equipment. The school uses a modular maths scheme, in which each fortnight is devoted to a particular topic, and pairs of pupils work their way at their own pace through a series of workcards and worksheets. Because there is not enough time to teach programming first and mathematics second, we are trying to introduce both in parallel, using our own worksheets containing LOGO-based material introduced at appropriate points in the sequence of normal workcards.

The main problems are practical, related to classroom management. With only 6 machines, and 24–30 pupils in each class, each pair can spend rather less than half of the five available half-hour lessons each week actually working at the machine. In order to prevent bottlenecks, the LOGO-based worksheets include a proportion of material that should be done away from the machine. However, this is hard to enforce, and demanding on the teacher. The children are now fairly adept at starting the system and using their own floppy disks — the first fortnight of the year was devoted to the rudiments of using the machines. Their most serious difficulty lies in seeing the computer-based work as a genuine part of mathematics; this has meant giving them tests on LOGO material, in order to allay anxieties about the control group getting "more marks".

The results of the project will be judged on several sets of information. We gave all six classes two standardised NFER tests at the start of the year; there will also be two post-tests, besides the results of the school's own tests set occasionally throughout the year. In addition, the LOGO system keeps a record of whatever is typed on the keyboard, together with timings, on the user's floppy disk; these are read and printed in the department at the end of each fortnight. Thus we have some record of what each pair has done at the key board. The impression at present is that the statistical distribution of childrens' progress is settling into a bimodal shape. This is more or less as expected—the interesting question is that of the correlation with initial ability in mathematics. On the practical side the bimodal distribution is emphasising the perpetual problems of managing a class of mixed and widely-varying ability. Ideally we would like to be able to introduce programming into mathematics classes S1, S2 and S3, and follow individuals' progress over several years, to observe any effects on mathematical and problem-solving skills.

SOME CONCLUSIONS

It seems likely that computers will spread their effect throughout schools in the next decade or so, making the benefits from computer modelling tools more apparent. One effect will be that teachers will have to cope with many levels of sophistication in computing and it seems sensible to use a language such as LOGO that can be tailored to many ability levels. This would reduce the demands on teachers to be familiar with two or more conventional languages such as BASIC or PASCAL, that are suited to particular age bands within the school. The knowledge required to be able just to run a simulation package is soon likely to increase greatly, as packages begin to take advantage of the power of currently available microcomputers. In addition to this, we foresee a demand for the teaching of the concepts and techniques of modelling and of computing, for which the current set of "educational" languages will be inadequate. We believe that the results of our present project will provide valuable information about the feasibility of this.

ACKNOWLEDGMENTS

The authors would like to thank the staff of James Gillespie's School for their cooperation, assistance and enthusiasm in their current project. All the authors, apart from J. A. M. Howe, are supported by a grant from the Social Science Research Council of Great Britain.

This article has been reprinted by permission of Pergamon Press.

REFERENCES

1. du Boulay J. B. H., Learning primary mathematics through computer programming. Ph.D. Dissertation, Edinburgh University (1978).
2. Feurzeig W., Papert S., Bloom M., Grant R. and Solomon C., Programming languages as a conceptual framework for teaching mathematics. Report No. 1889. Bolt Beranek & Newman Inc., Cambridge, MA, (1969).
3. Howe J. A. M., Learning through model building. In *Expert Systems in the Microelectronic Age* (Edited by D. Michie). Edinburgh University Press (1979).
4. Howe J. A. M., O'Shea T., and Plane F., Teaching mathematics through LOGO programming: an evaluation study: In *Computer-Assisted Learning—Scope, Progress and Limits* (Edited by R. Lewis and E. D. Tagg). North-Holland, Amsterdam (1979).
5. Statz, J. Problem solving and LOGO. In *Final Report of Syracuse University LOGO Project*. Syracuse University, New York (1973).

4

COGNITIVE CONSEQUENCES OF PROGRAMMING INSTRUCTION

MARCIA C. LINN
JOHN DALBEY
University of California, Berkeley

Increasingly, precollege students receive programming instruction. The avowed purpose of such instruction is typically to teach a computer language such as BASIC as well as to teach problem solving. In this paper, we describe an ideal chain of cognitive accomplishments from programming and examine the cognitive outcomes from a wide range of middle school programming courses.

Study of over 500 students in 17 classes reveals that the form of instruction, the access to computers, and the ability of the student influence outcomes from programming instruction. Specifically, exemplary instruction moves students further along the chain of cognitive accomplishments than does typical instruction. Furthermore, both access to computers and general ability are related to progress in typical classrooms. In exemplary classrooms, for medium and high ability students, neither ability nor computer access outside of class is related to programming performance.

RATIONALE

As precollege programming instruction becomes more and more widespread, it is useful to examine the potential and actual outcomes from such instruction (see Dalbey & Linn, 1985, for a review of research). The avowed purpose of precollege programming instruction typically is to teach a language such as BASIC as well as to teach problem solving. In this paper, we first identify an ideal chain of cognitive accomplishments from programming instruction and then assess the progress of students in programming classes at six diverse middle schools.

Because programming does involve solving problems, such instruction, at least superficially, teaches about problem solving. As recent research has shown, however, problem-solving skills appear to be much more discipline specific than had first been thought (e.g., Larkin, McDermott, Simon, & Simon, 1980; Linn, 1985a, in press; Resnick, 1983). Thus, the mechanisms that lead to generalization of problem-solving skill from one discipline to another require specification. The chain of cognitive accomplishments described in this paper is a preliminary approach to such specification.

Performance in precollege programming courses may be influenced by certain student characteristics. An important concern is whether instruction is equally effective for all students or whether some groups of students are more likely to benefit than others. In addition, there may be interactions between student characteristics and instruction. For example, schools serving high ability students may have offered courses for a longer period of time. To assess this question in our empirical studies, we measured: (a) general ability, (b) access to computers outside of school, (c) previous computer experience, and (d) interest in computers. We examined the relationships between these variables, gender, and progress along the chain of cognitive accomplishments.

THE CHAIN OF COGNITIVE ACCOMPLISHMENTS FROM COMPUTER PROGRAMMING INSTRUCTION

An ideal chain of cognitive accomplishments from programming instruction guided our investigations (Linn, 1985a, 1985c; Linn et al., 1983). This chain builds on earlier work describing the features of computer learning environments that make them cognitively demanding (Linn, 1985b; Linn & Fisher, 1983) and motivating (Lepper, 1985). It also builds on studies comparing expert and novice programmers (Atwood & Ramsey, 1978; Kurland, Mawby, & Cahir, 1984; Mandinach & Linn, in press) and on an examination of exemplary textbooks (Cooper & Clancy, 1982; Luehrmann & Peckham, 1983).

Identification of an ideal chain of cognitive accomplishments from programming instruction offers guidance for understanding what constitute appropriate precollege experiences and also provides a standard against which to measure current instruction. The chain is not intended to be an exhaustive list of all possible activities, but rather to identify those activities involving considerable cognitive skill. The chain has three main links: (a) single language features, (b) design skills, and (c) general problem-solving skills. We describe the earlier links on the chain in more detail than the final links because our empirical studies involve introductory courses.

Language Features

The first link consists of the features of the language being studied. In order to use a programming language, it is important to understand many of the language features or nondecomposable elements of the language. In programming courses, teachers typically introduce language features, explain how they work, and have students use them.

Students' knowledge of language features is often assessed by comprehension items asking them to predict how programs using the features will perform. In addition, language feature knowledge is assessed by asking students to reformulate or change a language feature in a program so that the program does something slightly different. For example, students might change the length of a loop or change the content of a print statement. Thus, comprehension and reformulation items can be used to asses understanding of language features.

Students need to learn language features. However, such knowledge is of little general use or benefit. Students with an understanding of language features cannot compose programs that feature groups of commands working in concert. These students can copy programs, they can change print messages in programs, they can modify games to award larger prizes for success, and they can in other ways alter single lines of programs. In spite of the limitations inherent in instruction that consists solely of language features, this is often the only topic of precollege texts and courses. It is especially common to find such instruction in middle school programming courses.

Design Skills

The second link on the chain consists of design skills. Design skills are the group of techniques used to combine language features to form a program that solves a problem. These include templates and procedural skills. Such skills are essential in order for students to write computer programs of any complexity.

Templates

Templates are stereotypic patterns of code that use more than a single language feature. Templates perform complex functions such as sorting names alphabetically, finding the least common multiple of a group of numbers, or counting the number of words in a text. Templates perform a function similar to weak schemata in the theoretical formulation of Anderson (1984) and to plans in the work of Soloway and Ehrlich (1984).

When students have a repertoire of templates, they have a set of flexible and powerful techniques that allow them to solve many problems without inventing new code. Furthermore, templates can help to reduce the cognitive demands of programming by providing obvious ways to decompose a problem. Students can decompose problems into pieces the size of their available templates. They then can implement the solution using their templates. Students who have a repertoire of templates, therefore, can write more complicated programs than those without such a repertoire.

Procedural Skills

Procedural skills are used to combine templates and language features in order to solve new problems. Procedural skills include planning, testing, and reformulating. Note that reformulating was mentioned as a technique for testing language feature knowledge, but it can also be used for modifying longer sequences of code. Programmers need a plan for combining language features and templates to solve a programming problem. Thus, they decompose the problem into component parts and plan how to combine those parts. Once a plan is implemented, programmers need to test the plan in order to ascertain its correctness. Testing involves determining whether a program meets specifications by deciding what data or other conditions might cause difficulty and then running the program under those conditions to see if it operates correctly. When the testing of a program reveals problems, the programmer decides whether it requires refinement. Programmers reformulate programs to make them work properly.

Planning.   Planning is required to solve complex programming problems. Novices rarely work on programs complex enough to demand planning. Programming assignments that involve only linear combinations of simple language features often fail to illustrate the advantages of planning. Thus, programming instruction must be carefully designed in order to insure that students understand the importance of planning and have the opportunity to practice it. Only then can they gain knowledge about the conditions under which a template will function.

Planning is an important component of the behavior of expert programmers. In some studies, experts spend much of their time engaged in planning (Kurland et al., 1984). In contrast, planning is not an aspect of novice behavior (Dalbey, Tourniaire, & Linn, 1986). Similar differences in the time spent planning problem solutions are reported for expert and novice physics problem solvers (Larkin et al., 1980).

Testing.   Testing is an important programming skill that can be enhanced by asking students to find out whether programs perform as intended. Experts and novices differ in this skill. Experts not only recognize the advantages of testing their programs but are good at designing tests to reveal possible problems. They have well-developed knowledge of antibugging strategies associated with their templates. For example, experts tend to test the boundary conditions, to insure that no division by zero is possible, and to consider difficulties resulting from interactions between parts of their programs. In addition, programs written by experts tend to have built-in tests for potential confusions such as tests to be sure that the input data meet the problem specifications. In contrast, novices often test only the obvious or usual forms of input and may fail to test all of the code (e.g., Mandinach & Linn, in press).

Reformulating.   Reformulating measures design skills when respondents are required to modify a program plan. It is another skill that differentiates experts and novices. Experts are likely to respond to the results of tests by considering large-scale as well as minor reformulations of their programs. In contrast, novices tend to seek localized "fixes" for their programs (e.g., Atwood & Ramsey, 1978), perhaps never learning how to revise larger programs. For novices, these efforts often result in what has been called "spaghetti" code.

Acquisition of design skills can be assessed by asking students to write programs to solve problems. To require planning, testing, and major reformulations, such problems must be reasonably complex. To measure template acquisition, problems must require commonly learned templates.

Problem-Solving Skills

The third link on the chain consists of problem-solving skills useful for learning new formal systems. These are templates and procedural skills common to many or all formal systems. For example, templates such as sorting in one programming language can often be used when programming in a new language. The procedural skills of planning, testing, and reformulating are applicable both in learning new programming languages and in learning to use other formal systems such as data-base management software, or word processors.

These general problem-solving skills may be acquired when students attempt to apply templates or procedural skills learned in one system to a new system (see Dalbey & Linn, in press, for an example). For example, students may identify aspects of templates or procedural skills that are central to their effectiveness as well as aspects that are peripheral to their effectiveness. These skills then become general enough to be used for problems in other programming languages and for nonprogramming problems. The acquisition of problem-solving skills can be assessed by asking students to solve problems using an unfamiliar formal system such as a new programming language. The chain of cognitive accomplishments that culminates in technological expertise is a long one. Students need to solve fairly complex problems before they use cognitively demanding skills such as planning. They probably need experience with several formal systems before they acquire general problem-solving skills.

EMPIRICAL STUDIES

Method

The studies reported here are part of the investigations of the Assessing the Cognitive Consequences of Computer Environments for Learning (ACCCEL) Project funded by the National Institute of Education. The project conducted an integrated set of studies to assess progress along the chain of cognitive consequences in middle school courses. These studies addressed both the effect of software (e.g., Mandinach, 1984; Stein & Linn, 1985) and the effect of programming (e.g., Dalbey & Linn, 1985). The study to be reported here specifically addressed the effect of instruction and of student characteristics on outcomes from programming classes.

When college instructors report that students with precollege experience have not gained skills that are useful for their college courses, this could reflect that: (a) students have not moved far enough along the chain of cognitive accomplishments to acquire any skills that are more generally applicable, (b) students have learned inefficient or incomplete templates, or (c) students have not followed the chain but have deviated from it in some inappropriate fashion. The empirical study was undertaken in order to assess how far along the chain of cognitive accomplishments students typically move in middle school programming instruction.

It is important to examine how programming instruction is currently conducted in order to make recommendations for change and to identify effective procedures (e.g., Salomon & Gardner, 1984). Field studies provide such opportunities but make it difficult to disentangle the effects of potentially important variables. In addition, studies of naturally occurring instruction document what is possible given the many constraints imposed by schools but may fail to characterize the full potential of the environment. As field studies, our investigations have these difficulties.

Site Selection

To maximize understanding of the potential of the middle school programming environment, we studied both typical and exemplary schools offering rigorous programming courses. To be identified as rigorous, classes had to: (a) be at least 12 weeks in duration, (b) have at least eight computers, and (c) have teachers who had participated in at least one workshop prior to offering the course and had at least 100 hr of on-line experience in programming. From among those schools offering rigorous instruction, we selected typical and exemplary classrooms. To be identified as exemplary, the programming course had to emphasize explicitly the design skills described earlier as part of the chain of cognitive accomplishments.

The language used for instruction in this study was BASIC because it is most prevalent in middle school classes. Most schools chose BASIC for economic reasons. It is resident on most computers and does not require additional software or hardware.

Sites were selected by surveying middle schools within 50 mi of the Lawrence Hall of Science, the University of California, Berkeley. A total of 10 schools met our criteria for typical sites. We selected the three schools (Sites 1 to 3) using Apple computers with color monitors to meet the needs of one related study (Dalbey & Linn, in press) and one school close to the Lawrence Hall of Science (Site 4) to meet the needs of another related study (Dalbey et al., 1986). We located two schools (Sites 5 and 6) with exemplary instruction (i.e., emphasizing design of programs). Characteristics of the six sites participating in the study are summarized in Tables 1, 2, and 3 (for more details about these sites, see Mandinach & Fisher, 1985).

At the two exemplary sites, explicit emphasis on program design was apparent. We sought sites that emphasized templates or procedural skills or both. These sites also had good access to machines, effective curriculum materials, experienced teachers, and students with moderate to high ability. No doubt, the machine access and student ability components of the situation made the teachers more willing to set up instruction explicitly emphasizing design. In addition, it seemed clear that experienced teachers were more likely to locate or develop curriculum materials emphasizing explicit design of programs. Thus, as might be expected, there was some confounding between site characteristics and exemplary instruction.

Student Characteristics

Student characteristics are the primary focus of another report (Mandinach & Fisher, 1985) and are considered here when appropriate for understanding response to instruction.

Table 1
Site Characteristics

Site	Number of Classes	Number of Students	Grade Level	% Female	Number of Computers	Out-of-Class Access	Total Possible School Access[a]	Text Title	% Emphasis
1	3	92	8	41	8	Some	25 hr	Kids & the Apple	100%
2	3	84	7/8	32	12	Some	26 hr	Comp Lit.[b]	75%
3	6	132	7/8	42	8	4 hr/wk	13 hr	Kids & the Apple	50%
								Own supp. materials	50%
4	3	51	7/8	26	11	None	53 hr	Teacher selected materials	100%
5	2	60	8	37	9	2 hr/wk	29 hr	Comp. Lit.	75%
								Own supp. materials	25%
6	1	28	8	39	10	15 hr/wk	84 hr	Teacher selected materials	100%

[a] Combined in-class and outside-of-class over duration of course.
[b] Luehrmann & Peckham, 1983.

Table 2
Student Characteristics

Site	Selection Criteria	Raven's Matrices Score		Access to Home Computer
		Mean	SD	
1	Required math/science class	8.28	2.6	34.8%
2	Elective No prereq.	8.49	2.1	46.4%
3	Elective No prereq.	6.76	2.7	30.3%
4	Elective No prereq.	9.04	1.9	56.9%
5	Elective No prereq.	9.62	1.9	43.3%
6	Elective B+ minimum English and Algebra	10.08	1.5	57.7%
	Further screening by teacher			

Table 3
Teacher Characteristics

Site	Previous Experience Teaching Programming	Specialization	Source of Computer Education	Classroom Instructional Format	Classroom Feedback Techniques[a]
1	None	Math/Science	Workshops	Self-paced Informal	Direct
2	2 years[b]	Math coord. (Masters)	Workshops and conferences	Self-paced	Direct
3	1.5 years	Industrial Education	Workshops	Daily assignments Frequent tests	Direct
4	2.5 years	Special Education	Workshops	Monitored/ Self-paced	Indirect
5	2 years	Gifted coord.	Workshops[c]	Daily assignments	Indirect, Modeled, Testing
6	Over 3 years	Math coord.	College degree	Projects with timelines	Indirect, Modeled, Debugging techniques

[a]Direct: gives answers to questions. Indirect: encourages student to find answers to questions.
[b]No previous experience with currently used curriculum.
[c]Worked with curriculum development team over a 2-year period.

General ability.   Many have hypothesized that general ability, or intelligence, is important for acquiring skill in programming. Studies of expert programmers reveal that a good predictor of success is high general ability (Corno & Haertel, 1982). In addition, the demands of current programming instruction might artificially exclude students who could learn programming.

The 12 items of the Advanced Progressive Matrices, Set I (Raven, 1956), were used as a measure of ability. The test had an alpha reliability of .77. At times in the analyses, students were divided into low, medium, and high ability groups. The low ability group scored between 0 and 6 on the Raven. Scores at this level reflect considerable difficulty in understanding the demands of a matrix item. Medium ability students were identified as those having scored between 7 and 10 on the Raven. These students understand the principles involved in solving a matrix item but cannot always apply them effectively. The high ability group was comprised of students scoring 11 or 12. These students understand the demands of matrix items and can apply them to complex figures.

Access to computers.   In typical precollege computer courses, students might have as little as 10 to 12 hr of in-class access to computers. Thus, out-of-class and out-of-school computer access could potentially be extremely important. It is possibile that students could double or even triple their computer access time by judicious use of out-of-class and out-of-school access opportunities.

Access to computers varies tremendously from one school district to another and probably from one geographic area to another (Becker, 1983, 1984). To examine the impact of access on acquisition of programming skill, we: (a) estimated in-school access for all students (see Table 1) and (b) asked students about access to computers at home and in other out-of-school settings (see also Mandinach & Fisher, 1985).

Four categories were established: (a) access neither at home nor elsewhere, (b) no access at home but access elsewhere, (c) home access but not other access, and (d) home and other access. At times these categories are collapsed into "high" and "low" access. High access includes categories c and d (i.e., home access). Low access includes categories a and b (i.e., no home access).

Interest and previous experience with computers.   Other indicators of response to programming instruction have been suggested. These include interest in learning to program and previous experience using computers for programming or other applications.

A locally developed test called Headlines was used to assess interest in computers, science, and nontechnical areas. Students were asked to rate, on a scale of 1 (definitely would) to 4 (definitely would not), whether they would read a newspaper article with a particular headline. The test contained 24 items: 12 computer, 8 science (1 item later was deleted), and 4 nontechnical. The alpha reliability for the total test was .83; $r = .78$ for the computer subscale, $r = .78$ for science, and $r = .56$ for the nontechnical items. Note that reliability reflects the length of each scale.

Experience with computers was established by combining answers to a series of 12 items that assessed use of computers for mathematics, science, programming, and other activities.

Gender.   It has been documented that females are less likely than males to enroll in programming courses (e.g., Linn, 1985b, 1985c). The responses of males and females were investigated in this study.

Programming Skill

Progress along the chain of cognitive accomplishments was assessed by a project-designed test called the Final Programming Assessment. This test was administered in two class periods and had three sections entitled: (a) comprehension, (b) reformulation, and (c) design. The 11 comprehension items asked students to produce the output for simple programs involving single language features. The alpha reliability was .93. The 6 reformulation items required students to modify programs involving simple language features likely to be encountered in introductory programming courses. These items generally assessed language feature knowledge rather than design skill. Reliability was .81. The 6 design items asked students to write programs. These ranged from short programs that required linear assembly of simple language features to complex programs that required a considerable amount of planning and were greatly facilitated by knowledge of certain rudimentary templates. Reliability was .91. The 23-item scale had an alpha reliability of .96.

Participating teachers reviewed the Final Programming Assessment and agreed that it assessed what they taught and what they would teach if time permitted. Thus, the test was viewed as having face validity for the programming content of courses involved in the study.

RESULTS

Programming Skill

How far along the chain of cognitive accomplishments from programming instruction did students at these six sites move? In general, students at typical sites made limited progress. As shown in Table 4, more progress was made in comprehension than in reformulation, and more progress was made in reformulation than in design.

Typical sites.   Typical programming instruction, offered at Sites 1 through 4, yielded considerable diversity in student outcomes on the Final Programming Assessment. The comprehension section was easiest. Site means ranged between 20% and 70% correct. Reformulation was possible for some students at each site. Site means ranged between 15% and 50%

Table 4
Performance of the Final Programming Assessment

	Typical Sites								Exemplary Sites			
	1 N = 79		2 N = 83		3 N = 115		4 N = 48		5 N = 53		6 N = 28	
Site	M	SD	M	SD	M	SD	M	SD	M	SD	M	SD
Comprehension (55 Possible)	27.9	13.9	17.0	15.3	11.1	13.7	37.6	15.6	40.0	11.6	50.5	6.3
Reformulation (30 Possible)	10.9	8.1	11.6	8.0	6.7	6.2	14.6	10.4	17.9	7.1	25.4	4.8
Design (50 Possible)	11.5	14.4	9.8	10.8	5.5	9.4	16.3	17.4	28.8	14.6	40.6	11.0
Total Score (135 Possible)	50.3	32.0	38.4	31.7	23.4	26.7	68.5	39.1	86.7	30.3	116.5	20.1

correct. Design was very difficult with mean success by site between 10% and 30% correct. Students at Sites 1, 2, and 4 outperformed those at Site 3. At Sites 1, 2, and 4, there was more in-class access, the curriculum was more developed, and students were of higher ability in comparison to Site 3.

Considerable variability in student performance within each site was found. For example, most students at Site 3 scored zero on design, but a few students had very high scores. However, most students at typical sites were at the language feature stage of the chain of cognitive accomplishments. Most students were in the process of mastering the language features and had not moved to the point where they could apply them to the design of programs (for more details, see Dalbey & Linn, 1985).

Exemplary sites. The exemplary instruction at Sites 5 and 6 moved students much further along the chain of cognitive accomplishments than at other sites. Students had mastered comprehension (mean scores between 78% and 95%) and were close to mastering reformulation (mean scores between 60% and 80% correct). In addition, students made considerable progress on the design of solutions to programming problems. On the average, 60% of the items were solved correctly at Site 5, and 80% of the items were solved correctly at Site 6. At these two sites, students moved beyond the language features part of the chain and gained design skills.

Because reliability of the 23-item test was extremely high and performance on the items was very consistent, subsequent sections of this paper discuss only the total score on the Final Programming Assessment.

Computer Access and Programming Skill

Students had access to computers both in school and out of school. In-school access was uniform within sites. Out-of-school access varied across students within each site.

In-school access.   The maximum amount of computer access during school was estimated and is shown in Table 1. These maximum times were correlated with performance on the Final Programming Assessment for all students in the sample. The correlation was .56. When ability was partialed out, it dropped slightly to .45.

For typical sites, in-school access to computers was directly related to level of performance. The highest scoring site had the most access, and the lowest scoring site had the least access. The two middle scoring sites had almost the same amount of access. In contrast, one of the exemplary sites has only about as much in-school access as was found in the median typical site. The other exemplary site offered by far the most access (over 15 hr per student per week).

Out-of-school access.   Much has been written about the potential of vast gaps between the performance level of students who have home computers and those who do not (e.g., Papert, 1980). In addition, because the amount of in-school access to computers is very limited at most sites (under 30 hr at all but two sites), it seems logical to assume that out-of-school access would contribute to success on the Final Programming Assessment.

Reasonable diversity from site to site in student reports of computer access out of school was apparent (Table 2). Thus, students were divided into groups reporting the same level of access. As shown in Figure 1, out-of-school access significantly influenced performance at typical sites but not at exemplary sites.

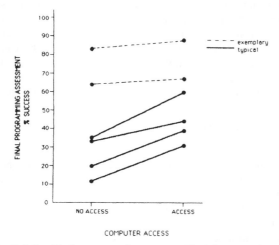

FIGURE 1   Relationship between performance on Final Programming Assessment and out-of-school computer access.

Implications. For typical sites, there is a significant relationship between both in-school and out-of-school access and performance on the Final Programming Assessment. Recall that students at these sites are mainly acquiring understanding of programming language features and have less than 30 hr of in-class computer access. Their on-line time is primarily devoted to drill on language features. Thus, the strong relationships may reflect benefits from opportunities for drill on language features.

At exemplary sites, no relationship between out-of-school access and performance on the Final Programming Assessment was found. Recall that at these sites the major contributor to student differences in performance is on the design section of the Final Programming Assessment. At both exemplary sites, teachers used in-school access efficiently by requiring that students plan their programs before going to the computer. Students at the site with extensive access were able to do longer and more complex class projects. Thus, teachers of these classes made a great effort either to provide extensive opportunities for in-school machine access or to make sure that in-school machine time was used effectively.

Perhaps students in exemplary classes had the access they needed in school to learn the design skills taught. It is interesting to note that when access is either extensive or efficient and when students are far enough along the chain of cognitive accomplishments that their concern is with the design of programs, then the influence of out-of-school access is small. Given the naturalistic nature of this investigation, no causal relationships can be established. However, the lack of relationship between out-of-school access and success for whatever reason is encouraging because it shows that home computers are not necessary for the acquisition of moderate skill in designing programs. This relationship is discouraging because it suggests that home computers are not being used for the acquisition of complex programming skills. Quite different results would no doubt be found for courses that were designed to capitalize on considerably greater machine access (e.g., access in the range of 200 to 1,000 hr). This level of access cannot be provided in class, and some other mechanisms must be identified.

Student Ability and Performance

Student ability was measured by the Raven Advanced Progressive Matrices (see Table 2). Diversity from school to school is a common occurrence, and site differences resulted. In order to assess the influence of ability on response to programming instruction, we grouped students of similar ability, as previously described.

Table 5 shows the number of students at each site who were of low, medium, and high ability. Very few students at Sites 5 and 6 fall in the low

Table 5
Performance on Final Programming Assessment by Ability Group and for All Students

| | Typical Sites | | | | | | | | | | | | Exemplary Sites | | | | | |
| | 1 | | | 2 | | | 3 | | | 4 | | | 5 | | | 6 | | |
Site	N[a]	M	SD	N	M	SD	N	M	SD	N	M	SD	N	M	SD	N	M	SD
High	17	80.1	32.2	13	68.5	36.7	6	80.2	44.2	6	87.0	43.8	17	90.3	32.0	12	120.8	13.3
Medium	44	40.5	25.3	52	37.4	29.8	61	25.4	22.6	32	66.7	39.0	30	89.4	28.8	12	116.6	12.3
Low	12	37.9	28.8	14	17.6	10.8	37	11.4	18.5	4	33.0	21.4	3	58.7	38.8	1	35.0	.0
Total	79	50.3	32.0	83	38.4	31.7	115	23.4	26.7	48	68.5	39.1	53	86.7	30.3	28	116.5	20.1

[a]Total is greater than sum of students in each group because some students missed the ability test.

ability group; hence, no analysis of this group seems justified. A reasonable number of students of medium and high ability were identified at each site, making parallel analyses possible. The relationship between ability and programming performance is summarized in Table 5 (see Linn, 1985a, for a graphic representation). At typical sites, there are significant differences between the means for all ability groups. At exemplary sites, there are no differences between groups of medium and high ability.

The importance of ability at typical sites but not at exemplary sites is consistent with the view that explicit instruction in program design reduces the cognitive demands of programming. Perhaps with this form of instruction other skills not necessarily tapped by a measure of general ability become important. In particular, skills such as perseverance and organization of complex tasks may become central when the cognitive demands of keeping track of a lot of information are relaxed.

Ability, Access, and Performance

Disentangling the influence of access and ability on performance in the Final Programming Assessment, although important, is complicated by the distribution of these factors across sites. As mentioned earlier, there are very few low ability students in the sites where explicit instruction in the design of programs was offered. In addition, at some sites there is a correlation between access to computers out of school and ability. These naturally occurring conditions make conclusions about the role of access and ability difficult, yet they are probably realistic and would no doubt occur in a larger sample.

To understand the relationship between performance on the Final Programming Assessment, access to computers, and ability as measured by the Raven Progressive Matrices, students were separated into the ability groups we have identified, and the relationship between access and performance was examined for typical and exemplary sites. For typical sites, both ability and access were related to performance on the Final Programming Assessment, and their influence was reasonably additive (see Figure 2). In general, low ability and low access students did not perform as well on the Final Programming Assessment as did students with high ability and high access; intermediate levels of ability yielded intermediate results. Thus, both access and ability appear to contribute substantially to performance on the Final Programming Assessment for these sites. Because performance reflects acquisition of the programming language features and is generally accompanied by limited in-school access to computers, the influence of both factors seems reasonable. For exemplary sites, ability and access had no clear relationship with performance.

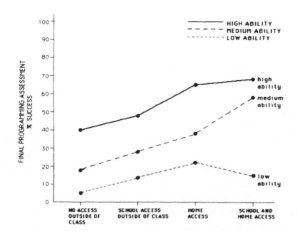

FIGURE 2   Relationship between Final Programming Assessment, ability, and computer access outside of computer class for typical sites.

Interest, Experience, and Performance

It has been hypothesized that interest in computers, global experience with machines, and experience specifically with programming might influence performance in programming courses. In general, these factors did not consistently influence typical or exemplary instruction (Mandinach & Fisher, 1985).

Gender and Performance

Another factor that has been hypothesized to covary with some of the previous factors, and which might be important in assessing response to programming instruction, is gender. Many have hypothesized that males are more responsive than females to programming instruction. Results from the present study contradict this suggestion. There are no gender differences in performance, and indeed, females outperformed males on the Final Programming Assessment at several sites.

In contrast, even at sites where programming was a required course, the enrollment of females in the course was generally less than the enrollment of males (see Table 1). Even at Site 6, where the teacher recruited females, only 39% of the students were female. It seems important to insure that both males and females enroll in programming courses in order for equitable future opportunities to be assured (Linn, 1985a, 1985c). The point where equity seems most central is in securing the participation of females in programming courses.

IMPLICATIONS FOR MIDDLE SCHOOL INSTRUCTION

The major finding of this investigation is the influence of explicit instruction in the design of computer programs on the ultimate success of students. Not only was such exemplary instruction effective compared to typical forms of instruction, but in addition, such instruction tended to minimize the influence of access to computers outside of school and the influence of student ability on outcomes for those of medium and high ability. Thus, a prime consideration in the design of future instructional programs for programming is to increase the access of students to exemplary instruction.

In order for more effective programming instruction to be developed and implemented, curriculum materials and teacher education programs are required. At the explicit design sites, the curriculum materials were refined and effective. At one site, a popular textbook was used, and the teacher had been a participant in the development of that text. At the other site, the teacher had developed her own curriculum materials over the last 3 years using her experience teaching programming at the community college as a guide. Both of these teachers had more experience than the other teachers in providing programming instruction. In contrast, teachers at typical sites complained that they needed better materials.

Unfortunately, a group of low ability students with excellent instruction was not located. We suspect that an instructional program emphasizing the explicit design of programs would succeed with low ability students provided that the teacher and the curriculum materials were carefully selected. For example, at Site 3, when the ACCCEL project provided augmentation to BASIC and offered instruction using the introductory language Spider World, students made progress in understanding a programming language and in the ability to design programs in that language (Dalbey & Linn, in press a). Thus, it appears possible to offer a challenging and effective educational program for students who have low scores on the Raven Advanced Progressive Matrices.

Perhaps we were unable to locate a site with low ability students and excellent instruction because such sites cannot allocate resources to this activity. Becker (1983) reports that low socioeconomic status schools (which often also have low ability students) are less likely to use computers for programming than are other schools. Perhaps schools serving a low ability population do not place a high priority on programming instruction. It seems clear that without effective instruction and well-planned curriculum materials, courses serving low ability students are unlikely to be very effective. Furthermore, it is possible that large payoffs could arise from small changes in the curriculm materials and teacher preparation for these courses.

Another striking finding was that the majority of students made very limited progress in programming. Mean success on the Final Programming

Assessment ranged between 15% of the items at Site 3 to 85% of the items at Site 6. Students at typical sites were still at the beginning of the chain of cognitive accomplishments from programming instruction. At the exemplary sites, the coincidence of many factors, including good in-school access and a refined curriculum with experienced teachers and high ability students, resulted in fairly dramatic movement along the chain of cognitive accomplishments. These large differences indicate the tremendous importance that must be placed on reform of programming instruction in order for it to have the potential of influencing problem-solving skill.

It is important to note that this study assessed only progress in learning programming. There are other possible objectives for precollege programming instruction. For example, this study did not assess possible affective outcomes such as confidence in using technological tools. These additional questions also deserve scrutiny.

Constraints on Outcomes

There are some serious constraints on programming instruction in precollege settings that placed restrictions on the possible outcomes of this study.

Computer access.   Middle school instruction typically involves students working on-line during a 40 to 50 min class period. In some schools, students can also gain access to the computer outside of class. Schools typically have 10 or 12 computers for all students. During the class day, students rotate through the computer room. Five or six classes of students are potential users of the 10 to 12 available computers during outside-of-class access periods. Thus, even fairly generous computer access time before, during, and after school may have limited impact for the large number of students enrolled in the course (see Table 1).

Typically, students in middle school programming classes receive between 6 and 30 weeks of instruction. It is also typical for classrooms to have one computer for every two or three students. Thus, enrollees could accumulate a maximum of 10 to 75 hr of on-line time. In contrast, adolescents who become expert programmers have typically spent over 500 hr on-line acquiring their skills (Kurland et al., 1984). Furthermore, although a growing number of students have out-of-school access to computers either at home, at recreation centers, or at libraries, current exemplary instruction does not appear to capitalize on these resources.

Language of instruction.   As mentioned, economics govern the decision to teach BASIC. BASIC is resident on most microcomputers and requires no additional memory or software.

There are many drawbacks to the use of BASIC as the language of instruction. Explicit instruction in the design of programs is difficult for a number of reasons. First, BASIC has a less than adequate subroutine structure: Students cannot pass parameters, nor can they define local variables for their subroutines. Second, the planning of effective programs in BASIC is thwarted by the poor flow of control structures characteristic of the language. The GOTO statement is particularly problematic because it encourages students to use undisciplined flow of control and form loops inappropriately; thus, it results in code that is difficult for others to understand.

Curriculum.   The curriculum materials available for precollege programming instruction often fail to offer opportunities for students to move along the chain of cognitive accomplishments. Many texts are limited to instruction in programming language features. A few, such as Luehrmann and Peckham's *Computer Literacy* (1983), offer instruction in design of solutions to programming problems and emphasize templates. Teachers are often obliged to augment available resources. They must develop their own curriculum materials on their own time with very restricted resources. To make programming courses worthwhile, this situation must be changed.

Teacher experience.   It is only recently that programming has been offered in precollege settings. Therefore, teachers tend to have limited training in teaching programming. Commonly, teachers have participated in summer institutes. Often, they have had limited on-line experience themselves. Teachers we contacted often had less than 200 hr of on-line programming experience and were not expert in programming. Especially when curriculum materials are limited, this lack of experience seriously hampers the likelihood that such courses can be effective.

Thus, the limited progress of students in typical classes is hardly surprising given the context in which this instruction occurs. The crucial elements of successful instruction, including curriculum materials, trained teachers, and reasonable access to computers, are largely lacking.

CONCLUSIONS

The most central finding of this study is that instruction strongly influences outcomes in introductory programming classes. Even the most able students, a group often thought of as likely to learn in spite of instruction, learned significantly more in exemplary classes than in typical classes. The greatest advantage was for the medium ability students who did as well as high ability students in exemplary classes and were far more successful than medium ability students in typical classes.

This finding coincides with those from other studies of middle school programmers. Mandinach and Linn (in press) report that the most successful programmers of middle school age have generally learned their skills in regular school classes and have strengths and weaknesses reflecting the nature of the instruction they received. Thus, even when the population is taken as all middle school students, not necessarily those who acquired their skills in regular classes, the successful students appear to be those who learned from good school instruction, not those who learned at home, at science centers, or at computer stores.

Stein and Linn (1985) demonstrate the importance of a particular aspect of exemplary instruction, namely, explicit instruction concerning how to benefit from the computer learning environment. Studying *Rocky's Boots* (The Learning Company, 1982), they found that students seem unlikely to take advantage of all the feedback features in the environment without explicit instruction. When required to use available feedback, students quickly learn complex skills. Similarly, exemplary classes explicitly address how to form templates and how to use procedural skills.

The role of the curriculum was also demonstrated in a study of the Spider World software (Dalbey, 1983a, 1983b) used in conjunction with instruction in BASIC (Dalbey & Linn, in press). Students learning Spider World and then BASIC made more progress in BASIC language features than those spending the same amount of the time learning BASIC alone. In this case, it seemed likely that students receiving the Spider World curriculum learned templates for loops that were not learned by those in the BASIC curriculum. Furthermore, they were able to use their loop templates to solve problems in another programming language.

A second important finding in this study is the similar progress of medium and high ability students in exemplary classes. Anderson, Boyle, Farrell, and Reiser (1984) suggest that effective instruction in programming can reduce the working memory load for the task. Perhaps this is what teachers who emphasize explicit design of programs actually accomplish, accounting for the similar progress made by medium and high ability students. As Doyle (1983) argues, explicit instruction can be particularly beneficial to medium ability students who may be unable to figure out how to solve complex problems on their own.

A third finding is that few students get beyond the language features link on the chain of cognitive accomplishments from programming instruction. Those who do acquire some skill in design, as Mandinach and Linn (in press) show, appear to have learned some skills for acquiring new programming language.

IMPLICATIONS

An important question concerns the likelihood that problem-solving skill will result from programming instruction. It is certainly unreasonable to expect progress in general problem solving from a first course in programming. If the proposed chain of cognitive accomplishments is an accurate depiction of how such learning might occur, considerable proficiency in programming will first be necessary. Students are probably more likely to develop problem-solving skills from learning several programming languages and developing some robust and general templates for programming.

Considerable reflection and research will be required to establish exactly how this chain of cognitive accomplishments can be effectively taught. Preliminary results suggest that relatively simple templates can be generalized from one programming language to another. We cannot yet ascertain how more complex templates might be generalized or how, indeed, procedural skills might be enhanced through programming instruction.

Efforts to teach complex problem-solving skills, such as those described by Piaget as formal operations (Inhelder & Piaget, 1985), have generally met with failure (e.g., Linn, 1980). When there has been success, it has often been limited to a single discipline (e.g., Kuhn & Angelev, 1976; Linn, in press). Taking advantage of the motivation associated with using computers and the emphasis on problem solving inherent in programming may allow us to make progress in teaching problem solving.

Is programming instruction beneficial? Given the lack of progress in typical programming classes, it may appear that such classes offer no benefit to students. But such a conclusion is premature. Exemplary classes clearly do provide considerable benefit to students in that they develop complex problem-solving skills in a particular discipline. Thus, programming courses do start students along a very promising chain of accomplishments.

Programming classes, compared to other middle school classes, also provide extensive opportunity to solve problems and to get feedback on the effectiveness of those solutions. Because the computer can provide precise feedback, students can improve their problem-solving skills on their own. Thus, compared to classes where most of the feedback comes from the teacher, programming can be a rich source of problem-solving experience.

A danger, which has perhaps been somewhat overrated, is that students might invent templates on their own for solving programming problems which interfere with later learning. For example, students come to rely on the GOTO structure in BASIC even though it is a poor mechanism for flow of control. Clearly, exemplary instruction and clever choice of software can avoid this problem. However, just as students in their personal experience gain alternative conceptions of physical phenomena, such as velocity, force, or density, so might they gain alternative conceptions of programming templates. It is neither possible nor desirable to control learning to such an extent that no incorrect ideas are acquired. Rather, the challenge to educators is to design instruction that will allow students to recognize and correct their faulty approaches to solving problems.

ACKNOWLEDGMENTS

We gratefully acknowledge the contributions of Charles Fisher, Ellen Mandinach, Corinne Nelson, and Joanne Stein, as well as other members of the ACCCEL staff whose helpful comments, assistance with instrument design, observations, data collection and analysis made this research possible. Thanks are due David Rogosa, who served as our consultant for data analysis. In addition, we appreciate the cooperation of the teachers and students who participated in the investigations.

This material is based upon research supported by the National Institute of Education under Grant 400–83–0017. Any opinions, findings, and conclusions or recommendations expressed in this publication are those of the authors and do not necessarily reflect the views of the National Institute of Education.

REFERENCES

Anderson, J. R., Boyle, C. F., Farrell, R., & Reiser, B. J. (1984). *Cognitive principles in the design of computer tutors.* Unpublished manuscript, Advanced Computer Tutoring Project, Carnegie-Mellon University, Pittsburgh.

Anderson, R. C. (1984). Some reflections on the acquisition of knowledge. *Educational Researcher, 13,* 5–10.

Arwood, M. E., & Ramsey, H. R. (1978). *Cognitive structures in the comprehension and memory of computer programs: An investigation of computer debugging* (Tech. Rep. TR-78-A210). Alexandria, VA: U.S. Army Research Institute for the Behavioral and Social Sciences.

Becker, H. J. (1983). *School uses of microcomputers.* Baltimore, MD: Johns Hopkins University, Center for Social Organization of Schools.

Becker, H. J. (1984, April). *The classroom context of microcomputers: How different schools manage the problems.* Paper presented at the annual meeting of the American Educational Research Association, New Orleans.

Cooper, D., & Clancy, M. (1982). *Oh! Pascal!* New York: Norton.

Corno, L., & Haertel, E. (1982). *Selection and validation of a problem solving test for use in Amdahl PS & S technical personnel selection.* Sunnyvale, CA: Amdahl Corporation.

Dalbey, J. (1983a). *Spider World Reference Manual and Teacher's Guide* (ACCCEL Report).

Dalbey, J. (1983b, November). *Teaching programming with Spider World.* Paper presented at the seventh annual Western Educational Computing Conference, San Franciso.

Dalbey, J., & Linn, M. C. (1985). The demands and requirements of computer programming: A review of the literature. *Journal of Educational Computing Research, 1* (3), 253–274.

Dalbey, J., & Linn, M. C. (in press). Cognitive consequences of programming: Augmentations to BASIC instruction. *Journal of Educational Computing Research.*

Dalbey, J., Tourniaire, F., & Linn, M. C. (1986). Making programming instruction cognitively demanding: An intervention study. *Journal of Research in Science Teaching, 23.*

Doyle, W. (1983). Academic work. *Review of Educational Research, 53*(2), 159–199.

Inhelder, B., & Piaget, J. (1958). *The growth of logical thinking from childhood to adolescence.* New York: Basic Books.

Kuhn, D., & Angelev, J. (1976). An experimental study of the development of formal operational thought. *Child Development, 47*(3), 697–706.

Kurland, D. M., Mawby, R., & Cahir, N. (1984, April). *The development of programming expertise in adults and children.* Paper presented at the annual meeting of the American Educational Research Association, New Orleans, LA.

Larkin, J. H., McDermott, J., Simon, P. P., & Simon, H. A. (1980). Expert and novice performance in solving physics problems. *Science, 208,* 1335–1342.

The Learning Company. (1980). *Rocky's Boots* [Computer software]. Menlo Park, CA: Author.

Lepper, M. R. (1985). Microcomputers in education: Motivational and social issues. *American Psychologist, 40*(1), 1–18.

Linn, M. C. (1980). Teaching children to control variables: Some investigations using free choice experiences. In S. Modgil & C. Modgil (Eds.), *Toward a theory of psychological development within the Piagetian framework* (pp. 673–697). Windsor, Berkshire, England: National Foundation for Educational Research Publishing Company.

Linn, M. C. (1985a). The cognitive consequences of programming instruction in classrooms. *Educational Researcher, 14,* 9–16.

Linn, M. C. (1985b). Gender equity in computer learning environments. *Computers and the Social Sciences, 1*(1), 19–27.

Linn, M. C. (1985c). Fostering equitable consequences from computer learning environments. *Sex Roles, 13*(3/4), 229–240.

Linn, M. C. (in press). Physical science curriculum design: Views from a psychological framework. In R. Dillon & R. J. Sternberg (Eds.), *Psychology and curriculum design.* New York: Academic.

Linn, M. C., & Fisher, C. W. (1983). The gap between promise and reality in computer education: Planning & response. In Far West Laboratories Staff (Eds.), *Proceedings of Making Our Schools More Effective: A Conference for California Educators* (pp. 51–73). San Francisco: Far West Laboratories.

Linn, M. C., Fisher, C. W., Dalbey, J., Mandinach, E. B., Burbules, N. C., & Reese, P. (1983). *The effects of learning to program and learning from cognitively demanding software* (ACCCEL Report). Berkeley, CA: University of California, Lawrence Hall of Science.

Luehrmann, A., & Peckham, H. (1983). *Computer literacy: A hands-on approach.* New York: McGraw Hill.

Mandinach, E. (1984). *The role of strategic knowledge and self-regulation in learning to solve an intellectual computer game.* Unpublished doctoral dissertation, Stanford University, Stanford, CA.

Mandinach, E., & Fisher, C. (1985). *Individual differences and acquisition of computer programming skill* (ACCCEL Report). Berkeley, CA: University of California, Lawrence Hall of Science.

Mandinach, E., & Linn, M. C. (in press). Cognitive consequences of programming: Achievements of experienced and talented students. *Journal of Educational Computing Research.*

Papert, S. (1980). *Mindstorms: Children, computers and powerful ideas.* New York: Basic Books.

Raven, J. C. (1958). *Advanced Progressive Matrices* (Set 1). New York: Psychological Corporation.

Resnick, L. B. (1983). Mathematics and science learning: A new conception. *Science, 220,* 477–478.

Salomon, G., & Gardner, H. (1984, April). *The computer as educator: Lessons from televison research.* Paper presented at the annual meeting of the American Educational Research Association, New Orleans, LA.

Soloway, E., & Ehrlich, K. (1984). Empirical studies of programming knowledge. *IEEE Transactions on Software Engineering, SE-10*(5), 595–609.

Stein, J. S., & Linn, M. C. (1985). Capitalizing on computer-based interactive feedback: An investigation of *Rocky's Boots.* In M. Chen & W. Paisley (Eds.), *Children and microcomputers: Formative studies* (pp. 213–227). Beverly Hills, CA: Sage.

5

A STUDY OF THE DEVELOPMENT OF PROGRAMMING ABILITY AND THINKING SKILLS IN HIGH SCHOOL STUDENTS*

D. MIDIAN KURLAND
ROY D. PEA
CATHERINE CLEMENT
RONALD MAWBY
Bank Street College of Education, New York

ABSTRACT

This article reports on a year-long study of high school students learning computer programming. The study examined three issues: 1) what is the impact of programming on particular mathematical and reasoning abilities?; 2) what cognitive skills or abilities best predict programming ability?; and 3) what do students actually understand about programming after two years of high school study? The results showed that even after two years of study, many students had only a rudimentary understanding of programming. Consequently, it was not surprising to also find that programming experience (as opposed to expertise) does not appear to transfer to other domains which share analogous formal properties. The article concludes that we need to more closely study the pedagogy of programming and how expertise can be better attained before we prematurely go looking for significant and wide reaching transfer effects from programming.

Psychologists, computer scientists, and educators have argued that computer programming can be a powerful means of enhancing thinking and the development of good problem-solving skills in children, in addition to being a powerful method for teaching students fundamental concepts in mathematics, physics, and logistics [1-3]. At first glance, the enthusiasm surrounding programming seems well-founded. Observations of expert adult programmers indicate that

* The work reported here was supported by the National Institute of Education (Contract No. 400–83–0016). The opinions expressed do not necessarily reflect the position or policy of the National Institute of Education and no official endorsement should be inferred.

programmers explicitly employ important problem-solving strategies such as decomposing problems into modules, use analogical reasoning, and systematically plan, code, and debug their programs. Programming seems to demand complex cognitive skills such as procedural and conditional reasoning, planning, and analogical reasoning [3-7].

In addition to problem-solving skills, programming utilizes fundamental concepts such as variables and recursive structures, which are important in math and physics. It is well-known that these concepts are difficult to teach with traditional media, and their employment in the functional context of a programming language may make them more easily comprehended [1, 3].

Motivated by this enthusiasm for the potential of programming, as well as by the pressure from business and the homes to make students "computer literate," schools have instituted programming courses or related activities at all grade levels. Yet, surprisingly, there has been very little research to date which has directly addressed the many broad claims that have been made for programming. And in addition, there has been very little research examining what students are learning about programming itself as the result of school-based instruction. We know far too little about what to expect students will learn in a reasonable period of time, how they learn, what conceptual difficulties they encounter, what forms of cognitive support they may require to guide them over these difficulties, or whether individual differences in learning styles are reflected in programming and need to be guided differently in instruction. And beyond what rational analyses suggest, we cannot say with much assurance what knowledge and skills that students bring with them when they first meet programming (e.g., natural language competencies; various reasoning skills) are likely to facilitate the acquisition of programming knowledge and skills.

Addressing the issue of how well students actually learn to program in precollege courses is thus an important matter. It is particularly important because of two relations between level of expertise and transfer of learning. First, it is primarily sophisticated programming activities that demand higher level thinking skills and problem-solving techniques, and these activities require expertise. They require a good model of the stucture of the language: you cannot write a modular program and use variables unless you understand how control is passed in the language and how logical tests operate on outputs of operations. Thus, the thinking skills we hope will develop and transfer out of programming depend upon students attaining certain proficiencies in programming [8]. Simple tasks such as a four-line graphics program to draw a box do not require the full range of complex reasoning skills that programming is purported to help develop.

Second, the transfer of concepts and skills across domains depends on the detection of potential similarities between a known and a new domain [9-13]. Brown, Bransford, Ferrara and Campione note that this fact implies differences in the abilities of novices and experts to transfer since novices and experts classify similarities between tasks differently [14]. Novices will be more limited in their abilities for recognizing problem similarity since they tend to classify tasks according to surface characteristics whereas experts focus on underlying conceptual properties or casual structures. For example, Chi *et al.* examined the categorization of physics problems by novice and experts [15]. Novices categorized problems in terms of particular objects referred to, terminology given in a problem statement, and physical configurations of problem elements. In contrast, experts ignored these superficial features of problems and categorized them in terms of physics principles relevant for problem solutions. Since the novice and expert represent domains differently, they have different information to use in classifying problems, and in accessing knowledge potentially useful in a new problem-solving situation. Similar findings have been obtained for novice and expert adult programmers [16].

Thus, in programming, even if novices begin to develop an understanding of the workings of the language and to write relatively sophisticated programs, they may represent programming in terms of the surface code, format and syntactic properties of a language, and in terms of particular tasks. Experts, on the other hand, are more likely to represent programming problems in terms of the general concepts which underlie particular programming constructs such as recursive routines and variables, the underlying structure of broad classes of problems, the solution strategies which crosscut many types of problems, or routinized plans [17] or "templates" [18] for solving common programming subproblems. Those aspects of programming problem-solving skills we hope will transfer, and that could transfer, involve the general structure of the problem-solving activity and general concepts. Further, the ability to transfer these techniques and concepts from programming will depend on recognizing problems in new domains where the techniques and concepts apply by analogical extension [11, 19].

Whether we are concerned about students learning to think better through programming, or in their learning to program, it is essential to recognize that we are in a very early state of knowledge about the psychology of programming. For this reason, any work in this area, has the nature of work in progress. The technologies available to schools, both hardware and software, are in great flux, and teachers' intuitions are being sharpened through their experiences in helping students learn programming, and to think through programming. So, as useful as any new findings in this area are likely to be for the educator, they must be treated with caution. At the same time, the influence on education of grandiose and optimistic pronouncements that have been made about the cognitive benefits of programming, and on the ease with which students can learn to program, cry out for empirical assessment, even in these early days in the field when the terrain changes faster then one's "research snapshot" develops.

THE PRESENT STUDY

To begin to examine more directly some of the many claims that are being made for and about programming we undertook a study designed to investigate the relation between thinking skills and programming, and to investigate the programming skills acquired by precollege students. We were interested in the development of programming skill among well taught precollege students with significantly more experience programming than most students who have participated in previous research studies.

Our study had three aims. The first was to document the impact of programming experience on a range of reasoning and math skills. The second was to observe the nature of the programming knowledge students attained. The third was to replicate findings from a previous study [20] that certain of these cognitive skills predict some aspects of programming skill acquisition.

Our choice of concepts and skills to investigate was based on a rational analysis of the cognitive components of programming and on correlations, found in previous research, between particular skills and programming mastery [6]. The tasks chosen involved procedural reasoning, decentering, planning, math understanding, and algorithm design.

Our particular task designs were based on an analysis of how the target skills are manifested in programming. Many of the skills we were interested in could not be assessed by standard cognitive ability measures, either because no measures of these skills exist or because existing measures demand skills in a form inappropriate to programming. For instance, standard tests of conditional reasoning examine comprehension of material implication as defined in standard logic. This is not particularly relevant to the use of conditionals in programming; rather the conditional reasoning skill practiced in programming involves reasoning through a complex chain of nested condition-action structures.

METHOD

Design

Three groups of high school students were tested at the beginning and end of the school year. One group of students, the *Experimental* group, was enrolled in their second year of programming. A second group, the *Some-CP* group, had taken one year of programming but had elected not to continue. A third group, the *No-CP* group, had no experience programming.

A battery of *posttests* administered at the end of the year was intended to assess the cognitive benefits resulting from the programming course, and for the *Experimental* group, programming knowledge and skill. Performance on these measures was compared among the three groups of students. The *pretests* administered at the beginning of the year were selected as potential predictors of

Table 1. Distribution of Subjects in Each Group According to Sex, Grade in School and Grade Point Average

Group	Sex		Grade			GPA	
	Male	Female	10th	11th	12th	Mean	Range
Experimental	11	4	9	3	3	74.3	40-93
No Prior Programming	9	7	8	2	6	78.0	68-96
Some Prior Programming	6	7	4	6	3	77.7	46-94
Total	26	18	21	11	12	76.6	40-96

performance in the programming class. These tests also served as measures of the initial ability level of students on many of the skills were were posttested.

Students

All students for the study were drawn from a large urban public high school with an ethnically and socio-economically mixed student body. The experimental group consisted of a full class of fifteen students who ranged widely in ability as indicated by their grade point average. Control students were selected from a pool of volunteers and matched with the experimental students on math background, overall GPA, and grade level. Students in the Some-CP group had taken an introduction to computers through the BASIC language course the previous year. Table 1 gives the breakdown of the three groups by sex, grade, and GPA.[1]

Programming Instruction

Students in the experimental group had taken the same introductory course as the Some-CP students. They were currently enrolled in a second, more intensive programming course taught by an excellent programming teacher with five years experience.[2] Class met for forty minutes, five days a week in one of the school's computer labs. Over the year students studied six programming languages. They spent nine weeks each on BASIC, COBOL, and Logo and three weeks each on FORTRAN, MACRO, and Pascal.

[1] The number of students reported for results of certain measures varies since we were unable to administer some tests to one or two students in each group.

[2] The teacher of the Experimental students had a B.A. in Mathematics from Yale University, an M.A. in Interactive Educational Technology from Harvard University, and five years of teaching experience. Her students have won the department's prize exam for first year students in each of her five years, and her AP students placed very highly in national competition and on the Advance Placement Exam.

The nine week Logo section came at the end of the year. While the programming teacher designed and taught the curriculum for the other five languages, we designed, then had the teacher teach, the Logo curriculum. Our aim in designing the Logo curriculum was to help students develop a richer mental model of Logo than students in our previous studies seemed to develop. The focus was on control structure. Work was done solely in list processing—no turtle graphics were taught. In turtle graphics it is too easy for students to continue to generate interesting screen effects without understanding the code [21]. In list processing work, to obtain interesting effects requires a deeper understanding of the language. This approach has its own costs—students need to understand more of the language before they can do much of interest in it.

In our design of the Logo curriculum, we emphasized comprehension over production. Students were given handouts covering concepts and commands, worksheets that stressed program comprehension, and a glossary of Logo primitives, written in flow-of-control language (i.e., in terms of inputs and outputs of Logo command operations). And we supplied utilities for file management to encourage a tool-kit approach.

We designed a series of weekly projects, each building on the previous ones, so that in principle each project could be a modular tool for the next project. The final project was to program a simple version of ELIZA, the program that mimics a non-directive psychotherapist [22]. Topics covered in the course included Logo commands (primitives, procedures, inputs, outputs, and outcomes, creating and editing procedures, words, lists, and list processing, input and output commands, workspace management commands, debugging, trace and error messages, subprocedures, procedures with input variables, naming and creating variables with the MAKE command, the OUTPUT command, conditionals, and tail and embedded recursion.

Measures

The specific rationale and design of each of the tasks used in the study is described fully elsewhere [23]. A brief review of the tasks is provided below.

Pretests – To assess the extent to which skills acquired in programming transfer to other domains, we developed transfer tasks in both "far" and "near" contexts. Our far transfer tasks (the majority of the tasks), demanded skills we believed to be deeply ingredient to programming, but they bore no obvious surface similarities to programming tasks. One near transfer task, in addition to bearing deep structural similarities to programming, resembled programming tasks in several surface features. The pretests were divided into three types: procedural reasoning, planning, and mathematics.

Procedural Reasoning Tests – Rational analysis suggests that programming requires instrumental reasoning, particularly procedural reasoning. Designing, comprehending, and debugging programs requires this type of means-ends reasoning.

Programmers must make explicit the antecedents necessary for different ends, and must follow through the consequences of different antecedent conditions. Designing and following the flow of control of a program requires understanding different kinds of relations between antecedent and consequent events, and organizing and interrelating the local means-end relations leading to the final end. Therefore we designed a set of tasks to measure procedural/conditional reasoning with conditional structures in complex contexts. One task was non-verbal and two were verbal. The tasks involved following the flow of control in systems having logical structures analogous to the logical structures in computer languages. The systems involved reasonable though arbitrary and artificial rules to make them analogous to a programming language and to prohibit students' use of prior world knowledge.

Nonverbal Reasoning Task One.   This task was designed using non-English symbolisms so that verbal ability and comprehension of the "if-then" connective would not be an inhibiting factor for students.

Students had to negotiate passage through tree diagrams having an embedded conditional structure. The task tapped ability to discover which goals could be legally reached given that a set of antecedents were true, and ability to determine the antecedents necessary to reach given goals.

Passage through the trees required satisfaction of conditions set by nodes in the tree. Each node required a differing logical combination of various shaped "tokens." Nodes with a *disjunctive* structure offered a choice of tokens to be used, and nodes with a *conjunctive* structure required a combination of tokens. Some nodes were combinations of disjuncts and conjuncts.

The task had two parts. In the first part (Part A), for each question students were given a set of tokens and were asked to determine all goals that could be legally reached with that set. The second part (Part B) included additional components aimed at hypothetical reasoning and planning abilities. In some instances many routes were legal but students were encouraged to find the most efficient route. Here we were interested in the student's sense for elegant problem solutions. In other cases students were required to test a large number of possibilities to discover the one legal path.

Verbal Reasoning Task One.   The first verbal procedural reasoning task was analogous to the Non-verbal Procedural Reasoning tasks, but given in verbal form. This task used the "if . . . then . . . else" structure often found in programming. The task assessed ability to follow complex verbal instructions consisting of nested conditionals. Students had to understand the hierarchical relations between instructions, e.g., that some condition was only relevant given the outcome of a prior condition.

The task involved following instructions within a precisely defined set of rules (determining a student's tuition from a complex set of rules based on the student's background and current academic level). Like the non-verbal task, students were given different types of questions to test their mastery of the complex logical structure. In some questions (Type A) students were given a set of antecedents and were asked for the consequence. In other questions (Type B), the goal or answer was given and the student had to determine what antecedent conditions must have been satisfied. Finally, other questions (Type C) asked what are all and only the decisions that must be made in order to determine a particular outcome given partial knowledge about the conditions. These questions required a good understanding of the structure of the instructions. Students had to separate irrelevant from relevant conditions and understand the hierarchical relation among conditions.

Verbal Reasoning Task Two.   This task had a complex conditional structure with a number of goals and conditions for satisfaction. The problem had two conditional structures, in addition to the "if . . . then . . . else" structure, that were isomorphic to programming conditionals. There was a "do-until" loop structure, and a structure isomorphic to an "on gosub" or "Jump match" structure where a match between variables determines what you do.

Planning Task.   Several analyses of the cognitive components of programming isolate planning as a central activity [4-7, 24]. After defining the problem to be solved, the programmer develops a plan or "structured description" of the processes required to solve the problem [5], that will then be written in programming code. Observations of expert programmers reveal that a major portion of their time is devoted to planning and that they have available many general plan-design strategies. Pea and Kurland provide an indepth discussion of the nature of planning as it is manifested in programming [24].

The task used to assess planning skill was a slightly modified version of that described in Pea, Hawkins and Kurland [21] (also see [24]). The task involved scheduling a set of classroom chores: students had to design a plan which specified the sequence in which chores should be completed in order to clean-up a classroom in as little time as possible. The chores were to be executed by a hypothetical "robot" who responded to a minimum set of commands, and required a specified amount of time to perform specific actions.

This was a computer-based task. A graphics interface depicted a classroom in which the chores were to be done. Students gave English commands to instruct the robot how to clean up the room and the experimenter typed the commands into the computer. Students designed three plans. After each plan, students were told how much time the Robot would take to actually execute the plan.

The programming and nonprogramming students were each further divided into two subgroups. One subgroup received "feedback" after each plan and the other subgroup did not. Although all students were told of the time that would be required to complete their plans, "feedback" students also received a paper print-out of their plan listing each action and the amount of time it required. They were also shown a screen display of the classroom, in which a step by step enactment of the student's plan (the path of the robot as he completed each chore) was carried out under the student's control. We proposed that there may be group differences in the extent to which students benefited from the feed-back information.

The planning task was administrated for both the pretests and posttest. Two types of data yielded by this task were used in the analyses to be reported. One was the time required to execute the students' plans. The second was the planning behavior of the students. This was assessed by their use of the plan monitoring aids, which was recorded by the computer, and the amount of time they spent thinking about their plan, also recorded automatically by the computer.

Math Test.   Math ability has been hypothesized to be both a cognitive demand and an outcome of programming experience [6, 25]. Similarities between high school math and programming exist at several levels. Math and programming languages are both formal systems with well-defined syntactic rules. Both employ the concepts of variable and algorithm. At the procedural level, both may demand representing relatively rich situations in relatively abstract formalisms, and then operating on these formalisms to compute an outcome. Math word problems require extracting essential relations from a prose description of a situation and representing them in mathematical terms. Programming involves giving an explicit procedural representation of a desired output.

Thus we included a math task that we felt would be relevant to programming. Since the math backgrounds of our students varied, and we did not want the task to demand special knowledge, we considered the most basic algebraic concept—the use of letters to represent variables. All students had enough math so that this notation was familiar. The task was designed to depend more on the ability to systematically operate with variables, and on insight during mathematical thinking, than on domain-specific mathematical knowledge.

These salient similarities guided our task design. We gathered a set of math problems that tested either grasp of variables, especially evaluating functions, which is analogous to keeping track of a variable in programming, or ability to relate a symbolic expression to a prose description.

We wanted the variables task to reflect the use of variables in programming. Since values of variables are often passed, modified and printed in programming, we chose problems in which students had to determine the values of variables which were defined in terms of other variables. They thus had to evaluate nested functions, following a chain of several variables to reach a constant. To follow the calculation through would be analogous to tracing the value of a variable through the execution of a program.

Posttests

The battery of posttests included mesures of procedural reasoning, decentering, planning, math ability, and algorithm design and comprehension. All but the algorithm test can be seen as measures of "far transfer:" the tests demanded skills and concepts we believed to be ingredient to programming, but the tests bore no obvious surface similarities to a programming task. The algorithm task was our measure of "near transfer;" in addition to deep structural similarities to programming, the task also resembled a programming task in several surface features.

Non-Verbal Procedural Reasoning Task Two — This was a slight modification of the non-verbal procedural reasoning pretest. The rationale was the same—to test procedural and conditional reasoning ability in a non-verbal situation in which reasonable though arbitrary rules must be followed.

This task, like the pretest, had two parts. Rules were similar to Part B of the original non-verbal task. However, unlike the previous task, there was no question designed to assess elegance. In Part A of the posttest students were given a set of passes and were asked to find all the goals they could reach with the passes. These questions assessed ability to exhaustively test conditions in order to discover all legal routes through the tree with the given passes.

In Part B, students were given a set of passes and were asked to find the correct path leading to a particular goal. There was only one legal path for each question. Again, students had to plan, and evaluate several possible routes in order to arrive at the legal route. For the first problem, possibilities could be easily reduced if students compared the number of passes they were given with the number required to reach the goal. The second problem was more difficult since more possibilities had to be tested.

Debugging Task — Programming, especially debugging, demands decentering—programmers must differentiate between their knowledge and intentions and the actual programming code the computer reads. This is a common problem for novice programmers [26]. In program construction the programmer must realize the level of explicitness required to adequately instruct the computer, and in debugging must distinguish expectations from what the computer actually executed. We hypothesized that after learning to program, students might be better at writing and debugging instructions in general.

The debugging task required both instrumental reasoning and decentering. Students were required to detect bugs in a set of driving instructions written for another person to follow. Students had to follow the given instructions, assess their accuracy, and correct "buggy" instructions. This required them to use means-ends analysis and temporal reasoning to assess the consequences and connections among temporally ordered actions. Students had to decenter, making a distinction between the subject's and the driver's knowledge, in order to tell whether instructions were sufficiently explicit and accurate. Bugs included were:

1. *Ambiguous information bug* — instructions not sufficiently explicit to enable the driver to correctly make a choice between alternative routes.
2. *Temporal order bug* — one instruction was stated at the wrong time.
3 *Insufficient or missing information bug.*
4. *Complex bugs* — problems due to unusual input conditions, and embedding, in which obvious corrections fail because they introduce and/or leave a bug.

For each line of instructions with a bug, students were scored for whether they caught the bug, and whether they correctly rewrote the instruction (fixed the bug). For lines of instruction not containing a bug, students were scored for whether they left the line unchanged, or instead inserted information which resulted in a new bug.

Math Test — The math posttest focused on calculating values of variables and translating prose descriptions into symbolic expressions. The rationale was that by programming in six different languages students would have explicit knowledge of variables and considerable practice in setting up equations with variables and tracing the calculation of values of variables.

We used three symbolic expression problems that have been used by Erhlich, Abbot, Salter, and Soloway in studying the transfer of programming abilities to math tasks [27]. The tasks gave prose descriptions and asked for an equation that expressed the same information. For one of the problems we gave students a partial equation to be completed. Ehrlich *et al.* gave programmers and nonprogrammers partial equations of different forms, and found that the advantage of a programming background was most evident when the equation was written with a single variable on one side, e.g., $R = 3/4 \times D$, rather than when written as a multiple expression, e.g., $4R = 3D$. Ehrlich *et al.* suggested that programmers benefited from the single variable expression because in programming one thinks of an active generation of a value, rather than a static description of a relationship.

Two of the three variable problems were the same as given on the math pretest. The third was a simpler problem, based directly on the sort of functional evaluation one finds in Logo list processing, i.e., "$A = B + 1; B = C + 10; C = D + 100; D = 0$; What is the value of A?" Because of poor average performance on the pretest we sought to reduce the difficulty of the easiest problems.

Algorithm Design and Analysis Task

This task assessed comprehension and production of an algorithm within a task designed to closely resemble a programming task. An *Analysis* part asked students to understand a program-like algorithm or "plan;" a *Design* part asked them then to develop an improved algorithm of their own. The task employed a meaningful rather than an abstract programming-language, but its structure resembled the structure of a computer program with sub-routines. The steps of the algorithms were functionally equivalent to programming language commands, as the task description will make clear. Thus, the task served both as: 1) a measure of general algorithmic concepts and skills employed in programming, which might develop through programming, and 2) a measure of "near" transfer to test whether skills employed in programming transferred more readily when the task structure is more transparently analogous to a program.

Students were presented with a goal and a series of legal operators (e.g., count, increment, decrement, test). The algorithms consisted of organizing the operations in such a way so as to achieve the goal efficiently. Efficient correct algorithms had to have a looping structure. Students were given one algorithm, a looping structure with two flaws that made it inefficient. They were asked to calculate the time required to achieve the goal if the algorithm were executed (assuming 10 seconds per operations). This required students to understand the algorithm. Students were then asked to devise a better algorithm. The students' algorithms were scored for the overall design, use of an iterative structure, accuracy, and conformity to the rules of the system.

Programming Skill Measures

Measures of the programming skills of students in the experimental group included both final scores on regular class tests given for each language, and a specially constructed test administered at the time of the posttest. The teacher designed the regular class tests with the exception of a "Conditional-Iteration" question designed by us and included on the final test for four of the languages.

The Conditional-Iteration question was designed to assess procedural reasoning and understanding of variables within each of the languages taught. For this question, students were asked to show the output (values of variables) of a short program which was structurally analogous, across the four languages tested (BASIC, FORTRAN, COBOL, Logo). Success required ability to follow the flow of control and keep track of variable values. Each program had an iterative (looping or recursive) structure, multiple variables, and conditional tests. The antecedent of each conditional test evaluated the value of a variable; the consequent either incremented a variable, stopped an iteration, or printed a statement. Like the problems on the math tests which asked students to evaluate variables, many variables in these programs were defined in terms of each other, rather than in terms of constants. To fully test students' understanding of how control is passed and of the order of execution of statements, each program contained a line of code designed to detect students' "order bugs," misconceptions of flow of control. This was a conditional test whose consequent prints a statement, but whose antecedent is never satisfied given the order of execution of commands. If students included the statement as output in their answer, they did not correctly follow the flow of the program. A correct answer to each problem displayed the correct values of three variables printed after three iterations.

Logo Test — The second programming measure was a comprehensive Logo test designed by us and administered by the classroom teacher as the students' final exam. This test assessed program comprehension and program production. The program comprehension questions included:

1. A *matching task*: examples of Logo expressions must be identified as expressions of a certain kind. For example, given the expression: "*A*, does Logo read this as a word, number, list, procedure, variable or primitive?

2. A *flow of control task*: students must show the screen effects for a procedure containing three subprocedures each of which prints a certain word.
3. Four *program comprehension tasks* which focused on list processing primitives, the MAKE and OUTPUT commands, tail recursion, and embedded recursion, respectively. Students needed to show the screen effects for four, 2- to 4-line programs, written with these structures. Each program contained local variables, and students were given particular input values.

The program production part of the task required students to write programs (on paper) to generate three given screen effects. They were told to use separate super-procedures to generate each display, but that the super-procedures could share subprocedures. They were also to give the appropriate run commands. An example task was given. The first screen effect the students were to generate was a display of two short English sentences; the second was identical to the first with two sentences added; the third screen effect was identical to the second with the exception that the subject and object of the added sentences was different. Thus, an ideal approach to this task involved the creation of two subprocedures. One would produce the first screen effect. The second would produce the remaining two sentences for the other two effects, by using variables for the subject and object of the sentence.

PROCEDURE

All groups of students received all the pre- and posttest measures, with the exception of the measures of planning skill, and programming skill. The planning task was only administered to the experimental group and to the *No-CS* control group.[3] The programming tests were only given to the *Experimental* group.

Pretests were given during the first month of classes in the fall and the posttests were given during the last month of classes in the spring. We were able to give the Experimental group and most control students the math and procedural reasoning tasks during class time; other students were given the math and reasoning tasks individually. The planning task was always individually administered. All tasks, with the exception of the Planning Task, were administered under time constrainted conditions (5 to 17 minutes per task).

RESULTS

The study was designed to address three questions:

1. Did learning programming for two years occasion advances in reasoning and math skills? Did these second-year programming students perform better, at

---

[3] The planning task was individually administered. Consequently, logistics did not permit administration of this task to both control groups.

the end of the year, on tasks assessing reasoning and math skills, than students who had only one introductory course?
2. Were certain math and reasoning skills good predictors of success in a programming course? What were the correlations between performance on reasoning, math and programming tasks?
3. Were students able to program at an advanced level after their second year of programming?

Performance of Programming and Nonprogramming Students on Pretest Measures of Reasoning, Math and Planning Skills

To make meaningful *posttest* comparisons between programmers and nonprogrammers, we first examined the comparability of the groups in terms of the skills measured. One purpose of our pretest battery was to make this assessment. The pretests were designed to measure many of the same skills as the posttests, and in two instances the pre and post measures were identical. We compared the three groups on the pretests using analyses-of-variance. Also, correlations between pre- and posttests were examined to provide evidence for the underlying equivalence of the measures.

To conduct these analyses, composite scores were computed for each pretest measure. The analyses-of-variance on each composite showed there were no significant differences between groups for any measures.

The means and standard deviations for the math pretest scores are shown in Table 2. One score consisted of the combination of the two variables problems. Another score consisted of performance on the remaining three questions. As shown in the table, performance was generally low and highly variable. Students had difficulty computing the values of variables except in the simplest cases. They were also generally unable to create the symbolic expression for a word problem.

Table 2. Performance on the Math Prestest: Mean Number of Points in Each Group

	Group					
	Experimental (N = 15)		Control (Some-CP) (N = 12)		Control (No-CP) (N = 16)	
	Mean	SD	Mean	SD	Mean	SD
Variables Questions (max = 8)	3.67	2.66	2.50	2.71	2.31	2.85
Other Questions (Max = 8)	1.60	1.12	2.00	1.86	3.06	2.69

Table 3. Performance on theNon-Verbal Procedural Reasoning Pretest:
Mean Number of Points in Each Group

	Group					
	Experimental (N = 15)		Control (Some-CS) (N = 13)		Control (No-CS) (N = 16)	
	Mean	SD	Mean	SD	Mean	SD
Part A (max = 60)	19.47	19.38	32.39	16.34	28.63	17.85
Part B (max = 6)	.73	1.10	.92	1.71	1.69	2.15

Table 4. Performance on the Verbal Procedural Reasoning Pretests:
Mean Number of Points in Each Group

	Group					
	Experimental (N = 15)		Control (Some-CS) (N = 13)		Control (No-CS) (N = 16)	
	Mean	SD	Mean	SD	Mean	SD
Verbal Task 1 Type A and B Questions (max = 18)	6.40	4.37	9.54	5.09	7.88	5.33
Type C Questions (max = 7)	1.00	.93	2.15	1.14	1.38	1.89
Verbal Task 2 (max = 6)	1.33	1.80	1.31	1.65	1.31	1.92

Table 3 shows performance on composite scores for Part A and Part B of the nonverbal reasoning task. Again performance was fairly low for each group. Students could discover some of the correct goals in Part A (which asked them to discover all possible legal goals given a set of tokens), but were often not exhaustive. For Part B, students were usually able to find a legal, but not the best, path to a goal.

Results for Verbal Reasoning Task One are shown in Table 4. For all of the verbal tasks, performance indicated that all groups of students had difficulty following the complex nested conditionals given in the verbal instructions.

Table 5 shows performance by each group on the planning task. There were no group differences due to feeeback condition, so scores were collapsed for this factor. Two general measures of performance are shown: the amount of time it

Table 5. Performance on the Planning Pretest

	Group			
	Experimental (N = 15)		Control (No-CS) (N = 16)	
	Mean	SD	Mean	SD
Plan Execution Time— In Minutes[a]				
Mean Plan Time (across 3 plans)	21.42	1.93	21.73	2.65
Best Plan Time	19.57	1.58	19.67	2.12
Planning Behavior Mean "Think" Time— In Minutes	33.34	13.12	30.02	9.34
Mean Number of Pauses	4.44	2.61	4.13	1.83
Mean Number of Reviews	1.02	1.19	.56	.69
Mean Number of Checks	.27	.38	.56	.71

[a] Optimal time = approximately 17 minutes.

would take to execute their plans (lower times indicate more efficient plans) and the amount of "planning behavior" on the part of the students. Measures of planning behavior include the amount of time students spent thinking about their plans while creating them, the number of pauses between commands (where a pause was defined as any time a student waited five seconds or more between two consecutive steps in their plan) and the extent to which they took advantage of the plan monitoring aids available: the number of times they *reviewed* a listing of their plan so far, and the number of times they *checked* a list of remaining chores. As shown in the table, there are no differences between groups on any of these measures. This allowed us to compare groups directly on the posttest.

Performance of Programming and Nonprogramming Students on Posttests of Reasoning and Math Skills

Non-Verbal Procedural Reasoning Posttest — Composite scores were developed for Part A and for Part B of the nonverbal reasoning test. Performance on these measures for each group is shown in Table 6. There were no significant between-group differences. As on the pretest, students were often able to discover some of the correct goals in Part A, but tended not to be exhaustive. For Part B, many students were unable to find the one legal path for either one or both of the questions asked.

Table 6. Performance on the Non-Verbal Procedural Reasoning
Posttest: Mean Number of Points in Each Group

	Group					
	Experimental (N = 15)		Control (Some CS) (N = 13)		Control (No CS) (N = 16)	
	Mean	SD	Mean	SD	Mean	SD
Part A (max = 90)	59.27	24.14	55.08	23.13	58.56	21.23
Part B (max = 2)	.73	.88	.85	.80	.88	.96

Debugging Posttest — Table 7 shows students' performance on the four specific types of bugs. The groups did not differ in their ability to detect or correct any of the classes of bugs. For all groups the temporal order bug was relatively easy to detect. For the remaining types of bugs, students in each group, on the average, were able to detect half of the bugs present. For these bugs, once a bug was detected, most students could successfully correct it. Few students were able to completely detect and correct the complex, embedded bugs.

Planning Posttest — Table 8 shows performance on the planning task. Again, there were no significant differences between groups on any of the measures of plan execution time or planning behavior.

It was of particular interest to compare the groups performance on this task to their performance on it at the beginning of the year. A repeated-measure ANOVA was carried out with Group and Feedback Condition as between-subject variables and Session (pre/post) as a within-subject variable. Mean plan-time (the average of the three plans) was the dependent measure. This analysis revealed that there was a main effect for session—mean plan-times improved slightly overall from the pre- to posttests—but there was no effect for Group, or Feedback Condition, and no interactions. Thus, there were improvements on the planning task over the year but the programming students did not improve any more than the non-programming students, nor did they respond differently to the feedback.

Math Test — As shown in Table 9, no significant differences between groups were found on either the variables problems or the symbolic expressions problems. Thus our findings were not consistent with previous results [27] in which college-level programming appeared to provide advantages for solving word problems given partial equations of the form used here.

A second analysis of performance on the math test involved comparing performance on the subset of those problems which were identical to problems on the pretest. There were eight variable value calculation questions in common between the two tests and the composite scores for these were compared. A

Table 7. Performance by Each Group on the Debugging Posttest: Mean Number of Bugs Detected and Corrected in Each Category

	Group					
	Experimental (N = 15)		Control (Some CS) (N = 13)		Control (No CS) (N = 16)	
	Mean	SD	Mean	SD	Mean	SD
Bug Types						
Ambiguous Information (max = 2)						
Detect	1.13	.83	1.15	.80	1.06	.85
Correct	1.07	.80	1.00	.82	.75	.93
Insufficient Information (max = 4)						
Detect	1.67	1.11	2.00	1.15	1.94	1.18
Correct	1.27	.96	1.77	1.17	1.75	1.24
Temporal Order (max = 1)						
Detect	.80	.41	.77	.44	.69	.48
Correct	.60	.51	.62	.51	.56	.51
Complex (max = 2)						
Detect	.73	.59	.92	.64	.88	.72
Correct	.40	.63	.62	.65	.56	.73

Table 8. Performance on the Planning Posttest

	Group			
	Experimental (N = 15)		Control (No CS) (N = 16)	
	Mean	SD	Mean	SD
Plan Execution Time— In Minutes[a]				
Mean Plan Time (across 3 plans)	20.22	1.69	21.04	1.78
Best Plan Time	18.85	1.23	19.17	1.23
Planning Behavior Mean "Think" Time—				
In Minutes	23.17	12.30	23.73	9.32
Mean Number of Pauses	2.87	2.11	2.79	1.34
Mean Number of Reviews	.40	.46	.56	.51
Mean Number of Checks	.49	.55	.31	.45

[a] Optimal time = approximately 17 minutes.

Table 9. Performance on the Math Posttest:
Mean Number of Points in Each Group

	Group					
	Experimental (N = 14)		Control (Some CS) (N = 13)		Control (No CS) (N = 15)	
	Mean	SD	Mean	SD	Mean	SD
Variables Problems (max = 9)	5.64	3.05	5.77	2.31	5.00	2.04
Equation Problems (max = 3)	1.29	1.20	1.15	1.14	1.20	.94

Table 10. Performance by Each Group on the Algorithm Analysis and
Design Task: Number of Subjects in Each Response Category
for Algorithm Analysis

	Group		
	Experimental (N = 14)	Control (Some CS) (N = 13)	Control (No CS) (N = 15)
Gave approximately correct time	5	2	2
Understood but calculated incorrectly	4	4	9
Response indicates no understanding	3	6	4
No answer	2	1	0

repeated-measures ANOVA (group by session) indicated that posttest performance was significantly better ($F(1,38) = 26.25$; $p < .00$). However, there was no main effect for group nor an interaction. This result was surprising given the degree to which students in the programming course had to work with variables, and the number of different ways they encountered them in their programming tasks.

Algorithm Design and Analysis Test – The two parts of this task—analysis and design of an algorithm—were analyzed separately. Students' ability to analyze an existing algorithm is shown in Table 10. No significant differences between groups were found.

Groups were compared for the style and adequacy of the algorithm they generated. Although there were no between-group differences on an overall composite

Table 11. Algorithm Analysis and Design Task:
Number of Algorithms in Each Group Receiving Each Score

	Group		
	Experimental (N = 14)	Control (Some CS) (N = 13)	Control (No CS) (N = 15)
Scoring Dimensions			
Scope of Intended Design[a]			
No design apparent	5	4	6
Specific to given input	5	4	2
Specific to input of a			
multiple of 4 coins	2	1	3
General Solution	2	4	4
Used Programming			
Structures			
Loop	5	2	1
Repeat	2	1	3
Conditional Test[b]	7	3	1
Counter[c]	10	3	2
Structural Errors Present			
In Counter/Counting	12	11	13
In Sequencing	7	5	9
Quality of Design[d]			
No design apparent	5	4	6
Many flaws	1	7	6
Few flaws	7	0	1
Working design	1	2	2

[a] Few algorithms would actually run if executed, but we assessed whether the attempted design was intended to be general or specific.

[b] Chi Square test on number of students using a conditional test = 7.13, $p < .05$.

[c] Chi Square on number of students using a counter = 11.95, $p < .05$.

[d] Chi Square on number of students falling into each quality of plan category = 16.04, $p < .01$.

score, there were differences on some subscores. As shown in Table 11, programming students were more likely to use three of the four programming structures possible: a loop, a conditional test, and a counter (differences in the frequency of use of the latter two structures were significant).

There was also a significant difference in the score for overall algorithm quality. While only one programming student wrote an algorithm that would actually work successfully, many more programming students than nonprogramming students wrote algorithms with only a few flaws. Only one programming student wrote an algorithm with many flaws, although six students in the nonprogramming groups wrote such algorithms.

The picture that emerges from these results is that programming students recognized this task as analogous to programming and could employ some of their knowledge from that domain to construct an algorithm. In comparison to non-programming students, they were better able to develop an algorithm which used efficient programming-like constructs, and which could be fairly easily debugged. However, their work was not flawless; there was usually at least one error either in the sequencing, in the use of the counter, or due to violation of the complex task constraints, which prevented their algorithms from actually working. They also did not usually write a general algorithm which would work for any number of input values.

Correlation of Math and Reasoning Pretests with Posttests

The math and reasoning pre- and posttests were almost all significantly correlated, even with grade point average partialed out. Results are shown in Table 12. (Math pretest scores are presented in Table 9.)

Correlation of Math and Reasoning Pre- and Posttests with Programming

We correlated performance on pre- and posttests with a composite of the test scores for each language and with subscores on the Logo tests. Table 13 shows correlations with the composite test scores. The procedural reasoning pretest scores and the math variables pretest score correlated significantly with the

Table 12. Correlations Between Pretests and Posttests
for All Subjects; Grade Point Average is Partialed Out ($N = 44$)

	PRETESTS Procedural Reasoning		
	Non-Verbal	Verbal	Math
Posttests			
Procedural Reasoning			
Non-Verbal 2	.45*	.64*	.72*
Debugging Test	.56*	.60*	.61*
Math	.39*	.69*	.74*
Algorithm			
Analysis	.35*	.50*	.56*
Design	.19	.39*	.23

*$p < .01$

Table 13. Correlation of Performance on Programming Tests
with Performance on Pre- and Posttests (Experimental Group) (*N* = 15)[a]

	Composite Programming Tests Score
Pretests	
Non-Verbal Procedural Reasoning	.48*
Verbal Procedural Reasoning	.66**
Math	.77**
Planning (mean time)	.09
Posttests	
Non-Verbal Procedural Reasoning	.65**
Debugging	.63**
Algorithm (analysis)	.85**
Algorithm (design)	.74**
Math	.77**
Planning (mean time)	−.65**

[a] *N* = 15 for correlations with all pretests, and the procedural reasoning and debugging posttests. *N* = 14 for correlations with the math and algorithm posttests.
 * $p < .05$
 ** $p < .01$

programming score. Of the posttests, the procedural reasoning, debugging, algorithm, and math scores correlated significantly with the programming tests. The math-variables pre- and posttest scores, and the algorithm task scores correlated particularly well with the programming measures.

Table 14 shows the correlation of the comprehension and production parts of the Logo Test with the pre- and posttests. Almost all correlations are significant. With grade point average partialed out, the pattern of significance remains essentially unchanged.

The correlations found between procedural reasoning, decentering and programming replicate findings of an earlier study of high school students learning Logo [20]. These skills, as well as the ability to evaluate the values of variables, to translate word problems into symbolic equations, and to design and comprehend an algorithm, appear to be centrally related to the development of programming skill.

Programming Ability in the Experimental Group

All measures of programming skill showed that most students had gained only a modest understanding of any of the languages taught. Only performance on the Logo test will be reported here along with the conditional flow of control question which we included on each of the tests for three other languages. Performance on the Logo test is representative of understanding of other languages

Table 14. Correlation of Performance on Logo Test with Performance
on Pre- and Posttests (Experimental Group) ($N = 13$)

	Logo Scores		
	Production	Comprehension	Total
Pretests			
Non-Verbal Procedural Reasoning	.59*	.68**	.69**
Verbal Procedural Reasoning	.62**	.67**	.66**
Math	.68**	.69**	.70**
Planning (mean time)	.02	−.11	.01
Posttests			
Non-Verbal Procedural Reasoning	.73**	.58*	.70**
Debugging	.71**	.69**	.72**
Algorithm			
Analysis	.84**	.80**	.84**
Design	.66**	.63**	.68**
Math	.57*	.65**	.61**
Planning (mean time)	−.34	−.59*	−.44

* $p < .05$
** $p < .01$

Table 15. Performance of the Experimental Group on the Final
Programming Tests in Each Language

	Mean Scores on Each Test	
	Mean	SD
BASIC	69.80	18.60
COBOL	64.07	22.91
FORTRAN	57.40	22.26
Logo	53.47	25.08

	Correlations Among Test Scores		
	BASIC	COBOL	FORTRAN
BASIC			
COBOL	.80*		
FORTRAN	.88*	.74*	
Logo	.88*	.91*	.72*

* $p < .01$

by the students; as shown in Table 15, performance in each language is highly correlated.

Logo Proficiency Test – In general, students exhibited a somewhat confused overall understanding of Logo. For example, when asked to identify Logo expressions as variables, procedure names, words, lists, or numbers, on the average only half of the students correctly identified the expressions. They had greatest difficulty recognizing a variable. On following the flow of control through a short Logo program only five of the students were successful. Several students showed understanding of the passage of control among subprocedures, but they failed to exhaustively follow the passing of control. The remaining students demonstrated no understanding of how the order of execution of the lines in a program is determined by particular flow of control commands and the current value of variables.

On the program comprehension problems, students were successful on a program which required understanding of a simple use of list processing primitives and an input variable. When the problem, requiring understanding of *Make* and *Output*, several understood that the OUTPUT command in a subprocedure passes information to a calling procedure, but they did not understand that the OUTPUT command ends the execution of a procedure. Only four students showed a good understanding of tail recursion and none could follow a program involving embedded recursion (also see [28]).

On the program production part of the Logo Test, approximately half of the students could produce the correct screen effects. Only three students used variables and only five students used subprocedures, even though much of the content for the three screen effects was similar or identical, and effectively created a demand for use of subprocedures and variables. The reamining students wrote linear "brute force" programs (lists of outputs preceded by the print command) or were unable to approach a successful program.

Overall, more students evidenced comprehension of variables and flow of control when given short simple programs than when asked to produce their own programs. This may indicate both the fragility of their understanding, and a lack of appreciation of the utility of variables and subprocedures.

Conditional Iteration Problems in Four Languages – Few students could successfully produce the output of short programs given in each language which had an iterative structure with conditional tests and multiple variables to be incremented. Many did understand lines of code which contained a conditional stop rule, incremented a variable, or created a global variable (in Logo). However, they often seemed to evaluate these lines out of context; many could not follow the flow of control and did not demonstrate understanding of the order of execution. A few students followed the order correctly but stopped the programs too soon (wrong number of iterations); they seemed to interpret the comparatives in the stop rule incorrectly, or to have some other difficulty with flow of control.

With the exception of the Logo version of this task, most students could not systematically keep track of values of variables. This was easier in Logo, where the program did not compare variables to each other (i.e., IF $X = Y$) but instead compared them to constants (i.e., IF $X = 3$). Also, the Logo task had only three variables whereas the other tasks had a fourth, counter variable. It is important to note that the "variables" problems on the math pre- and posttests were analogous to this programming problem. There were four variables, most of which had values defined in terms of other variables. Each of these tasks demanded a systematic approach in order to reduce working memory load. Students did not demonstrate skills for such systematic reasoning in their programming nor in their solving of the math problem.

DISCUSSION

Programming students were found to range greatly in their understanding of even basic programming principles and commands. For the most part they exhibited a weak understanding of flow of control or of the structure of the languages in which they worked. Observations of the students as they worked in their programming class indicated that students frequently shared ideas and code (compare [29]). While exploiting pre-written code is an honorable programming technique among professionals, in schools it is a double-edged sword. Some students relied on the understanding of a few good students and never bothered to learn the material themselves. Many students used a trial-and-error approach to a task, or immediately asked for help when stuck. Though several were concerned with understanding what to do, they did not seem to have techniques or rules for systematically analyzing buggy programs and for developing corrections.

Given the generally low level of programming understanding, even after two years of instruction, it did not come as a major surprise that there were no significant differences between the experimental and control groups for any of our measures of "far" transfer. This was the case even though our reasoning and math measures correlated with programming mastery indicating, as expected, that programming taps a number of specific complex cognitive skills.

The transfer tasks all proved to be fairly difficult for most students regardless of programming experience. Students had difficulty with exhaustive and accurate procedural reasoning, evaluating variables defined in terms of other variables, setting up an equation for a word problem expressing proportional relations, decentering sufficiently to exhaustively detect "buggy" instructions and constructing and monitoring a plan for efficient chore execution.

One reason postulated for previous failures to find far transfer still reigns central: students did not attain a very high level of expertise in programming. The significant gains we did find for programming students on the near transfer task—the Algorithm Design and Analysis Task—highlight the important relationship between the nature of knowledge transferred and the acquisition of expertise.

The algorithm task, to which programming students did apply some of their skills, was different from our other transfer measures in two ways: First, the possible knowledge to be transferred included specific programming concepts such as a "counter" and a conditional stop rule, as well as cognitive *operations* used in programming (such as procedural reasoning, or the systematic evaluation of variables). Second, it bore relatively obvious similarities to a programming task (the goal was to perform numerical computations given a set of functions analogous to programming commands or subprocedures). We found that students recognized the conditions for application of some of their programming concepts to the task. Also, to some extent they showed superior procedural reasoning ability; their overall plan quality was better than the nonprogramming students though many still made procedural errors.

These positive results exemplify the tight relation between transfer and what has been learned. The *concepts* transferred—the use of a counter, a loop and a conditional stop rule—are salient features of programming, explicitly represented in the code, and presented early in programming instruction. Thus they are familiar to, even if not fully mastered by, most novices. Given the transfer of the operational skills here and not to our other tasks, it is apparent that relatively context specific rather than general operations were learned.

Because most students' knowledge of the fundamental aspects of programming was quite limited, we do not conclude that development and *far* transfer of skills from programming cannot in principle occur. We can conclude, however, that such far transfer is unlikely to occur given the type of programming curriculum and amount of experience provided for these students, which if anything is misrepresentatively rigorous and unrealistically more intensive than that found in most schools today. Such experience is insufficient for mastery of the programming concepts and practices that engage and make more probable the far transfer of high level thinking skills. Until a population with greater programming expertise is studied longitudinally, the far transfer question remains open.

In conclusion, two things seem clear. First, mastery of at least basic programming skills appears to be essential for transfer, but is hard to achieve within the constraints imposed by the organization of schools. And second, if programming is to continue to play such a major role in the school curriculum, we need to develop much more effective ways of teaching children to program. Explicit devices for helping students see how flow of control structures work appear promising [30-33]. But better programming environments are not enough by themselves. Instruction must explicitly focus on helping the student build a model of how the programming language works. If the operation of the language is a mystery [26], then students cannot write complex and cognitively demanding programs. Early on and throughout instruction, understanding the control and data structures should be stressed. Trial-and-error creation of screen effects typical of pure discovery learning environments common in precollege programming should be tempered with directed teaching of the principles which underlie the effects.

Trial-and-error generation of screen effects neither engages high level thinking skills nor supports increased mastery of the language.

Another possibility often proposed is that, since transfer of thinking skills may involve representation of knowledge at a high level of abstraction, divorced from particular contexts, one might teach thinking skills at this general level of abstraction. Perhaps in this way the need for domain expertise can be bypassed. Unfortunately, we know from previous research that "methods without content are blind," that students have great difficulty deducing examples to which general thinking skills or rules they are taught will apply if they are presented with abstractions alone [34-38]. Insofar as instruction in general thinking skills programs has been effective in promoting transfer, it appears that there have been *explicit conditions for transfer designed into the instructional programs*, including multiple examples of skill application, links to real-world problem solving situations, content area instruction, abstract descriptions of thinking skill methods, and so on [39, 40]. These issues are too complex for treatment here, but will be important to systematically consider in future instruction and research with the aim of helping students learn generalizable thinking skills such as planning and problem solving methods through computer programming activities.

From our perspective, based on data from the present study and others [20, 21, 41-43], we do not believe that the current hope for *incidental* learning of generalizable thinking skills through programming is realistic, and would take these broader lessons about conditions for transfer of learning from the psychological literature into account in designing for transfer in the future. Whether with better programming environments, better instruction, and more explicit attention to designing instruction for transfer, programming will begin to more fully live up to its potentials and promises remains to be seen.

REFERENCES

1. S. Papert, *Mindstorms*, Basic Books, New York, 1980.
2. W. Feurzeig, S. Papert, M. Bloom, R. Grant, and C. Solomon, *Programming Languages as a Conceptual Framework for Teaching Mathematics* (BBN Report No. 1889), Bolt, Beranek, and Newman, Cambridge, Massachusetts, 1969.
3. R. S. Nickerson, Computer Programming as a Vehicle for Teaching Thinking Skills, *Thinking: The Journal of Philosophy for Children, 4*, pp. 42-48, 1982.
4. R. E. Brooks, Towards a Theory of the Cognitive Processes in Computer Programming, *International Journal of Man-Machine Studies, 9*, pp. 737-751, 1977.
5. R. Jeffries, A. A. Turner, P. G. Polson, and M. E. Atwood, The Processes Involved in Designing Software, in *Cognitive Skills and Their Acquisition*, J. R. Anderson (ed.), Erlbaum, Hillsdale, New Jersey, pp. 255-283, 1981.

6. R. D. Pea and D. M. Kurland, *On the Cognitive Prerequisites of Learning Computer Programming*, (Technical Report No. 18), Center for Children and Technology, Bank Street College of Education, New York, 1983.

7. N. Pennington, *Cognitive Components of Expertise in Computer Programming: A Review of the Literature*, (Technical Report No. 46), University of Michigan, Center for Cognitive Science, Ann Arbor, 1982.

8. R. Mawby, *Proficiency Conditions for the Development of Programming Skill*, paper presented at the International Conference on Thinking, Harvard University, Cambridge, Massachusetts, August, 1984.

9. J. G. Carbonell, *Derivational Analogy: A Theory of Reconstructive Problem Solving and Expertise Acquisition*, Technical Report CMU-CS-85-115, Carnegie-Mellon University, Computer Science Department, Pittsburgh, March 1985.

10. D. Gentner, Are Scientific Analogies Metaphors? in *Metaphor: Problems and Perspectives*, D. Miall (ed.), Harvester Press Ltd., Brighton, England, 1982.

11. _____, Structure-Mapping: A Theoretical Framework for Analogy and Similarity, *Cognitive Science*, 1983.

12. M. B. Hesse, *Models and Analogies in Science*, University of Notre Dame Press, Notre Dame, 1966.

13. K. J. Holyoak, Analogical Thinking and Human Intelligence, in *Advances in the Psychology of Human Intelligence*, Vol. 2, R. J. Sternberg (ed.), Erlbaum, Hillsdale, New Jersey, 1983.

14. A. L. Brown, J. D. Bransford, R. A. Ferrara, and J. C. Campione, Learning, Remembering, and Understanding, in *Cognitive Development* (Vol. III), J. H. Flavell and E. M. Markman (eds.), of P. H. Mussen (ed.), *Handbook of Child Psychology* (4th edition), Wiley, New York, 1983.

15. M. T. H. Chi, P. J. Feltovich, and R. Glaser, Categorization and Representation of Physics Problems by Experts and Novices, *Cognitive Science*, 5, pp. 121-152, 1981.

16. B. Adelson, Problem Solving and the Development of Abstract Categories in Programming Languages, *Memory and Cognition*, 9, pp. 422-433, 1981.

17. E. Soloway, *From Problems to Problems via Plans: The Content and Structure of Knowledge for Introductory LISP Programming*, Technical Report No. 21, Cognition and Programming Project, Yale University, Department of Computer Science, New Haven, Connecticut, 1984.

18. M. C. Linn, The Cognitive Consequences of Programming Instruction in Classrooms, *Educational Researcher*, 14, pp. 14-29, 1985.

19. D. N. Perkins and G. Salomon, Transfer and Teaching Thinking, in *Thinking: Progress in Research and Teaching*, J. Bishop, J. Lochhead, and D. Perkins (eds.), Erlbaum, Hillsdale, New Jersey, in press.

20. D. M. Kurland, C. A. Clement, R. Mawby, and R. D. Pea, Mapping the Cognitive Demands of Learning to Program, in *Thinking: Progress in Research and Teaching*, J. Bishop, J. Lochhead, and D. Perkins (eds.), Erlbaum, Hillsdale, New Jersey, in press.

21. R. D. Pea, J. Hawkins, and D. M. Kurland, LOGO and the Development of Thinking Skills, in *Children and Microcomputers: Research on the Newest Medium*, M. Chen and W. Paisley (eds.), Sage, Beverly Hills, California, 1985.

22. J. Weizenbaum, *Computer Power and Human Reason: From Judgment to Calculation*, W. H. Freeman, San Francisco, 1976.
23. D. M. Kurland, R. D. Pea, C. Clement, and R. Mawby, *A Study of the Development of Programming Ability and Thinking Skills in High School Students*, Technical Report, with Appendices, Center for Children and Technology, Bank Street College of Education, New York, 1985.
24. R. D. Pea and D. M. Kurland, *Logo Programming and the Development of Planning Skills*, (Technical Report No. 16), The Center for Children and Technology, Bank Street College of Education, New York, 1984.
25. ____, On the Cognitive Effects of Learning Computer Programming, *New Ideas in Psychology*, 2:1, pp. 137-168, 1984.
26. R. D. Pea, Language-Independent Conceptual Bugs in Program Understanding, *Journal of Educational Computing Research*, 2:1, pp. 25-36, 1986.
27. K. Ehrlich, V. Abbot, W. Salter, and E. Soloway, Issues and Problems in Studying Transfer Effects of Programming, in *Developmental Studies of Computer Programming Skills*, D. M. Kurland (ed.), (Technical Report No. 29), The Center for Children and Technology, Bank Street College of Education, New York, 1984.
28. D. M. Kurland and R. D. Pea, Children's Mental Models of Recursive Logo Programs, *Journal of Educational Computing Research*, 1:2, pp. 235-243, 1985.
29. N. M. Webb, Microcomputer Learning in Small Groups: Cognitive Requirements and Group Processes, *Journal of Educational Psychology*, 76:6, pp. 1076-1088, 1984.
30. D. duBoulay, T. O'Shea, and J. Monk, Presenting Computing Concepts to Novices, *International Journal of Man-Machine Studies*, 14, pp. 237-249, 1981.
31. B. duBoulay, Children Learning Programming, *Journal of Educational Computing Research*, in press.
32. D. Mioduser, R. Nachmias, and D. Chen, *Teaching Programming Literacy to Non-Programmers: The Use of Computerized Simulation*, (Technical Report No. 15), The Computers in Education Research Lab, Center for Curriculum Research and Development, School of Education, Tel Aviv University, Tel Aviv, Israel, 1985.
33. R. Nachmias, D. Mioduser, and D. Chen, A Cognitive Curriculum Model for Teaching Computer Programming to Children, in *Computers in Education*, K. Duncan and D. Harris (eds.), Elsevier Science Publishers, B. V. North Holland IFIP, 1985.
34. N. Frederiksen, Implications of Cognitive Theory for Instruction in Problem Solving, *Review of Educational Research*, 54, pp. 363-407, 1984.
35. R. M. Gagne, Learnable Aspects of Problem Solving, *Educational Psychologist*, 15, pp. 84-92, 1980.
36. R. Glaser, Education and Thinking: The Role of Knowledge, *American Psychologist*, 39, pp. 93-104, 1984.
37. R. E. Mayer, The Elusive Search for Teachable Aspects of Problem Solving, in *A History of Educational Psychology*, J. A. Glover and R. R. Ronning (eds.), Plenum, New York, in press.
38. A. Schoenfeld, *Mathematical Problem Solving*, Academic Press, New York, 1985.

39. R. D. Pea, *Transfer of Thinking Skills: Issues for Software Use and Design*, paper presented at a national conference on "Computers and Complex Thinking," National Academy of Sciences, Washington, D.C., 1985.

40. L. B. Resnick, *Education and Learning to Think: Subcommittee Report*, National Research Council Commission on Behavioral and Social Sciences and Education, Washington, D.C., NRC, 1985.

41. D. H. Clements and D. F. Gullo, Effects of Computer Programming on Young Children's Cognition, *Journal of Educational Psychology*, 76, pp. 1051-1058, 1984.

42. J. D. Milojkovic, "Children Learning Computer Programming: Cognitive and Motivational Consequences," Doctoral dissertation, Department of Psychology, Stanford University, 1983.

43. C. Clement, D. M. Kurland, R. Mawby, and R. D. Pea, *Analogical Reasoning and Computer Programming*, paper presented at the Conference on Thinking, Cambridge, Massachusetts, 1984.

6

LEARNING TO PROGRAM AND LEARNING TO THINK: WHAT'S THE CONNECTION?

RICHARD E. MAYER
JENNIFER L. DYCK
WILLIAM VILBERG
University of California, Santa Barbara

Many strong claims have been made concerning the relationship between learning to program and learning to think. In the process of learning to program a computer, it is assumed, students will also learn about their own thinking processes. This premise underlies many assertions concerning the usefulness of teaching computer programming in schools. For example, Papert [21] claims that, when children are allowed to write Logo programs, "powerful intellectual skills are developed in the process." Similarly, Bork [4] sees "computer programming as a vehicle for . . . training . . . analytic thinking applicable to broad classes of problems." Nickerson [20] argues that we should view "computer programming as a vehicle for teaching thinking skills."

Despite these claims, there have been very few relevant research studies and almost no convincing support of this connection [7, 8, 13, 17, 22]. This article presents research on three assertions concerning the relationship between learning to program and learning to think, based on a cognitive analysis of programming [17]. Each assertion is defined, available literature is reviewed, and an empirical study from our laboratory in Santa Barbara, California, is summarized to assess the current state of knowledge concerning the relationship between learning to program and learning to think.

In order to accomplish this goal, it is necessary to define what is meant by "learning to program" and "learning to think." In the context of this article, learning to program refers to the initial learning of a novice's first programming language. In particular, we focus on changes in people who initially know nothing about programming and who engage in approximately 10–50 hours of experience with Basic. Learning to think refers to improvements in problem solving in domains beyond the programming language that is taught. Linn [13] has suggested three possible "cognitive accomplishments" from learning programming in a language such as Basic: (1) learning the features of the language, such as the statements LET, PRINT, and INPUT; (2) learning to solve programming problems, such as designing programs in Basic; and (3) learning problem-solving skills applicable to other formal systems, such as problem solving in other languages. The third category, which represents "transfer" of learning to new domains, is the focus of this article.

As a brief historical prelude, it must be pointed out that the search for methods to teach problem solving has been an elusive one [14, 18]. For example, the Latin School movement, which originated in the 1600s in the United States, was one of the first large-scale attempts to teach "proper habits of mind." The curriculum focused on teaching students to read, write, and speak Latin, as well as teaching some Greek and geometry [23], the aim being to build logical and disciplined minds. However, the practical demands of an emerging industrialized society and the negative results of educational research studies eventually helped to bring on the demise of Latin Schools. Thorndike's classic "transfer of training" studies also found that learning Latin did not produce strong transfer to other domains [26]. Similar failures to produce transfer have been observed for modern curricula aimed at teaching general thinking skills [5, 15] and for compensatory training in general intellectual development [6]. Transfer is even rare when students who have learned problem-solving strategies within one domain are asked to solve formally identical problems presented within a different domain [5, 18]. It is from this historical context — of strong claims for transfer coupled with little or no research support — that we now address each of the three assertions discussed below.

ASSERTION 1: LEARNING A PROGRAMMING LANGUAGE WILL ENHANCE A PERSON'S THINKING SKILLS

Does learning a programming language enhance thinking skills in domains beyond programming? Preliminary studies involving Logo have offered mixed results. Although Papert [21] offers case studies and testimonials, the unreliability of such reports is notorious. In a research study, Pea and Kurland [22] failed to find support for the idea that a year of Logo activities improved children's strategic planning skills. Similarly, Gregg [11] found that four- and five-year-old children had great difficulty both in learning to program a turtle and in transferring what they had learned. Gorman and Bourne [10] found, however, that third graders who learned Logo with one extra hour of computer time per week performed better on tests of logical reasoning than third graders who learned Logo with just one half hour of extra computer time per week. Apparently, gains in thinking skills depend on the student being given heavy doses of Logo rather than just minimal exposure. The most encouraging study found that first graders who learned Logo during a 12-week course performed better on tests of creative problem solving than first graders who were exposed to computer-assisted instruction (CAI) over the same period [7]. This study involved very few students, however, so replications are needed.

Preliminary studies involving Basic have also yielded mixed results. Bayman and Mayer [3] and Bayman [2] have found that students who learn Basic in traditional hands-on, mastery courses often harbor serious misconceptions of Basic statements. Furthermore, students who are able to use Basic creatively in problem solving tend to have fewer misconceptions than students who are unable to solve problems [2]. Linn [13] attempted to investigate the idea that learning Basic would enhance students' problem-solving skills, but methodological problems such as students' difficulty in learning Basic precluded the study. One promising piece of evidence is that students who know and use Basic are better able to comprehend word problems, such as "There are six times as many students as professors at this university" [25]. These results suggest that there may be a connection between programming and problem solving in other domains.

In order to more closely examine the effects of novices' initial learning of Basic on their thinking skills, we conducted a study using 57 computer-naive college students who took a course in Basic. Before taking the course, all students took a battery of thinking skills pretests; at the end of the term, all students took versions of the same tests. A comparison group, consisting of 54 computer-naive students, took the same thinking skills pretests at the beginning of the term, and were retested toward the end. Both groups consisted of nonengineering students who had no plans to become professional programmers.

The left column of Table I lists eight thinking skills tests: *word problem translation* required translating word problems into equations, *word problem solution* involved giving the correct numerical answer for word problems, *following procedures* involved predicting the output for a procedure stated in English, *following directions* involved predicting the consequences of following one or more directions, *logical reasoning* involved solving a series of oddity problems, *visual ability* involved a series of paper folding tasks, *verbal ability* involved decoding of verbal messages, and *arithmetic computation* involved a series of addition and division problems. Test-retest reliability correlations were computed for each test, yielding a significant correlation at $p < 0.001$ for each test. Sample items from each test are shown in the sidebar.

TABLE 1
Eight Thinking Skills: Net Proportion Change after Learning Basic
and Predictive Correlation with Basic Exam Score

Thinking skill	Net change after learning Basic	Correlation with Basic exam score
Problem translation skil		
Word problem translation	+0.08*	0.55*
Word problem solution	+0.07*	0.56*
Procedure comprehension skill		
Following procedures	+0.18*	0.44*
Following directions	+0.04*	0.44*
General ability		
Logical reasoning	−0.01	0.29*
Visual ability	−0.05*	0.31*
Verbal ability	−0.01	0.16
Other skills		
Arithmetic computation	−0.01	0.26

The asterisk (*) indicates that gain score for Basic group is significantly different from gain score for comparison group based on a t-test ($p < 0.05$), or that correlation between pretest score and Basic exam score is significant ($p < 0.05$).

Some of the tests were designed to evaluate two skills that are specifically related to learning Basic: the problem translation skill — as measured by the word problem translation test and the word problem solution test; and the procedure comprehension skill — as measured by the following procedures test and the following directions test. These two skills, which can be called specific thinking skills or specific cognitive components of Basic programming, were identified by carrying out a cognitive task analysis of Basic programming [17]. Other tests were designed to evaluate general intellectual abilities such as logical reasoning, spatial ability, and verbal ability. Finally, the arithmetic computation test was included to evaluate a thinking skill — making rapid computations — that is not closely related to Basic programming.

Students in the Basic and comparison groups were matched for pretest score, so that mean scores on each pretest were identical for the two groups. Gain scores were computed by subtracting the proportion correct on the pretest from the proportion correct on the second test. The first column of numbers in Table I shows the net gain score for each thinking skill test for the Basic group, determined by subtracting the gain score for the comparison group from the gain score for the Basic group. As indicated, the Basic group gained significantly more than the comparison group on the two specific component thinking skills: problem translation (as measured by word problem translation and word problem solution) and procedure

Examples of Items from Eight Cognitive Tests

PROBLEM TRANSLATION

Word Problem Translation Test   (6 problems)
A car rental service charges 20 dollars a day and
15 cents a mile to rent a car. Find the expression for
total cost C, in dollars, of renting a car for D days to
travel M miles.

a. $C = 20D + 0.15M$
b. $C = 15D + 0.20M$
c. $C = 20D + 15M$
d. $C = 0.15D + 20M$
e.   None of the above

Word Problem Solution Test   (9 problems)
One day Mrs. Arnold worked 3½ hours in the morning,
took a ½ hour for lunch, and worked 4½ hours in the
afternoon. If she began work at 8:30 A.M., at what time
did she finish?

a.   4:30
b.   5:00
c.   5:30
d.   6:00
e.   6:30

PROCEDURE COMPREHENSION

Following Directions Test   (8 problems)

		Column		
	1	2	3	4	5
Row 1	A	B	C	D	E
Row 2	B	D	E	A	C
Row 3	C	E	D	A	B
Row 4	B	A	C	E	D
Row 5	A	C	E	B	D

Start in the lower left-hand corner, and follow the letters
up Column 1, down Column 2, up Column 3, and so on,
until you reach the upper right-hand corner. What is the
first letter to appear four times?

A   B   C   D   E

Following Procedures Test   (8 problems)

1.   Put 5 in Box A.
2.   Put 4 in Box B.
3.   Add the number in Box A and the number in Box B,
     and put the result in Box C.

4.   Add the number in Box A and the number in Box C,
     and put the result in Box A.
5.   Write down the numbers from Box A, B, and C.

What is the output of this program?

a.   5, 4, 9
b.   14, 4, 9
c.   14, 9, 9
d.   9, 4, 9
e.   None of the above

GENERAL ABILITIES

Logical Reasoning Test   (10 problems)
Draw an X through the set of letters that is different.

BCDE   FGHI   JKLM   PRST   VWXY

Spatial Ability   (10 problems)
Draw an X through the correct answer.

Verbal Ability   (9 problems)

black sheep = dag kip
white dog   = tin bud
black cow   = dag stam
white sheep =

a.   dag kip
b.   tin kip
c.   stam dag
d.   bud tin
e.   tin bud

OTHER

Computation   (60 problems)

```
  36
  20
+ 54
```

comprehension (as measured by following procedures and following directions). The results of the word translation test are consistent with the results
of Soloway and his colleagues [25] in that the learning of Basic programming seems to be related to improved skill in representation of word
problems. In contrast, the Basic group did not show significantly greater
statistical gains than the comparison group on tests of general intellectual
ability, including logical reasoning, spatial ability, and verbal ability. As
expected, learning Basic did not tend to increase students' computational
speeds.

These results encourage the idea that learning a programming language —
even a language with as many critics as Basic has — can result in changes in
thinking skills. The improvements appear to be limited to thinking skills
that are specifically tied to specific concepts underlying Basic, however, and
there is no evidence of any enhancement of intellectual ability in general.
The conclusion that can be drawn concerning this assertion is a modest one:

Under appropriate conditions, learning to program may result in increases for specifically related thinking skills, but there is not strong support for the idea that it will radically improve general thinking skills.

ASSERTION 2: CERTAIN THINKING SKILLS WILL ENHANCE THE LEARNING OF PROGRAMMING

The question of what students need to know in order to learn a programming language has motivated many studies, which find that general measures of nonverbal intellectual ability such as in the IBM Programmer Aptitude Test (PAT) or Aptitude Assessment Battery Programming (AABP) can correlate with programming test scores in the range of $r = 0.3$ [1, 8, 9, 12, 19]. However, as Webb [27] points out, "it is unclear which specific abilities included in these tests relate most strongly to performance."

It is not particularly surprising or useful to find that measures of general intelligence are related to students' learning of programming, as general intelligence tests are designed to predict success in academic learning under a wide variety of situations. The fact that such tests tend to predict success in initial programming ability simply points to the tests' predictive validity: Success on the test is related to success in learning to program. A theoretically more important form of validity is construct validity—that is, determining the underlying cognitive mechanisms to explain why performance on a test is related to success in learning to program. The search for construct validity requires a search for tests that measure theoretically meaningful thinking skills, such as specific component processes required for programming in Basic [17].

Accordingly, our analysis of whether or not thinking skills enhance programming ability is concerned mainly with construct validity (in addition to predictive validity). Another way of stating this focus is to say that our analysis of this assertion is concerned with identifying specific thinking skills (in addition to general thinking skills).

The issue of which specific thinking skills are related to the learning of programming has been examined in only a few studies. Snow [24] reports that success in learning Basic is more strongly related to "diagraming" ($r = 0.66$)—a problem representation skill specifically related to programming— than to general verbal intellectual ability ($r = 0.17$). In addition, tests measuring nonverbal logical reasoning and mathematics problem solving correlated with learning Basic ($r = 0.54$). Similarly, Webb [27] found that the best predictor of success in learning Logo was a mathematics test consisting of word problems and computation problems ($r = 0.81$). In addition, tests of nonverbal logical reasoning correlated strongly with learning Logo ($r = 0.49$); spatial ability correlated with learning Logo in Webb's study, but not with learning Basic in Snow's report.

The picture that emerges from this work is that success in learning a language such as Basic may depend on such specific skills as ability to translate a word problem into an equation or answer (problem translation), and ability to follow directions listed as a procedure (procedure comprehension). In fact, tests based on these specific thinking skills, or cognitive components, provide the basis for construct validity and may provide even better predictive validity than traditional measures of general skills, such as logical reasoning, and spatial and verbal ability.

In order to test these hypotheses concerning predictive thinking skills for Basic, we conducted a series of studies that each generated similar results, but will focus on the study previously described, in which we administered a battery of tests to 57 college students before and after a course in Basic.

The second column of numbers in Table I (p. 606) summarizes the correlations between pretest score and Basic exam score for each pretest. Tests of the two specific thinking skills and two of the three general abilities tests tended to predict success in learning Basic. A subsequent stepwise multiple regression analysis revealed that tests measuring the two specific thinking skills were better predictors of success than tests measuring general ability: word problem translation, word problem solution, and following directions were selected for the regression equation. Performance on these three tests accounted for approximately 50 percent of the variance in Basic exam scores. It is significant that the most highly predictive thinking skills are logically related to Basic programming (i.e., are specific thinking skills or component skills), but not identical to information taught in Basic instruction. These results are consistent with a single study reported by Snow [24], in which skill at problem representation was related to learning Basic.

This part of our study demonstrates how it is possible to pinpoint specific thinking skills that are related to learning a programming language. As expected, success in learning Basic was related to general intellectual ability, especially logical reasoning and spatial ability. More importantly, this study identified two specific thinking skills that are based on a cognitive task analysis of Basic [17]: ability to translate word problems into equations or answers (problem translation skill), and ability to predict the outcome of a procedure or set of directions that is stated in English (procedure comprehension skill). The search for additional specific thinking skills represents a potentially fruitful direction for future research.

ASSERTION 3: PRETRAINING ON CERTAIN THINKING SKILLS WILL ENHANCE THE LEARNING OF PROGRAMMING

The first two sections of this article provide empirical support for the idea that the ability to learn Basic is predicted in part by two specific thinking skills, and that an outcome of learning Basic is improvement in these two skills. The next logical step is to determine if direct instruction in these predictive thinking skills can foster the learning of Basic.

This issue has not been convincingly addressed in existing published research. In some of our previous work [2, 16], we have given pretraining in appropriate mental models for various programming languages. Pretraining tended to enhance students' subsequent learning of programming languages, especially for those who lacked computer programming aptitude. This line of research only indirectly informs our analysis of this issue, since the pretraining is not on specific thinking skills.

A preliminary study, conducted in our labs at Santa Barbara by Jenny Dyck, addresses this issue. In Dyck's study, 23 randomly selected college students (no pretraining group) learned Basic by reading a manual and through exercises in predicting the outputs of simple Basic programs. For example, a typical problem was the following:

Determine the output of this program:

```
10 LET A = 3
20 LET B = A + 5
30 PRINT B
40 END
```

If the student gave the right answer, the next program was given. If the student made an error, the correct answer was given, and the student could refer to the manual. In all, students solved 100 such problems.

In contrast, 23 other randomly selected college students (pretraining group) first received practice in predicting the output of procedures that were stated in English (see also the following procedures test described in the sidebar). For example, a typical problem was the following:

1. Put the number 3 in Box A.
2. Add 5 to the number in Box A; put the result in Box B.
3. Write down the number from Box B.
4. Stop working on this.

If the student gave the correct answer, the next problem was presented. If an error was made, the correct answer was given, and the student could refer to an English version of the manual. After solving 60 similar problems, students in the pretraining group were transferred to learning Basic by predicting the output of 40 simple Basic programs, as described above.

The results indicated that the students who were given pretraining in predicting the output of English procedures learned Basic much faster than those with no pretraining. For example, on the first set of 40 Basic problems, the pretrained group averaged about 6 seconds per answer to predict the output of Basic programs compared to over 12 seconds per answer for the students who had received no pretraining. A t-test revealed that this difference was statistically significant at $p < 0.001$. When we compared the group with no pretraining after 60 Basic problems to the pretraining group (who received 60 equivalent English procedure problems), the pretrained group averaged about 6 seconds per answer to predict the output of Basic programs, whereas those with no pretraining averaged about 6.5 seconds. A t-test here failed to reveal any significant difference between the groups. The results may be summarized by saying that pretraining in procedure comprehension is at least as effective as isomorphic pretraining in Basic. These findings are interesting because they show that pretraining in procedure comprehension (involving English) provides a foundation for learning Basic. A straightforward conclusion is that procedure comprehension is a component skill in learning Basic, and that this skill can be taught to novices.

CONCLUSION

Several scholars, including many proponents of Logo, have asserted that learning to program will enhance thinking skills in domains outside of programming. Anecdotal and personal introspective data are the two principal sources of evidence. Unfortunately, both are notorious for their unreliability and thus their unsuitability as scientific evidence. Methodologically sound experimental studies in this area are almost nonexistent. Our study encourages the idea that learning to program can have positive effects on thinking skills that are directly related to the language to be learned. At present, however, there is no convincing evidence that learning a program enhances students' general intellectual ability, or that programming is any more successful than Latin for teaching "proper habits of mind."

The assertion that certain thinking skills will enhance a person's learning of programming has also spawned a line of research that is subject to both methodological and logical flaws. A common methodological flaw is the "shotgun approach," in which many predictor variables are used so that a small number might reach statistical significance. A common logical flaw is the "correlation implies causation fallacy": If A predicts B, it does not mean that A causes B. To avoid these problems, we suggested using predictor tests that are selected on the basis of construct validity, that is, theoretically related to learning a particular language. Although prior studies have often found evidence that general abilities, such as logical reasoning, are predictive of learning programming, such research does not explain the underlying mechanisms of that learning process. The exemplary predictor study presented in this article demonstrates that it might be possible to identify specific information processing skills, based on a cognitive analysis of a programming language, that serve as predictors of learning programming. At present, problem representation and procedure comprehension are two likely specific thinking skills related to learning Basic; future research should be directed at lengthening the list.

The issue of pretraining follows from the foregoing two assertions. Although the concept of "readiness skills" has received wide acceptance in mathematics and language arts, very little is known concerning what a person needs to know to successfully learn to program. At the present time, it appears that pretraining in procedure comprehension skills transfers to learning of Basic. Additional research is needed, however, to determine which other "predictor skills" might also serve as "readiness skills."

Careful empirical research can inform the controversy concerning the teaching of Basic in schools, by evaluating assertions concerning the relation between programming and problem solving. The empirical research presented in this article suggests that there is an important — albeit limited — relationship between a person's thinking skills and ability to learn Basic. These preliminary results suggest that the most fruitful way to search for a relation between thinking skills and programming is to focus on thinking skills that are cognitive components of programming — specific thinking skills that are elements in a cognitive task analysis of programming — rather than to focus on general intellectual ability.

ACKNOWLEDGMENT

This project was supported by the National Science Foundation under grant MDR84-70248. This article also has been reprinted by permission of The Association for Computing Machinery.

REFERENCES

1. Bauer, R., Mehrens, W.A., and Visonhaler, J.R. Predicting performance in a computer programming course. *Educ. and Psychol. Meas. 28* (1968), 1159-1643.
2. Bayman, P. Effects of instructional procedures on learning a first programming language. Ph.D. dissertation, Dept. of Psychology, Univ. of California, Santa Barbara, 1983.
3. Bayman, P., and Mayer, R.E. A diagnosis of beginning programmers' misconceptions of Basic programming statements. *Commun. ACM 26,* 9 (Sept, 1983), 677-679.
4. Bork, A., *Learning with Computers.* Digital Press, Bedford, Mass., 1981.
5. Bransford, J.D., Arbitman-Smith, R., Stein, B.S., and Vye, N.J. Improving thinking and learning skills: An analysis of three approaches. In Vol. 1, *Thinking and Learning Skills,* J.W. Segal, S.F. Chipman, and R. Glaser, Eds. Erlbaum, Hillsdale, N.J., 1985, pp. 133-206.
6. Caruso, D.R., Taylor, J.J., and Detterman, D.K. Intelligence research and intelligent policy. In *How and How Much Can Intelligence Be Increased?* D.K. Detterman and R.J. Sternberg, Eds. Ablex, Norwood, N.J., 1982, pp. 45-65.
7. Clements, D.H., and Gullo, D.F. Effects of computer programming on young children's cognition. *J. Educ. Psychol. 76,* 6 (Dec. 1984), 1051-1058.
8. Dalbey, J., and Linn, M.C. The demands and requirements of computer programming: A literature review. *J. Educ. Comput. Res, 1,* 3 (Summer 1985), 253-274.
9. Denelsky, G.Y., and McKee, M.G. Prediction of computer programmer training and job performance using the AABP Test. *Pers. Psychol. 27* (1974), 129-137.
10. Gorman, H., and Bourne, L.E. Learning to think by learning LOGO: Rule learning in third grade computer programmers. *Bull. Psychonomic Soc. 21* (1983), 165-167.
11. Gregg, L.W. Spatial concepts, spatial names, and the development of exocentric representations. In *Children's Thinking: What Develops?* R. Siegler, Ed. Erlbaum, Hillsdale, N.J., 1978, pp. 275-290.
12. Hollenbeck, G.P., and McNamara, W.J. CUCPAT and programming aptitude. *Pers. Psychol. 18* (1965), 101-106.
13. Linn, M.C. The cognitive consequences of programming instruction in classrooms. *Educ. Res. 14,* 5 (May 1985), 14-16, 25-29.
14. Lochhead, J. An introduction to cognitive process instruction. In *Cognitive Process Instruction.* J. Lochhead and J. Clement, Eds. Franklin Institute Press, Philadelphia, Pa., 1979, pp. 1-4.
15. Mansfield, R.S., Busse, T.V., and Krepelka, E.J. The effectiveness of creativity training. *Rev. Educ. Res. 48,* 3 (Summer 1978), 517-536.
16. Mayer, R.E. The psychology of how novices learn computer programming. *Comput. Surv. 13,* 1 (Mar. 1981), 121-141.
17. Mayer, R.E. Learning in complex domains: A cognitive analysis of computer programming. *Psychol. Learn. Motiv. 19* (1985), 89-130.
18. Mayer, R.E. The elusive search for teachable aspects of problem solving. In *History of Educational Psychology.* J. Glover and R. Ronning, Eds. Academic Press, New York. To be published.
19. McNamaer, W.J., and Hughes, J.L. A review of research on the selection of computer programmers. *Pers. Psychol. 14* (1961), 39-51.
20. Nickerson, R.S. Computer programming as a vehicle for teaching of thinking skills. *Thinking 4* (1982), 42-48.
21. Papert, S. *Mindstorms.* Basic Books, New York, 1980.
22. Pea, R.D., and Kurland, M.K. On the cognitive effects of learning computer programming. *New Ideas in Psychol. 2,* 2 (Spring 1985), 137-167.

23. Rippa, S.A. *Education in a Free Society: An American History.* Longman, New York, 1980.
24. Snow, R.E. Aptitude processes. In Vol. 1, *Aptitude, Learning, and Instruction,* R.E. Snow, P. Federico, and W.E. Montague, Eds. Erlbaum, Hillsdale, N.J., 1980, pp. 27–63.
25. Soloway, E., Lochhead, J., and Clement, J. Does computer programming enhance problem solving ability? Some positive evidence on algebra word problems. In *Computer Literacy,* R.J. Seidel, R.E. Anderson, and B. Hunter, Eds. Academic Press, New York, 1982, pp. 171–185.
26. Thorndike, E.L. The influence of first-year Latin upon the ability to read English. *Sch. Soc. 17* (1923), 165–168.
27. Webb, N.M. Microcomputer learning in small groups: Cognitive requirements and group processes. *J. Educ. Psychol. 76,* 6 (Dec. 1984), 1076–1088.

SECTION III:
LEARNING PROGRAMMING CONCEPTS

Given that programming is to be taught in the schools, the next questions to address are what programming concepts should be taught and how should the concepts be taught so that students can effectively learn the material? The papers in this section examine the following six concepts commonly presented in introductory programming classes:

Concrete machine — the model underlying a language
Variables — storing, changing, and testing values
Conditionals — performing actions when appropriate
Looping — performing actions many times
Recursion — decomposing a problem in terms of itself
Output — printing out patterns of symbols

Each paper presents the results of empirical studies that illuminate what novices are actually learning (or failing to learn) when taught these concepts. The final paper in this section discusses some of the important differences in problem-solving and learning styles that exist between novice programmers.

Mayer's paper examines the instructional techniques of providing a concrete model of the computer to the novices as well as encouraging the novices to put technical information into their own words. The results of Mayer's studies show that, under certain conditions, both of these techniques can have a positive impact on the students' ability to solve new problems that were not explicitly taught. A further discussion of concrete models or "notional machines" can be found in the paper by du Boulay, O'Shea, and Monk in the section Designing Programming Environments in this volume.

In the next paper, a "fill in the blanks" study is used to understand the nature of novices' conceptions about the use of programming variables. Samurcay finds, among other things, that using variables in contexts that are similar to previously learned domains (e.g., $X = 0$ makes sense as an algebraic equation) is easier for novices than using variables in contexts that somehow violate those previously learned domains (e.g., $COUNT = COUNT + 1$ does not make sense as an algebraic equation). Samurcay's observations about the influence of previously learned domains agree with Hoc's observation that: "the construction of a program is never done from tabula rasa." Hoc's study identifies important similarities and differences between non-programming use of conditional reasoning and the use of conditionals in programs. In their paper in the section Bugs, Bonar and Soloway examine how pre-programming knowledge can lead to various bugs in novice programs.

Three papers in this section deal with the topics of looping and recursion. The Soloway, Bonar, and Erhlich paper finds that programmers are more likely to generate correct programs when the looping constructs in the language they are using more closely match the "natural" looping strategies subjects prefer. Kahney's paper explores many alternative mental models of recursion that novices adopt, and finds that novices tend to incorrectly view recursion as a form of looping. Kahney uses excerpts from thinking-aloud protocol data as evidence for the alternative models of recursion. Kessler and Anderson performed experiments that found that learning to write iterative functions first helped novices later learn to write recursive functions, but not vice versa. Analysis of thinking-aloud protocol data revealed that if recursion was taught before iteration the novices' poorly formed mental models of recursion actually interfered with the novices' ability to learn iteration second. In the section Bugs, Kurland and Pea examine in detail the types of bugs novices make when learning about the concept of recursion.

Perkins and his colleagues at the Harvard Educational Technology Center are concerned with the question "Why is there such a wide range in competence between novice programmers?" Some students take to programming like ducks to water, while others seem almost totally lost. Their research traces much of the variability to different patterns of learning that each individual brings with them to the programming task. Specifically, they identify two different learning styles: *stoppers* and *movers*. Stoppers tend to disengage from the programming task at the first sign of trouble, whereas movers will begin tinkering with a partial solution. Perkins suggests that one way to help stoppers become movers is to encourage them to use neglected strategies (such as tinkering, close tracking, and problem decomposition) when the stopper hits a problem, instead of simply disengaging.

This section presents a wide range of findings on what novices are learning when they are taught about programming concepts. In addition to the specific findings, the research presented here is interesting because the results were obtained using such a diverse set of experimental procedures (e.g., "fill in the blanks" studies, controlled experiments, thinking-aloud protocols, clinical interviews, etc.).

7

THE PSYCHOLOGY OF HOW NOVICES LEARN COMPUTER PROGRAMMING

RICHARD E. MAYER

Department of Psychology, University of California, Santa Barbara

This chapter examines the current state of knowledge concerning how to increase the novice's understanding of computers and computer programming. In particular, it reviews how advances in cognitive and educational psychology may be applied to problems in teaching nonprogrammers how to use computers. Two major instructional techniques are reviewed: providing a concrete model of the computer and encouraging the learners to actively put technical information into their own words.

INTRODUCTION

This paper focuses on the question, "What have we learned about how to increase the novice's understanding of computers and computer programming?" In particular, it reviews ideas from cognitive and educational psychology that are related to the problem of how to teach nonprogrammers to use computers. Since people who are not professional programmers will have to learn how to interact with computers, an important issue concerns how to foster meaningful learning of computer concepts by novices.

Meaningful learning is viewed as a process in which the learner connects new material with knowledge that already exists in memory [Bran79]. The existing knowledge in memory has been called a "schema" and the process of connecting new information to it has been called "assimilation." However, there is not yet agreement concerning the specific mechanisms that are involved in "assimilation to schema" [Ande77, Ausu77, Bart32, Kint74, Mins75, Rume75, Scha77, Thor77].

129

Figure 1 provides a general framework for a discussion of the process of meaningful learning (or assimilation to schema) of technical information [Maye75a, Maye79a]. In the figure the human cognitive system is broken down into

- *short-term memory*—a temporary and limited capacity store for holding and manipulating information;
- *long-term memory*—a permanent, organized, and unlimited store of existing knowledge.

New technical information enters the human cognitive system from the outside and must go through the following steps for meaningful learning to occur:

(1) *Reception*. First the learner must pay attention to the incoming information so that it reaches short-term memory (as indicated by arrow a).
(2) *Availability*. Second, the learner must possess appropriate prerequisite concepts in long-term memory to use in assimilating the new information (as indicated by point b).
(3) *Activation*. Finally, the learner must actively use this prerequisite knowledge during learning so that the new material may be connected with it (as indicated by arrow c from long-term memory to short-term memory).

Thus, in the course of meaningful learning, the learner must come into contact with the new material (by bringing it into short-term memory), then must search long-term memory for what Ausubel [Ausu68] calls "appropriate anchoring ideas" or "ideational scaffolding," and then must transfer those ideas to short-term memory so they can be combined with new

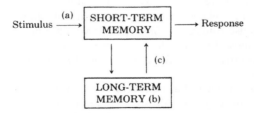

FIGURE 1 Some information processing components of meaningful learning. Condition (a) is transfer of new information from outside to short-term memory. Condition (b) is availability of assimilative context in long-term memory. Condition (c) is activation and transfer of old knowledge from long-term memory to short-term memory.

incoming information. If any of these conditions is not met, meaningful learning cannot occur; and the learner will be forced to memorize each piece of new information by rote as a separate item to be added to memory. The techniques reviewed here are aimed at ensuring that the availability and activation conditions are likely to be met.

The goal of this paper is to explore techniques for increasing the novice's understanding of computer programming by exploring techniques that activate the "appropriate anchoring ideas." Two techniques reviewed are (1) providing a familiar concrete model of the computer and (2) encouraging learners to put technical information into their own words. Each technique is an attempt to foster the process by which familiar existing knowledge is connected with new incoming technical information. For each technique a brief rationale is presented, examples of research are given, and an evaluative summary is offered.

1.   UNDERSTANDING OF TECHNICAL INFORMATION BY NOVICES

1.1   Definitions

For our present purposes *understanding* is defined as the ability to use learned information in problem-solving tasks that are different from what was explicitly taught. Thus understanding is manifested in the user's ability to transfer learning to new situations. *Novices* are defined as users who have had little or no previous experience with computers, who do not intend to become professional programmers, and who thus lack specific knowledge of computer programming.

1.2   Distinction Between Understanding and Rote Learning

The Gestalt psychologists [Wert59, Kato42, Kohl25] distinguished between two ways of learning how to solve problems—rote learning versus understanding. With respect to mathematics learning, for example, a distinction often is made between "getting the right answer" and "understanding what you are doing."

In a classic example Wertheimer suggests that there are two basic ways to teach a child how to find the area of a parallelogram [Wert59]. One method involves dropping a perpendicular line, measuring the height of the perpendicular, measuring the length of the base, and calculating area by use of the formula, Area = Height × Base. Wertheimer calls this the "rote learning" or "senseless" method, because the student simply memorizes a formula and a procedure. The other method calls for the student to explore the parallelogram visually until he sees that it is possible to cut a triangle from one end, put it on the other end, and form a rectangle. Since the student already knows how to find the area of a rectangle, the problem is solved. Wertheimer calls this method "structural understanding" or "meaningful apprehension of relations," since the learner has gained insight into the structure of parallelograms.

According to Wertheimer, if you give a test involving parallelograms like the one used during instruction, both groups of children will perform well. However, if you give a transfer test that involves unusual parallelograms, the rote learners will say "We haven't had this yet," while the understanders will be able to derive answers. Thus the payoff for understanding comes not in direct application of the newly learned material, but rather in transfer to new situations. This example suggests that when creative use of new technical information is the goal, it is important to use methods that foster understanding.

2.   DO CONCRETE MODELS AID MEANINGFUL LEARNING OF COMPUTER PROGRAMMING?

2.1   Statement of the Problem

Since novices lack domain-specific knowledge, one technique for improving their understanding of new technical information is to provide them with a framework that can be used for incorporating new information. This technique is aimed at ensuring availability of knowledge in long-term memory (see Figure 1). The present section explores the effects of concion models on people's understanding and learning of new technical information such as computer programming. The major research questions concern how concrete models influence the learning process and how to choose an effective model.

2.2   Concrete Models in Mathematics Learning

One technique for providing the appropriate prerequisite knowledge is the use of familiar, concrete models. For example, Brownell and Moser [Brow49] taught third graders how to use a subtraction algorithm, employing two different methods. One group of several hundred children was taught by means of concrete objects like bundles of sticks. For these children, concepts like "borrowing" and "place value" were described in terms of rearranging bundles of sticks into groups of tens. The other group was taught in a "purely mechanical rote fashion"; these children were explicitly given the rules for subtraction at the start and provided with plenty of "hands on" experience in executing the procedures on standard two-digit subtraction problems. Although both groups of students learned to perform equally well on standard two-digit subtraction problems, the students who learned with bundles of sticks performed better on tests involving transfer problems (e.g., more complicated subtraction problems).

In current instructional practice, *manipulatives,* such as coins or sticks or blocks, are used in mathematics teaching in order to make computational procedures more concrete [Weav72, Resn80]. In a careful set of interviews with children who were learning to subtract, Resnick and Ford [Resn80] noted that the children often invented a concrete model to help them understand the procedure. Since computer programming shares many of the characteristics of computational procedures in mathematics, it seems possible that the use of manipulatives in computer programming might be as successful as in mathematics.

2.3 Models, Titles, and Advance Organizers in Text

There is also encouraging evidence that similar techniques may be used to increase the meaningfulness of technical information presented in text. For example, Bransford and Johnson presented the following passage to subjects:

> The procedure is actually quite simple. First you arrange items into different groups. Of course, one pile may be sufficient depending on how much there is to do. If you have to go somewhere else due to lack of facilities, that is the next step; otherwise, you are pretty well set. It is important not to overdo things. In the short run this may not seem important, but complications can easily arise. A mistake can be expensive as well. At first, the whole procedure will seem complicated. Soon, however, it will become just another facet of life. It is difficult to foresee any end to the necessity for this task in the immediate future, but then, one never can tell. After the procedure is completed one arranges the materials into different groups again. Then they can be put into their appropriate places. Eventually they will be used once more and the whole cycle will have to be repeated. However, this is part of life [Bran72, p. 721] .

Subjects who read this passage without a title rated it low in comprehensibility (2.3 on a 7-point scale) and recalled an average of only 2.8 out of 18 ideas from the passage. However, some subjects were given a description of the topic — washing clothes — before the passage. These subjects rated the passage much higher in comprehensibility (4.5 on a 7-point scale) and recalled more than twice as much information (5.8 idea units out of 18). In addition, a third group was given the washing clothes topic after the passage was presented. However, this group performed at about the same low level as the subjects who were given no topic (rating the passage at 2.1 in comprehension and recalling an average of 2.7 idea units). Similar studies [Bran72, Dool71, Dool72] also found that students' recall of ambiguous and technical passages was enhanced when an organizing title, diagram, or sentence was given prior to reading. However these techniques did not have the same facilitating effect when presented after the student had read the passage. These results sugest that the learner must have an appropriate assimilative set available at the time of learning. Even though the same total amount of information may be presented, the students' ability to recall and use the information in the passage is much higher when the clarifying title or picture is given before rather than after reading.

Ausubel [Ausu68] has argued that learning of new technical prose may be enhanced by providing an *advance organizer* — a short expository introduction, presented prior to the text, containing no specific content from the text, but providing the general concepts and ideas that can be used to subsume the information in the text. The first advance organizer studies conducted by Ausubel and his colleagues in the early 1960s [Ausu60, Ausu63, Ausu68] provided some support for this assertion. For example, in a typical study [Ausu60] 120 college students read a 2500-word text on metallurgy after reading either a 500-word advance organizer that presented the underlying framework for the information or a control 500-word historical passage. The advance organizer presented the abstract principles involved in the text. On a reading comprehension posttest covering the basic information in the passage, the advance organizer group performed significantly better than the control group, with scores of 47 percent correct versus 40 percent correct, respectively.

More recently, reviews of the advance organizer literature reveal that advance organizers tend to have their strongest effects in situations where learners are unlikely to already possess useful prerequisite concepts — namely, for technical or unfamiliar material, for "low-ability" or inexperienced students, and for a test involving transfer to new situations [Maye79a, Maye79b]. For example, to study the effects of advance organizers on different kinds of materials, Lesh [Lesh76] asked 48 college students to watch a four-hour videotape on finite geometry. An organizer that gave concrete examples and models was provided either before or after instruction. The instructional lesson was organized either in an order of increasing difficulty (hierarchical order) or in an order that repeated key concepts and related new material to previous material (spiral order). Results of a standard posttest indicated that the advance organizer group outperformed the postorganizer group for the hierarchical unit, but the difference was much less for the spiral unit. Similar treatment × material interactions were obtained using social studies lessons [Schu75] and mathematics lessons [Grot68]. Similarly, Raye [Raye73] reported that the title biasing effects obtained by Bransford and Johnson [Bran72] with the washing clothes passage were eliminated when the passage was made more concrete and familiar. Thus there is consistent evidence that organizers have stronger effects for unfamiliar, abstract information than for familiar, concrete information.

In a study investigating the effects of advance organizers on students with high and low ability (or knowledge), physics material was taught to high school students [West76]. Advance organizers consisting of concrete models tended to improve test performance of low-ability students but had a much smaller effect for high-ability subjects. Similar group × ability interactions were obtained by several other researchers [Ring71, Fitz63, Ausu62, Ausu61, Ausu63, Ausu77, Smit69]. Thus there is evidence that advance organizers have a stronger effect on low-knowledge or low-ability learners as compared with high-knowledge or high-ability learners.

Finally, in studies involving transfer tests (i.e., problems that are different from those in instruction), there is consistent evidence that advance organizers have a stronger effect on transfer performance than on simple retention. For example, this pattern was obtained with material on mathematical topology [Scan67], number bases [Grot68, Maye77], and an imaginary science [Merr66].

Many of the apparent conflicts in the advance organizer literature [Barn75, Lawt77] can be accounted for by the idea that advance organizers find a way of connecting new information with existing knowledge — organizers are not needed for familiar material, experienced learners, or when the test does not involve transfer.

While there is at present no foolproof procedure for generating useful advance organizers, a careful review of the existing literature suggests the following guidelines [Maye79a]: (1) The organizer should allow the reader to generate all or some of the logical relations in the text. (2) The organizer should provide a means of relating the information in the text to existing knowledge. (3) The organizer should be familiar to the learners. (4) The organizer should encourage the learner to use prerequisite knowledge that the learner would not normally have used. To date, advance organizers have been most effectively used in mathematics and science topics [Maye79a].

Royer and his colleagues [Roye75, Roye76] have demonstrated that concrete models may serve as effective advance organizers in learning new scientific information. In their studies, subjects read two passages, such as a passage on electrical conductivity followed by a passage on heat flow. For some subjects the first passage contained several concrete analogies, such as electrical conduction being described as a chain of falling dominoes. For other subjects the first passage presented the same information in abstract form without any concrete analogies. Reading of the second passage was facilitated if students had been given concrete models in the first passage (e.g., recall of the information in the second passage was about twice that of control groups). Appararently, the models presented in the first passage could be used by learners during the reading of the second passage to help relate the technical terms to familiar concepts.

Similarly, White and Mayer [Whit80] analyzed physics textbooks to determine how concrete models were used. For example, many textbooks explain Ohm's law by describing water flowing in pipes, or a boy pushing a heavy load up an inclined street, or electron flow through a circuit. Recent results [Maye81] show that when concrete analogies are embedded in a technical text, novices tend to perform best on recalling these familiar models and tend to recognize the information adjacent to the model in the text.

2.4   Concrete Models in Computer Programming

In previous sections research was presented concerning the role of manipulatives in mathematics instruction, titles and pictures in remembering ambiguous passages, and advance organizers and models in science text. In each case there was evidence that these techniques serve to provide the learner with appropriate anchoring knowledge that is required for comprehension of new technical information. The present section focuses on research related specifically to computer programming.

Du Boulay and his colleagues [DuBo76, DuBo80] have provided a concrete model for teaching LOGO to children. The model consists of a conceptual LOGO machine with concrete memory locations, switches, and work space, which allow the learner to "work" the machine.

Du Boulay and his colleagues have argued that there are two basic approaches to learning to interact with a computer. The first approach could be called the *black box approach*. In this approach the user develops the attitude that the computer is a black box — you put in commands and data and out comes the answer as if by magic. The mechanisms by which the computer operates are hidden from the user, and the user is likely to assume that computers are just not understandable. Such users are likely to memorize algorithms that "work;" that is, that generate the desired answers. However such users are not able to relate the commands to an understanding of what goes on inside the black box.

The second approach is what can be called the *glass box approach*. In this approach the user attempts to understand what is going on inside the computer. Each command results in some change in the computer and these changes can be described and understood. The level of description need not — indeed should not — be at the "blood and guts" level. Users do not need to become electronics experts. There is an appropriate level of description that Mayer [Maye79c] refers to as the "transaction level." Similarly, du Boulay et al. [DuBo80] offer two important properties for making hidden operations of a language clearer to a novice: (1) *simplicity* — there should be a "small number of parts that interact in ways that can be easily understood"; (2) *visibility* — novices should be able to view "selected parts and processes" of the model "in action." The LOGO model appears to fit these specifications because it is a simple, familiar model of the computer operations involved in LOGO; in short, it allows the user to develop intuitions about what goes on inside the computer for each line of code. Unfortunately, however, du Boulay and his colleagues have not provided empirical tests concerning whether the LOGO machine model actually influences the problem-solving performance of new learners as compared with traditional methods that emphasize only hands-on experiences.

2.5   Effects of Models on Transfer Performance

In order to provide some information concerning the effects of concrete models on learning computer programming, a series of studies was conducted [Maye75b]. In the studies, subjects were either given a concrete model of the computer, or they were not given such a model. Then subjects read a manual on a BASIC-like language and took a transfer test on the material.

Method.   Figure 2 shows the model of the computer that was used to explain elementary BASIC-like statements to novices. The model provides concrete analogies for four major functional units of the computer: (1) Input is represented as a ticket window at which data are lined up waiting to be processed and placed in the finished pile after being processed; (2) output is represented as a message note pad with one message written per line; (3) memory is represented as an erasable scoreboard in which there is natural destructive read-in and nondestructive read-out; (4) executive control is represented as a recipe or shopping list with a pointer arrow to indicate the line being executed. This model is similar to du Boulay's model of the LOGO machine in the way it makes the basic operations of the computer visible to the learner. A two- by four-foot diagram containing these parts and a brief one-page description were provided to subjects in the model group (see Figure 2), but no model was given to the control group.

All subjects then were given a ten-page manual that described seven statements modified from BASIC and FORTRAN (see Table 1). For each

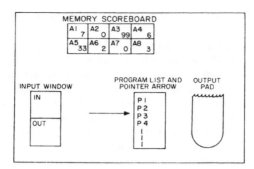

```
              MEMORY  SCOREBOARD
        A1    A2    A3    A4
           7     0    99     6
        A5    A6    A7    A8
          33     2     0      3
```

```
                        PROGRAM LIST AND    OUTPUT
                        POINTER ARROW        PAD
    INPUT  WINDOW
         IN                    P 1
                               P 2
                               P 3
                    ─────►     P 4
         OUT                    I
                               I
                               I
```

FIGURE 2   A concrete model of the computer for a BASIC-like language [Maye76].

DESCRIPTION OF MODEL PROVIDED TO SUBJECTS

The figure above represents a simple computer system which you will learn about in this experiment. The computer is made up of three main parts: (1) INPUT and OUTPUT WINDOWS, which allow communication between the computer's memory and the outside world; (2) MEMORY SCOREBOARD, which stores information in the computer; and (3) PROGRAM LIST and POINTER ARROW, which tell the computer what to do and what order to go in. Each of these three parts will now be explained.

Input and Output Window. Notice that to the far left is an input window divided into two parts. A pile of computer cards with numbers punched into them can be put in the left part of the window; as the computer finishes processing each card, it puts the card on the right side of the input window. Thus when the computer needs to find the next data card, it takes the top card on the left side of the input window; when it is done with the card, it puts it on the right side.

On the far right is the output window. This is where printed messages (in this case only numbers can be printed) from the computer's memory to the outside world appear. Each line on the printout is a new message (i.e., a new number).

Thus the computer can store in memory a number that is on a card entered through the input window, or it can print out what it has in memory onto a printout at the output window. The statements which put the input and output windows to work are READ and WRITE statements, and each will be explained later on.

Memory Scoreboard. Inside the computer is a large scoreboard called MEMORY. Notice that it is divided into eight spaces with room for one score (one number) in each space. Also notice that each space is labeled with a name—A1, A2, A3, A4, A5, A6, A7, A8. These labels or names for each space are called "addresses" and each of the eight addresses always has some number indicated in its space. For example, in our figure A1 shows a score of 81 and A2 has the number 17.

It is possible to change the score in any of the eight spaces; for example, the score in box A1 can be changed to 0, and you will learn how to change scores in memory later on when we discuss EQUALS statements and CALCULATION statements.

Program List and Pointer Arrow. Inside the computer to the right of the MEMORY is a place to put a list of things to do called PROGRAM LIST and an arrow which indicates what step in the list the computer should work on.

Notice that each line in the PROGRAM LIST has a number so that the first line is called P1, the second step is P2, and so on. When a program is inserted in the step, the indicator arrow will point to the first line (P1); when the first step is finished, the arrow will go to the next step on the list (P2); and so on down the list. You will learn how to control the order of steps later on when the IF statement, GOTO statement, and STOP statement are discussed.

138

TABLE 1.   SEVEN STATEMENTS USED IN BASIC-
LIKE INSTRUCTIONAL BOOKLET

Name	Example
READ	P1 READ (A1)
WRITE	P2 WRITE (A1)
EQUALS	P3 A1 = 88
CALCULATE	P4 A1 = A1 + 12
GOTO	P6 GO TO P1
IF	P5 IF (A1 = 100) GO TO P9
STOP	P9 STOP

statement the manual presented the statement, provided the grammar rules for the statement (e.g., definitions of legal address names), and gave an example of the statement as it might occur in a line of a program. Subjects in both groups were given the same manual to read at their own rates, which averaged 20 to 30 minutes.

Following the reading the same test was given to all subjects. The test consisted of six types of problems: (1) *Generate-statement* problems gave a problem in English and required a one-statement program as the solution; (2) *generate-nonloop* problems gave a problem in English and required a short nonlooping program for solution; (3) *generate-looping* problems gave a problem in English and required a looping program for solution; (4) *interpret-statement* problems gave a single-statement program and asked the student to describe what the computer would do; (5) *interpret-nonloop* gave a nonlooping program and asked for a description of what the computer would do; (6) *interpret-looping* problems gave a looping program and required a description of what the computer would do. Examples of the six problems are given in Table 2.

Results.   The proportion of correct responses by type of problem for each of the treatment groups is given in Table 3. As can be seen, the control group performs as well or better on problems that are very much like the material in the instructional manual, for example, generate-statement and generate-nonloop. However, on problems that require moderate amounts of transfer[1] — for example, generate-loop and the shorter interpret problems — the model group excels. Both groups do poorly on the very complex

---

[1]Transfer problems are problems that are different from those given in the text but can be solved using the information provided. Since information about how to generate single statements and simple programs is given, these two kinds of problems are not transfer problems. Since looping is not mentioned explicitly, problems that require the generation of a looping program are transfer problems. Similarly, since interpretation of programs is not dealt with explicitly, interpretation problems are transfer problems in this study. However, looping interpretation may require much more transfer than the others, since it is most different from this discussion.

TABLE 2. Examples of Six Types of Test Problems for a BASIC-like
Language

Generation-Statement	Interpretation-Statement
Given a number in memory space A5, write a statement to change that number to zero	A5 = 0
Generation-Nonloop	Interpretation-Nonloop
Given a card with a number on it is input, write a program to print out its square	P1 READ (A1) P2 A1 = A1 * A1 P3 WRITE (A1) P4 STOP
Generation-Looping	Interpretation-Looping
Given a pile of data cards is input, write a program to print out each number and stop when it gets to card with 88 on it	P1 READ (A1) P2 IF(A1 = 88) GO TO P5 P3 WRITE (A1) P4 GO TO P1 P5 STOP

TABLE 3. Proportion of Correct Answers on Transfer
Test by Type of Problem for Model and Control Groups[a]

Group	Generation			Interpretation		
	State-ment	Nonloop	Looping	State-ment	Nonloop	Looping
Model	.63	.37	.30	.62	.62	.09
Control	.67	.52	.12	.42	.32	.12

[a] Adapted from Maye75b.
Note. 20 subjects per group; interaction between group and problem type, $p < .05$.

interpret-looping programs. The difference in the pattern of performance is consistent with earlier results in other domains in which models enhance transfer performance but not simple retention of presented material. Apparently the model provided an assimilative context in which novices could relate new technical information in the booklet to a familiar analogy. This learning process resulted in a learning outcome that supported some transfer.

2.6 Locus of the Effect of Models

One problem with the foregoing study is that the model subjects received more information than the controls. However, assimilation theory (see Introduction) predicts that presenting a model prior to learning will enhance learning because it provides a meaningful context, but presenting the model after the text will not enhance learning because students will have already encoded the material in a rote way. In further studies [Maye76] subjects read the same BASIC-like manual, but some subjects were shown a concrete model of the computer before reading while others were shown the same model after reading the manual. Thus subjects in the before group (i.e., those who received the model first) were able to use the model while encoding the material in the text, but the after group (i.e., receiving the model last) was not.

Method.   The booklet, model, and test were similar to those used in the previous experiment. The before group received the model first, then the booklet, and then the test. The after group received the booklet first, then the model, and then the test.

Results.   The proportion of correct answers by type of problem for the two groups is given in Table 4. As can be seen, the after group (like the controls in the previous study) excelled on retention-like problems (i.e., generation-statement and generation-nonloop), but the before subjects excelled on problems requiring creative transfer to new situations (i.e., generation-loop, interpretation-statement, interpretation-nonloop). Thus these results provide further support for the claim that subjects who use a concrete model during learning develop learning outcomes that support broader transfer. As predicted, the locus of the effect is before rather than after instruction.

2.7   Effects of Models on Recall Performance

The foregoing studies used transfer tests as a measure of what is learned under different instructional techniques. Another technique involves asking subjects to try to write down all they can remember about certain statements. In a follow-up study [Maye80b] subjects read the same manual and were given the model either before or after reading as in the previous study. However, as a test, subjects were asked to recall all they could about portions of the manual.

TABLE 4.   PROPORTION OF CORRECT ANSWERS ON TRANSFER
TEST BY TYPE OF PROBLEM FOR BEFORE AND AFTER GROUPS[a]

Group	Generation			Interpretation		
	State-ment	Non-loop	Looping	State-ment	Non-loop	Looping
Before	.57	.50	.20	.47	.63	.17
After	.77	.63	.13	.27	.40	.17

[a] Adapted from MAYE76.
Note. 20 subjects per group; interaction between group and problem type, $p < .05$.

Method.   The same booklet and model were used as in the previous experiments, with some minor modifications. The before group received the model, then the manual, then the recall test; the after group received the manual, then the model, and then the recall test.

Results.   In order to analyze the recall protocols, the information in the manual was broken down into "idea units." Each idea unit expressed one major idea or action. There were three kinds of idea units in the manual: (1) *conceptual idea units* related to the internal operation of the computer, (2) *technical idea units* that gave examples of code, and (3) *format idea units* that gave grammar rules. Table 5 gives examples of each type of idea unit.

Table 6 shows the average number of correctly recalled idea units from each category for the two groups. As can be seen, the before group recalled more conceptual information, while the after group recalled more technical and format information. This pattern is consistent with the idea that good retention requires recall of specific code, whereas good transfer requires understanding of conceptual ideas. Also, Table 6 shows that the before group included more intrusions about the model and about other idea units from other sections of the booklet, thus suggesting that they integrated the information better. For example, an intrusion is "An address is a slot in the memory scoreboard." The after group, however, included more vague summaries and connectives which served as "filler." For example, a

TABLE 5.   EXAMPLE OF CONCEPTUAL, FORMAT,
AND TECHNICAL IDEA UNITS

Type	Idea Unit
Technical	READ is one kind of statement
Format	The format is READ ( )
Format	An address name goes in the parentheses
Conceptual	An address name is a space in the computer's memory
Conceptual	There are eight memory spaces
Technical	The spaces are called A1, A2 ...
Technical	An example is READ (A2)
Conceptual	First the computer checks the number from the top data card
Conceptual	Then that number is stored in space A2
Conceptual	The previous number in A2 is destroyed
Conceptual	Then the data card is sent out of the computer
Conceptual	This reduces the pile of data cards by one
Conceptual	Then go on to the next statements

TABLE 6. AVERAGE NUMBER OF RECALLED IDEA UNITS FOR THE
BEFORE AND AFTER GROUPS[a]

Group	Idea Units			Intrusions		
	Techni-cal	Format	Concep-tual	Inap-pro-priate	Appro-priate	Model
	(14)	(12)	(35)			
Before	5.0	1.9	6.6	1.5	1.3	3.1
After	6.0	2.9	4.9	2.5	.8	.5

[a] Adapted from MAYE80b.
Note. 30 subjects per group; interaction between group and problem type, $p < .05$. Numbers in parentheses indicate total possible.

connective is "And that's how READ statements work." Thus, as with the transfer test, subjects given the model before learning showed evidence of more integrated and conceptual learning of technical information.

2.8 Effects of Models on Transfer and Recall Using a Different Language

Although the above results are consistent and were obtained in a long series of studies, their generality is limited by the fact that just one type of language was used. Thus a follow-up study [Maye80a] was conducted using a file management language based on SEQUEL [Goul74, Reis77]. The goal of this study was to determine whether the results from previous studies generalize to a new domain.

Method. Subjects read a manual that presented the file management language. For one group of subjects, the model group, the manual began with discussion of a concrete model and related each statement to the model (see Figure 3), but no model was given to the control group. The manuals were informationally equivalent. Each page of the booklet presented one of the eight statements shown in Table 7, along with examples of how the statement fit into a program. Figure 3 presents the concrete model that was used: Long-term memory is represented as a file cabinet; the sorting function is represented as an in-, out-, and save basket; temporary memory is represented as an erasable scoreboard; executive control is represented as a list and pointer arrow; output is represented as a message pad. The entire model was presented on a two- by three-foot diagram in order to enhance the learner's ability to visualize the system.

After reading the manual, all subjects took the same 20-item test. Problems varied in complexity from generating or interpreting a sort-1

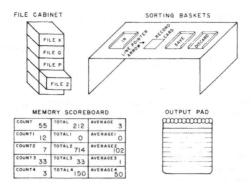

FIGURE 3   A concrete model of the computer for a file management language.

Description of Model Provided to Subjects

The computer is capable of three main functions: sorting record cards into sorting baskets, remembering numbers on its memory scoreboard, and outputting information to the world through its message pad.

To understand the sorting function of the computer, you could think of an office worker sitting at a desk with three sorting baskets, a line pointer arrow, and file cabinet with many drawers. Each drawer of the file cabinet contains a different set of records; the name of the file is indicated on each drawer. If the worker needs all the records in a particular file, all the worker needs to do is open that drawer and take out all the records. To avoid mixups, the clerk can take out all the records of only one file at a time; if the clerk needs to bring records from a certain file drawer to his desk, first all the records from all other files must be put back in their proper drawers. Thus a worker may have all the records for only *one* file on his desk at a time. These could be placed in the "in-basket" which is on the left side of the clerk's desk—it thus contains all of the to-be-processed record cards, waiting for the office clerk to look at them. In the middle of the desk is a work area with a line pointer arrow; the clerk may place only one card in the work area at a time, and the pointer arrow points to just one line at a time. To the right are two more baskets—the "save basket" and the "discard basket." If a record card passes the clerk's inspection, it is placed on top of the pile of cards in the "save basket"; but if it fails, it is placed in the top of the pile of cards in the "discard basket." The procedure the office worker uses is to take the top card from the "in-basket," place it in the work area with a pointer arrow aimed at one line, and on the basis of inspection of this line move that card to either the "save" or "discard basket." The worker continues until all of the records in the "in-basket" have been processed so that the "in-basket" is empty and the "save" and "discard baskets" contain all the records; then the worker may sometimes be asked to take the pile in either the "save" or the "discard basket" and put it in the "in-basket" for further processing.

To understand the memory function of the computer, think of a memory scoreboard. The scoreboard consists of 15 rectangular spaces like a classroom blackboard, divided into 15 spaces. Each space has a label, such as COUNT2, and each space has one number (of any length) in it. The office worker may count all the records that have been stored in the save basket, and this number could be stored in one of the spaces on the scoreboard. When a new number is stored in a space on the scoreboard, the old number is erased. However, when the office worker copies a number from one of the memory spaces onto the output pad, the number is not erased.

To understand the output function of the computer, think of a telephone message pad. To communicate with the outside world, the computer can write one piece of information on each line of the pad. If it fills all the lines on one page, it will just turn to the next page and begin with the top line. The office worker may write down two kinds of information on the output pad: a number may be copied from one of the spaces on the scoreboard onto the pad (but this does not alter the number on the scoreboard), or information that is on each card in the save basket can be copied onto the output pad.

144

TABLE 7. Eight Statements Used in File
Management Language Booklet

Name	Example
FROM	FROM *AUTOMOBILE*
FOR	FOR *WEIGHT* IS CALLED *3000 OR MORE*
AND FOR	AND FOR *COLOR* IS CALLED *GREEN*
OR FOR	OR FOR *MAKE* IS CALLED *FORD*
LIST	LIST *NAME*
COUNT	COUNT
TOTAL	TOTAL *CURRENT VALUE*
LET	LET *TOTAL ÷ COUNT* BE CALLED *AVERAGE*

program (with very few operations) to a compute-2 program (with many different statements integrated into one large program). Table 8 lists the five different kinds of programs used.

Results. Table 9 gives the proportion of correct answers by type of problem for the two treatment groups. As can be seen, the control group performed as well as the model group on very simple problems like those in the manual, but the model group excelled on longer problems that require

TABLE 8. Examples of Test Problems for a File Management Language[a]

Sort 1
List the owners' names for all cars weighing 3000 pounds or more.

FROM *AUTOMOBILE*
FOR *WEIGHT* IS CALLED *3000 OR MORE*
LIST *NAME*

Sort 2
List the owners' names for all model green Fords.

FROM *AUTOMOBILE*
FOR *YEAR* IS CALLED *1976 OR MORE*
AND FOR *COLOR* IS CALLED *GREEN*
AND FOR *MAKE* IS CALLED *FORD*
LIST *NAME*

Count
How many cars are registered in Santa Barbara County?

FROM *AUTOMOBILE*
FOR *HOME COUNTY* IS CALLED *SANTA BARBARA*
COUNT
LIST *COUNT*

Compute 1
What is the average current value of all cars?

FROM *AUTOMOBILE*
COUNT
TOTAL *CURRENT VALUE*
LET *TOTAL ÷ COUNT* BE CALLED *AVERAGE*
LIST *AVERAGE*

Compute 2
What percentage of 1977 cars are Chevrolets?

FROM *AUTOMOBILE*
FOR *YEAR* IS CALLED *1977*
COUNT
LET THIS BE CALLED *COUNT 1*
AND FOR *MAKE* IS CALLED *CHEVROLET*
COUNT
LET THIS BE CALLED *COUNT 2*
LET *COUNT 2 ÷ COUNT 1* BE CALLED *AVERAGE*
LIST AVERAGE

[a] From Maye80a.

TABLE 9.   PROPORTION OF CORRECT ANSWERS ON
TRANSFER TEST FOR MODEL AND CONTROL
GROUPS—FILE MANAGEMENT LANGUAGE[a]

Group	Type of Test Problem				
	Sort-1	Sort-2	Count	Com-pute-1	Com-pute-2
Model	.66	.66	.63	.58	.45
Control	.63	.44	.43	.33	.22

[a] Adapted from MAYE80a.
Note. 20 subjects per group; group × problem-type interaction, $p < .07$.

creatively integrating all of the statements in the booklet. Thus, as in the studies with BASIC-like materials, a familiar model serves to enhance performance on creative transfer when it is presented prior to technical instruction.

2.9   Ability

The pattern of results described above tended to be strongest for low-ability subjects [Maye75b] where ability is defined in terms of SAT mathematics scores. For example, for low-ability subjects the advance organizer increased transfer test performance (55 percent correct) as compared with the control group (45 percent correct), but for high-ability learners the advance organizer group performed more poorly than the control group (55 percent versus 62 percent correct, respectively). Apparently high-ability learners already possess their own useful "models" for thinking about how a computer works, but low-ability students are more likely to lack useful prerequisite knowledge.

2.10   Text Organization

The pattern of results described above also tended to be strongest when material was poorly organized [Maye78]. For example, the BASIC-like manual was presented either in its original order or in a random order. In the random order, presentation order of paragraphs was randomized. For the randomized version of the manual the advance organizer group performed better on a transfer test than a control group (41 percent versus 31 percent correct, respectively), but for the logical version of the manual the advance organizer group performed as well as but did not outperform the control group (36 percent versus 44 percent correct, respectively). Apparently the model is more useful when material is poorly structured because it helps the reader to hold the information together.

2.11 Conclusion

These results provide clear and consistent evidence that a concrete model can have a strong effect on the encoding and use of new technical information by novices. These results provide empirical support to the claims that allowing novices to "see the works" allows them to encode information in a more coherent and useful way [DuBo76, DuBo80]. When appropriate models are used, the learner seems to be able to assimilate each new statement to his or her image of the computer system. Thus one straightforward implication is: If your goal is to produce learners who will not need to use the language creatively, then no model is needed. If your goal is to produce learners who will be able to come up with creative solutions to novel (for them) problems, then a concrete model early in learning is quite useful. More research is needed in order to determine the specific effects of concrete models on what is learned, and to determine the characteristics of a useful model.

3. DOES STUDENT ELABORATION ACTIVITY AID MEANINGFUL LEARNING?

3.1 Statement of the Problem

The previous section presented evidence that concrete models may influence learning of computer programming because they provide a familiar context for assimilating the new material. The second major technique for increasing the meaningfulness of technical information is elaboration — encouraging the learner to explain the information in his or her own words and to relate the material to other ideas or concepts. Elaboration techniques may influence meaningful learning because they encourage the activation of existing knowledge that is relevant for comprehending the newly presented material; that is, elaboration may affect the activation process (see Figure 1).

3.2 Putting It in Your Own Words

There is some evidence that asking subjects to put ideas into their own words during learning can enhance the breadth of learning. For example, Gagne and Smith [Gagn62] asked subjects to give a verbal rationalization for each step as they learned to solve a three-disk version of the Tower of Hanoi problem [Ewer32]. These subjects took longer to learn than did those who did not verbalize; however they were able to transfer what they had learned to different problems, such as a six-disk version, much more efficiently (e.g., 3.8 minutes to solution) than the nonverbalizers (e.g., 10.0 minutes to solution).

More recently, Wittrock (Witt74] proposed the idea that "learning is a generative process" — that is, learning occurs when the learner actively generates associations between what is presented and what he already has in memory. As an example, Wittrock presented a study in which elementary school children read a passage and either generated a one-sentence summary for each paragraph or did not. Recall by the students who generated summary sentences was nearly double that of the control group. Apparently, when students are actively encouraged to put information in their own words, they are able to connect the new information to existing knowledge.

Elaboration techniques have long been used by experimental psychologists to enhance the learning of paired associates (such as HOUSE-CASA). For example, when students are asked to actively form mental images or a sentence involving word pairs, paired associate recall is greatly enhanced [Bowe72, Paiv69]. More recently, elaboration techniques have been used in school curricula [Dans78, Wein78]. For example, in studying human physiology students are asked "How do arteries differ from veins?" Several researchers have argued that students should be given explicit training in "learning strategies" for actively processing new material [ONei78].

The following is a series of studies that explore the role of elaboration techniques in learning computer programming. The main theme of this research is to determine how "putting it in your own words" influences the learning of a new computer language.

3.3   Effects of Model Elaboration on Transfer Performance

The first set of studies [Maye80a] addresses the question of whether elaboration activity influences students' ability to engage in problem solving. In these studies subjects learned a new computer programming language and either were or were not encouraged to describe what they learned in their own words by relating it to a concrete familiar situation.

Method.   Subjects read an instructional manual covering an information management language similar to that described in the previous section (see Tables 7 and 8). For subjects in the model elaboration group, there was an elaboration page after each page in the manual, while for subjects in the control group there was no elaboration exercise. The elaboration exercises asked the subject to describe the newly learned statement in terms of operations within a concrete model of the computer. Table 10 provides a

TABLE 10.   Example of the Model
Elaboration Exercise in the Programming
Text

Model Elaboration
Consider the following situation. An office clerk has an in-basket, a save basket, a discard basket, and a sorting area on the desk. The in-basket is full of records. Each one can be examined individually in the sorting area of the desk and then placed in either the save or discard basket. Describe the FOR statement in terms of what operations the clerk would perform using the in-basket, discard basket, save basket, and sorting area.

TABLE 11.   Proportion of Correct Answers
on Transfer Test by Type of Problem for
Model Elaboration and Control Groups[a]

Group	Type of Test Problem				
	Sort-1	Sort-2	Count	Com- pute-1	Com- pute-2
Model elabora- tion	.65	.58	.64	.64	.45
Control	.66	.64	.41	.38	.27

[a] Adapted from Maye80a.
Note. 20 subjects per group; group × problem-type interaction, $p < .05$.

typical exercise. Then all subjects took the same 20-item problem-solving test as described in the previous section.

Results   Table 11 shows the proportion of correct responses by type of problem for the two groups.[2] As can be seen, the control group performed well on simple retention-like problems, but the model elaboration group performed considerably better on problems requiring creative transfer. Thus there is evidence that requiring the learners to put technical information in their own words through relating the material to a familiar situation results in broader learning outcomes. The results are similar to those given in Table 9 and suggest that model advance organizers and model elaboration have similar effects.

---

[2]These tables are broken down by problem complexity, wth more complex problems requiring transfer. The same general pattern is found for both generation and interpretation problems. Table 13 shows data for interpretation problems only, in order to avoid unnecessary complexity. However this table cannot be directly compared with Table 11.

3.4   Effects of Comparative Elaboration on Transfer Performance

In the previous study a concrete situation was presented and the learner asked to relate the new information to it. However, the results are ambiguous in the sense that they may be attributed either to elaboration activity per se or to the fact that additional information (about the concrete model) was presented to the model elaboration group. The purpose of the present studies was to use a kind of elaboration activity that does not add new information [Maye80a]. Thus a set of studies was conducted in which some subjects were asked to compare newly learned statements in their own words.

Method.   Subjects read the same manual about an information management language as in the previous study. However some subjects were given an elaboration page after each page in the booklet (comparative elaboration group), while for other subjects there was no elaboration (control group). The elaboration activity asked subjects to tell in their own words how two statements were similar and different. Table 12 provides a typical exercise. Then all subjects took the same test as in the previous study.

Results.   Table 13 shows the proportion of correct answers by type of problem for the two groups. As can be seen, the control group excelled on retention-like problems, but the comparative elaboration groups excelled on the more complex transfer problems. Thus there is evidence corresponding to that found in the model elaboration studies that asking learners to put technical information in their own words (through making comparisons) results in broader learning that supports transfer.

3.5   Effects of Model and Comparative Elaboration on Recall

The previous studies suggest that elaboration activity can influence transfer performance. As a further test [Maye80a] subjects were given manuals

TABLE 12. EXAMPLE OF THE COMPARATIVE ELABORATION EXERCISE IN THE PROGRAMMING TEXT

Comparative Elaboration
How is the FOR command like the FROM command? How is the FOR command different from the FROM command?

TABLE 13. PROPORTION CORRECTION TRANSFER
TEST FOR COMPARATIVE ELABORATION AND
CONTROL GROUPS[a]

Group	Type of Problem				
	Sort-1	Sort-2	Count	Com-pute-1	Com-pute-2
Compara-tive elab-oration	.90	.90	1.00	.75	.55
Control	.90	.90	.65	.65	.25

[a] Adapted from MAYE80a.
Note. Data are for interpretation problems only; 13
subjects per group; group × problem-type interaction,
$p < .05$.

either with no elaboration questions, model elaboration questions, or
comparative elaboration questions. It can be predicted that the elaboration
subjects should recall more information that supports transfer — such as
conceptual information — while the control group should recall more information about specific statements — such as technical information.

Method.   As in the previous study subjects read a manual explaining
the information management language that contained either no questions
(control group), model questions (model elaboration group), or comparative questions (comparative elaboration group). Then subjects were asked
to recall portions of the text.

Results.   For purposes of scoring the recall protocols the text was
divided into idea units. Some of the idea units presented information about
how the computer operated (conceptual idea units), and others emphasized
the grammar and technical aspects of each statement (technical idea units).
Table 14 shows the average number of idea units recalled by type for the
three groups. As can be seen, the control group recalled equal amounts of
both types of information, but the elaboration groups each tended to
emphasize recall of conceptual as compared with technical information.
These results are consistent with the results of the transfer studies in that
conceptual information is likely to be needed to support transfer.

3.6 Effects of Note Taking on Transfer and Recall Performance

The foregoing series of studies provides some evidence that elaboration
techniques influence the breadth of learning. However, the generality of the
results is limited by the fact that just one type of manual and two types of
elaboration activity were used. In addition, previous studies did not control

TABLE 14.   AVERAGE NUMBER OF RECALLED IDEA
UNITS FOR MODEL ELABORATION, COMPARATIVE
ELABORATION, AND CONTROL GROUPS[a]

Group	Type of Idea Units	
	Technical	Conceptual
	(19)	(52)
Model elaboration	5.3	13.9
Comparative elaboration	9.4	14.1
Control	7.5	7.5

[a] Adapted from MAYE80a.
Note. 20 subjects per group; group × type interaction, $p < .05$, for low-ability subjects. Numbers in parentheses indicate total possible.

for amount of reading time. Thus an additional series of studies [Pepe78] was conducted using a different language (a BASIC-like language) and a different elaboration activity (note taking).

Method.   Subjects watched a 20-minute videotape lecture, similar to the manual described earlier, describing seven BASIC-like statements. Some subjects were asked to take notes by putting the basic information in their own words. Other subjects simply viewed the lectures without taking notes. At a test subjects were given problems to solve or asked to recall portions of the lesson. Videotape presentations were controlled for presentation time in the two groups.

Results.   Table 15 gives the proportion of correct answers on generative problems (similar to those in the lesson) and on interpretation problems

TABLE 15.   PROPORTION OF CORRECT ANSWERS
ON TRANSFER TEST FOR NOTES AND NO-NOTES
GROUPS[a]

Subjects	Problem Type	
	Generative	Interpretive
Low ability		
Notes group	.39	.56
No-notes group	.49	.33
High ability		
Notes group	.67	.62
No-notes group	.60	.60

[a] From PEPE78.
Note. 15 subjects per group; effect of ability, $p < .01$; interaction between group ability and problem type, $p < .025$.

(which were not in the lesson). As can be seen, for low-ability subjects (based on SAT mathematics scores) there is a pattern in which note taking helps performance on transfer but hurts performance on the retention-like problems. For high-ability subjects note taking has no effect, presumably because high-ability learners already possess strategies for actively assimilating the new information.

Table 16 shows recall of the lecture by type of idea unit for the two groups. As can be seen, the note takers recalled more conceptual information, but there is no difference between the groups in recall of technical information. Thus the results are consistent with the model elaboration and comparative elaboration studies concerning the effects of asking subjects to put new technical information in their words during learning.

3.7 Conclusion

The goal of elaboration is to help the learner describe the key concepts in his own words, using his existing knowledge. Unfortunately there is no foolproof way to design useful elaboration activities. Emphasis on format or grammatical details and emphasis on errorless verbatim recall of statements will not produce the desired effects. The learner should be able to describe the effects of each program statement in his own words.

4.   UNDERSTANDING COMPUTER PROGRAMMING

The previous sections have focused on the issue of *how* to teach novices. This section briefly examines the issue of *what* to teach. Greeno [Gree76] has argued that instruction for problem-solving tasks should be based on *cognitive objectives*—statements of what the learner should have in his or

TABLE 16. AVERAGE NUMBER OF RECALLED IDEA
UNITS FOR NOTES AND NO-NOTES GROUPS[a]

| Group | Type of Idea Units | | |
	Technical	Conceptual	Intru-sions
	(28)	(36)	
Notes	10.4	7.2	3.9
No-notes	9.4	4.7	2.4

[a] Adapted from PEPE78.
Note. 20 subjects per group; interaction between group and type of recall, $p < .025$. Numbers in parentheses indicate total possible.

her head at the end of instruction. Two major objectives that are relevant to enhancing a novice's understanding of computer programming are knowledge for understanding a statement and knowledge for understanding a program.

4.1   Understanding a Statement

What does it mean to say that someone "understands" a certain statement? In a recent analysis of BASIC each statement is described as a "transaction" [Maye79c]. A transaction consists of an action, an object, and a location in the computer. For example, the statement LEFT $X = 5$, consists of the following six transactions:

1. Find the number indicated on the right of the equal sign (ACTION: Find; OBJECT: Number; LOCATION: Program).
2. Find the number in the memory space indicated on the left of the equal sign (ACTION: Find; OBJECT: Number; LOCATION: Memory).
3. Erase the number in that memory space (ACTION: Destroy; OBJECT: Number; LOCATION: Memory).
4. Write the new number in that memory space (ACTION: Create; OBJECT: Number; LOCATION: Memory).
5. Go on to the next statement (ACTION: Move; OBJECT: Pointer; LOCATION: Program).
6. Do what it says (ACTION: Allow; OBJECT: Command; LOCATION: Program).

Thus there is a general structure for each transaction: some action can be expected to be carried out on some object in some location in the computer. The two techniques cited in previous sections can be applied to teaching a transaction-type analysis of statements. It may be noted that statements with the same name may actually consist of different actions. For example, a "Counter Set LET" as given above is different from an "Arithmetic LET" such as LET $X = 5/2$. Explicit naming and describing of different types of statements with the same keyword may become a part of computer instruction.

4.2   Understanding a Program

What do experts know about computer programming that beginners do not know? One answer is that experts possess much more information and that the information is organized more efficiently. For example, a review of research on teaching people how to become better problem solvers concludes that good problem solving requires that the user have domain-specific knowledge: "All problem solving is based on knowledge" [Gree80]. Similarly, Simon [Simo80] estimates that a person needs 50,000 chunks of domain-specific information to become an expert in some domain.

In a classic study subjects were asked to view briefly presented chessboard configurations and then to reconstruct them [Chas73]. Chess masters performed much better than less experienced players on reconstructing board configurations if the board positions came from actual games; however the advantage was lost when random board patterns were presented. This finding suggests that experts in chess do not necessarily have better memories, but rather a repertoire of many meaningful patterns of board positions. They can chunk several pieces together into one meaningful pattern, while a less experienced player must try to remember each piece separately. In an analogous study reported by Shneiderman [Shne80], experienced and inexperienced programmers were given programs to study. Experienced programmers were able to recall many more lines of code than inexperienced programmers when the program was a meaningful running program; however, when the program consisted of random lines of code, the two groups performed at similar levels. Apparently, the experts were able to chunk lines of code together into chunks, while less experienced users were less able to form such chunks.

For example, Atwood and Ramsey [Atwo78] suggest that experienced programmers encode a segment such as

```
SUM = 0
DO 1 I = 1, N
    SUM = SUM + (I)
1 CONTINUE
```

as "CALCULATE THE SUM OF ARRAY X." An experienced programmer has a "schema" for this task and is able to generate a variety of lines of code to accomplish it. In order to provide a more precise description of the "schemata" that are involved in understanding programs, Atwood and Ramsey [Atwo80] used a modified version of Kintsch's [Kint74] propositional analysis. Each statement in the program can be written as a predicate with arguments, and a macrostructure can be constructed. Although a detailed description of Atwood and Ramsey's system is beyond the scope of this paper, their work is promising in that it suggests that knowledge can be represented precisely.

One implication of this work is that it might be possible to teach the major "chunks" or "schemata" involved in computer programming explicitly using the techniques cited in previous sections. Explicit naming and teaching of basic schemata such as these may become part of computer programming curricula.

5. SUMMARY

This paper is concerned with how to make computers and computer programming more understandable for novices. Two instructional techniques from educational and cognitive psychology are described — using concrete models to represent the computer system and encouraging the learner to describe technical information in his own words. A review of the effectiveness of these techniques reveals that, under certain conditions, both techniques may enhance the learner's understanding as measured by ability to solve problems that were not explicitly taught. Finally, two major objectives of computing instruction are suggested — enhancing the novice's ability to understand (1) the meaning of individual program statements and (2) the program schemata that give the statements a higher level meaning.

ACKNOWLEDGMENTS

I wish to thank Tom Moran for his editorial comments. A shorter version of this paper was presented at the National Science Foundation Conference on National Computer Literacy Goals for 1985, held in Reston, Va., on December 18–20, 1980. Preparation of this paper was supported by Grant NIE-G-0118 from the National Institute of Education and Grant SED-80-14950 from the National Science Foundation.

The quotation on page 124 is reprinted from "Contextual Prerequisites for Understanding: Some Investigations of Comprehension and Recall," by J. D. Bransford and M. K. Johnson, in *J. Verbal Learn. Verbal Behav.* **11** (1972); © Academic Press. Figure 2 and Table 4 are, respectively, reproduced and adapted from "Some Conditions of Meaningful Learning for Computer Programming: Advance Organizers and Subject Control of Frame Order," by R. E. Mayer, in *J. Educ. Psychol.* **68** (1976), 143–150; © 1976 American Psychological Association. Table 3 is adapted from "Different Problem-Solving Competencies Established in Learning Computer Programming with and without Meaningful Models," by R. E. Mayer, in *J. Educ. Psychol.* **67** (1975), 725–734; © 1975 American Psychological Association. Table 6 is adapted from "Different Recall Protocols for Technical Text Due to Advance Organizers," by R. E. Mayer and B. Bromage, in *J.*

Educ. Psychol. **72** (1980), 209–225; © 1980 American Psychological Association. Tables 9, 11, 13, and 14 are adapted from and Table 8 is reproduced from "Elaboration Techniques for Technical Text: An Experimental Test of the Learning Strategy Hypothesis," by R. E. Mayer, *J. Educ. Psychol.* **72** (1980), 770–784; © 1980 American Psychological Association. Tables 15 and 16 are, respectively, reproduced and adapted from "Note Taking as a Generative Activity," by R. J. Peper and R. E. Mayer, in *J. Educ. Psychol.* **70** (1978), 514–522; © 1978 American Psychological Association. All of the material from the *Journal of Educational Psychology* is reproduced by permission of the American Psychological Association and the Association for Computing Machinery.

REFERENCES

Anderson, R.C. "The notion of schemata and the educational enterprise," in *Schooling and the acquisition of knowledge,* R.C. Anderson, R.J. Spiro, and W.E. Montague, Eds., Erlbaum, Hillsdale, N.J., 1977.

Atwood, M.E., and Ramsey, H.R. "Cognitive structure in the comprehension and memory of computer programs: An investigation of computer programming debugging." ARI Tech. Rep. TR-78-A210, Science Applications, Englewood, Colo., Aug. 1978.

Ausubel, D.P. "The use of advance organizers in the learning and retention of meaningful verbal material." *J. Educ. Psychol.* **51** (1960), 267–272.

Ausubel, D.P., and Fitzgerald, D. "The role of discriminability in meaningful verbal learning and retention." *J. Educ. Psychol.* **52** (1961), 266–274.

Ausubel, D.P., and Fitzgerald, D. "Organizer, general background, and antecedent learning variables in sequential verbal learning." *J. Educ. Psychol.* **53** (1962), 243–249.

Ausubel, D.P. *The Psychology of meaningful verbal learning,* Grune and Stratton, New York, 1963.

Ausubel, D.P. *Educational psychology: A cognitive view,* Holt, Rinehart and Winston, New York, 1968.

Ausubel, D.P., Novak, J.D., and Hanesian, R. *Educational psychology: A cognitive view,* 2nd ed., Harper and Row, New York, 1977.

Barnes, B.R., and Clawson, E.U. "Do advance organizers facilitate learning? Recommendations for further research based on an analysis of 32 studies," *Rev. Educ. Res.* **45** (1975), 637–659.

Bartlett, F.C. *Remembering,* Cambridge University Press, Cambridge, England, 1932.

Bower, G.H. "Mental imagery and associating learning," in *Cognition in learning and memory,* L. Gregg, Ed., Wiley, New York, 1972.

Bransford, J.D., and Johnson, M.K. "Contextual prerequisites for understanding: Some investigations of comprehension and recall," *J. Verbal Learn. Verbal Behav.* **11** (1972), 717–726.

Bransford, J.D. *Human cognition,* Wadsworth, Monterey, Calif., 1979.

Brownell, W.A., and Moser, H.E. "Meaningful vs. mechanical learning: A study in grade III subtraction," in *Duke University Research Studies in Education, no. 8,* Duke University Press, Durham, N.C., 1949, pp. 1–207.

Chase, W.G., and Simon, H.A. "Perception in chess," *Cognitive Psychol.* **4** (1973), 55–81.

Dansereau, D. "The development of a learning strategies curriculum," in *Learning strategies,* H.F. O'Neal, Ed., Academic Press, New York, 1978.

Dooling, D.J., and Lachman, R. "Effects of comprehension on the retention of prose," *J. Exp. Psychol.* **88** (1971), 216–222.

Dooling, D.J., and Mullet, R.L. "Locus of thematic effects on retention of prose," *J. Exp. Psychol.* **97** (1973), 404–406.

du Boulay, B., and O'Shea, T. "How to work the LOGO machine," Paper No. 4, Dep. Artificial Intellligence, Univ. Edinburgh, Scotland, 1976.

du Boulay, B., O'Shea, T., and Monk, J. "The black box inside the glass box: Presenting computing concepts to novices," Paper no. 133, Dep. Artificial Intelligence, Univ. Edinburgh, Scotland, 1980.

Ewert, P.H., and Lambert, J.F. "The effect of verbal instructions upon the formation of a concept," *J. Gen. Psychol.* **6** (1932), 400–411.

Fitzgerald, D., and Ausubel, D.P. "Cognitive versus affective factors in the learning and retention of controversial material," *J. Educ. Psychol.,* **54** (1963), 73–84.

Gagne, R.M., and Smith, E.C. "A study of the effects of verbalization on problem solving," *J. Exp. Psychol.* **63** (1962), 12–18.

Gould, J.D., and Ascher, R.M. "Query by non-programmers," IBM Research Rep., Yorktown Heights, N.Y., 1974.

Greeno, J.G. "Cognitive objectives of instruction," in *Cognition and instruction.* D. K. Dahr, Ed., Erlbaum, Hillsdale, N.J., 1976.

Greeno, J.G. "Trends in the theory of knowledge for problem solving," in *Problem solving and education: Issues in teaching and research,* D.T. Tuma and F. Reif, Eds., Erlbaum, Hillsdale, N.J., 1980.

Grotelueschen, A., and Sjogren, D.D. "Effects of differentially structured introductory materials and learning tasks on learning and transfer," *Am. Educ. Res. J.* **5** (1968), 277–202.

Katona, G. *Organizing and memorizing,* Columbia University Press, New York, 1942.

Kintsch, W. *The representation of meaning in memory.* Erlbaum, Hillsdale, N.J., 1974.

Kohler, W. *The mentality of apes,* Liveright, New York, 1925.

Lawton, J.T., and Wanska, S.K. "Advance organizers as a teaching strategy: A reply to Barnes and Clawson," *Rev. Educ. Res.* **47** (1977), 233–244.

Lesh, R.A. "The influence of an advance organizer on two types of instructional units about finite geometrics," *J. Res. Math. Educ.* **7** (1976), 82–86.

Mayer, R.E. "Information processing variables in learning to solve problems," *Rev. Educ. Res.* **45** (1975), 525–541.

Mayer, R.E. "Different problem-solving competencies established in learning computer programming with and without meaningful models," *J. Educ. Psychol.* **67** (1975), 725–734.

Mayer, R.E. "Some conditions of meaningful learning for computer programming: Advance organizers and subject control of frame order," *J. Educ. Psychol.* **68** (1976), 143–150.

Mayer, R.E. "Different rule system for counting behavior acquired in meaningful and rote contexts of learning," *J. Educ. Psychol.* **69** (1977), 537–546.

Mayer, R.E. "Advance organizers that compensate for the organization of text," *J. Educ. Psychol.* **70** (1978), 880–886.

Mayer, R.E. "Can advance organizers influence meaningful learning?" *Rev. Educ. Res.* **49** (1979), 371–383.

Mayer, R.E. "Twenty years of research on advance organizers: Assimilation theory is still the best predictor of results," *Instr. Sci* **8** (1979), 133–167.

Mayer, R.E. "A psychology of learning BASIC," *Commun. ACM* **22** (1979), 589–594.

Mayer, R.E. "Elaboration techniques for technical text: An experimental test of the learning strategy hypothesis," *J. Educ. Psychol.* **72** (1980), 770–784.

Mayer, R.E., and Bromage, B. "Different recall protocols for technical text due to advance organizers," *J. Educ. Psychol.* **72** (1980), 209–225.

Mayer, R.E., and Cook, L. "Effects of shadowing on prose comprehension and problem solving," *Memory and Cognition* **8** (1981).

Merrill, M.D., and Stolurow, L.M. "Hierarchical preview vs. problem oriented review in learning in imaginary science," *Am. Educ. Res. J.* **3** (1966), 251–261.

Minsky, M. "A framework for representing knowledge," in *The psychology of computer vision,* P. Winston, Ed., McGraw-Hill, New York, 1975.

O'Neil, H.F. *Learning strategies,* Academic Press, New York, 1978.

Paivio, A. "Mental imagry in associative learning and memory," *Psychol. Rev.* **76** (1969), 241–263.

Peper, R.J., and Mayer, R.E. "Note taking as a generative activity," *J. Educ. Psychol.* **70** (1978), 514–522.

Raye, C. "Considerations of some problems of comprehension," in *Visual information processing,* W.G. Chase, Ed., Academic Press, New York, 1973.

Reisner, P. "Use of psychological experimentation as an aid to development of a query language," *IEEE Trans. Soft: Eng.* SE-3 (1977), 218–229.

Resnick, L.B., and Ford, S. *The psychology of mathematics learning,* Erlbaum, Hillsdale, N.J., 1980.

Ring, D.G., and Novak, J.D. "Effects of cognitive structure variables on achievement in college chemistry," *J. Res. Sci. Educ.* **8** (1971), 325–338.

Royer, J.M., and Cable, G.W. "Facilitated learning in connected discourse," *J. Educ. Psychol.* **67** (1975), 116–123.

Royer, J.M., and Cable, G.W. "Illustrations, analogies, and facilitative transfer in prose learning," *J. Educ. Psychol.* **68** (1976), 205–209.

Rumelhart, D.E. "Notes on a schema for stress," in *Representation and understanding,* D.B. Bobrow and A. Collins, Eds., Academic Press, New York, 1975.

Scandura, J.M., and Wells, J.N. "Advance organizers in learning abstract mathematics," *Am. Educ. Res. J.* **4** (1967), 295–301.

Schank, R.C., and Abelson, R.P. *Scripts, plans, goals and understanding,* Wiley, New York, 1977.

Schumacher, G.M., Liebert, D., and Fass, W. "Textual organization, advance organizers, and the retention of prose material," *J. Reading Behav.* **7** (1975), 173–180.

Shneiderman, B. *Software psychology: Human factors in computer and information systems,* Winthrop, New York, 1980.

Simon, H.A. "Problem solving and education," in *Problem solving and education: Issues in teaching and research,* D.T. Tuma and F. Reif, Eds., Erlbaum, Hillsdale, N.J., 1980.

Smith, R.J., and Hesse, K.D. "The effects of prereading assistance on the comprehension and attitudes of good and poor readers," *Res. Teach. Engl.* **3** (1969), 166–167.

Thorndyke, P.W. "Cognitive structures in comprehension and memory of narrative discourse," *Cognitive Psychol.* **9** (1977), 77–110.

Weaver, F., and Suydam, M. "Meaningful instruction in mathematics education," in *Mathematics Education Reports,* 1972.

Weinstein, C. "Elaboration skills as a learning strategy," in *Learning strategies,* H.F. O'Neil, Ed., Harper and Row, New York, 1978.

Wertheimer, M. *Productive thinking,* Harper and Row, New York, 1959.

West, L.H.T., and Fensham, D.J. "Prior knowledge or advance organizers as effective variables in chemistry learning," *J. Res. Sci. Teach.* **13** (1976), 297–306.

White, R.T., and Mayer, R.E. "Understanding intellectual skills," *Instr. Sci* **9** (1980), 101–127.

Wittrock, M.C. "Learning as a generative process," *Educ. Psychol.* **11** (1974), 87–95.

8

THE CONCEPT OF VARIABLE IN PROGRAMMING: ITS MEANING AND USE IN PROBLEM-SOLVING BY NOVICE PROGRAMMERS*

RENAN SAMURÇAY
Laboratoire de Psychologie du Travail EPHE/CNRS, Paris France

Our general aim is to study the cognitive problems encountered by students in their acquisition of programming concepts. In this paper we focus our attention on the concept of variable and its use in problem-solving by novice students (15–16 year) who had previously followed a didactical experience. A set of incomplete program text in which one or more lines have been left blank is presented to students at the end of teaching sessions. The students were asked to complete these lines. The results are discussed in terms of the nature of the solution given by the students, the properties of the conceptual field and the way in which these concepts were introduced.

INTRODUCTION

Teaching and learning to program at school is an important issue in education today. Programming instruction is given at different levels: from the primary school to the professional level. Given this context many questions arise: How to teach programming? What is necessary to teach? At which level?

The answers are not immediately available; we have to know more about how students at different levels learn to program and which kind of difficulties they encounter, and how the instruction may help them to go beyond these difficulties.

---

*The first version of this paper is published in French with the title: "SIGNIFICATION ET FONCTIONNEMENT DU CONCEPT DE VARIABLE INFORMATIQUE CHEZ DES ELEVES DEBUTANTS," Educational Studies in Mathematics 16 (1985) 143–161.

During the last ten years many research works have investigated the psychological study of learning programming, but only few of them pay attention to the content of programming knowledge and to the characteristics of meaningful teaching situations in which novices can acquire this knowledge. The identification of the specific components of that underlying knowledge is necessary in order to teach programming better and in order to build up didactical situations which help students to learn programming. The study presented here is a part of a larger research project in which our aim is to identify, analyze and describe the cognitive difficulties encountered by students in learning programming concepts in relation to the nature of the teaching situation. In this paper we will focus on the programming concept of variable and its use in problem-solving by novice students.

The organization of this paper is as follows. We will first explain the theoretical framework which serves as a basis for our experimental study. We will then describe the particular tasks we have developed to examine the novices' representations about the variable concept. The analysis of the experimental data will then be presented. We conclude with some remarks about the implications of our findings.

LEARNING PROGRAMMING

The specific nature of programming as a problem-solving situation can be summarized in a few points: the goal of the activity is not only to produce a solution as in classical problem solving situations, but also to make explicit the procedure producing the solution; the activity is highly mediated by a technological tool for which the subject has to construct functional representations; the elaboration and the expression of the procedure in a specific "action code system" necessitate the acquisition and the use of specific programming concepts.

These characteristics have important effects on the learning process. One cannot consider programming learning only in terms of the acquisition of syntax or method. For instance, the research works on learning programming methodology (Hoc, 1981; 1983) suggest that the lack of a "Representation and Processing System" (RPS), closely related to the computer operation, constitutes an obstacle for novice programmers in learning and using these methods by requiring higher level representations. This kind of result suggests that a way to conceive the initial stage of programming learning is to permit students to construct a RPS organized by a hierarchy of plans.

The notion of plan is used (Soloway et al., 1982) to describe the organisation of the expert knowledge with the aim of analyzing the novices' behaviour by referring to this organization. Here a plan is defined as a catalogue of stereotypic action sequences that the expert programmers have and select and use by adapting them to the need of the current situation. According to this approach the novices' bugs are analyzed in terms of their distance from the expert plans and they may have several explanation systems such as the inappropriate use of natural language plans (Bonar & Soloway, 1985) or the use of a simple plan to achieve multiple goals (Soloway et al., 1982). Then, learning programming is seen as an acquisition of a catalogue of plans through programming experience. Although the notion of plan describes well the structure of the expert programming knowledge, it seems to us that its references to the conceptual aspects (content) of this knowledge are insufficient. The question of what kind of experiences the novices need to have before they construct a catalogue of plans, is still open.

We consider programming as a complex domain of knowledge and practice corresponding both to a scientific field and to a professional practice field. We assume that learning programming means the acquisition of specific programming concepts mediated by a technological tool which necessitates the construction of high-level representations and conceptual invariants. Our aim is to identify and to describe the programming concepts in terms of their epistemological meaning (i.e., what are the theoretical and practical programming problems for which these concepts constitute an answer?) and their relative complexity. The notion of complexity is not only defined in terms of the quantity of information processed simultaneously, but also in terms of the conceptual difficulty which is defined by three components: intrinsic analysis of a concept, observable behaviours and properties of the situations in which the behaviours are produced.

Our general hypothesis is that the initial representations of novices in programming are characterized by the transfer of familiar procedures of the problem domain and the mental execution of these procedures. These procedures may or may not be compatible with the functioning of the computer with respect to the complexity of the problem and with respect to the level of competency of the programmer. It is then important to characterize the familiar procedures associated with different concepts.

In the following section, we will present an analysis of programming variables in order to describe the different levels of conceptual complexity which can be associated with this concept.

COGNITIVE AND EPISTEMOLOGICAL ANALYSIS OF PROGRAMMING CONCEPT OF VARIABLE

From the programming point of view a variable is defined as an address but this formulation is not sufficient to analyse this concept in its functional meaning for the student. In fact when the values of a variable change, its naming and its functional relationships with other elements of the program are invariant. In the programming activity with procedural languages such as Pascal, Basic, Fortran etc..., this property of invariance appears particularly in the looping problems, in which variables are involved with a particular status such as

sum→sum + number

We will call this type of variables "accumulator" to distinguish them from other ones. With respect to their meaning for the student, we distinguish four forms of occurrence of the assignment sign when operating on variables.

1. Assignment of a constant value
   a := 3
   list := 'word'
   test := false
2. Attribution of a calculated value
   a := 3 + 5
   b := 3 * k
3. Duplication
   k := m
4. Accumulation
   x := x + 5
   sum := sum + number
   expox := expox * x

It is obvious that the concepts of variables and assignment take their full programming meaning in the last case. In the other cases the student may use his existing mathematical conception of variable and equality, i.e., a unique value can be associated to the name of the variable. The understanding and the construction of the symbolic representations associated with the accumulation form makes it necessary to consider a variable in its temporal definition: "the value of variable sum at $n+1$.th step is equal to its value at n.th step plus the value of variable number". The student has to designate by the same name both the preceeding value and the present value which is a function of the former and has to process the assignment sign as an asymmetric relation. The mathematical model of variable and the equality relation constitutes for a novice an initial but unsufficient model for operating on the programming variables when these are involved in the loop construction. The mathematical description of a variable is a static one and it designates either a generic name of a set

$x \epsilon$ a,b

or an unknown in an equation

$$3x = x + 10$$

The programming variable is a new concept for the student and we hypothesize that processing with variables in loop problems is a difficult task for students.

We distinguish two kinds of variables as regard to their functional meaning for the students' model of action planning. *External variables* are corresponding to the values controlled by the program users: i.e., variables which are explicit inputs and outputs of the problem. *Internal variables* are corresponding to the values controlled by the programmers: i.e., variables which are necessary only for the programmed solution of the problem. For example, consider the problem of permutation of numbers; the variable corresponding to two given numbers are external, the intermediary variable which should be used to keep one of the variable in the change is internal.

We hypothesize that internal variables are conceptually more difficult to construct than external variables. They require representations of the computer operation in terms of system states.

Based on Ehrlich and Soloway's definition of variable plans (1982), we distinguish three types of variable processes when solving loop problems: update, test and initialization. In the problem-solving these various processes are intimately related to each other, and the cognitive task of the student can be defined as following:

- update: identification, elaboration and expression of the rule of definition of the accumulation variables. The values of these variables are transformed in the loop-body.
- test: identification and expression of the condition for terminating the loop in relation to the functional role of the test-variable. By which variable is the loop controlled and for which particular value?
- initialization: identification of the initial values of the variables involved in the loop-body.

We hypothesize that these operations will not be on the same level of complexity for the students. For instance, the initialization (make an hypothesis on the initial state of the system) will be more difficult than the operations of updating and test, because it is not a relevant operation for the "hand solution" of the problem. Moreover these operations may be more or less complex with respect to the type of variable on which they will operate. For instance updating the counter variables is easier than updating the accumulation variable. One of the reasons is the fact that updating a counter variable involves adding a constant counter → counter + 1

although updating an accumulation variable necessitates adding another variable to the last one.

GOAL OF THE EMPIRICAL STUDY AND METHODOLOGY

To understand the difficulties encountered in the teaching of a concept, to interpret the strategies used by students in the problem-solving, it is necessary to have a precise image of the students' conceptions about this concept. Hence, it is important to collect information about the students' conceptions and their evolution during the learning process.

There are various methods for collecting information about students' conceptions. These conceptions may be represented with respect to two dimensions:

- synchronous dimension which describes the state of the competencies of the subjects at a given moment of acquisition;
- diachronous dimension which describes the evolution of the concepts and the procedures during a period of time.

In this study we are using the first kind of analysis. To collect the data we use a technique similar to those used by Ehrlich and Soloway (1982): an incomplete fragment of a program in which one or more critical lines have been left blank is given to the students. The students' task was to fill in the blank lines with one or more lines of code. The only difference in our study is that information is given about what problem the program was intended to solve. This difference is introduced with the aim of observing the transfer effects of familiar procedures from the problem domain.

With this technique the task of the student is a program completion task and it is different from the program construction task: it involves also a program understanding task as a sub-task. Although there exist some research works on the program understanding by expert programmers (Detienne, 1985; Letovsky, 1986), a very few things are known concerning the novices. Some informal observations suggest that the novices try to execute mentally the program when they have to understand it in order to say what problem the program solves. This fact is another reason why we have changed the original technique with the hypothesis that the knowledge of the problem text will lead the students to focus more on the relations between the variables than on the execution of the program.

POPULATION

The question sheet is given to 26 college students (in the fifth year of the French secondary school) in the classroom situation. They were at the end of their 15 hours of programming course in Pascal (1 hour per week). During this period the following concepts are introduced on simple arithmetic problems: variables, operations on the variables and two loop strategies: repeat- and for-loop (Samurçay, 1985). The students were not all at the same level in terms of their competency in programming; we distinguish three groups and note them by G1 "strong", G2 "average" and G3 "weak".

TASK ANALYSIS AND HYPOTHESIS

There are three types of task in the question sheet (4 problems).

Initialization Tasks

Two rules may be announced about this operation: (1) each variable for which the values are transformed in a loop should be initialized; (2) the way to initialize a variable (read or asignment) is determined in general by the manner in which it is updated.

However the use of these rules is not sufficient to determine the initial value of the variable: this value is determined both by the problem text and the identification of the transformations operating on the variables. There are three initialization tasks in question sheet

1. The first one concerns three accumulation variables of a program (cf. Fig. 1).

To answer the question, the student has to identify both the variables and their initial value. We expect a large distribution of responses, in particular for variables EXPOX and EXPOY. According to our hypothesis, we would expect that the initialization of the COUNTER variable will be easier than the two others. On the other hand the initialization of counter variable to zero may correspond to a pragmatic rule introduced in the teaching session "before each calculus get empty the corresponding variables". The initialization of the variables EXPOX and EXPOY to 1 makes a deeper understanding of their function in relation with the problem text necessary.

2. The second problem (cf. Fig. 2) concerns a program containing only one variable with double functions.

The following program has to calculate and print out the value of
$x^n - y^n$. x, y, are positive integers.

```
program expo;
var
  x, y, n, expox, expoy, counter, result : integer;

begin
  read(x);
  read(y);
  read(n);
**  ─────────────────────→  counter := 0;
                             expox := 1;
                             expoy := 1;

  repeat
    begin
      expox := expox * x;
      expoy := expoy * y;
      counter := counter + 1;
    end
  until counter = n;

  result := expox - expoy;
  write(' the result is: ', result);
end.
```

Are there some missing lines in the program where you see ** ?
        yes   no

If yes, please complete the program.

FIGURE 1   Problem 1: Initialization problem note: the missing lines are indicated in
the box.

The following program has to calculate and print out a series of
strictly positive integers. One line is missing, where you see **.
Please complete the program.

```
program integerseries;
var
  x : integer;

begin

**  ─────────────────────→  x := 1;

  repeat
    begin
      writeln(x);
      x := x + 2;
    end
  until x = 32767 (* 32767 is the largest integer! *)

end.
```

FIGURE 2   Problem 2: Initialization problem note: the missing lines are indicated in
the box.

The variable x is at the same time an explicit given data (external) of the problem and the counter variable (internal). But this last function may not be immediately identified by students. For solving the initialization problem of this variable, the student has to coordinate two pieces of information: the transformational rule in updating and the particular value of the variable in the test (the particular value chosen here is well known by students as a maximum integer of the system). The standard solution of the problem is the initialization of the variable via assignment of an odd number (this should be deduced from the two pieces of information noticed above). However, a solution via the read statement is also acceptable if the number entered by the user is always odd. We would expect that the solution adopted by the students will be initialization via an assignment statement.

3. The third initialization task is involved in the fourth problem (cf. Figure 4) combined with the updating task. We will analyze it in the following sections in relation with the updating task.

Test Tasks

For solving the test tasks of our questions which concern only repeat-loop problems, a general rule may be announced: a loop is a finite process, it involves the begin and end statements. The use of this rule allows only the identification of the conditonal statement's place in a program. The construction of the test as a conditional expression necessitates also the identification of the test variable and its value in order to realize the end condition at least once. Thus an exact representation of the functional roles of the different variables in the program is necessary. This task is involved in two questions:

1. The first one (cf. Fig. 3) concerns a variable with a double function: the variable y is at the same time, an external variable as a given data and an internal variable as a decreasing counter variable. This decreasing form is unusual for the students who have worked usually with an increasing form.

The algorithm of the multiplication has been already encountered by the students at the beginning of the teaching sessions. In this version there was an explicit increasing counter variable and the test consisted of comparing the value of this variable with the read value. Although, in this version the initial value of the variable y is read, this value is modified by the execution of the program.

2. In the second test task, the variable on which the student has to operate is an explicit counter variable and the student may use an analogical model to construct the test (cf. Figure 4).

The following program has to calculate and print out the product of
two positive integers x and y. One line is missing, where you see **.
Please complete the program.

```
program multiple;
var
   x, y, result : integer;

begin
   read(x);
   read(y);
   result : = 0;
   repeat
      begin
         result := result + x;
         y := y - 1;
      end
   **  ─────────────────────────►│until y = 0;│

   write(result);
end.
```

FIGURE 3   Problem 3: Test problem note: the missing lines are indicated in the box.

```
program division;

(* this program calculates the division of a number by two for a certain number
of times and prints out the result; the initial number and the number of divisions
are chosen by the user *)

var
   number, ntimes, counter : integer;
   result : real;
begin
   read(number);
   read(ntimes);
   counter := 0;
   result := number;
   repeat
      begin
         result := result / 2;
         counter := counter + 1;
      end
   until counter = ntimes;
   write('the result of the divisions is: ');
   write(result);
end.
```

By using the above program as a model, please complete the following program
(program triple) which multiplies the square of a number by 3 a given number
of times and prints out the result; the initial number and the number of divisions
are chosen by the user.
Hint: the square of a number is the product of this number with itself (x*x).

```
program triple;
var
   number, ntimes, counter : integer;
   result : real;

begin
   read(number);
   read(ntimes);
   counter := 0;
   result := ─────────────────────►│number * number;│
   repeat
      begin
                  ─────────────────►│result := result * 3;│
                                    │counter := counter + 1;│
      end
   until counter = ──────────────►│ntimes;│
   write('the result is: ');
   write(result);
end.
```

FIGURE 4   Problem 4: Update and initialization problem note: the missing lines are
indicated in the box.

170

Updating Tasks

This task arises in problem 4 (cf. Fig. 4) in which the students have to construct the whole variable plans in a loop by using the problem text and an analogical model.

The program to complete and the model are different from each other only with respect to the transformation rule of the accumulation variable (RESULT). To solve the problem, the students have to identify the respective roles of the variables NUMBER, RESULT and NTIMES and the relationships between them as regard to the problem text. The model may help them only in terms of the plan structure's form. In terms of the "relational calculus" (i.e., mental operations on relations), the students have to consider four relations:

A1:   "divide a number by 2 a given number of times"
A2:   "multiply by 3 the square of a number a given number of times"
B1:   "result : = number
        result : = result /2"
B2:   "result : = number * number
        result : = result * 3"

The relationship between B2 and B1 translate the relationship between A1 and A2. The task is not a simple copying task. The student has to reproduce not only a form but also a relationship between two different systems of representation and process: arithmetic problem domain and programming domain.

RESULTS

The results are analyzed in two parts. In the first part we examine for each problem the different responses given by the students. In the second part we compare different results with respect to the types of variables, types of operations and types of student groups.

Analysis of Each Question

Table 1 shows the distribution of responses for problem 1 (Fig. 1).

Only one student has correctly initialized the three variables. The most interesting finding concerns partially correct initializations. As expected, the variables COUNTER and RESULT play a privileged role in the program for students. The variable RESULT was initialized by 3 students when it was not necessary. Initialization of the accumulation variables is the most difficult problem. The difficulty concerns both the function of the

Type of answer to Problem 1		Number of Responses
correct initialization on 3 variables		1
answer "no missing lines"		4
answer "yes" without adding missing lines		3
partial initialization		12
– only COUNTER	7	
– only EXPOX	1	
– only EXPOX and COUNTER	1	
– only RESULT	3	
erroneous initialization		4
– read(EXPOX), read (EXPOY)	2	
– read(EXPOX)	1	
– n := 0	1	
no answer		2

TABLE 1. Answers to Problem 1.

initialization in the definition of a variable and the representation of its function in the calculation. The initialization of the accumulation variables via the read statement (by 3 students) reflects the idea expressed by some students "you have to say to the computer the values of variables, because it cannot understand what are the names". This idea is also supported by the non-initialization of the variable COUNTER by the same students who think that the value of variable is known: it is always zero. Table 2 shows the distribution of responses for problem 2 (Fig. 2).

As hypothesized above, the dominant responses amongst the novices was to initialize the variable x via the read statement instead of an assignment statement. In the case of assignment, the use of zero as initial value is more frequent: this result confirms the a priori analysis we have done. Note also the case of two students who use both an assignment and a Read to initialize the variable x: it looks as if the Read was insufficient to give a value to a variable. This answer reflects, in our opinion, a residual conception about the Read statement in which

Read(x)

corresponds only "to take the value from the screen" but not to assign it to the address labelled by the x. The subject completes this second function by using the assignment.

Type of answer to Problem 2		Number of Responses
initialization		
via read "read(x)"		16
via assignment		6
– x := 0	5	
– x := 1	1	
via read and assignment		2
no answer		2

TABLE 2. Answers to Problem 2.

The distribution of responses for problem 3 (Fig. 3) is shown on the Table 3.

The results allow us to distinguish four hierarchical types of responses. The first type corresponds to the exact answer: "the test variable is y". In one of the 11 answers of this kind, the only error concerns the value of the variable: it is equal to 1, instead of 0.

The second type of answer reflects a conception for which "the repetition will be stop when the product x * y will be obtained". There are three responses of this kind.

The third type of answer corresponds to a more primitive conception than the two others: "the repetition will be stopped when the result will be obtained" without the precision of the nature of this nature.

Finally the fourth type of answer is characterized by the use of only syntactical rules: "to each REPEAT (begin statement) corresponds an UNTIL (end statement). This association is well established by the majority of students (22 out of 26).

Table 4 shows the distribution of answers for problem 4 (Fig. 4).

The data indicate that 11 students out of 26 gave correct answers to the updating task. Two minor errors are observed in the update of the variable RESULT. The first one concerns a simple syntactic error: "number^2" corresponds to the lack of the exponential notation in Pascal language. In the second erroneous answer, in addition to the syntactical aspect, there is also a conceptual difficulty concerning the use of NUMBER as a variable name in an algebraic calculation for which x is still a consecrated symbol.

It is important to notice that there is a significant difference between the treatment of two variables RESULT and COUNTER both in terms of success and erroneous procedures. Updating the variable RESULT is more difficult.

The most dominant type of errors corresponds to copying of the initialization part of the analogical model without modification and to

Type of answer to Problem 3		Number of Responses
test on variable y and its particular value		11
– until y = 0	10	
– until y = 1	1	
until the result is equal to the multiplication		3
– until y * x	1	
– result = y * x	1	
– result = result + x * y + 1	1	
until to obtain result		3
– until y = result	1	
– until result	1	
– result different from 0	1	
until without test		8
no answer		1

TABLE 3. Answers to Problem 3.

Type of answer to Problem 4		Number of Responses
correct procedure and expression		9
correct procedure and erroneous code		2
– result := number^2	1	
– result := x^2	1	
error on initialization: use of assignment as equality		5
– result := number;		
repeat		
begin		
result := result * result * 3		
counter := counter + 1;		
end		
until counter = ntimes		
use of analogical model without modification		3
– result := result / 2	2	
– result := number; result := result * 3	1	
algebraic model: update operations in loop are		
processed as successive algebraic operations		3
– result := x^2 * 3	1	
– result := (3 * (number * number) * ntimes)	1	
– repeat	1	
result := number * number		
result := result * 3		
other answers		3
– repeat x * x	1	
– result := number; repeat result := number	1	
– result := number * number	1	
repeat result := number * 3		
no answer		1

TABLE 4. Answers to Problem 4.

updating the variable RESULT in relation to this initialization. One of the plausible interpretations is that the subjects use the assignment sign as an equality sign, and the program represents for them a sequence of algebraic equations. In fact in this form, the program works for the value 1 of the variable NTIMES.

Three other erroneous answers reproduce the analogical model with very few modifications. If we don't report here the students' reactions observed during the correction session of the questions, the explanation of these answers will not be complete. During the correction phase we have observed that at least half of the students have some difficulties in translating the word problem "multiplying by 3, the square of a number a given number of times" into its algebraic formulation. Various formulations proposed by students before writing the exact formula x^2*3^y were:

—multiply $3x^2$ by NTIMES
—$3x^2y$ (corresponding to the idea of $(3x^2)$ y times)
—(x^2y) 3y
—$x^2*3*3*\ldots\ldots*3 = x^2y^3$

The difficulties concerning the translation of the word problems into the algebraic form are also pointed out by other research work (Ehrlich et al.,

1982). Hence the nature of the difficulties encountered by students in this last problem become more understandable. However, we argue that the problem here is not purely an algebraic formulation problem; the students have to conceive the formula as an image of the calculation necessary to express the relation

from $x^2\ 3^P$ to $(...(((x^2*3)*3)*3)...*3)$

In the other terms, updating the variable RESULT requires a particular functional representation of the relation described by the word problem. It is necessary for students to make an algorithmical reading of the algebraic formula. This example shows the importance of the representations transferred by students from the problem domain into the programming domain. Nevertheless, we need more specific research in order to characterize different RPSs in relation to different problem domains.

Students' Conceptions about Variables

In this part we will organize the data in order to compare the differences between the processing, by the students, with the different types of variables we have distinguished. We were interested also in the manner in which different operations are used on these different types of variables.

Table 5 shows the data organized in order to compare the number of correct responses with respect to the functional characteristics of variables, types of operations on variables and levels of competency of students.

Concerning the operations on variable, the data confirms our predictions: the initialization task is more difficult than the update and test

Operation	Variable types	G1 N=8	G2 N=10	G3 N=8	Total N=26
Initialization	Internal accumulation variables	1	–	–	1
	Counter variable	3	3	3	9
	External variable read	4	7	5	16
	multiple function assign.	4	1	1	6
Update	Counter variable	8	8	6	22
	Accumulation variable	5	2	5	12
Test	Explicit counter variable	8	8	4	20
	Implicit counter variable	7	3	–	10

TABLE 5. Distribution of answers in terms of functional characteristics of variables.
Note: G1, G2, and G3 indicate "strong", "average", and "weak" groups, respectively.

operations which seem to be on the same level of complexity. The conceptual difficulty concerning the initialization is observed also in a more general context than the programming context: make an hypothesis on the initial state of a variable while the transformation and the final state are known. Similar difficulties are observed when solving addition-subtraction problems (Vergnaud, 1982).

Moreover, from the two types of initialization, the meaning of the Read statement seems to be better constructed by students than the assignment statement. Two arguments may be put forward to explain this difference:

- the relationship between the statement and its effects on the screen may be more easily established in the case of Read, because the subject is involved him/her-self when the program is running: s(he) enters data by using the key board. The representation of the same statement-effect relationship in the case of assignment is more complex.
- the students have probably an implicit rule according to which "each program has to contain a Read statement to process the particular values".

Concerning the manner in which the students treat the different types of variables, the data shows that they operate better with COUNTER variable than with the other ones. We assume that there is a canonical schema constructed by students about the COUNTER variable: "it has to be initialized to 0 and incremented by 1". When a variable which plays the role of counter does not conform to this model as in the problem 3 (cf. Fig. 3), the performances decrease as for instance in the test task. Operating on the accumulation variables which are the internal variables is difficult in all of the tasks.

If we compare now the performances of different groups of students, we note that the most difficult tasks are those for which the weak group has obtained the poorest performances. This last phenomenon is observed in particular in the initialization and the test tasks. The difference between the students' groups is observed in particular in the processing with different types of variables. The weak group has more difficulties than the other groups in the representation of the functional role of the internal variables and the processes associated with them.

CONCLUDING REMARKS

The experimental study was designed to provide an exploratory examination of the early conception of novice programmers about the concept of programming variables which we outlined in Section 3. In the study, the responses of the novice students were consistent with predictions based on our analysis about the conceptual complexity of different types of variables and operations we have distinguished. The main results may be summarized as follows:

- The students are more able to process variables for which they have already a representation and processing system constructed in domains other than programming. For instance, they have a canonical schema constructed about the counter variable. This schema is also institutionalized by teaching. By "institutionalization" we characterize a teaching procedure which defines a concept or a procedure by underlying it as knowledge to be retained.
- Initialization of variables is a complex cognitive operation and the meaning of the Read statement is more easily constructed than the meaning of the assignment statement. This complexity has different components. The first one is the difficulty of making a hypothesis about the initial state of a system and it concerns more general cognitive activities than programming. The second is more specific to the programming and concerns difficulties with making the procedures which are not relevant for the hand-solution of the problem explicit. In general, initialization is an operation which is done automatically when solving problems, its awareness by the subject is not needed for the hand-solution.
- The difficulties concerning the updating and the test operations in the loop problems seem to be on the same level of complexity. More research is needed in this field before we can fully understand their respective roles in the loop construction. However many cues indicate that the difficulties of students in updating are also intimately related to the complexity of the problem domain.

We are well aware that the data we obtained do not cover the whole field of the conceptualization of the variables in learning programming. Nevertheless, we have studied an important aspect of the concept acquisition in programming. The data is consistent with the hypothesis we have tried to specify, and we think that our findings are significant in the early period of acquisition.

Our general hypothesis is also supported by the data: the novices transfer their representation and processing systems constructed in the problem domain into the programming domain. As we have seen below, many of the students' errors may be characterized by the transfer of their knowledges from the problem domain which are the algebraic conceptions of variable and equality. Moreover the novices' representation of the program is based on the mental execution of the procedure which corresponds to a dynamic model of computer functioning. In contrast, to obtain a good level in programming, the students have to develop a more static model in which the variables are represented in terms of their invariant inter-relations and not in terms of their successive values obtained in the execution process. We think that this is one of the important question of teaching and learning programming.

ACKNOWLEDGMENTS

This work was done in collaboration with A. Rouchier, J. Rogalski, G. Vergnaud, C. Landré, J.C. Despland, J.M. Laubin, J.F. Pigeonnat, Y. Ferrand, G. Sarfati. This chapter has been reprinted by permission of Kluwer Academic Publishers.

I am grateful for the comments which Rosamund Sutherland made on the English version of this paper.

REFERENCES

Bonar, J., Soloway, E. (1985). Preprogramming knowledge: A major source of misconceptions in novice programmers. *Human-Computer Interaction, 1,* 133–161.

Détienne, F. (1985). *Program expertise and program understanding.* 9th Congress of the International Ergonomics Association.

Ehrlich, K., & Soloway, E. (1982). *An empirical investigation of the tacit plan knowledge in programming.* New Haven: Yale University.

Hoc, J.M. (1981). Planning and direction of problem-solving in structured programming: an empirical comparison between two methods. *International Journal of Man-Machine Studies, 15,* 363–383.

Hoc, J.M. (1983). Analysis of beginner's problem-solving strategies in programming. In T.R.G. Green, S.J. Payne, & G. van der Veer (Eds.), *The psychology of computer use,* (143–158). NY: Springer Verlag.

Letovsky, S. (1986). Cognitive process in program comprehension. In E. Soloway (Ed.), *Empirical studies of programmers.* Norwood, N.J.: Ablex.

Samurçay, R. (1985). Learning programming: An analysis of looping strategies used by beginning students. *For the Learning of Mathematics, 5*(1), 37–43.

Soloway, E. Ehrlich, K., Bonar, J., & Greenspan, J. (1982). What do novices know about programming? In A. Badre & B. Shneiderman (Eds.), *Directions in Human-Computer Interactions.*

Vergnaud, G. (1982). A classification of cognitive tasks and operations of thought involved in addition and subtraction problems. In T.P. Carpenter, J.M. Moser, & T.A. Romberg (Eds.), *Addition and subtraction: A cognitive perspective.* Hillsdale, NJ: Lawrence Erlbaum Associates.

9

DO WE REALLY HAVE CONDITIONAL STATEMENTS IN OUR BRAINS?[1]

JEAN-MICHEL HOC

Laboratoire de Psychologie du Travail de l'EPHE (ERA CNRS), Paris France

INTRODUCTION

Programs which beginners are asked to write, more often than not, correspond to tasks that can be executed by hand. The programming strategy usually employed is one in which a well-known procedure is adapted to adhere to the rules of operation of the formal machine underlying the programming language being used (Hoc, 1983a).

However, it is not enough to simply adapt a procedure, it must be explicited as well. This requires an awareness of the control structure, in other words, data identification operations and transfers of control. This paper will examine the nature of the control structures on which this awareness is based, and not the complex mechanisms involved in becoming aware (Piaget, 1974a, b).

In procedural programming language control is expressed by means of tests. It has been shown however (Miller, 1981), that beginners find it difficult to construct those test statements in conditional structures or at the ends of iterations. Several research papers have been devoted to this question and in particular to the facilitating effects of different languages (Sime et al., 1977; Green, 1980; Van der Veer and Van de Wolde, 1983). But it is possible to go even further and to examine the effect of such tests in control structures of procedures which seem to be algorithmic and which are executed by hand. If not, this would explain one of the reasons for the difficulties experienced by beginners. This hypothesis can be considered in the light of two current areas of research in psychology:

---

[1]This research was supported by the "Agence de l'Informatique."

1. Research on attention (Richard, 1980) which has highlighted the importance of states of preparation (expectation phenomena) linked, in particular, to frequency and recency effects;

2. Research on typicality (Cordier & Dubois, 1981) which exploits the delay in decision-making in class-sorting problems in order to show that, in the subject's representations, there are typical (short delay) and atypical (long delay) examples which are not necessarily linked to frequency effects.

If such effects exist, it can be expected that certain identifications will be omitted during the execution of the procedure, either:

1. because the subject adapts to the frequency of events or he is sensitive to the recency effect or,

2. because the data being processed are represented semantically in the long-term memory, implying typicality effects.

This experiment mainly examines the second phenomenon by comparing the control structures during the execution of procedures in two different situations. In the first, the subjects rely on a strongly semantic representation of the data and in the second, on a much more abstract representation. In both situations, the data to be processed have the same "objective" structure. In the "semantic" situation we anticipate that the subjects will not be able to deal with certain identifications which could have been made in the "abstract" situation in which exhaustive search is possible.

The subjects are placed in a command situation in front of an interactive computer device. The data transformations are controlled by function keys so that the control structures can be identified by response latencies. The different representations are achieved by modifying certain characteristics of the device which affect neither the data structure nor the commands available but only the way in which the data can be accessed.

METHOD

Subjects and Task Type

Twenty adults with no particular computer skill took part in the experiment. They were first presented with a task comparable to the task (of using a keyboard and screen device) they would have to do in the real test situation. It concerned the updating of a stock (fig. 1).

The subjects had at their disposal: the stock position the evening before (Old Stock file: AS) and the following day's transactions (Transaction file: MVT). The items were listed according to their classification numbers —

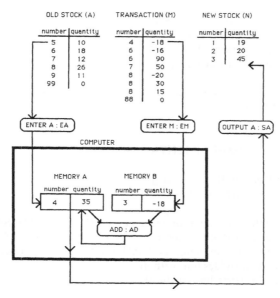

FIG. 9.1   Task of reference

lowest first. The subjects had to construct a new file (New Stock, NS) similar to the file Old Stock (AS) but including the quantities actually in stock after the day's transactions. The subjects were then shown how to use the transformations common to the two experimental devices. They had to learn how to use the keyboard display, the system presenting data files and the processor, together known as a "computer".

The computer contains two memories, each containing one item from one of the corresponding files (memory A for the file AS and memory M for the file MVT). The subject gives the computer commands using one of 4 keys, each key corresponding to a possible transformation:

EA: to enter the first item of the file As in memory (this item is thus cleared from the file);

EM: Same operation between file MVT and memory M;

AD: to add the contents of memory M to that in memory A (clearance of memory M) and the total appears in A;

SA: to write the contents of memory A in the file NS (clearance of memory A);

The result of each transformation appears on the screen. The subject is shown how to proceed before taking part in the actual experiment:

item without transaction: EA − SA
item with one transaction: EA − EM − AD − SA
item with "n" transactions: EA −[EM − AD]^n − SA
where [...]^n indicates n times [...]

Finally, each subject is assigned at random to one of the two experimental devices described below.

EXPERIMENTAL DEVICES

Device Compatible with a Strong Semantic Representation of the Data

The subject, using the commands described above (EA, EM, AD, SA), only has access to the immediate states of memories A and M. After each operation EA (entry of an item) and AD (addition of a transaction), however, memory M provides him with information about the nature of the following transaction (first line of the file MVT):

1. if the word MVT appears (ex: "6 18 MVT") it means that the item which is currently being processed (ex: Item 6 in memory A) will be involved in the next transaction. The subject must therefore type the command sequence EM − AD until further information is supplied.
2. if, however, the word MVT does not appear, the processing of this item has been completed and the system is waiting for the next item to be processed. The subject inserts the commands sequence SA − EA and again further information is supplied (ex: "9 11   " which means here that there is no transaction for item 9).

The correct procedure can therefore be illustrated by the following rules:

IF		THEN EXECUTE
R1: presence of indication MVT	⟶	EM − AD
R2: absence of indication MVT	⟶	SA − EA

This device is compatible with a semantic representation of data in terms of transactions nested in items. The following goal stack is the result:

Goal Stack:	Procedure:
File AS updating	$[EA-[EM-AD]^n-SA]^p$
item updating	$EA-[EM-AD]^{n-}SA$
transaction processing	$EM-AD$

Device Incompatible with a Strong Semantic Representation of the Data

This device is identical to the previous one except there is not indication MVT. The experiment is therefore exactly the same as before, but the item number in memory M is masked if it is different to that in memory A. The subject having just processed the transaction of one item and having entered a transaction concerning another item, without this masking, may have calculated the number of intermediary items without transactions. This would have been impossible with the compatible device. The subject could process the masking (after EA or EM) in the following way:

1. if the transaction number in memory M is legal (ex: "6 18 6 − 16") it means it is the same as the item number being currently processed (in memory A): the subject can therefore use the command sequence AD − EM until further information is supplied by the following indication.

2. if however, the number in memory M is illegal ("6 92 XXX 50") it means a different item is being processed and that the command sequence SA − EA will lead to further information.

The correct procedure can be written by a system of rules analogous to the rules previously mentioned with just one inversion, namely of the sequence EM − AD to AD − EM:

IF		THEN EXECUTE
R1: unmasked	⟶	AD − EM
R2: masked	⟶	SA − EA

The inversion of the sequence EM − AD makes no difference to those items without transaction. They will still be processed by the sequence EA − SA. This inversion does however affect the items with transactions as these are now processed by a sequence EA − $[AD - EM]^n$ − SA. The device is now incompatible with the previous goal stack. The subject can only identify the final transaction of an item by entering a transaction which is foreign to this item. The processing sequence of this transaction is thus interrupted: [EM − [SA −...−EA] −AD]. The nesting of the earlier goal stack no longer corresponds to a complete nesting by this procedure. At various moments the subject has to change to a higher level goal (item) whilst already seeking a lower level goal (transaction) without having accomplished it.

The subject is forced to change his semantic representation into a more successful abstract representation in which the data are structured as a list of pairs (content of memory A, content of memory M). From now on he employs simple rules of passage from one pair to another without having to consider the nature of the objects being processed (items, transactions).

The objective being to study control structures used in executing procedures, the elaboration of these procedures is deliberately accelerated by telling the subject (using either the compatible or the incompatible device) the correct procedure in terms of a semantic representation of the data.

Design

The subjects (factor S) are divided into two groups of 10 — each group corresponding to a device type (factor D). During the execution of a procedure, eight possible types of transitions (factor T) between commands are defined (Figure 2). Each procedure being represented by a two rule system, a distinction is made between: inter-rule transitions (t1 to t4) which correspond to identifications and intra-rule transitions (t5 to t8) which are simple links between commands. The response latency is measured for each correct transition.

The data to be processed are divided into eight successive blocks. The frequency with which each of the four types of inter-rule transition appear is equally balanced. There are 80 transitions for each block which means

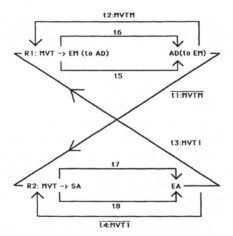

FIG. 9.2   Transition types for the two devices. Meaning of the transitions:

t1:   transition at the end of processing an item with transaction: there is no other transaction: $\overline{\text{MVTM}}$: SA __t7__ EA.

t2:   transition to the following transaction: there is another transaction (MVTM) : EM (or AD) __t6__ AD (or EM).

t3:   transition to processing an item with transaction: there is a first transaction (MVTI): EM (or AD) __t5__ AD (or EM).

t4:   transition to processing an item without transaction: there is no transaction $\overline{\text{MVTI}}$: SA __t8__ EA that each subject executes 640 (8 × 80) transitions. The factor "Block" has been introduced to examine the effects of a potential modification of the control structure on time. The data have been analysed by analysis of variance followed by "fiducial inference" using the design formula:

$$S_{10} < D_2 > \star T_8 \star B_8$$

(subjects nested in devices and crossed with transitions which are themselves crossed with blocks). (For fiducial inference and notation of design formula, see Rouanet et al., 1976; Hoc, 1983b, c).

RESULTS

In order to define the control structure employed in each block and to evaluate the inter-individual variability within each group of subjects the individual protocols were analysed. As the variability proved to be very small, analysis per group for each device was completed, the results of which are presented here.

Figure 3 shows the evolution of the response latencies corresponding to each transition type for all the blocks. We would like to point out, that independent of the blocks, all eight transition types show the same response latencies pattern. Response latencies for the intra-rule transitions (links) are the shortest and have the smallest variance. For the response latencies of the inter-rule transitions (identifications: see also figure 2):

1. with a guarantee of .98 it is inferred that the response latencies for t3 are shorter by at least 160 msec. (22% of the latency observed for t3) to those for t4, over all the blocks.[2] Therefore, after EA the subject is prepared to process an item with transaction.

2. with the same guarantee of .98 it is inferred that the response latencies for t2 are at least 140 msec. (21% of t2) shorter than those of t1, over all the blocks. Therefore after AD the subject is prepared to process another transaction.

In addition, we note that if the latencies corresponding to preparation phases (t2 and t3) are similar to those for the intra-rule links (t5 to t8), then

---

[2]The meaning of this formulation is the following: Without any other information than the one provided by the two samples, an uncertainty distribution on the set of possible values for the difference between the two population means can be defined. From this distribution, the following statement (fiducial conclusion) can be derived: "the probability that the population mean latency for t3 is shorter by at least 160 msec. to the population mean latency for t4 is .98": $p \star (\mu \star_4 -_\mu \star_3 < 160$ msec.$) = .98$. To evaluate its importance the difference (160 msec) is related here to the latency observed for t3: 22%.

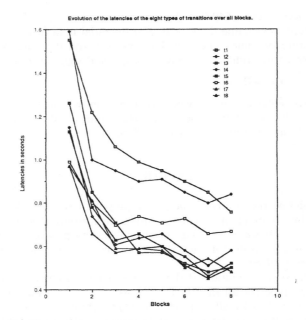

FIG. 9.3   Response latencies for the compatible device (d1):
abscissa: successive blocks.
ordinate: mean latency in seconds.
Evolution of the latencies of the eight types of transition over all the blocks.

the data are compatible with the hypothesis that those conditions, which correspond to the states of preparation, are not explicitly identified by the subject.

The frequency of errors is revealing in this respect: a prepared transition (t2 or t3) is more often triggered off in error (11.3% and 27.5% respectively) than an unprepared transition (t1 : 2,5%; t4 : 0%).

Incompatible Device (Abstract Representation)

Figure 4 is analogous to figure 3 for the incompatible device. The preparations observed for the compatible device have now almost entirely disappeared:

1. response latencies for t3 and t4 are very similar to each other over all the blocks. Absolute value of the difference is smaller than 80 msec. (8% of t3 and t4) with a guarantee of .95.

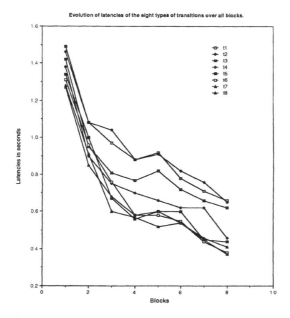

FIG. 9.4   Response latencies for the incompatible device (d2) (see sub-title of figure 3)

2. the same can be said for t1 and t2 for the blocks b1 to b4, and b7: ther absolute value of the difference is smaller than 130 msec. (14% of t1 and t2) with a guarantee of .90. Nothing can be concluded for the other blocks which implies that abstract representation is not always stable. Error frequencies are small and similar to each other when there is no preparation.

The data are compatible with the hypothesis that the subject now explicitly identifies all the conditions.

DISCUSSION

The existence of different preparation states leads to a distinction between two types of identification to be found in the control structure of the procedure executed by each subject:

1. Specific Identifications:
   They are based on well defined conditions of validity and occur at precise moments in the execution.

2. Identifications of Invalidity:
They are more diffuse and capable of halting the execution at any time to return the control to the specific identifications.

The procedures employed by the subjects can be modelised as systems of rules in which the component "condition" only brings out the specific identifications (Hoc, 1982). The model for the observed procedure with the compatible device would therefore be of the following type (transition numbers are the same as in figure 2):

$$
\begin{array}{llllll}
t4 & t8 & t3 & t5 & t2 & t6 \\
\text{no initial transaction} \rightarrow SA - EA & -EM & -AD & -[EM & - & AD]^n \\
\text{no following transaction} \rightarrow SA - EA & -EM & -AD & -[EM & - & AD]^n \\
t1 & t7 & t3 & t5 & t2 & t6
\end{array}
$$

We note that t2 and t3, which correspond to the two preparation states, are processed as simple links which are only interrupted when invalidity (considered a "demon") is identified. As these identifications of invalidity are diffuse, it may happen that they don't operate correctly and so don't prevent the release of inappropriate actions. This results in mistakes such as these examined above.

The procedure does not include conditionals, such as those known in informatics: all the identifications do not by way of specific identifications (left side of the rules) such as was the case for the incompatible device.

What now remains to be considered is the difference in the control structure between a situation in which the semantic representation of the data can be retained and one in which the subject has to adopt a more abstract representation.

In the first case (semantic representation), there is double preparation: for an item with transaction and for the presence of another transaction. Two reasons can be put forward to explain this preparation for an item with a possibility of transaction:

1. a phenomenon of typicality — this property is more typical in an updating task
2. a more satisfactory nesting of the transactions in the items. (items without transaction are not considered).

On the other hand the preparation for another transaction concerns the absence of specific identifications of the condition for continuing the iteration (that of processing the transactions).

It should be noted that the semantic features of the data to be processed (items, transactions) create effects which are extremely resistant to any temporal adaptation. This could have led for example to the removal of the preparation states for the later blocks.

In the second case (abstract representation), it is precisely this temporal adaptation which works with the incompatible device. As a result of adopting an abstract representation of the data in the form of a list of pairs, with rules for passing from one pair to another, the phenomena observed in the previous situation disappear:

1. the lack of typicality and of a nesting form of representation take away the necessity for the preparation of a particular item.

2. this same lack of nesting removes the iteration on the transaction and, by that, the absence of any explicit identification of a stopping condition.

CONCLUSION

Although this experiment has only a limited significance, we feel that it highlights the need for a deeper study of the control structures used in carrying out procedures so that the mechanisms of becoming aware can be better understood. The construction of a computer program is never done from a *tabula rasa* — the subject always knows some parts of the procedure and, using the mechanisms of becoming aware, he will try to express them in the programming language.

This experiment certainly shows that the equivalent of computer tests can be found in the control structure of a procedure carried out by a subject, but at the price of an abstraction which it is not always possible to achieve. Programming problems convey semantic representations which are not easily made abstract. These phenomena can be used to understand beginners' difficulties. The effects of typicality are, for example, the source of certain programming errors even for experienced subjects, e.g., authors of programming manuals, as it has been shown by Lesuisse (1983).

It has also been noted that even when a procedure seems algorithmic, the subject will work according to a heuristic which ensures a certain economy of identification by treating the procedure sequentially. This can be seen in some of the results obtained by Miller (1981) in his studies on programming in natural language.

The question to be asked is whether it is fruitful to construct programming languages which use "natural" control structures. On one hand these "natural" structures are not always reliable but on the other it is probably impossible to be aware of certain components of these structures. If the presence of diffuse identifications of invalidity is a viable hypothesis, they are doubtless outside our realm of awareness.

In order to answer these questions and to improve our definition of the basic constructions of our own control structures, further research is necessary. The tools introduced by artificial intelligence could be very useful in this type of analysis.

ACKNOWLEDGMENTS

This chapter has been reprinted by permission of Springer-Verlag Publishing Co.

REFERENCES

Cordier, F. & Dubois, D. (1981). Typicalité et représentation cognitive. *Cahiers de Psychologie Cognitive, 1,* 299–333.

Green, T.R.G. (1980). Ifs and thens: is nesting just for the birds? *Software Practice and Experience,* n. 10.

Green, T.R.G., Payne, S.J., & Van der Veer, G.C. (1983). *The psychology of computer use.* Academic Press, London.

Hoc, J.M. (1982). Représentation des données et structure de contrôle d'un processus de traitement. *Cahiers de Psychologie Cognitive, 2,* 389–419.

Hoc, J.M. (1983a). Analysis of beginner's problem-solving strategies in programming. In Green et al., *The psychology of computer use.* London: Academic Press.

Hoc, J.M. (1983b). Evaluation of different modalities of verbalisation in a sorting task. *International Journal of Man-Machine Studies, 18,* 293–306.

Hoc, J.M. (1983c). *L'analyse planifiée des données en psychologie.* PUF, Paris.

Lesuisse, R. (1983). Analyse des raisonnements faits et des erreurs commises dans des programmes publiés de recherche dichotomique. *Le Travail Humain, 46,* 239–254.

Miller, L.A. (1981). Natural language programming: styles, strategies, and contrasts. *Perspectives in Computing, 1,* 22–33.

Piaget, J. (1974a). *La prise de conscience.* PUF, Paris.

Piaget, J. (1974b). *Réussir et comprendre.* PUF, Paris.

Richard, J.F. (1980). *L'attention.* PUF, Paris.

Rouanet, H., Lépine, D., & Pelnard-Considère, J. (1976). Bayes-fiducial procedures as practical substitutes for misplaced significance testing: an application to educational data. *Advances in psychological and educational measurements.* D.N.M. de Gruiter, L.J.T. van der Kamp, H.F. Crombag (eds.). Wiley, New York.

Sime, M.E., Arblaster, A.T., & Green, T.R.G. (1977). Reducing programming errors in nested conditionals by prescribing a writing procedure. *International Journal of Man-Machine Studies, 9,* 119–126.

Van der Veer, G.C., & Van de Wolde, G.J.E. (1983). Individual differences and aspects of control flow notations. In Green et al., *The psychology of computer use.* London: Academic Press.

10
COGNITIVE STRATEGIES AND LOOPING
CONSTRUCTS: AN EMPIRICAL STUDY

ELLIOT SOLOWAY, JEFFREY BONAR, KATE EHRLICH
University of Michigan
University of Massachusetts
Yale University

In this paper, we describe a study that tests the following hypothesis: A programming language construct that has a closer "cognitive fit" with an individual's preferred cognitive strategy will be easier to use effectively. After analyzing Pascal programs that employed loops, we identified two distinct looping strategies: 1) on the ith pass through the loop, the ith element is both read and processed (the READ/PROCESS strategy); and 2) on the ith pass, the ith element is processed and the next ith element is read (the PROCESS/READ strategy). We argue that the latter strategy is associated with the appropriate use of the Pascal **while** construct. In contrast, we feel that a construct that allows an exit from the middle of the loop (e.g., loop . . . leave . . . again) facilitates the former (READ/PROCESS) strategy. Our results indicate that subjects overwhelmingly preferred a READ/PROCESS strategy over a PROCESS/READ strategy. When writing a simple looping program, those using the loop . . . leave . . . again construct were more often correct than were those using the standard Pascal loop constructs.

INTRODUCTION

The need for the public to be literate in computing is rapidly being recognized. One aspect of such literacy is programming. While we do not believe that everyone needs to become a professional programmer, it is increasingly important to be able to describe to the computer how it is supposed to realize one's intentions. The characteristics of the language in which novice or casual programmers describe their plans are of critical importance. We might well expect professional programmers to adapt to the constraints and implicit strategies facilitated by a particular language. However, if the language does not "cognitively fit" with the non-professionals' problem-solving skills, then a barrier has been erected to their use of computers.

Concern for finding a better match between a language and an individual's natural skills and abilities is reflected in some recent empirical research. For example, Ledgard et al. [6] compared an editing language whose syntax was based on English with a standard notational editing language, and found that the English-based language was preferred by the subjects and led to better performance. Miller [4] examined the natural problem-solving strategies of nonprogrammers in order to explore the potential for "natural language" programming. One conclusion he draws that is particularly relevant to this paper is that programming language constructs could be developed that were closer to how people "naturally" specified problem solutions. Claims have also been made (e.g., [7]) that the procedurality in programming taps into novices' preexisting cognitive notions. In support of this claim, Soloway et al. [9] have shown that students write correct equations more often when solving simple word problems using a procedural programming language as opposed to using algebra, a non-procedural language. Similarly, Welty and Stemple [12] compared the performance of novices using a procedural query language with those using a non-procedural query language; they found that subjects performed at a higher level of accuracy with the procedural language when writing moderate to difficult queries.

We report here on an experiment that explores the relationship between the preferred cognitive strategies of individuals and programming language constructs. By *preferred strategy,* we mean the strategy that individuals *spontaneously* use when solving a problem. We will focus on looping strategies and examine the impact they have on the use of looping constructs.

TWO STRATEGIES: READ/PROCESS VERSUS PROCESS/READ

Consider the following problem:

The Averaging Problem
Write a program that repeatedly reads in integers, until it reads the integer 99999. After seeing 99999, it should print out the **correct** average. That is, it should not count the final 99999.

This problem is certainly neither tricky nor esoteric; one would expect this problem to be easy for students at the end of a semester course on Pascal.

```
program Example1;
    var Count, Sum, Number : integer;
        Average : real;
    begin
        Count := 0;
        Sum := 0;
        Read (Number);
        while Number <> 99999 do
            begin
                Sum := Sum + Number;
                Count := Count + 1;
                Read (Number)
            end;
        if Count > 0
            then
                begin
                    Average := Sum / Count;
                    Writeln (Average);
                end
            else
                Writeln ('No numbers input:
                          average undefined');
    end.
```

FIGURE 1   A Stylistically Correct Pascal Solution to the Averaging Problem.

In fact, we found that students do surprisingly poorly on this and related problems.[1] In this problem, the loop is dependent on the variable that holds the new values as they are successively read in.[2] In this situation, the loop may not be executed even once, and thus the Pascal loop construct most appropriate is the **while** construct [13]. In Figure 1, we depict the stylistically correct Pascal solution to this problem.

Stepping back from the code, the strategy that this program embodies can be characterized as:

```
Read (first value)
while Test (ith value)
    do begin
        Process (ith value)
        Read (i + 1st value)
    end
```

---

[1]In an earlier study [10], we asked students to write a program that solves the averaging problem stated above. In grading their problems, we overlooked syntax errors; only 38% were able to produce a correct program. This test was given to students on the last day of classes after a semester course on Pascal programming.

[2]Loops can also be dependent on variables playing other roles, e.g., the counter, the running total. If the counter variable controls the loop, then Pascal's **for** loop is most appropriate; if the running total variable (Sum, in Figure 1) controls the loop, then the loop can reasonably be expected to be executed at least once, hence the **repeat** loop is most appropriate (see [10]).

Since the loop may not be executed if the first value read is 99999, a *Read* outside the loop is necessary in order to get the loop started. However, this results in the loop processing being one step behind the *Read;* on the *i*th pass through the loop, the *i*th value is processed and *then* the *i*th + 1 value is read in. We call this strategy "process *i*/read next *i*" (henceforth referred to as PROCESS/READ).

We felt this strategy to be unnecessarily awkward and confusing [3, 11]. In effect, processing in the loop would be "out of sync" with reading in the loop. From a cognitive perspective, we speculate that such a strategy puts an extra burden on memory and processing resources. We suggest that a more natural cognitive strategy would be to read the *i*th value and process it on the *i*th pass through the loop; we call this the "read *i*/process *i*" strategy (henceforth referred to as READ/PROCESS). For example:

```
loop
   do begin
      Read (ith value)
      Test (ith value)
      Process (ith value)
   end
```

This strategy would have the reading and processing "in sync", and should require less cognitive resources than the PROCESS/READ strategy.

Although the PROCESS/READ strategy is facilitated by Pascal's **while** loop, a READ/PROCESS can be encoded using either the **while** or the **repeat** loop. For example, Figure 2 depicts three Pascal programs that use **while** and **repeat** loops and implement the READ/PROCESS strategy.[3] These are actual student programs generated in an earlier experiment [10]. The programs in Figures 2a and 2b use an embedded **if** statement to effect the READ/PROCESS strategy. In the former case, a Boolean variable is used to control the outside **while** loop; in the latter case the same test is performed twice. In Figure 2c, we see a program in which a **repeat** loop is used to implement the READ/PROCESS strategy; the stop value is simply subtracted from the total. While correct, all three programs need to employ a considerable amount of additional code in order to compensate for not employing the appropriate PROCESS/READ strategy.

Consider, then, the following looping construct, that is similar to one in Ada, the new DOD language:

```
loop;
   S;
   if B then leave;
   T;
again
```

---

[3]The **goto** was not taught to students in this class; thus, it does not appear in the students' programs.

```
program Example2a;
    var N, Sum, X : integer;
        Average : real;
        Stop : boolean;
    begin
        Stop := false;
        N := 0;
        Sum := 0;
        while not Stop do
            begin
                Read (X);
                if X = 99999
                    then Stop := true
                    else
                        begin
                            Sum := Sum + X;
                            N := N + 1
                        end
            end;
        Average := Sum / N;
        Writeln (Average)
    end.
                    2(a)
```

```
program Example 2b;
    var Num, Sum, N : integer;
        Avg : real;
    begin
        Num := 0;
        N := 0;
        Sum := 0;
        while Num <> 99999 do
            begin
                Read (Num);
                if Num <> 99999 then
                    begin
                        Sum := Sum + Num;
                        N := N + 1
                    end
            end;
        Avg := Sum / N;
        Writeln (Avg)
    end.
                    2(b)
```

```
program Example 2c;
    var Count, Sum, Num : integer; Average : real;
    begin
        Count := -1;
        Sum := 0;
        repeat
            Count := Count + 1;
            Read (Num);
            Sum := Sum + Num
        until Num = 99999;
        Sum := Sum - 99999;
        Average := Sum / Count;
        Writeln(Average);
    end.
                    2(c)
```

FIGURE 2   Effecting a READ/PROCESS Strategy. (a) Using a Boolean Variable and a Nested Condition to Effect a READ/PROCESS Strategy. (b) Using a Nested Conditional and a Repeated Test to Effect a READ/PROCESS Strategy. (c) Using a Repeat Loop and Backing Down to Effect a READ/PROCESS Strategy.

where S and T are zero or more statements and B is the test condition. This construct clearly facilitates a READ/PROCESS strategy, since the test can come in the middle of the loop, between the read and the process. In Figure 3, we depict the averaging problem, described above, encoded using "Pascal L," a version of standard Pascal in which the only looping construct is **loop . . . leave . . . again**. Note that unlike the programs in Figure 2, no extraneous machinery is required to encode the READ/PROCESS strategy. Note, too, however, that the **loop . . . leave . . . again** construct can also be used to encode a PROCESS/READ strategy: If S is empty, then the test is at the top of the loop, thereby creating a standard Pascal **while** loop.

HYPOTHESES

As stated above, we are interested in the strategies that people prefer to use to solve problems and the degree to which those strategies are compatible

```
program Pascal L;
    var Count, Sum, NewValue: integer;
            Average: real;
    begin
        Count := 0;
        Sum := 0;
        loop
            Read (NewValue);
            if NewValue = 99999 then leave;
            Sum := Sum + NewValue;
            Count := Count + 1;
        again
        if Count > 0
            then
                begin
                    Average := Sum / Count;
                    Writeln (Average);
                end
            else
                Writeln ('No numbers input:
                          average undefined');
    end.
```

FIGURE 3   The Averaging Problem Using Pascal L.

with the constructs of programming languages. In particular, we hypothesize: *People will find it easier to program correctly when the language facilitates their preferred strategy.*

Pascal, with the normal **while** and **repeat** constructs, can be used to implement either the READ/PROCESS strategy or the PROCESS/READ strategy. Moreover, Pascal L (Pascal with only the **loop . . . leave . . . again** construct) can also be used to encode either strategy. However, for problems in which the loop test is dependent on the values read in, Pascal's **while** construct facilitates a PROCESS/READ strategy whereas Pascal L facilitates a READ/PROCESS strategy. Our claim, then, is that for the type of problem discussed above, people should find Pascal L easier to program correctly than Pascal.

Our hypothesis leads us to ask three particular questions: 1. *Which strategy do people naturally use?* To answer this question we need to examine which strategy people adopt when they think about the problem and commit their thoughts to paper using a natural language—English— that is neutral with respect to READ/PROCESS OR PROCESS/READ.

Once having determined whether people will adopt a READ/PROCESS OR A PROCESS/READ type of strategy, we can go on to ask: 2(a). *Will people write correct programs more often when using the language that facilitates their preferred strategy?* Thus, if people use a READ/PROCESS strategy in their initial thinking, we would predict that they should write correct programs more often when using Pascal *L,* since this language facilitates a READ/PROCESS strategy, as compared with Pascal.

An ancillary question to 2(a) is: 2(b). *Irrespective of whether a strategy is preferred or not, will people write correct programs more often when using the strategy facilitated by the language?* That is, will people who use a READ/PROCESS strategy in Pascal *L* write correct programs more often than those using a PROCESS/READ strategy in Pascal *L*? Similarly, will people who use a PROCESS/READ strategy in Pascal write correct programs more often than those using a READ/PROCESS strategy in Pascal?

A third question of interest concerns the influence of programming experience on performance. We expect accuracy to improve when people have more experience in using a particular language. It is less clear, however, whether this experience will change the way people think about a problem. We need to ask: 3. *Do the following vary with experience: accuracy of solution, preference for a particular strategy, sensitivity to the strategy facilitated by a language.*

EXPERIMENTAL DESIGN

In order to gather empirical data on these questions, we designed the study described below. Students were given a two-part test, the first part of which is reproduced in Figure 4, where we asked them to write a plan that would solve the stated problem. The second part of the test is depicted in Figures 5 and 6. Half the students were asked to write a Pascal program that solved the problem, while the other half were asked to solve the problem using

---

Please write a PLAN which solves the problem described below, and which you would use to guide eventual program development. The plan should NOT be in a programming language; other than that restriction, the choice of "plan language" is up to you.

PLEASE SHOW ALL YOUR WORK!!!!! DO NOT ERASE!!!!!!

PROBLEM:
Write a plan for a program which reads in a series of integers, and which computes the average of these numbers. The program should stop reading integers when it has read the number 99999. NOTE: the final 99999 should NOT be reflected in the average you calculate.

FIGURE 4   All Subjects Were Asked to Produce a Plan.

Standard Pascal provides three looping statements: WHILE, REPEAT, and FOR. Below is a brief review of these statements. Please read the review carefully

```
WHILE expression
    DO statements
```

A WHILE loop repeatedly does the *statements* while the *expression* is true. In other words, *expression* is tested initially and after each execution of the *statements*.

```
REPEAT
    statements
UNTIL expression
```

A REPEAT loop repeatedly does the *statements* until the *expression* is true. That is, *statements* are executed initially and then expression is tested for each repetition of the loop.

```
FOR identifier :=
    expression-alpha TO expression-
beta
    DO statements
```

A FOR loop does the statements for each value of the identifier from *expression-alpha* to *expression-beta*. First, *identifier* is set to the value of *expression-alpha* and the *statements* are executed. Then, *identifier* is set to the value of *expression-alpha* + 1 and the *statements* are again executed. This continues until *identifier* is finally set to the value of *expression-beta* and the *statements* are executed for the last time.

PROBLEM

Write a Pascal program which reads in a series of integers, and which computes the average of these numbers. The program should stop reading integers when it has read the number 99999. NOTE: the final 99999 should NOT be reflected in the average you calculate.

REMEMBER, you should use standard Pascal.
(Please use the program outline provided. DO NOT ERASE ANY WORK. If you want to start fresh, use a new program outline. *Turn in all work*.)

```
PROGRAM PROBLEM (INPUT OUTPUT);
VAR
(* BEGIN YOUR STATEMENTS HERE ... *)
```

FIGURE 5   The Pascal Version of the Study.

Pascal *L*. Each group was given a one-page discussion of the respective loop constructs, i.e., the Pascal *L* group was given a one-page description of the **loop . . . leave . . . again** construct (Figure 6), while the Pascal group was given a one-page description of the **for, repeat,** and **while** constructs (Figure 5). The one page on the **loop . . . leave . . . again** construct of Pascal *L* contained three examples; we were careful to include an instance of using

We have just designed a new language called Pascal L. It is just like standard Pascal except that it does NOT have the WHILE, REPEAT, and FOR looping statements. Rather, Pascal L has a new kind of statement: LOOP..LEAVE..AGAIN.

The following describes how this new looping statement works:

```
LOOP
    statements-alpha
    IF expression LEAVE
    statements-beta
AGAIN
```

means:
• execute *statements-alpha*, which could be zero or more legal Pascal statements,
• then, test *expression*,
    ▶ if *expression* is TRUE, skip to the statement AFTER the AGAIN
    ▶ if *expression* is FALSE, continue through the loop and execute *statements-beta*, which could be zero or more legal Pascal statements, and do the loop all over again.

In other words, as long as the *expression* stays FALSE, all the statements before LOOP and AGAIN will continue to be executed.

For example, the following Pascal-L programs print out the numbers 1 through 10 and only use the LOOP . . . LEAVE . . . AGAIN loop construction:

```
PROGRAM example1(output);      PROGRAM example2(output);      PROGRAM example3(output);
    VAR i : INTEGER;               VAR i : INTEGER;               VAR i := INTEGER;
    BEGIN                          BEGIN                          BEGIN
    i := 1;                        i := 1;                        i := 1;
    LOOP                           LOOP                           LOOP
        Writeln(i);                    IF i > 10 LEAVE;               Writeln(i);
        IF i >= 10 LEAVE;              Writeln(i);                    i := i + 1;
        i := i + 1                     i := i + 1                     IF i > 10 LEAVE
    AGAIN                          AGAIN                          AGAIN
END.                           END.                           END.
```

We would like you to use the LOOP..LEAVE..AGAIN statement in the program you write for the problem described on the next page. Thank you for your cooperation.

PROBLEM

Write a Pascal-L program which reads in a series of integers, and which computes the average of these numbers. The program should stop reading integers when it has read the number 99999. NOTE: the final 99999 should NOT be reflected in the average you calculate.
REMEMBER, you may only use the
LOOP . . . LEAVE . . . AGAIN looping statement.

(Please use the program outline provided. DO NOT ERASE ANY WORK. If you want to start fresh, use a new program outline. *Turn in all work*.)

```
PROGRAM PROBLEM (INPUT, OUTPUT)
    VAR
    (* BEGIN YOUR STATEMENTS HERE ... *)
```

FIGURE 6   The Pascal *L* Version of the Study.

the **if . . . leave** that branched off the top of the loop (that is equivalent to a **while**), an instance of using the **if . . . leave** that branched at the bottom of the loop (that is equivalent to a **repeat**), as well as an instance that branched in the middle. As much time as necessary was given to students taking this test although subjects typically finished in 10–15 minutes.

This test was administered to three different groups: novices, intermediates, and advanced students. Novices were students currently taking a first programming course in Pascal. The test was administered after the novices had been taught about and had experience with the **while** loop and the other two looping constructs; this occurred three-quarters of the way through the semester. Intermediates were students currently two-thirds through a second course in programming (e.g., either a data structures course using Pascal or an assembly language course). The advanced group were juniors and seniors in systems programming and programming methodology courses.

RESULTS

Question 1: Which Strategy Do People Naturally Use?

In Table I, we display the results from the first part of the test where we asked people to write down their plans for solving the averaging problem. (Half of the intermediate group were asked to write a *plan* and half were asked to write a *flowchart*. We found no reliable difference between the two groups in their choice of strategies. Thus, for reporting purposes, we have combined the results of these two groups.) These results clearly indicate that all three populations had a strong preference for the READ/PROCESS strategy when it was possible for us to discern any strategy at all. Across all three groups, of those students who had a discernible strategy, 80% used the READ/PROCESS strategy, while only 20% used the PROCESS/READ stratgy in their plans.[4]

Now consider Table II, where we show the strategy choice on the program, irrespective of language (see Table V). Except for the advanced group, we again see a strong preference for the READ/PROCESS strategy. That is, over all three groups, of the subjects who had a clearly discernible strategy, 73% of them used the READ/PROCESS strategy while only 27% used the PROCESS/READ strategy. These data support the claim that given the two alternatives, the preferred strategy is READ/PROCESS rather than PROCESS/READ.

It is also illuminating to look at the students who used the same strategy on both plan and program, and those who did not, i.e., those that changed strategies. Of the 158[5] students who had a discernible strategy for both plan and program, 78% (123) used the same strategy on both plan and program, while only 22% (35) switched strategies. Of the ones who did not switch, 82% (101) used a READ/PROCESS strategy on both plan and program. Again, this supports our claim that READ/PROCESS is the preferred strategy.

---

[4]The category of "Miscellaneous" was made up of those plans in which we could not discern a clear READ/PROCESS or PROCESS/READ strategy. Of the 77 novices and 22 intermediates with miscellaneous plans, 40 novices and 11 intermediates had plans that were too sketchy for categorization; 18 novices and 5 intermediates wrote nonprocedural plans— typically they simply restated the problem; 17 novices and 3 intermediates solved the wrong problem, and 2 novices and 3 intermediates wrote no plan. Clearly, the large number in this category is interesting in its own right; however, we feel that explanations for these data can reasonably be decoupled from the specific issues raised in this paper.

[5]There were fewer plans (177) than programs (202) in which we could clearly detect a strategy. However, of the former group, there were 19 students who did not have a discernible strategy on their programs; hence, there were only 158 students who had discernible strategies on both plan and program.

TABLE I: Strategy on Plans

	READ/ PROCESS[1]	PROCESS/ READ[1]	N	Misc.[2]
Novices	82%	18%	39	77
Intermediates	91%	9%	90	22
Advanced	67%	33%	48	4

A Chi-square test was used to analyze these data: $\chi^2 = 12.96, p < 0.01$
[1] The percentages are based on N, the number of people who had an identifiable strategy, (i.e., they do not include those in the Misc. category).
[2] This column depicts the number of individuals for which we could not identify a strategy in their plan.

TABLE II: Strategy on Programs

	READ/ PROCESS[1]	PROCESS/ READ[1]	N	Misc.[2]
Novices	86%	14%	64	52
Intermediates	72%	28%	89	23
Advanced	60%	40%	49	3

[1] The percentages are based on N, the number of people who had an identifiable strategy (i.e., they do not include those in the Misc. category).
[2] This column depicts the number of individuals for which we could not identify a strategy in their program.

TABLE III: People Who Did and Did Not Switch Strategies

	People Switching Strategies from Plan to Program	People NOT Switching Strategies from Plan to Program	Statistical Significance[1]
Pascal Group	23	50	$\chi^2 = 6.89$
Pascal L Group	12	73	$p < 0.01$
	35	123	

[1] A Chi-square test was used in this comparison.

Interestingly, some students appeared to be sensitive to the strategy faciliated by the programming language: in Table III we show a breakdown by language type for those subjects who did (and did not) switch strategies between the plan and the program. These data indicate that subjects in the Pascal group switched more often than did subjects in the Pascal L group. This is as expected: by comparison, there were many more READ/PROCESS plans than there were PROCESS/READ plans; thus, Pascal L subjects could stay with a READ/PROCESS strategy, while Pascal subjects who were sensitive to the fact that the appropriate strategy for the problem was PROCESS/READ needed to switch strategies.

Question 2a: Will People Write Correct Programs More Often When Using the Language That Facilitates Their Preferred Strategy?

While it seems clear that people prefer a READ/PROCESS strategy, the key question is whether or not this preference can lead to program correctness. From the data shown in Table IV, it can be seen that more people wrote a correct program using Pascal *L*, the language that facilitates a READ/PROCESS strategy, than did those using Pascal. The incorrect programs exhibited a number of standard bugs, in particular the "off-by-1" bug. Students would typically employ a READ/PROCESS strategy and thus include the final 99999 both in the sum and in the count of numbers. Almost none of the students, introductory or advanced, tested to see if the count was zero. For the purposes of our experiment, we did not count such programs as incorrect, if that were the only bug. Also, we did not count as incorrect programs that were only syntactically incorrect (e.g., missing semicolons).

Except for the novice group, all other groups showed significant improvement with respect to correctness when using Pascal *L* as compared to standard Pascal. (Although the novices show the same direction of effect as the other groups, the difference in their performance is not significant due to the large number of incorrect programs.) Given that students were exposed to the **loop . . . leave . . . again** construct of Pascal *L* for only a few minutes, and given that they had much more familiarity and experience with Pascal's standard loop constructs, we were quite impressed with the high performance of the Pascal *L* users. Thus, these data support the claim

TABLE IV: Program Correctness with Respect to Language

	Correct[1]	Incorrect[1]	N	Statistical[2] Significance
Novices				
Pascal *L* Group	24% (14)	76% (44)	58	Not Significant
Pascal Group	14% (8)	86% (50)	58	
Intermediates				
Pascal *L* Group	61% (36)	39% (23)	59	$(\chi^2 = 7.08)$
Pascal Group	36% (19)	64% (34)	53	$p = 0.01$
Advanced				
Pascal *L* Group	96% (25)	4% (1)	26	$(\chi^2 = 6.58)$
Pascal Group	69% (18)	31% (8)	26	$p < 0.02$
Novices + Intermediates + Advanced				
Pascal *L* Group	52% (75)	48% (68)	143	$(\chi^2 = 10.98)$
Pascal Group	33% (45)	67% (92)	137	$p < 0.001$

[1] The numbers in parentheses represent actual numbers, not percentages.
[2] A Chi-square test was used in this comparison.

that people will write correct programs more often if they use the language that facilitates their preferred strategy.

Question 2b: Irrespective of Whether a Strategy Is Preferred or Not, Will People Write Correct Programs More Often When Using the Strategy Facilitated by the Language?

In order to answer Question 2a we needed to compare performance across languages (Pascal versus Pascal L). However, in order to answer Question 2b, we need to look at correctness within a language as a function of strategy (Table V). First consider the intermediate group's performance; there we see quite clearly that those in the Pascal L group who used a READ/PROCESS strategy on their program were able to write a correct program more often than those who used a PROCESS/READ strategy. Similarly, those in the Pascal group who used a PROCESS/READ strategy on their program were able to write a correct program more often than those who used a READ/PROCESS strategy. Thus, it seems that a sensitivity to the strategy facilitated by the language constructs can have a significant effect on performance.

Question 3: Does Preference for a Strategy Vary with Experience? Does Program Accuracy Vary with Experience?

As expected, accuracy improves from 19% for the novice group to 49% for the intermediate group to 83% for the advanced group ($x^2 = 61.3$, $p < 0.001$). We also examined whether the difference in performance between Pascal and Pascal L was affected by the level of experience of the group (see Table IV). The significance of level of experience and language type was only marginal,[6] suggesting that all levels of experience benefited equally from Pascal L.

We can also see a shift in strategy preference: the trend in the data in Table I suggests that the more experienced programmers were beginning to more consistently adopt a PROCESS/READ strategy. Finally, sensitivity to the strategy that implicitly underlies a language construct also seems to increase with experience. This trend can be seen by asking the following question of the data in Table V: what percentage of programmers used the strategy appropriate to the language (irrespective of language type and irrespective

---

[6]Novice vs. expert: $z = 1.62$, $p = .10$; intermediate vs. (expert + novice) $z = .91$, not significant. The interaction was analysed using an arcsin transformation (see [1] p. 368).

TABLE V: Program Correctness with Respect to Language and Strategy

	Strategy on Program[3]	Correct[1]	Incorrect[1]	N	Statistical[2] Significance
Novices					
Pascal L Group	* READ/PROCESS	48% (14)	52% (15)	29	See note[4]
	PROCESS/READ	0% (0)	100% (1)	1	
	Misc.			28	
Pascal Group	READ/PROCESS	0% (0)	100% (26)	26	See note[4]
	* PROCESS/READ	100% (8)	0% (0)	8	
	Misc.			24	
Intermediates					
Pascal L Group	* READ/PROCESS	79% (34)	21% (9)	43	$(x^2 = 7.62)$ $p < 0.01$
	PROCESS/READ	29% (2)	71% (5)	7	
	Misc.			9	
Pascal Group	READ/PROCESS	14% (3)	86% (18)	21	$(x^2 = 21.6)$ $p < 0.001$
	* PROCESS/READ	89% (16)	11% (2)	18	
	Misc.			14	
Advanced					
Pascal L Group	* READ/PROCESS	96% (23)	4% (1)	24	See note[4]
	PROCESS/READ	100% (2)	0% (0)	2	
	Misc.			0	
Pascal Group	READ/PROCESS	40% (2)	60% (3)	5	$(x^2 = 5.50)$ $p < 0.02$
	* PROCESS/READ	89% (16)	11% (2)	18	
	Misc.			3	

[1] The numbers in parentheses represent actual numbers, not percentages.
[2] A Chi-square test was used in this comparison. Note that the *Misc.* category was not used in the Chi-square calculation.
[3] Asterisks indicate the strategy that was appropriate for the language.
[4] Although the numbers are in the predicted direction, there are too few individuals in some of the cells to permit a Chi-square analysis.

of program correctness)? The answers are that 58% (37/64) of the novices, 68% (61/89) of the intermediates, and 80% (42/49) of the advanced programmers employed the strategy appropriate to the language, e.g., a PROCESS/READ strategy for Pascal, and READ/PROCESS strategy for Pascal L (χ^2 = 10.20, $p < 0.01$).

In summary, the data gathered in this study support the following claims:

- people's preferred cognitive strategy seems to be READ/PROCESS as opposed to PROCESS/READ, at least on problems of the sort used in this study.
- people can write correct programs more often using a language that facilitates their preferred cognitive strategy; and
- people's accuracy, sensitivity to underlying strategy, and preference for a particular strategy can shift with experience.

CONCLUDING REMARKS AND IMPLICATIONS

In this study, we have documented some of the difficulties that arise when a programming language construct requires a cognitive strategy that differs from the preferred strategy. In particular, we have focused on Pascal's **while** construct, and have shown that the strategy that underlies the correct use of that construct — a PROCESS/READ strategy — is clearly not the preferred strategy. Moreover, we have demonstrated the significant increase in performance that results when subjects are given a construct, e.g., the **loop ... leave ... again** construct, that facilitates the READ/PROCESS strategy, their preferred cognitive strategy. Clearly, care must be taken in generalizing our results: the task used in our study required only a small program and the subjects were not professional programmers. However, at a minimum, programming instruction needs to attend to the bugs and misconceptions that arise in this sort of situation. For example, students need to be made aware of the existence of the different strategies. Also, students need to be taught explicitly about the characteristics of problems that require the unusual strategy. In this way, students might be made more conscious of the potential pitfalls. It would be an interesting experiment to see if, with such explicit instruction, the number of bugs and misconceptions could be reduced.

Another observation can also be drawn from our study: students write programs correctly more often using a construct that permits them to exit from the middle of the loop. Strong claims have been made against this sort of construct as it is argued that one should exit a loop from the top or the bottom, not the middle. For example, Ledgard [5], argues that *"forcing loop exits to the beginning or end of a loop in the long run is superior. In particular, it forces the programmer to state the loop-terminating condition at the entrance to or exit from the loop. While this may be more difficult to write initially, in the long run it forces a good program structure and leads to more maintainable programs. Exiting from the middle of a loop, while convenient, may readily lead to confusing program logic."* It is further claimed that the readability of a program is hampered if exits from the middle of the loop are allowed. (See also [2, 13].) Our study did not examine the readability claim, since we looked only at program generation. However, a series of studies by Sheppard et al. [8] suggest that in fact a construct that permits an exit in the middle does not interfere with readability. They compared a "strictly structured" looping construct [2], that did not permit an exit from the middle with a "naturally structured" construct, that did permit an exit from the middle, and found that their programmers showed no reliable difference in performance between these two constructs on a program comprehension task. They also examined these constructs in modification and debugging tasks and again found no statistical difference between the programmers' performance. Moreover, their studies were with professional programmers. Thus, there appears to be empirical evidence that an exit from the middle of the loop is not as harmful as was conjectured.

Finally, our study suggests that insights can come from looking beyond the syntax and semantics of language constructs to the cognitive demands that those constructs place on programmers. This appears to be especially relevant to the training of non-professional programmers since programming is a demanding skill and unnecessary hurdles serve only to complicate the learning process further. By being sensitive to the problem-solving skills that people bring to programming, and to those required by programming, we might be better able to assist people in making the necessary transitions.

ACKNOWLEDGMENTS

The authors would like to thank the reviewers of this paper for their constructive comments. We would also like to thank Lewis Johnson, Steve Draper, Jerry Leichter, Jim Galambos, and John Black for their helpful comments on earlier drafts of this paper.

This work was supported by the Army Research Institute for the Behavioral and Social Sciences, under ARI Grant No. MDA903-80-C-0508. This work was also supported by the National Science Foundation under NSF Grant SED-81-12403.

This chapter has been reprinted by permission of the Association for Computing Machinery.

REFERENCES

1. Bishop, Y.M.N., Feinberg, S.E., and Holland, P.W. *Discrete Multivariate Analysis: Theory and Practice.* MIT Press, Cambridge, Massachusetts, 1975.
2. Dijkstra, E.W. Notes on structured programming. In *Structured Programming.* O.J. Dahl, E.W. Dijkstra, C.A.R. Hoare, (eds.). Academic Press, New York, 1972.
3. Knuth, D. Structured programming with GOTO statements. *Comput. Surv. 6,* 4 (December 1974), 261–301.
4. Miller, L.A. Natural language programming: styles, strategies, and contrasts. *IBM Syst. J. 20,* 2 (1981), 184–215.
5. Ledgard, H.F. and Marcotty, M. A genealogy of control structures. *Commun. ACM 18* 11 (1975), 629–638.
6. Ledgard, H., Whiteside, J., Singer, A., and Seymour, W. The natural language of interactive systems. *Commun. ACM 23,* 10 (1980), 556–563.
7. Papert, S. *Mindstorms, Children, Computers and Powerful Ideas.* Basic Books, Inc., New York, 1980.
8. Sheppard, S.B., Curtis, B., Milliman, P., and Love, T. Modern coding practices and programmer performance. *Computer* (December 1979), 41–49.
9. Soloway, E., Lochhead, J., and Clement, J. Does computer programming enhance problem solving ability? Some positive evidence on algebra word problems. In *Computer Literacy,* R. Seidel, R. Anderson, B. Hunter (eds.), Academic Press, New York, 1982, pp. 171–215.
10. Soloway, E., Ehrlich, K., Bonar, J., and Greenspan, J. What do novices know about programming? In *Directions in Human-Computer Interactions,* B. Shneiderman and A. Badre (eds.), Ablex, Inc., 1983.
11. Wegner, P. Programming languages—Concepts and research directions. In *Research Directions in Software Technology,* MIT Press, Cambridge, Massachusetts, 1979.
12. Welty, C. and Stemple, D. Human factors comparison of a procedural and a nonprocedural query language. *ACM Trans. Database Syst. 6,* 4 (1981), 626–649.
13. Wirth, N. On the composition of well-structured programs. *ACM Comput. Surv. 6,* 4 (1974).

11

WHAT DO NOVICE PROGRAMMERS KNOW ABOUT RECURSION?

HANK KAHNEY
Human Cognition Research Laboratory
The Open University
Milton Keynes, MK7 6AA, UK

INTRODUCTION

The task discussed in this chapter was designed 1) to test the hypothesis that novices and experts differ in terms of their respective models of recursion as a process, and, 2) to try to discriminate the models of recursion which novices actually do possess.

The conceptual model presented to students in the D303 Programming Manual defines recursion as a process that is capable of triggering new instantiations of itself, with control passing forward to successive instantiations and back from terminated ones. This is the model of the recursive process that experts are hypothesized to have. A graphic representation of the model provided in the Manual is depicted in Figure 11.1.

Students, on the other hand, are hypothesized to have a 'looping' model of recursion. That is, they view a recursive procedure as a single object instead of a series of new instantiations, having the following features:

1. an 'entry point', the constituents of which are the procedure's name and a parameter slot;

2. an 'action part', which is designed to add information to the database (by way of the 'NOTE <pattern>' in Figure 11.2, below);

3. a 'propagation-mechanism' for generating successive database nodes and feeding the values of these successive nodes back to the 'front part', or 'entry point' of the procedure. This 'looping' model is illustrated in Figure 11.2.

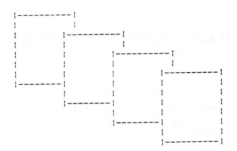

FIG. 11.1   A graphic depiction of the 'Copies' model of recursion.

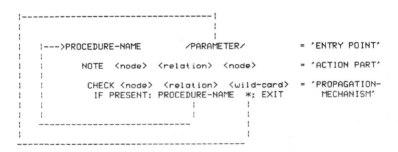

FIG. 11.2   A graphic description of the 'Loop' model of recursion.

THE BEHAVIOUR OF PROGRAMS PREDICTED BY THE DIFFERENT MODELS

The hypothesis about differences between novice and expert models of recursion was tested by presenting Subjects with the Questionnaire in Figure 11.3, below. As may be seen, the Questionnaire contains three programs, called SOLUTION-1, SOLUTION-2, and SOLUTION-3, respectively. Two of these solutions are critical to determining a Subject's model of recursion, and in order to make clear to the reader the predictions being made I shall in this section demonstrate the reasoning processes presumed to occur when Subjects with different models of recursion are confronted with the critical two of the three programs presented in the problem statement, or Questionnaire. The text of the Questionnaire is:

PROPAGATING INFERENCES

Recently I needed a programme which would make the following inference: if somebody 'X'; has 'flu, then whoever 'X' kisses also has 'flu, and whoever is

```
SOLUTION-1:

TO INFECT /X/
1 CHECK /X/ KISSES ?
 1A If Present: NOTE * HAS FLU ; EXIT
 1B If Absent:  EXIT
DONE


SOLUTION-2:

TO INFECT /X/
1 NOTE /X/ HAS FLU
2 CHECK /X/ KISSES ?
 2A If Present: INFECT * ; EXIT
 2B If Absent:  EXIT
DONE


SOLUTION-3:

TO INFECT /X/
1 CHECK /X/ KISSES ?
 1A If Present: INFECT *; CONTINUE
 1B If Absent:  CONTINUE
2 NOTE /X/ HAS FLU
DONE
```

FIG. 11.3   The full text of the Questionnaire task.

infected spreads the infection to the person he or she kisses, and so on.
Starting with the database given in Figure A, I needed a programme which
would change the Figure A database into the Figure B database.

```
JOHN ISA MAN                      JOHN ISA MAN
 !                                 !
 !...KISSES MARY                   !...KISSES MARY
                                   !
                                   !...HAS FLU

MARY ISA WOMAN                    MARY ISA WOMAN
 !                                 !
 !...KISSES TIM                    !...KISSES TIM
                                   !
                                   !...HAS FLU

TIM ISA MAN                       TIM ISA MAN
 !                                 !
 !...KISSES JOAN                   !...KISSES JOAN
                                   !
                                   !...HAS FLU

JOAN ISA WOMAN                    JOAN ISA WOMAN
                                   !
                                   !...HAS FLU


     Figure A                          Figure B
```

I have been provided with three solutions to the problem, all called 'TO INFECT /X/' and these are labelled SOLUTION-1, SOLUTION-2, and SOLUTION-3, below. I want you to consider each programme in turn and say (A) whether or not the programme will do what I want it to do, and (b) if it will, say how it does it (in your own words), or, if it won't, say why it doesn't (again in your own words).

Please write your answers on the pages provided overleaf. Thank you for cooperating.

SOLUTION-1 will not achieve the required effect. As may be seen, its outcome would be to add 'HAS FLU' to the node MARY after which the procedure would be terminated. SOLUTION-2 and SOLUTION-3 would both achieve the required output database. SOLUTION-2 works by side-effecting the database on the node first given as the argument to INFECT (= JOHN), and then generating the next node on the 'KISSES' list, which triggers the recursion. SOLUTION-3 works by creating a stack of bindings for /X/, i.e. (JOHN MARY TIM JOAN) and side-effecting each on return from the recursive creation of the list (i.e., side-effects the listed nodes in reverse order).

The Effects of Running the Programs Under the Copies Model

Call the conceptual model presented in the Programming Manual the 'Copies' model of recursion, and the model hypothesized for students the 'Loop' model of recursion. Consider programs SOLUTION-2 and SOLUTION-3 from the perspective of either model.

A person possessing the Copies model should select SOLUTION-2 and SOLUTION-3 as programs that would achieve the intended results. Figures 11.4 and 11.5 provide a graphic display of the reasoning process which the Copies model was designed to inculcate, for SOLUTION-2 and SOLUTION-3 respectively.

Figure 11.4 shows the first two instantiations of the INFECT procedure. The parameter slot, at the first instantiation (marked (1) in the figure), has the value, 'JOHN'. At the first step of the procedure, the node 'JOHN' is side-effected by the addition of the description 'HAS FLU'. At the second step, the wild-card pattern match succeeds, binding 'MARY' to the wild-card variable, and at step 2A a new instantiation (marked (2) in the figure) of the INFECT procedure is triggered. The same process is repeated each time the pattern-match succeeds. Ascent from the recursion is indicated by the backwards pointing arrows in the figure, demonstrating when each instantiation is terminated.

Figure 11.5 shows the last and penultimate instantiations of the INFECT

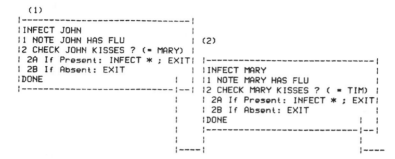

FIG. 11.4   The behaviour of the SOLUTION-2 program under the Copies model of recursion.

FIG. 11.5   The behaviour of the SOLUTION-3 program under the Copies model of recursion.

procedure given in SOLUTION-3. The unwinding of the recursion is terminated (in (4)) when the wild-card pattern match (CHECK JOAN KISSES ?) fails. The 'If Absent' branch of the conditional contains the instruction to continue, and step 2 results in side-effecting the node 'JOAN' with the description 'HAS FLU'. Control is then returned to the flow of control statement at step 1A of the previous instantiation, (3), and the result is that the node 'TIM' is side-effected at step 2. The same process occurs for the two previous instantiations, of course.

The Effects of Running the Programs Under the Loop Model

Figures 11.6 and 11.7 depict the operation of the Loop model in reasoning about SOLUTION-2 and SOLUTION-3, respectively.

In Figure 11.6 (a) the procedure's paramater slot is first instantiated with 'JOHN'. At step 1, the side-effect to that node is accomplished, and at step

```
FIGURE 4.6(a)                    INFECT JOHN
                                 1 NOTE JOHN HAS FLU
                                 2 CHECK JOHN KISSES ? (= MARY)
                                 2A If Present: INFECT * ; EXIT


FIGURE 4.6(b)                    INFECT MARY
                                         !
                                         !---->JOHN
                                 1 NOTE MARY HAS FLU
                                 2 CHECK MARY KISSES ? (= TIM)
                                 2A If Present: INFECT * ; EXIT


FIGURE 4.6(c)                    INFECT TIM
                                         !
                                         !---->MARY
                                 1 NOTE TIM HAS FLU
                                 2 CHECK TIM KISSES ? (= JOAN)
                                 2A If Present: INFECT * ; EXIT


FIGURE 4.6(d)                    INFECT JOAN
                                         !
                                         !---->TIM
                                 1 NOTE JOAN HAS FLU
                                 2 CHECK JOAN KISSES ? (NIL)
                                 ------------------------
                                 2B If Absent: EXIT
                                 DONE
```

FIG. 11.6   The behaviour of the SOLUTION-2 program under the Loop model of recursion.

```
FIGURE4.7(a)        INFECT JOHN
                    1 CHECK JOHN KISSES ? (= MARY)
                    1A If Present: INFECT * ; CONTINUE


FIGURE4.7(b)        INFECT MARY
                            !
                            !---->JOHN
                    1 CHECK MARY KISSES ? (= TIM)
                    1A If Present: INFECT * ; CONTINUE


FIGURE 4.7(c)       INFECT TIM
                            !
                            !---->MARY
                    1 CHECK TIM KISSES ? (= JOAN)
                    1A If Present: INFECT * ; CONTINUE


FIGURE 4.7(d)       INFECT JOAN
                            !
                            !---->TIM
                    1 CHECK JOAN KISSES ? (NULL)
                    --------------------
                    1B If Absent: CONTINUE
                    2 NOTE JOAN HAS FLU
                    DONE
```

FIG. 11.7   The behaviour of the SOLUTION-3 program under the Loop model of recursion.

2 the wild-card pattern match succeeds, binding the value 'MARY' to the variable. As a result, at step 2A recursion is triggered, which, in terms of the Loop model, means looping back to the beginning of the procedure, taking along the value of the wild-card variable as the new value of the parameter slot. Since the parameter can contain only one value, the previous value is swept aside, as indicated in Figures 11.6(b)–11.6(d).

Strong evidence for possession of the Copies model would be selection of both SOLUTION-2 and SOLUTION-3 as correctly designed programs for the task in hand, plus some comment on the order in which the side-effect to the database occurs when SOLUTION-3 is run: since the side-effect occurs as the recursion unwinds, one would expect anyone who recognized this fact would mention it. Selection of SOLUTION-3 by itself would be weak evidence, at best, for possession of the Copies model, unless, again, some comment about the order of side-effects to the database is made. SOLUTION-2 should be easier for students to understand than SOLUTION-3, even if they have the Copies model, since SOLUTION-2 is in a form with which the students should be familiar: this program is an exact copy of the program used as an example of recursive procedures in the Programming Manual. Thus, it would seem improbable that anyone selecting SOLUTION-3 and rejecting SOLUTION-2 actually understood either program. In all cases, however, the Subjects' reasons for selecting or rejecting one and another of the programs were examined for direct evidence about the model possessed.

The behaviour of the SOLUTION-3 program, under the Loop model, is depicted in Figure 11.7. In Figure 11.7(a), at step 1 of the procedure, 'MARY' is generated by the wild-card pattern match, triggering recursion at step 1A. The result of this is that the value 'MARY' is 'fed back' to the beginning of the program. In 11.7(b), with the new value of the parameter slot = MARY, the value 'JOHN' is swept aside and the operation of the procedure produces 'TIM'. Figures 11.7(c) and 11.7(d) show the procedure looping through the chain of 'KISSES' relations until the wild-card pattern match (CHECK JOAN KISSES ?) fails. At that point (Figure 11.7(d)) the 'If Absent' branch of the conditional is taken, and the node 'JOAN' is side-effected with the addition of the description 'HAS FLU'.

Strong evidence for possession of the Loop model would be:

1. selection of SOLUTION-2 as correctly designed, and,
2. rejection of SOLUTION-3, especially if this program is rejected on the grounds that only JOAN would be affected by running this program.

Method: The full intake of students (approximately 90) for the first week of the Cognitive Psychology Summer School (July, 1981) were given the Questionnaire in Figure 11.3 and asked to fill it in at their leisure and to return it to the experimenter. Students' previous experience of programming is not known. Nine experts also acted as Subjects in the experiment. The experts were Subjects S13–S20, plus a research assistant, S21, who works in the psychology laboratory. S21 had a year of experience in writing Lisp and PASCAL programs. In the remainder of this Chapter, novice Subjects who took part in this experiment will be referred to as 'Respondents', to avoid confusion over which experimental Subjects are being referred to: the Subjects who were studied in depth and are referred to in other Chapters as, e.g., S5 or S8, or the different Subjects for this particular experiment. Experts are still referred to in terms of their identifying labels (e.g., S14). Respondents have been labelled R1 through R30.

Results: Eight of the nine experts selected both SOLUTION-2 and SOLUTION-3, and one (S14) selected only SOLUTION-2 as the programs that would achieve the required output for the Questionnaire task. A typical expert's comments were those of S17:

> (Commenting on SOLUTION-2): "Yes. This procedure will transform the database to the required form from one call of INFECT JOHN. It does this by NOTEing that the node called as the procedure's parameter, /X/, 'HAS FLU' as the first step. At the next step the database is CHECKed for a relation linking /X/ and another node by the relation KISSES. If such a 'triple' is found then INFECT is called recursively with the new node as the parameter /X/. This depth first search continues (like a real infection — although iteration must be involved in the real case, but not here) until the '/X/ KISSES?' triple cannot be found and the EXIT route is taken (back through each level of recursion to the top). This solution is the most plausible representation of propagating inferences about infection given the database here."

> (Commenting on SOLUTION-3): "Yes. This procedure will also transform the database as required using the single call INFECT JOHN. It does it in essentially the same recursive manner as SOLUTION-2 except that here '/X/ HAS FLU' is added to the database after the search for 'KISSES ?' has terminated. That is, the procedure recurses until no more '/X/ KISSES' ? triples can be found and as it EXITs back up through the recursions '/X/ HAS FLU' is added for each call of INFECT. This means of propagating is less psychologically plausible than SOLUTION-2 because of the high STS load imposed in this case."

Of the 90 or so novices who were given the Questionnaire, 30 completed and returned it. In Figure 11.8 the graph represents the percentages of novices (the stars on the graph) and experts (the plus signs on the graph) selecting particular programs as correctly designed solutions to the Questionnaire problem.

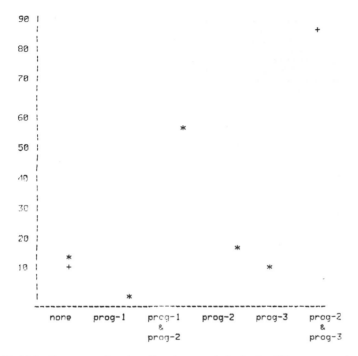

FIG. 11.8   Percentage of novices (*) and experts (+) selecting different categories of 'correct programs'.

The actual number of Respondents represented by these percentages is provided in square brackets for each category of response, in Table 11.1.

Table 11.2 shows the numbers of novices (N) and experts (E) who chose either SOLUTION-2, or both SOLUTION-2 and SOLUTION-3 as programs that would achieve the required effect. All other responses were collapsed into the category named OTHER. The difference in selection between novices and experts is highly significant (chi-squared = 21.40 p < .001).

Table 11.3 shows the number of novices and experts who selected only either SOLUTION-2, or SOLUTION-2 and SOLUTION-3 as correct solutions to the problem (the category OTHER has been removed). Novices chose SOLUTION-2 and SOLUTION-3 significantly less often than experts (chi-squared = 10.78, p < .01).

Discussion: These results suggest that just over half the Respondents have adopted the Loop model of recursion (selected SOLUTION-2 and

```
1) None of the programs would behave as intended [4].
2) Only SOLUTION-1 would work [1].
3) Both SOLUTION-1 and SOLUTION-2 would achieve the intended
     output database [1].
4) Only SOLUTION-2 would work [16].
5) Only SOLUTION-3 would work [5].
6) Both SOLUTION-2 and SOLUTION-3 would achieve the intended
     output database [3].
```

TABLE 4.1

	N	E
SOLUTION-2	16	1
SOLUTION-2 & 3	3	8
OTHER	11	0

```
chi-squared with 2 degrees of freedom = 21.40
contingency coeff. = .59
```

TABLE 4.2

	N	E
SOLUTION-2	16	1
SOLUTION-2 & -3	3	8

```
chi-squared with 1 degree of freedom = 10.78
cont. coeff. = .52
```

TABLE 4.3

rejected SOLUTION-3), and that only three of the 30 Respondents have acquired the Copies model (selected both SOLUTION-2 and SOLUTION-3). Six of the Respondents appear to have understood little, if anything, about any of the programs (Respondents in categories 1, 2, and 3 in Table 11.1). There is also 'weak' evidence that a further one sixth of all Respondents have the Copies model (selected SOLUTION-3 as the only program that would do the task required). In order to determine more precisely how the different Respondents thought the programs behaved, an examination of their reasons for selecting and rejecting programs must be examined.

The Evidence for the Copies Model

Of particular interest to us for the present is the small percentage (10%) of Respondents who thought both SOLUTION-2 and SOLUTION-3 were successful, indicating that just one in ten of the Respondents had the Copies model of recursion. And even this assumption may not be soundly based. The reasons given for selecting SOLUTION-2 and SOLUTION-3 by the three Respondents were the following.

> R23, commenting on SOLUTION-2, thought:
> Yes, this programme will solve the problem, but will try to INFECT all but JOAN twice, so Step 2 is unnecessary.

> On SOLUTION-3, R23 thought:
> Yes, this is the correct solution for this problem but could be achieved more easily by just using 'NOTE /X/ HAS FLU' because the 'KISSES' CHECK is not vital to the change, e.g., 'JOAN HAS FLU' but does not KISS anyone. It's a 'Heads you win, tails I lose' flu situation!

Whatever R23 might mean by his comments on SOLUTION-2, I am not convinced he understands the program at all. Step 2 is, of course, necessary, as it carries the recursion. An explanation for this respondent's misconception that all nodes would be side-effected twice by the operation of SOLUTION-2, and that the "KISSES CHECK" in SOLUTION-3 is unnecessary, wold be purely speculative and therefore no explanation will be attempted.

Here are R24's comments on both SOLUTION-2 and SOLUTION-3:

> Solution 2 and 3 look okay but I don't know if just typing in causes SOLO to change the database or whether the operator has to put in the new data — after which SOLO will INFECT new nodes who are kissed? P.S. Well I was told that 2 & 3 were okay! Before that I was wondering how JOAN got infected, but looking carefully I see TIM KISSES JOAN. As my favourite sport is jumping [to conclusions] I'm not very good at AI.

R24's response should fail to convince anyone that this Respondent has any understanding of the behaviour of either program.

The last Respondent, R29, commenting on SOLUTION-2, and subsequently on SOLUTION-3, thought:

> (SOLUTION-2): Yes. Infects first argument, finds link, infects second argument and follows chain of infection.

> (On SOLUTION-3): Yes. Infects first argument and follows link as above. Only difference is order of carrying out instructions. (And, incidentally, of inferring.)

Only this Respondent, of the three, has a convincing story to tell, convincing especially in his determination of the order of the side-effects that occur as a result of running the procedure.

Summary: Three Respondents out of thirty selected both SOLUTION-2 and SOLUTION-3 as correct programs, which was argued to be strong evidence for possession of a Copies model of recursion. However, the comments made by two of the three Respondents cast doubts on their level of understanding of either of these solutions. In the end the data suggest that only one in thirty Respondents after their initial training in SOLO programming, has acquired an expert's understanding of recursion, the Copies model. The 'weak evidence' for the Copies model will be discussed later in this chapter, in a subsection on 'Odd Models', because, rather than suggest that more Respondents possess the Copies model than indicated by the evidence examined in this section, the comments made by the Respondents who selected only SOLUTION-3 as correct suggest: 1) that many Respondents may have acquired idiosyncratic notions about recursive procedures, and 2) that some Respondents may have difficulty even recognizing recursive procedures.

The Loop Model

Most of the Respondents chose SOLUTION-2 as the only program that behaved as required, which is considered to be only weak evidence that the Loop model has been acquired by just over half (53%) of those who filled in the Questionnaire. Unfortunately, again, most of the comments made by these Respondents are less informative than necessary to work out their model in detail. A typical response was this:

Follows 3 stages of:
NOTE a) statement "X has flu"
CHECK b) consequence kisses flu
INFECT c) spread of flu via kiss.

Only three or four Respondents made comments longer than a couple of sentences, and only one of these (R13) made specific reference to looping as a mechanism of recursion. (This alone, of course, does not by itself mean that this Respondent actually has the Loop model.)

This does solve the problem. When asked to infect John it adds the relation 'has flu' to John, checks who he kisses, loops back to infect that person, noting first that the person has flu and looking for any person that this new person kisses. It continues to loop the routine until all the nodes that attach the kisses relation have been infected. This will change the database in Fig. 1 to that in Fig. 2.

The Strong Evidence for the Loop Model

Of the sixteen Respondents who selected SOLUTION-2, four rejected SOLUTION-3 on the grounds that only JOAN would get 'flu. Since it has been argued that this is the strong evidence for possession of the Loop model, the figures indicate that just 13% of all Respondents have this model of recursion.

Here are some of the comments of those who thought only JOAN would be side-effected by the operation of SOLUTION-3. (Note that two of the Respondents name 'JOAN' while it is inferred that the other two mean 'JOAN' by their comments.)

R7 commented:

Won't work because of sequence — SOLO is shortsighted — follows one line at a time. Infect John & Step 1a proceeds to Check Mary for 'kisses', finds it, checks Tim, then Joan. Only then, when "Joan kisses ?" is not present, will step 1b activate step 2 & give flu to Joan, then stop. John, Mary & Tim remain fluless.

R11 commented:

No one has flu to begin with. This will simply check who kisses who, flu is not passed on. It cycles through 1 and 1A, /X/ only gets flu if /X/ KISSES is absent.

R13 commented:

This does not solve the problem. The program will loop its way through the database in a similar fashion to solution 2 but will only note that Joan has 'flu.

R14 commented:

The procedure will search through the database repeatedly checking who /X/ kisses? However, the procedure will not use the database to note who has flu when kissed by /X/ because of the position in the procedure of NOTE /X/ has flu. Only the last value of /X/ will be infected.

Summary: The Copies model is not a viable candidate for what our students know about recursion. Only three out of thirty Respondents on the Questionnaire showed evidence for the copies model, and tow thirds of this evidence did not stand up to scrutiny. On the other hand, only four of the Respondents appear to have the Loop model, on the evidence of the strong indicants of that model. Thus, what the Respondents know about recursion can be accounted in terms of either the Copies or the Loop model in only five out of thirty cases. The comments of many of the Respondents who have been classified as providing only weak evidence for the Loop model suggest that they have acquired something other than either the Loop or the

Copies models, and so the weak evidence will be discussed in a subsection, below, on 'Syntactic', or 'Magic' models of recursion.

Other Models of Recursion

A possibility not yet considered, of course, is that students (or some of them) have no model of recursion, or a model different from either the Copies or the Loop model. Some of the Respondents clearly do not understand recursion at all. The evidence for this will be discussed in the subsection below on the 'Null' model. Some of the evidence suggests that a few Respondents have slightly idiosyncratic Copies or Loop models, and this will be discussed in the subsection on 'Odd' models. Another possibility, for which there are fragments of evidence in the comments of some of the Respondents is that there is a sort of 'Magic' model of recursion — that a procedure having a particular structure just is a recursive procedure, and it performs a certain sequence of operations, although the actual behaviour of the process is a complete mystery. This model will be discussed in the subsection on the 'Syntactic', or 'Magic' model.

The 'Null' Model

In this class would fall those Respondents who said that none of the programs would work (category 1 in Table 11.1), and the single Respondents who claimed that only SOLUTION-1 would work (category 2). Typical comments made by Respondents falling into these categories were these:

R16: Won't work. This is because as a definition of the procedure "infect", it can hardly use that very procedure as part of the initial definition. This would probably be refused by the computer.

R21 thought:

No. The procedure is cyclic (i.e. it uses itself) and hence illegal.

One of the Respondents in category 3 (the weak evidence for the Copies model category) rejected SOLUTION-2 on the grounds:

Will not work. Fans out from /X/ i.e. iteration but selected SOLUTION-3 on the grounds:

Will work. Goes in depth through the kissing, i.e. recursion.

The Respondents is correct in the latter statement but not correct in the former. A possible explanation for these comments is that the Respondents understood the behaviour of neither program, and perhaps thought he was being tested on his ability to discriminate recursive and iterative processes, and just made a guess. The Respondent's comments on SOLUTION-1 offer no help; he merely comments: "Will not work".

The 'Odd' Model

It was stated above that the comments of many of the Respondents classified as providing weak evidence for either the Copies or Loop model suggested that they had various odd notions about recursion. In this subsection some of the comments of these Respondents will be given and interpreted. The interpretations suggest that these Respondents do have models of the behaviour of the procedures given in the Questionnaire, but because they have idiosyncratic ideas about some features of the programs they do not correctly predict the behaviour of the programs.

R27 (from category four in Table 11.1) sounds as though he has the Copies model when talking about SOLUTION-3:

Yes. Programme will go through Infection process till last person kissing anybody has been found — then will note all four as having flu.

(Note that R27 states that the procedure recurses until "last person kissing anybody has been found" (= TIM, not JOAN). R27 then indicates that 'all four' will be Noted as having 'flu. What R27 means by the first comment is that SOLUTION-3 recurses as long as the pattern '/X/ KISSES ?' returns a value for the wild-card pattern-match.)

When discussing SOLUTION-2, R27 has this to say:

No. The programme would add 2 persons who had flu to the database, but EXIT prevents further infection occurring.

An unimpeachable interpretation of R27's thinking about these programs is not possible, but this last comment provides us with a vital clue. R27 apparently believes that step 2A of SOLUTION-2:

   If Present: INFECT * ; EXIT
 is read by SOLO as:
   'INFECT * and EXIT immediately.

That is, the stopping rule for the recursion is not the absence of a pattern in the database but the flow of control statement 'EXIT'. R27's model of the behaviour of SOLUTION-2 is something like:

   INFECT JOHN
   INFECT MARY and EXIT.

If so, his model of the behaviour of SOLUTION-3 would be:

    INFECT JOHN
    INFECT MARY and CONTINUE [the INFECT process]
    INFECT TIM
    INFECT JOAN.

The comments indicate that R27 has an idiosyncratic model of the stopping rule for recursion, but exactly which model of recursion the Respondent possesses is impossible to determine. The fact that R27 points out that the side-effect to the database will occur last is some evidence for his possessing the Copies model.

Other Respondents also seem to have R27's particular problem about recursion's stopping rule. Here are a couple of their comments.

R1: (Commenting on SOLUTION-2):

It's not this solution, because it would only INFECT one person, then EXIT.

R25: (Commenting on SOLUTION-2):

Solution 2 will not do the job either. Although /X/ has flu, the EXIT in 1A & 1B stops the infection process.

In all these cases, the notion acquired is that the flow of control statement, rather than the absence of a particular pattern in the database, acts as the stopping rule for recursion. Recall that in Chapter 2 we found that a number of student programmers opted for a 'Continue Regardless' solution to the 'Guilt By Association' problem. In Chapter 2 it was suggested that students conceptualized the 'bug' in 'Termination problem' programs as 'unreachable code', and that some characterized the fault in terms of the control statement 'EXIT' while others characterized the fault in terms of the non-equivalence of patterns associated with different database nodes. The former group, it was suggested, thus changed the 'EXIT' instruction on the 'If Absent' branch of a conditional segment to be 'CONTINUE', the result of which would be a 'Continue Regardless' type of program. A different possibility is that the 'Continue Regardless' programs were designed that way in the first place. R25's comments, above, on the SOLUTION-2 program, relate termination of the program to the 'EXITs' on the two branches of the conditional statement. It is possible that some of our students think that both branches require 'CONTINUE' for the program to work properly.

Among the Respondents who have been classified as providing weak evidence for the Loop model there are a number of comments suggesting that some have a variant of that model. For example, although only four of the Respondents who rejected SOLUTION-3 named JOAN specifically, six other Respondents indicated that this program would succeed in giving only one person 'flu. Two Respondents thought 'JOHN' would get 'flu. For example, commenting on SOLUTION-3, R10 said:

> All we will get is John has flu added to the database. We will follow through procedure finding out only who kisses who and not using the fact to infect anyone so the procedure is not making any inference at all.

It may be that the Respondents who chose 'JOHN' as the only person to get 'flu have a 'matching bias' — that is, they match the '/X/' in 'INFECT /X/' to the '/X/' in 'NOTE /X/ HAS FLU' at the second step of the procedure. The Respondents correctly determined that the procedure would work its way through to the end of the chain of 'KISSES' relations, but presumably thinks that successive values of the wild-card variable somehow 'get lost' and that the original value of the parameter is saved and operated upon by the action at step 2 of the procedure.

The comments of three other Respondents were too obscure on the point to determine which node they thought would be side-effected, but they apparently have some model of the behaviour of the program, as they all predict that only one (or, "at most only one") node will be affected by the operation of the procedure. Here, for example, is a typical comment which fails to specify which node is affected:

> (R30, commenting on SOLUTION-3): No, at most only one person gets flu for no apparent reason.

Finally, one Respondent R15, also thought only one node would be affected, but the claim was that it would be 'MARY'. Here are R15's comments on SOLUTION-3:

> Won't work. Only Mary gets flu. Only one node is affected.

This Respondent's comments may be based in the judgment that the design only allows one node to pass to the second step of the program, plus an priori model of the spread of 'flu — 'JOHN' kisses 'MARY'; 'MARY' is the first person to get kissed; kissing can cause the spread of infection; if anyone does 'get' 'flu, it should be 'MARY'.

The 'Syntactic', or 'Magic', Model

The possibility to be considered next is that there is a 'syntactic' or 'magic' model of recursion which a number of our students may possess. A syntactic model would be based in the structure of the 'INFECT' program (SOLUTION-2 in the Questionnaire), which was used in the Programming Manual as an example of a recursive procedure. Any program having the same structure as the 'INFECT' program would be 'recognized' as a recursive procedure. It is a 'magic' model in that, although the student may know what the procedure does, he has no idea how the procedure achieves its effects.

The memorized framework for recursive procedures would look like that in Figure 11.9. The single quotation marks indicate the variable features — such as 'PROCEDURE-NAME' — which the novice would have to fill from elements of different problems.

```
'PROCEDURE-NAME' /X/
1 NOTE /X/ '<relation1> <node>'
2 CHECK /X/ '<relation2>' ?
  2A If Present: 'PROCEDURE-NAME' * ; EXIT
  2B If Absent: EXIT
DONE
```

FIG. 11.9   A program frame for the Magic Model of recursion.

Hints that some students do base their judgments about the behaviour of programs in the syntactic structure of the program come from many of the comments made by different Respondents. For example, R12 thought:

> The procedure will search through the database repeatedly checking who /X/ kisses. However the procedure will not use the database to note who has flu when kissed by /X/ because of the position in the procedure of NOTE /X/ has flu.

R14's comments were these:

> Won't work. When at 2 /X/ has flu, it is after the event at 1, therefore cannot affect it.

R17 commented, on SOLUTION-3:

> This will not give correct printout because the triple /X/ has flu needs to be before the Check procedure.

These Respondents appear to be sensitive to the position of program segments, and, if they have no model of the actual behaviour of recursion, such indicants may be vitally important in their judgments about programs.

Summary: Different novices may acquire a wide range of models of processes like recursion, or may achieve no understanding at all of such processes, or may simply be able to identify a program as a member of a class if it has expected features in expected configurations. The bad news is that as many as four out of five may fall into the latter two of these three categories if the responses of this self-selecting group (they chose to fill in and return the Questionnaire) accurately reflect the level of understanding of one major concept by the entire population of novices who have had limited experience of SOLO programming.

Conclusion

A range of abilities is demonstrated in these results. Novices can be distributed into different classes according to the internal structure of the individual concepts they have acquired. The data show that at least some novices — probably a quarter — can, after a fairly brief training period in SOLO programming, identify and mentally simulate the behaviour of recursive procedures. That is, they have mental models of the way recursion behaves. The notion that concretization of abstract concepts is an essential component of successful problem solving is suggested by the experimental results of Mayer (1981). Mayer was able to show that less able, novice BASIC programmers performed better on a variety of tasks if they were given a concrete system model before they began to learn about the system. Able novices, in Mayer's study, did not improve their performance as a result of being given such a model: they presumably had their own means of devising such models. Mayer also discusses a finding of Resnick & Ford (1980) showing that young children often invent their own concrete models of processes such as subtraction when they are first introduced to such concepts.

The results indicate that different knowledge bases need to be 'plugged in' to an adequate model of novice programming behaviour. The average of the novice with a Copies model of recursion and the novice with a Null model is not the novice with the Loop or the Odd model. On a given task some performances will be severely memory data-limited (Bobrow & Norman, 1975), such as those given by novices with either Null, Syntactic, or Odd models of recursion. There will be many tasks, on the other hand, on which some novices will perform very well. If a person has a mental model of a process, even if it is at variance with the conceptual model of the process, he will be able to make predictions about the behaviour of the process, although perhaps not all the behaviour, and perhaps inaccurately (Norman, 1982; Collins & Gentner, 1982). That is, students who are able to develop a Loop model of recursion will be able to design procedures in terms of the model and understand unfamiliar programs by mentally simulating their behaviour in terms of the model. More importantly, possession of a model provides a person with a basis for debugging the model when confronted with a counterexample (Jeffries, 1982). Thus, some novice performances may be indistinguishable from expert performance (with the possible exception of the comments made by novices and experts about the knowledge they are using: experts are notoriously concise, in contrast to the commenting performance of novices (Byrne, 1977; Simon & Simon, 1980). The terseness of the experts' comments has been attributed to the experts' lack of self knowledge (Soloway; Byrne) and to the suggestion that experts have 'compiled' processes (Simon & Simon). The two explanations may come down to the same thing in the end. A difference to be expected, then, is not in the overall structure of the performance between 'able' novices and experts, but the length of the protocol given, because of the copious comments of the novice, which is presumably possible because the processes of the novice have not yet become compiled.

REFERENCES

Bobrow, D. G., & Norman, D. A. Some principles of memory schemata. In D. G. Bobrow & A. M. Collins (Eds.), *Representation and understanding: studies in cognitive science.* New York: Academic Press 1975.

Byrne, R. Planning meals: problem solving on a real data base. *Cognition, 5,* 287–332. 1977.

Colins, A. & Gentner, D. Constructing runnable mental models. *Proceedings of the Fourth Annual Conference of the Cognitive Science Society,* Michigan 1982.

Jeffries, R. A comparison of debugging behaviour of expert and novice programmers. Paper presented at AERA annual meeting. March, 19782.

Mayer, R. E., The psychology of how novices learn computer programming, *Computing Surveys,* 13, 1, March 1981.

Norman, D. A., Some observations on mental models. In D. Gentner & A. Stevens (Eds.), *Mental models.* Hillsdale, N.J.: Lawrence Erlbaum Associates, 1982.

Resnick, L. B., and Ford, S., *The psychology of mathematics learning,* Erlbaum, Hillsdale, N.J., 1980.

Simon, D. P. & Simon, H. A. Individual differences in solving physics problems. In Siegler (ed.), Children's thinking: what develops? Hillsdale, N.J.: Lawrence Erlbaum Associates, 1978.

Soloway, E.,Ehrlich, K., Bonar, J., & Greenspan, J. What do novices know about programming? In B. Shneiderman & A. Badre (Eds.) *Directions in human-computer interactions.* Norwood, N.J., Ablex, 1982.

Learning Flow of Control:
Recursive and Iterative Procedures

Claudius M. Kessler and **John R. Anderson**
Carnegie-Mellon University

ABSTRACT

Two experiments were performed to study students' ability to write recursive and iterative programs and transfer between these two skills. Subjects wrote functions to accumulate instances into a list. Problems varied in terms of whether they were recursive or iterative, whether they operated on lists or numbers, whether they accumulated results in forward or backward manner, whether they accumulated on success or failure, and whether they simply skipped or ejected on failure to accumulate. Subjects had real difficulty only with the dimensions concerned with flow of control, namely, recursive versus iterative, and skip versus eject. We found positive transfer from writing iterative functions to writing recursive functions, but not vice versa. A subsequent protocol study revealed subjects had such a poor mental model of recursion that they developed poor learning strategies which hindered their understanding of iteration. It is argued that having an adequate model of the functionality of programming is prerequisite to learning to program, and that it is sensible pedagogical practice to base understanding of recursive flow of control on understanding iterative flow of control.

Authors' present addresses: Claudius M. Kessler and John R. Anderson, Department of Psychology, Carnegie-Mellon University, Pittsburgh, PA 15213.

CONTENTS

1. INTRODUCTION: PREVIOUS EXPERIMENTS ON RECURSION AND ITERATION

Over the last few years there have been many attempts to foster and facilitate the acquisition of programming skills. A central research topic within this context is the issue of how novices acquire knowledge about control structures. For programming languages like Pascal, understanding the different kinds of iteration and their appropriate uses presents a major problem to the beginning student. A major problem when teaching novices a language like LISP is to find an effective way to teach recursion. Most students seem to have little trouble acquiring the language until recursive programming constructs are introduced. At this point, many students exhibit unusually strong comprehension problems that jeopardize their further progress.

Previous work comparing the acquisition of recursive and iterative procedures has shown that novices tend to understand the recursive process as an iterative one. Kahney and Eisenstadt (1982), for example, let novices and experts judge recursive programs. The subjects had to decide if the programs actually did what they were supposed to do and give an explanation of their answers. Nearly all of the novices' answers gave evidence of a wrong or inadequate model of recursion. The most popular misconception was to represent recursion as a loop structure that iterates through a problem.

Kurland and Pea (1983) showed that the same kind of misconception underlies children's understanding of recursive LOGO programs. Although subjects could mentally trace a tail-recursive procedure, they could not evaluate programs that included embedded recursive calls. The children's verbal protocols of their evaluation processes clearly showed that they viewed recursion as iteration.

Anzai and Uesato (1982) got subjects to write simple recursive constructs with about 1 hr of instruction. Subjects were taught a paper-and-pencil method to simulate a factorial function and then had to build factorial functions of their own. One group started with a recursive procedure and then switched to an iterative one, while a second group received the opposite order. The results show that writing iterative functions first facilitated the writing of recursive functions more than writing recursive functions first facilitated the writing of iterative functions. It was difficult for the subjects in the experiment to interpret recursive calls in the recursive procedures. Anzai and Uesato hypothesized that learning iteration first helps with recursion because iteration provides a model for what a recursive call does. However, learning recursion first does not help with iteration because iteration is easily mastered, and the recursive construct is not understood well enough to serve as the basis for transfer.

Unfortunately, Anzai and Uesato did not run control conditions that would allow them to distinguish the amount of facilitation due to increased practice from the effect of transferring from one procedure to another. It may be that subjects improve in the iteration-to-recursion condition because of general practice. In the recursion-to-iteration condition, there could be negative transfer combined with the effects of general practice. These possible explanations could be investigated if the transfer results of their conditions are compared with the improvement that would occur in conditions that transfer from recursion to further recursion and from iteration to further iteration.

With respect to the relevance of this study to computer programming, it should be noted that the subjects in the Anzai and Uesato experiment did not have to learn a computer language to execute the recursive procedures. The fact that one normally learns about recursion in the context of learning a computer language might introduce further factors in the process of skill acquisition that are not addressed by Anzai and Uesato.

The experiments reported in this article are designed to further investigate how novices learn about recursion and iteration and to test their ability to transfer from learning one construct to learning the other. Because we are interested in the acquisition of programming skills, our subjects learned about these constructs within the context of a programming language.

2. EXPERIMENT 1: NOVICE DIFFICULTIES WITH RECURSION AND ITERATION

The programming language used in this experiment, SIMPLE (Shrager & Pirolli, 1983), was designed especially for the purpose of studying the acquisition of recursive programming skills. SIMPLE does a few LISP-like operations whose implementations read as close to English as possible. Subjects learned this language and then solved a set of problems in a recursive and/or iterative fashion.

The tasks were designed to address the following questions:

- Is it easier to learn iteration than it is to learn recursion?
- Is there transfer from learning one of these constructs to learning the other?
- What factors influence the difficulty of writing recursive or iterative functions?

2.1. Method

The Programming Problems.   The programming tasks specified a set of constraints to extract certain book titles from a catalog. Each title was associated with a catalog number and a subject area.

The functions that had to be written differed on five dimensions (in parentheses, we give the name of the dimension as it will be used throughout this article):

1. whether they were recursive or iterative (recursion/iteration),
2. whether subjects had to search over a list of names or over numbers, that is, whether they had to work with the book titles or the catalog numbers (list/number),
3. whether the answers were accumulated in a forward or reverse manner when doing the recursive call or iterative loop (forward/reverse),
4. whether success or failure instances were accumulated in the answer, that is, whether a book title did or did not belong to a certain category (success/ failure), and
5. whether the answer was returned as soon as the accumulation test was negative or whether the function worked its way through the whole database by skipping negative instances (eject/skip).

The last four task dimensions were selected because they interacted with the recursion/iteration dimension to produce variations of code with which students in programming courses experience difficulty. We hoped to get at the heart of these difficulties with a systematic study of the variations.

Figure 1 gives an example of a recursive function that works on a list, accumulates successful instances in a forward manner, and ejects on a positive nonaccumulation test. The example in Figure 2 is its iterative analog on numbers.

All functions were patterned similarly: The first line contained a function header, the second line a test for termination. Lines 3 and 4 carried out the tests and accumulated the appropriate answer according to the function specifica-

Figure 1. **A recursive function.**

The following is an illustration of a SIMPLE function called **FIRST-SCIENCE** which takes a list of book titles and returns an answer list that contains all science titles from the first of the list to the first nonscience title. The answer list contains the titles in the order they appear in the variable. For example, **FIRSTSCIENCE [basic logic faust lisp dune]** returns the answer **[basic logic]**.

    1. firstscience list IS
    2. IF (list = [ ]) THEN [ ],
    3. IF ((FIRST list) ISA? science) THEN
         ((FIRST list) PRE (firstscience (REST list))),
    4. ELSE [ ].

Comments:
1. Header: function-name ("firstscience") and variable ("list").
2. Termination condition: If the list is empty, then return the empty list.
3. Conditional branch: If the first item of the list is a science title, then return the first item and put it in front of the result of the recursive call on the rest of the list.
4. Conditional branch: Else return the empty list.

Figure 2. **An iterative function.**

The following is an illustration of a SIMPLE function called **FIRST-SCIENCE** which takes a list of book catalog numbers and tests numbers less than and including the given number. The function returns an answer list that contains all science catalog numbers from the given number to the first nonscience number. The answer list contains the numbers in descending order. For example, **FIRST SCIENCE 7** returns the answer **[7 6]**, if number 5 is a nonscience title.

    1. firstscience num IS
    2. UNTIL (num = 0),
    3. IF (num ISA? science) THEN
         (ANSWER BECOMES (num POST ANSWER)),
    4. ELSE DONE,
    5. REPEAT WITH (num BECOMES (SUB1 num)).

Comments:
1. Header: function-name ("firstsciene") and variable ("num").
2. Loop termination: Test if the number has reached 0.
3. Conditional branch: If the number is a science title, then include it at the end of the answer-variable.
4. Conditional branch: Else eject from the function.
5. Repeat statement: Repeat the loop with the number decremented by 1.

---

tion. For the iterative function, a fifth line contained the repeat statement. Of all the dimensions varied, the difference between recursion and iteration was the most profound on the level of the actual code. As can be seen by comparing Figures 1 and 2, it affected every line of code but the first.

Differences on the list/number and forward/reverse dimensions involved simple term replacement. When working with a list, the constructs **FIRST**

< list > and **REST** < list > were needed. For numbers, the analogical constructs were a number variable < num > and **SUB1** < num >. The termination test was **list** = [] for the list and **num** = 0 for the numbers. Otherwise, the function remained unchanged when going from list to number.

The forward/reverse dimension only affected the answer accumulation. For recursion, the function word **PRE** signified forward accumulation, **POST** signified reverse accumulation. For iteration, **POST** signified forward accumulation, and **PRE** signified reverse accumulation. In both cases, the change from forward to reverse accumulation involved only changing one function word.

On the success/failure dimension, going from accumulation of success cases to accumulation of failure cases involved exchanging the then- and else-actions of Lines 3 and 4 of the code (see Figures 1 and 2) for each other. This was true in both iteration and recursion.

The eject/skip dimension required more subtle changes. In recursion, a function ejected the answer after the empty list, [], had been returned. A function skipped over cases when a recursive call was made without an accumulation action for the element the function currently was working on. For iteration, the function word **DONE** after a test made the program eject from a loop, while **ANSWER BECOMES ANSWER** was used for skipping the construct.

Instructions.   The instructions about how to write the recursive and iterative functions emphasized three aspects. First, a theoretical explanation of the recursive or iterative construct was given. Then, a template for writing the function was presented. Finally, the subjects obtained an example of a recursive or iterative function.[1]

Design.   There were two phases in the experiment, training and transfer. In each phase, some of the task dimensions were varied systematically. There were 16 conditions overall, obtained by having subjects transfer from programming any of number-iteration, number-recursion, list-iteration, or list-recursion in training to any of these in transfer. In each condition, there were two subjects. One subject did forward accumulation in training and reverse accumulation in transfer, while the other subject did the opposite.

Within each condition, subjects had to solve four tasks that were obtained by crossing the two task dimensions success/failure and eject/skip. The four tasks obtained in this fashion were given to the subjects in a fixed order. This order was kept constant over all subjects.

As an example, the subjects in the training condition recursion-list-forward obtained problems they had to solve recursively, by working on a list and by doing forward accumulation in the answer. Given this, the four problems they had to solve were ordered in the following way: First, subjects had to accumu-

---

[1] A transcript of the instructions can be obtained from the authors.

late successful instances while ejecting at the first positive nonaccumulation test (success-eject). The second task accumulated failure instances and had the same eject-condition (failure-eject). The third task also accumulated failure instances, but it worked through the whole list given, skipping the nonaccumulated elements (failure-skip). Finally, the fourth task accumulated successful instances and skipped nonaccumulated elements (success-skip). The same task sequence was employed in the transfer conditions.

Procedure. The participants in the experiment were Carnegie-Mellon University undergraduates who had little or no programming experience. The maximum programming experience allowed was one introductory programming course. The subjects were assigned randomly to conditions. Because it proved difficult to assess differences in programming proficiency prior to the experiment, we employed analyses of covariance (ANCOVAS) to control for differences in programming skills (see the Results section).

The whole experiment took place in two sessions over two consecutive days. In the first session, subjects were familiarized with the commands of the programming language and wrote four simple three-line function definitions which employed no recursive or looping structure. One of the tasks, for example, was to test if the first book title of a list belonged to a given category. This first session was identical for all subjects.

In the second session, the subjects obtained instructions according to the condition they were assigned. In the training phase, they learned either about recursion or iteration and then had to solve the four tasks described above. Each subject was given the first task he or she had to solve as an example. After completing the training phase, subjects went directly into the transfer phase. The procedure for the transfer phase was identical.

The experiment was self-paced. Subjects learned from an instruction booklet and did the tasks on a computer terminal. After typing in the code for a problem, the subjects could change, delete, or insert a line of code to correct errors they had noticed. After subjects signaled that they were done with a problem, their code was tested for correctness. If it was correct, the subjects got positive feedback; otherwise they got an error message and an example of a correct function which they could examine for as long as they wanted. Subjects did not necessarily have to write the same function as was presented to them, but most subjects chose to do so.

The learning criterion set for the subjects was to solve each of the four functions correctly. If they made a mistake, they had to rewrite the function. Subjects could solve the functions with the example present in their first pass. If they made any mistakes, the example function was taken away, and they had to solve the tasks on their own on their second pass. It took the subjects between 2 and 5 hr to finish the entire experiment. Nine subjects could not finish the experiment and gave up prematurely. The reasons for their failure ranged from genuine difficulties in understanding the task to fatigue and insufficient time to finish the experiment. The data of two subjects were discarded because they showed unusually high differences between the training and the transfer phase (> 30 min). One of the subjects was faster in the training phase, the other in the transfer phase. Both of the subjects were in the recursion-iteration transfer condition. Additional subjects were run to replace these 11 subjects.

2.2. Results

The data collected included the time for each line of code written and a record of the subjects' terminal interactions, including all editing operations. This section will present results about overall response times and response times on individual tasks. Response time for each problem was defined as the time between the presentation of the problem and the typing of the final function terminator (a period), including all the editing operations a subject might have performed. The overall response times were the sums of all the individual problem response times.

An ANCOVA was performed on the overall response times with programming construct (recursion-recursion, recursion-iteration, iteration-recursion, iteration-iteration) and datatype (list-list, list-number, number-list, number-number) as between-subjects factors and phase (training, transfer) as within-subjects factor. The response times in the definition phase were used as the covariate because the phase captured subject attributes such as typing speed and basic understanding of programming and the SIMPLE language, but not skills related to recursion or iteration. The product-moment correlation between the times of the definition and training phases was .83, between the definition and transfer phase, .76. The ANCOVA yielded a main effect for phase, $F(1, 16) = 11.28, p < .01$, and a significant interaction between construct and phase, $F(3, 16) = 3.5, p < .05$. The main effect indicates that there was a general speed-up from the training to the transfer phase; the interaction indicates that the speed-up was not uniform over the four groups that worked with a different sequence of constructs. All other effects or interactions were not significant. Because the factor datatype was not significant, $F(3, 15) = 1.26, p = .33$, further results will be discussed with respect to the four groups obtained by crossing recursion/iteration with the training and transfer phases.

Figure 3 presents the total time to criterion and mean number of incorrect functions in the training and transfer phases for the four training-transfer conditions recursion-recursion, recursion-iteration, iteration-recursion, and iteration-iteration. The data are the actual time taken, not adjusted for the ANCOVA. It is obvious that the recursion-iteration condition behaved differently from the other three conditions. Post hoc comparisons revealed significant differences below the 5% level for tests between recursion-iteration and the three other conditions with respect to the total time taken in the transfer

Figure 3. **Experiment 1: Total time to criterion in seconds (means) and number of errors (in parentheses).**

Condition	Definition	Training	Transfer	Training/Transfer Difference
Recursion-recursion	1305	1799	1125	674
	(3.9)	(3.6)	(1.4)	(2.2)
Recursion-iteration	1702	2031	2244	− 113
	(2.9)	(3.1)	(4.6)	(− 1.5)
Iteration-recursion	1013	1852	1162	690
	(2.9)	(4.4)	(1.5)	(2.9)
Iteration-iteration	882	1270	908	362
	(2.1)	(1.1)	(1.6)	(− .5)

Note. n = 8 for each cell.

Overall (*N* = 32)	1211	1738	1360	
	(2.9)	(3.0)	(2.3)	

phase. There were no significant differences between groups in the training phase.

The speed-up for the recursion-recursion and iteration-recursion conditions was significant, $t(7)$ = 3.23, p < .05, and $t(7)$ = 3.09, p < .05, respectively; the speed-up for the condition iteration-iteration fell just short of significance, $t(7)$ = 2.01, p = .085. Because this condition was the fastest overall, the lack of significance for iteration-iteration might have been due to a ceiling effect. The recursion-iteration condition actually slowed down, although not significantly, $t(7)$ = 1.02, p = .34. The difference in speed-up between the iteration-recursion and recursion-iteration conditions was significant, $t(14)$ = 2.91, p < .01.

The results reported so far were obtained through the manipulation of between-subjects factors. We now want to turn to the results of our within-subjects manipulation. Recall that within each condition and phase, subjects had to solve four problems that were given to them in a fixed order. These problems were success-eject (Task 1), failure-eject (Task 2), failure-skip (Task 3), and success-skip (Task 4).

Figure 4 shows the mean time to criterion for these four problems, split according to construct group and phase. An analysis of variance (ANOVA) on the total time to criterion for each task, with construct as a group factor and task as a within-subjects factor, revealed a significant main effect for task in the training phase, $F(3, 84)$ = 7.50, p < .001. The group factor and the interaction were not significant. Post hoc comparisons showed that the third task (failure-skip) took longer than the other three tasks (Task 1–Task 3: $t(31)$ = 3.15, p < .01; Task 2–Task 3: $t(31)$ = 2.82, p < .01; Task 4–Task 3: $t(31)$ =

Figure 4. **Experiment 1: Mean time to criterion for single tasks (in seconds).**

TRAINING (n = 8 for each cell)				
Task	Success-Eject	Failure-Eject	Failure-Skip	Success-Skip
Recursion-recursion	429	340	705	324
Recursion-iteration	441	468	650	459
Iteration-recursion	335	510	641	379
Iteration-iteration	361	346	369	194

TRANSFER (n = 8 for each cell)				
Task	Success-Eject	Failure-Eject	Failure-Skip	Success-Skip
Recursion-recursion	240	401	277	196
Recursion-iteration	452	620	684	489
Iteration-recursion	175	259	509	218
Iteration-iteration	293	245	192	178

5.65, $p < .001$). There were no significant differences among the other three tasks.

For the transfer phase, the analogous ANOVA revealed a significant main effect both for group and task, $F(3, 28) = 6.40$, $p < .01$, and $F(3, 84) = 3.02$, $p < .05$, respectively. The interaction was not significant. The group main effect was due to recursion-iteration, which took significantly longer to respond than the other groups (see Figure 3).

The task main effect was caused by Task 3 taking significantly longer than Task 1 and Task 4 (Task 1–Task 3: $t(31) = 2.16$, $p < .05$; Task 4–Task 3: $t(31) = 2.72$, $p < .05$), and Task 2 taking significantly longer than Task 4 ($t(31) = 2.74$, $p < .01$). Although the other t tests for differences between tasks were not significant, the results give the following rank ordering of time to criterion, longest to shortest response time: Task 3 (failure-skip), Task 2 (success-skip), Task 1 (success-eject), and Task 4 (failure-eject). This ordering, however, might be slightly misleading, for if the groups are collapsed according to the criterion "same or different construct from training to transfer," the interaction of group and task becomes significant, $F(3, 90) = 2.88$, $p < .05$. Figure 4 shows that only the groups that change constructs exhibited the longer response times with Task 3. Thus changing constructs seemed to aggravate the difficulty subjects have with Task 3.

We also analyzed the times to write each line of code, but these analyses did not provide any significant results. The data seemed to reflect some individual differences in solution style, but there did not seem to be any systematic relation to our task manipulations. For example, some subjects took very long to write the first line of code, whereas other subjects spent a large amount of time editing. We will try to point out some systematic relations between tasks and solution styles in Section 4.

The error data was analyzed in the same way as the response time data but did not yield any significant results. However, an analysis of the distribution of errors within the first four trials of each phase (i.e., the subjects' first tries at each of the problems) showed some interesting patterns. In the training phase, the subjects working with the recursive construct made significantly more errors than the subjects working with the iterative construct (32 vs. 18 errors; $\chi^2(1) = 6.43, p < .05$). Also, subjects made significantly more errors on Task 3 than on the other tasks (20 vs. an average of 10 errors; $\chi^2(1) = 11.68, p < .01$). For the transfer phase, the four groups distinguished themselves significantly only on Task 3. Here, the groups that did not change constructs made significantly less errors on their first try than the groups that did change constructs (4 vs. 13 errors, $\chi^2(1) = 10.42, p < .05$).

We classified errors into semantic versus other, where semantic refers to programs that were syntactically correct and free of typing errors but for some reason did not do the right operation. Overall, 68% of the errors were semantic, with 52% involving problems getting programs to skip or eject.

2.3. Discussion

There seem to be two major effects responsible for the results obtained in this experiment. One is the difficulty the recursion-iteration group had in the transfer phase. This group showed longer response times and higher error rates in the transfer phase than any other group. The second effect is the difficulty subjects had with the skip/eject dimension in the training phase which re-emerges if they had to change constructs in the transfer phase.

There are two obvious features we can try to use to explain the strange behavior in the recursion-iteration condition. One is the greater conceptual difficulty of recursion. Perhaps dealing with recursion in some way hurt subjects when they came to iteration. The second is the greater syntactic complexity of iteration. Perhaps, subjects were not prepared to deal with the syntactic complexity after recursion. Before elaborating on either of these explanations, we will consider the result of Experiment 2, which tried to equate the syntactic complexity of recursion and iteration.

Because doing the first skip-problem was so difficult, it is interesting to examine what exactly the subjects had to do to solve the problem of skipping an element. In the recursive condition, skipping involved introducing a second recursive call without an answer accumulation after the test for negative instances. Subjects had never seen a function with two recursive calls in this experiment, nor had they been told explicitly that this was possible at all. Given the success-eject example, it required some creative effort and a good understanding of recursion to come up with the correct solution without being given the example. Only 4 out of 16 subjects succeeded in doing so in the training phase, and 1 out of 8 in the transfer condition iteration-recursion.

For the iterative skipping construct, there were two immediate solutions for going from the example given (success-eject) to the skip case. One solution involved omitting the fourth line of code (**ELSE DONE**, see Figure 2). The loop would still work and would accumulate only successful cases. To get it to accumulate failure cases involved a second, rather idiosyncratic change. Because no negative test was available in SIMPLE and because there were only three categories, one could write two tests to accumulate the two categories other than the negated category. Only two subjects in the iterative conditions came up with this solution. Six more subjects actually generated the skipping construct that was used in the feedback given to the subjects, **ANSWER BECOMES ANSWER**, which left the answer variable unchanged if the test failed on a given iteration.

Given this interaction of the skip/eject and the recursion/iteration dimensions, it is a reasonable assumption that the subjects who changed constructs were exposed to most of the difficulties involved in the skip/eject dimension twice. There obviously is not much opportunity for transfer because changing constructs also altered the way the skip/eject dimension had to be written. Thus, exactly these subjects had difficulty with the failure-skip problem in transfer.

It should be emphasized that although subjects had to create something new to deal with the skip case, they were given sufficient information from which, in principle, they could create the program. They equally had to create something new to deal with the failure dimension and had much less difficulty. The basic point is that this dimension, which is concerned with flow of control, is harder to master.

It is also worth noting two null effects we obtained. First, there was no difference in the solution times between the iterative and recursive group in the training phase. In our view, the equal solution times seem to result from a trade-off between syntactic complexity in iteration and semantic difficulty in recursion. As noted before, subjects made more errors in their first pass at recursive functions compared to iterative functions. If we accept this as an indication that subjects had a harder time understanding recursion, the question becomes one of accounting for the comparatively long time it took for subjects to do the iterative problems. In order to give this account, it is necessary to look at the iterative construct at the level of code the subjects had to write. The iterative construct in SIMPLE is rather awkward and looks very complicated compared to a recursive SIMPLE function. This is reflected in the high number of edits with iteration (110 vs. 62 for recursion). If the number of edits is an indication of subjects' syntax problems, as opposed to comprehension problems, the trade-off hypothesis is supported: In recursion, subjects spent their time trying to understand what they are asked to do on the algorithmic level, while in iteration, subjects knew the algorithm but had a hard time getting the code right.

The second null effect deals with one of the other task dimensions tested in the experiment, list/number. This dimension was systematically varied because we expected it to be relevant to the subjects' representation of the programming constructs. However, it seems that the kind of problems we used were sufficiently easy to understand with both lists and numbers. There was no operation required that did any mathematical operation other than subtracting, and the lists had all very simple one-level structures that did not require any complex list structure manipulations.

3. EXPERIMENT 2: A CLOSER LOOK AT TRANSFER ISSUES

This experiment is essentially a replication of the previous one. Although the basic design remained the same as in the first experiment, a few changes were made to improve its shortcomings. This included changes to SIMPLE, such as simplifying the iterative construct so that the syntactic complications present in the first experiment were reduced. Additionally, the possibility of a negative test was introduced, which further simplified the task of writing the functions. To get better data on the subjects' learning, we made the task harder by changing the example problem given to the subjects. In the first experiment, the first task subjects had to solve was given to them as an example. Now, the example was a function that demonstrated the recursive or iterative construct but was not one of the experimental problems.

Two further changes were made to the design of the experiment. Because the first experiment showed that list/number did not influence the results and we did not know the impact of the forward/reverse factor, we exchanged these two dimensions in the design. In addition, the task sequence within each of the two phases, which had been kept constant in the first experiment, now was varied to test for differences between the individual tasks.

With respect to the forward/reverse dimension, we expected subjects to slow down if they changed constructs, because changing from recursion to iteration or vice versa elicits a counterintuitive change in the forward/reverse dimension on the code level. If the construct value changes, subjects have to use the same function word (**pre** or **post**) to change the order of accumulation. On the other hand, if the construct value remains the same, subjects have to change the function word. This is not an artifact of the SIMPLE language, but involves the difference between recursion and iteration. Thus, varying this dimension provides an additional test for subjects' understanding of the programming constructs.

3.1. Method

Programming Problems.   The tasks used were the same as in Experiment 1. Some features of SIMPLE were changed in order to simplify the language. The first two features dealt with the looping construct in iteration. The function word LOOP was used to indicate the beginning of an iterative loop, and the termination test for the loop was approximated as much as possible to the termination test for recursion. Manipulation of the eject/skip dimension was made substantially easier with the iterative construct. Skipping could now be achieved by simply doing nothing — the **ANSWER BECOMES ANSWER** construction of Experiment 1 became obsolete. The success/failure dimension could now be manipulated by exchanging only the function words **ISA?** and **ISNOTA?**. It was no longer necessary to exchange whole lines as in Experiment 1. Figure 5 shows an iterative function written in the new version of SIMPLE.

Instructions.   The instructions were nearly identical to those in Experiment 1, with some changes made to accommodate the new features mentioned above. In addition, subjects were no longer shown an example of a task they actually had to solve. Rather, this time the example was a sorting function that exhibited all the features of the problems in the experiment except for the negative test (see Figure 6).

Design.   The design was basically the same as the design of Experiment 1. There was a training and a transfer phase, and 16 between-subjects conditions. The only difference was the exchange of the factors list/number and forward/reverse. The factor forward/reverse now was crossed with recursion/iteration to obtain the four transfer conditions for each of the four training conditions. Thus, subjects transferred from programming any of forward-iteration, forward-recursion, reverse-iteration, or reverse-recursion in training to any of these in transfer. The factor list/number was always changed to the opposite of the training condition for each subject.

Within each of these conditions, subjects again were given the four problems obtained by crossing the factors success/failure and eject/skip. In this experiment, the sequence of the four tasks was varied according to the following criterion: In going from one task to the next, one and only one value on one of the two dimensions was changed. The eight sequences fitting this criterion were counterbalanced with the four between-subjects training conditions. The eight subjects in each of the four training conditions obtained a different task sequence. In the transfer phase, the four tasks for each subject were presented in the same sequence as in the training phase.

Procedure.   The procedure was identical to that of the first experiment except that the two sessions of the experiment were held either one or two days apart, rather than on consecutive days. In addition, subjects were now allowed to keep the example problem and were free to work with it until the end of the experiment.

Subjects were Carnegie-Mellon University undergraduates with little or no programming experience. It took the subjects between 3 and 5.5 hr to go through the whole experiment. Seven subjects could not finish the experiment or gave up prematurely. Additional subjects were run to replace them.

Figure 5. A new iterative function.

The following is an illustration of a SIMPLE function called **NOSCIENCE**, which takes a list of book catalog numbers and tests numbers less than and including the given number. The function returns an answer list that contains all nonscience catalog numbers less than and including the given number. The answer list contains the numbers in descending order. For example, NOSCIENCE 7 returns the answer [7 6 2 1], if numbers 3 to 5 are science titles.

      1. noscience num IS
      2. LOOP,
      3. IF (num = 0) THEN DONE,
      4. IF (num ISNOTA? science) THEN
           (ANSWER BECOMES (num POST ANSWER),
      5. REPEAT WITH (num BECOMES (SUB1 num)).

Comments:

1. Header: function-name ("nosciene") and variable ("num").
2. Start of loop.
3. Loop termination: If the number has reached 0, then eject.
4. Conditional: If the number is not a science title, then include it at the end of the answer-variable.
5. Repeat statement: Repeat the loop with the number decremented by 1.

Figure 6. The new example function.

The following is an illustration of a function called **SORT**, which sorts a list of book titles so that all science titles are at the beginning of the list. For example, Sort [dune faust zorba lisp] returns the answer [lisp zorba faust dune].

Recursive example:

      1. sort list IS
      2. IF (list = [ ]) THEN [ ],
      3. IF ((FIRST list) ISA? science)
           THEN ((FIRST list) PRE (SORT (REST list))),
      4. ELSE ((FIRST list) POST (SORT (REST list))).

Iterative example:

      1. sort list IS
      2. LOOP,
      3. IF (list = [ ]) THEN DONE,
      4. IF ((FIRST list) ISA? science)
           THEN (ANSWER BECOMES ((FIRST list) PRE ANSWER)),
      5. ELSE (ANSWER BECOMES ((FIRST list) POST ANSWER)),
      6. REPEAT WITH (list BECOMES (REST list)).

3.2. Results

The ANCOVA on the overall response times was done with programming construct and accumulation type (forward-forward, forward-reverse, reverse-forward, reverse-reverse) as between-subject factors and phase as within-subjects factor. The response times of the definition phase were taken as the covariate. The product-moment correlation between definition and training phase was .19, between definition and transfer phase, .26. These correlations are substantially lower than the ones obtained in Experiment 1. Two explanations for this can be offered. On the one hand, the problems in the training and transfer phases were more difficult to solve in Experiment 2 than in Experiment 1, while the definition phase remained the same in both experiments. On the other hand, the variance of the subject sample in Experiment 2 was lower than in Experiment 1. As in Experiment 1, analyses on error data did not produce any significant results.

The analysis of covariance on response times yielded a main effect for phase, $F(1, 16) = 27.48$, $p < .001$, and a significant interaction between phase and construct, $F(3, 16) = 4.14$, $p < .05$, signifying (as in Experiment 1), a general speed-up between training and transfer phase, except for the recursion-iteration condition. All other effects or interactions were not significant. Because the factor accumulation type was not significant, $F(3, 15) = 2.08$, $p = .15$, further results will be discussed in the same way as in Experiment 1, by refering to the four groups: recursion-recursion, recursion-iteration, iteration-recursion, and iteration-iteration.

Figure 7 presents the total time to criterion and mean number of errors for these four conditions. As in the first experiment, there were no significant differences between the conditions in the training phase. In the transfer phase, the following comparisons proved significant: recursion-recursion versus recursion-iteration, $t(14) = 5.67$, $p < .001$; recursion-recursion versus iteration-recursion, $t(14) = 2.40$, $p < .05$; and recursion-iteration versus iteration-iteration, $t(14) = 4.05$, $p < .001$.

It seems that changing constructs in the transfer phase had a more marked influence in Experiment 2. If analyzed in terms of whether groups changed constructs or not, that is, by collapsing the recursion-recursion and the iteration-iteration groups into a same-construct group, and the recursion-iteration and the iteration-recursion groups into a different-construct group, a t test of the transfer phase times was highly significant, $t(30) = 4.22$, $p < .001$. The group that changed constructs took longer overall to go through the transfer phase.

With respect to speed-up from the training to the transfer phase, the first experiment was nearly replicated: The conditions recursion-recursion, $t(7) = 8.55$, $p < .001$, iteration-recursion, $t(7) = 3.75$, $p < .01$, and iteration-iteration, $t(7) = 3.17$, $p < .05$, exhibited speed-up, while the recursion-iteration condition did not, $t(7) = -.27$, $p = .80$. Specifically, the difference

Figure 7. Experiment 2: Total time to criterion in seconds (means) and number of errors (in parentheses).

Condition	Definition	Training	Transfer	Training/Transfer Differences
Recursion-recursion	1193	2678	1225	1453
	(1.5)	(3.1)	(1.1)	(2.0)
Recursion-iteration	1512	2219	2329	−110
	(4.1)	(5.1)	(4.9)	(.2)
Iteration-recursion	1521	2893	1784	1109
	(4.2)	(4.1)	(4.2)	(−.1)
Iteration-iteration	1208	2385	1304	1081
	(2.9)	(3.6)	(2.9)	(.7)
Note. n = 8 for each cell.				
Overall (N = 32)	1358	2530	1608	
	(3.2)	(4.0)	(3.3)	

in speed-up between recursion-iteration and iteration-recursion was significant, $t(14) = 2.84, p < .05$.

Thus we have replicated the asymmetry in transfer despite efforts to equate syntactic complexity. It does appear that our changes to the iterative construct to make it of comparable syntactic complexity were successful. Subjects made almost the same number of edits with the iterative programs (158) as with the recursive programs (148).

We performed two ANOVAs for the within-subjects manipulation. One used task sequence as a factor, the other used task type. The first of these analyses, with task sequence as within-subjects factor and construct as between-subjects factor, showed a main effect of speed-up from the first task to the last task in both phases regardless of the construct subjects worked with (training: $F(3, 90) = 31.81, p < .001$; transfer: $F(3, 90) = 18.79, p < .001$). Although the group factor was not significant in the training phase analysis, it was in the transfer phase analysis, $F(1, 30) = 13.51, p < .001$, reflecting the fact that groups that changed constructs took longer on each of the four tasks than groups that did not change. The interaction was not significant in either phase.

In the first experiment, because task type and task sequence were confounded, it was unclear whether the two task dimensions manipulated within the sequence of tasks were contributing to the variance of the response times. In the current experiment, we separated these two factors. An ANOVA for each phase with group as between-subjects factor and the four task types as within-subjects factors revealed no significant effects. Thus it can be assumed that none of the four tasks was more or less difficult than any other. Furthermore, the task dimensions success/failure and skip/eject seemed to be equally difficult in recursion and iteration.

Although the four tasks were of equal difficulty, it is still possible that a change in the value of the dimensions skip/eject or success/failure could have caused difficulties. Recall that, as subjects progressed from one task to the next, only one of the binary values on the two dimensions skip/eject and success/failure was changed. Because there was no overall difference between the tasks, tests for sequence effects depending on changes on one of the two task dimensions could be performed. Half of the subjects changed values on the skip/eject dimensions from Task 1 to Task 2, while the other half changed values from Task 2 to Task 3. The same is true for the success/failure dimension. Task 1 and Task 4 had all subjects in the same condition with respect to experienced value change. Thus, the crucial differences should be found with response times to Tasks 2 and 3. Figure 8 presents the times to criterion according to this analysis.

The interaction between point of change for the skip/eject dimension (whether subjects changed on Task 2 or 3) and task sequence was significant (training: $F(1, 30) = 6.06, p < .05$; transfer: $F(1, 30) = 16.19, p < .001$). The main effect of point of change was not significant. The interaction is due to a significant difference in solution time on Task 2. The group that changed the value on the dimension skip/eject on Task 2 took longer on this task than the other group (training: $t(30) = 2.34, p < .05$; transfer: $t(30) = 2.39, p < .05$). In addition, only the change-on-2 group exhibited speed-up from Task 2 to Task 3 (training: $t(15) = 3.08, p < .01$; transfer: $t(15) = 2.79, p < .05$). The change-on-3 group actually slowed down, although significantly only in the transfer phase, $t(15) = 3.06, p < .01$.

In doing this analysis for the skip/eject dimension, we implicitly have done it for the success/failure dimension, too. Remember that changes on the success/failure dimension were complementary to changes on the skip/eject dimension: If one dimension changed its value from one task to the next, the other did not. Thus our results show that subjects were faster overall if the dimension success/failure changed from one task to the next, while they slowed down if this dimension did not change. Taken together, this implies that the skip/eject change was the more difficult factor.

As in the previous experiment, most of the errors could be classified as semantic (68%), and a large fraction of these (36%) involved errors with skip/eject. The next most common semantic error concerned confusions of success and failure (22%).

3.3. Discussion

The pattern of results obtained in Experiment 2 replicates the major outcomes of Experiment 1. Subjects had problems transferring from recursion to iteration and difficulty with the skip/eject dimension. The complexity of the iterative syntax is not the reason for the peculiar behavior of the recursion-

Figure 8. Experiment 2: Mean time to criterion for trial sequence (in seconds), with groups divided according to location of first change on the skip/eject dimension.

Trial	1	2	3	4
TRAINING				
Change2 (n = 16)	1159	657	413	359
Change3 (n = 16)	1116	465	534	384
TRANSFER				
Change2 (n = 16)	695	495	277	278
Change3 (n = 16)	637	278	440	214

Note. Change2 = Group changes value on the skip/eject dimension on Trial 2. Change3 = Group changes value on the skip/eject dimension on Trial 3.

iteration group, as this syntax was simplified in Experiment 2. As a matter of fact, there is nothing in the data of the second experiment that hints at an explanation for the difficulty experienced by this group.

To return to our original questions, this experiment showed that subjects actually can acquire the skill of writing recursive functions within a few hours of instruction, thus confirming the result of Anzai and Uesato (1982). In addition, it was shown that subjects could acquire the recursive construct as easily as they acquired the supposedly more natural iterative construct. When subjects did learn both constructs, the sequence of acquisition was crucial. When the subjects learned iteration first, and transferred to recursion, their speed-up was significant. When they started with recursion, there was no speed-up after they were transferred to iteration.

The claim of Anzai and Uesato that knowing iteration facilitates learning recursion is not really supported by these results. Our control group, which practiced recursion only, arrived at the same performance level in the second phase as did the iteration/recursion group. Therefore, all that can be said about the effect of learning iteration before learning recursion is that it seems to be as effective as increased practice on recursion itself. This, of course, does not change the pedagogical implication that it is beneficial to learn iteration before learning recursion.

In order to understand the peculiar behavior of the recursion-iteration group, it is important to look at the kind of problem solving the subjects actually were doing in this experiment. As Pirolli and Anderson (1985) showed, if the instructional environment permits, subjects generally solve their first recursive problems by analogy to examples. The instructions given in this experiment did provide an example and so the analogy process was available. Subjects' informal comments suggested they did make a good deal of use of analogy to the example. It is possible that they solved the recursive problems by analogizing from the surface structure of the example without really understanding how it worked.

If this were true, we could hypothesize that the recursion-iteration subjects did not really learn anything about the control construct in the training phase. Rather, they learned a set of surface templates by analogy. If subjects did not understand flow of control in recursion, they would have no basis for any transfer to a new construct. Therefore, the null transfer from recursion to iteration may be because subjects actually had to learn the iterative construct in the transfer phase as if they had had no previous experience with the task. This explanation could account for the lack of speed-up in our recursion-iteration subjects. In addition, it fits in with the fact that their error data in the transfer phase is not significantly different from the error data of subjects who learn iteration in the training phase.

Our third initial question was how other factors influence the acquisition of control constructs. Of the task dimensions we varied, only the skip/eject dimension proved to have any influence. Changing on this dimension was difficult and interacted with the recursion/iteration dimension. Although we cannot be sure if this is an artifact of our particular problems and/or programming language, it is interesting to note that the skip/eject dimension is the one dimension besides recursion/iteration that most influences flow of control.

4. PROTOCOL ANALYSES

In order to test our speculations about subjects' representations and strategies, we collected protocols of four subjects in the recursion-iteration and iteration-recursion conditions. In taking the protocols, the procedures of Experiment 2 were followed. The only difference was that the experimenter stayed in the room while the subjects solved the problems. His task was to prompt the subjects if they kept quiet for a long period of time. Otherwise, he did not interfere with the subjects' behavior. The experimenter's presence had one important consequence, however. Although subjects in Experiment 2 were told they could ask the experimenter for help if they did not understand the instructions or the feedback given to them, they hardly ever did so. The protocol subjects, on the other hand, were much more likely to ask questions. In these cases, the experimenter reiterated the information given in the instruction until the subjects decided that they had received a satisfactory answer. As a result, the protocol subjects showed less random behavior than some subjects in Experiment 2 (i.e., they never copied a previous function to solve the next problem, and they never went right to the feedback without trying to solve the problem).

There were eight protocols overall, four from subjects in the recursion-iteration condition (Subjects 1 to 4) and four from subjects in the iteration-recursion condition (Subjects 5 to 8). All subjects worked with lists in the training phase and with numbers in the transfer phase. A comparison with the data of Experiment 2 shows that all iteration-recursion subjects approximated the behavior of the subjects in the same condition of Experiment 2. Mixed results were obtained with the recursion-iteration subjects. One subject (S4) slowed down, while another one (S1) exhibited a slight speed-up. The other two subjects (S2 and S3) did not finish the transfer part of the experiment, although they finished their third and fourth trials, respectively, in the transfer phase. In both cases, subjects were unwilling to cooperate further due to fatigue. All subjects in the recursion-iteration condition took longer overall than would have been expected from Experiment 2.

There are two reasons why we did not exclude Subjects 2 and 3 from the analysis. First, except for taking longer, they did not exhibit any obvious behavior differing from that of Subjects 1 and 4. Second, we concentrated our analysis of the protocols on the first four problems in each phase. It became clear from the protocols that subjects had established their problem-solving strategy at about the third or fourth trial, as discussed in the following section.

4.1. General Characteristics of the Protocols

The protocols of both groups show some common characteristics supporting the findings of Anderson, Farrell, and Sauers (1984) in their analyses of protocols from subjects learning to program in LISP. In general, the knowledge subjects had acquired prior to the training phase of the experiment was not sufficient to allow them to solve the programming problems directly. The knowledge consisted of three parts: practice in the basic commands of the SIMPLE language; instruction about the construct, including a template showing the structure of the resulting function; and an example. When starting out, the main information that was used was the example that was given with the instructions. Subjects never made any reference to the template and frequently did not remember basic SIMPLE commands, the knowledge of which they had demonstrated earlier.

As subjects went through the training phase, they usually became more accurate and faster in solving the problems. After two or three exposures to the feedback consisting of correct functions, subjects were able to keep these correct functions in working memory and to adjust them to the given problem. References to the example were made only for syntactical questions such as parenthesization and argument ordering.

For the most part, errors committed after Problem 3 were mere lapses, (e.g., forgetting a comma or mistyping a word) or working memory failures (e.g., misremembering the previous function and falsely copying it). Subjects seemed to have developed a successful procedure for doing the problems at that point.

This general characterization of the training phase also holds for the transfer phase. That is, subjects showed reliance on the example in Trial 1, developed a solution procedure over Trials 2 and 3, and finally made a smooth application of this procedure.

Differences in the protocols obtained from the recursion-iteration and iteration-recursion groups show that subjects differ in their use of the example, and, more generally, in the way they approach the problem-solving process. These differences are examined in detail in the following section. Although such protocol evidence is necessarily opportunistic, we would like to argue that these dissimilarities account for the observed performance differences between the groups in the transfer phase. This account will schematize the protocols, and thus make them look more similar than they really are, but we feel that it captures the major differences that can be detected between the two groups. In order to support the hypothesis about different solution strategies given in the next section, we later present some quantitative analyses about utterances in the protocols which support our account.

4.2. Transferring From Recursion to Iteration

A typical solution process in the training phase was given by Subject S4. When solving his first problem, the subject was able to map the first three lines of code from the example to his solution. Although he was not very verbal about the mapping process, he took considerably more time to write the first three lines of code than would be necessary for straightforward copying. Rather, he tried to check each line of the example with regard to its relevance to the problem specification. He was able to convince himself that he could take over the first three lines of code without modification. This solution process broke down for the fourth line of code. There, the subject clearly stated what he had to do — skip the nonscience elements — but he also remarked that he did not know how to do it. Because the example did not provide a clue here, the subject finally tried a construction that he did not expect to work.

The reliance on the example varied markedly between subjects, as shown by other protocols from subjects in this group. One subject (S1) pursued a stubborn word-by-word mapping from the example to the problem. She went through several iterations of trying to understand the example and mapping it to the problem. Although she pursued a variety of dead ends, she finally succeeded in getting the function right by finding a mapping for each piece of code in the example. Another subject (S3) virtually ignored the example because she was convinced that she did not understand it. She tried to solve the problem by applying the knowledge she extracted out of the instructions. Although she did not succeed in solving the problem in this way, she maintained this strategy throughout the training phase. Her improvement was due to repeated exposures to the correct functions which she could approximate better after each trial.

What unites these different ways of using example and feedback is the fact that none of the subjects in this group demonstrated any sign of abstracting information about the flow of control from the example and/or the problem solutions. Their reasoning remained at the surface level of actual code; their strategy could be characterized as a form of means–ends analysis. Subjects tried to detect the difference between the problem and the example or the previous solution shown to them and then tried to reduce this difference doing a local repair consisting of exchanging a small part of the code.

What the subjects seemed to take away from the training phase was a strategy that proved reasonably effective, although it neither required nor created an understanding of the construct. Most subjects initially used the same approach in the transfer phase. Three of the four subjects tried to solve the first iteration problem by mapping from the example. Because the example was a function working on lists and the subjects now had to work with numbers, none of the lines, except for the loop statement, could be copied directly. Although all subjects failed to write this first problem correctly, they seemed to grasp the iterative control structure much better than the recursive structure once they received feedback.

In order to provide a demonstration of how subjects neglected consideration of an algorithm and stuck to the code when doing the iterative problems, Figure 9 gives an excerpt from the protocol of S1 coding the second problem in the transfer phase. It illustrates how the subject used the example and her memory of the previous problem to do a line-by-line generation of the code, without being able to devise a working algorithm before she started coding. Although the subject demonstrated an intuitive understanding of the control structure, she still relied on the step-by-step approach carried over from the training phase. Each line of code was treated as a separate entity, without consideration of the relationship between the code and the control structure. The claim is made here that this coding strategy is typical for the subjects in this group. After presenting an analysis for the iteration-recursion group, more quantitative evidence will be presented to support this claim.

4.3. Transferring From Iteration to Recursion

Subjects starting out with iteration also made heavy use of the example in the first problem. With increasing experience, the subjects became more independent of the example and used it mostly for reference to syntax problems. A good example is Subject S6 doing the second problem in the training phase. She started out immediately writing the first two lines, then went through the loop mentally before she wrote the next line. She made the decision which test to use and wondered how to accumulate and where to put the repeat statement. Only then did she start writing out code. All this was done without reference to the example, which led her to write a false repeat statement, the only mistake in her code.

Figure 9. **Protocol excerpt: Subject 1, transfer phase, Trial 2.**

Problem Statement:
Write a function that takes a science ID as a variable. The function should return an answer list that contains all science IDs less than and including the variable. Answer list IDs should be in descending order.

---

1. "The first thing that we're doing here is function, and then the number . . ."
   Writes: func num is
        loop,
2. "and then we have our all purpose if . . ."
   Writes: if (num = 0) then done,
3. "Alright, if number is a science — if the number, yes, is a science then the answer becomes number, and while I'm in descending order, that would be post answer — yes I think."
4. "If number, now number is a function, right. So, number — I'm not sure about the syntax of this. Does it have to have . . . take an argument? I don't know. Am I supposed to have a paren there? I don't think so."
5. "Then — if the number is a science then answer becomes — that would be the number — . . . so it's number which is the function, and then pre answer."
6. "So is it pre or post? Pre."
7. "Alright, I'm rereading the instructions. . . . Answer becomes the number displayed in front of the answer. I don't really understand all that, but I'm going to continue."
   Writes: if (num isa? science) then (answer becomes (num pre answer))),
8. "Now I have to do the sub1. No, no I need an else. If the number is not a science, that's my else."
9. "Now at the last time at this point I just said done."
10. (Rereading the instructions) "I wonder if this means it contains only science IDs. Alright, so I can't say else done, I have to say take out the first number, which would be first num, that would be answer becomes . . ."
11. "Alright, the answer becomes. . . . Now this one, the example gives everything back. I don't want it to give everything back. I want it to take that out."
12. "Now I'm not sure if this is gonna do that. If the number is a science then — answer becomes and is displayed — that's very circular. Else, if it is not a science, you extract it."
    Writes: else (answer becomes (first num))
13. "Now I am at the repeat. At this point, I've forgotten how to write this, but I want to tell the number, and I'm hoping this is right. Here I use sub1. So I am telling it to subtract number. The parens are wrong. I didn't put sub1 in its parens."
14. "Now . . .," (rereading the instructions) "I think I'm supposed to have — I wonder if I'm supposed to have pre answer in there. It doesn't say that in the example."
15. "I don't know how these things are arranged. We are assuming that these things in the catalog are arranged in descending order. If they are, this will skip over anything that is bigger. I expect it would go look for the next sub1. Well, I'm not going to worry about that."
17. "Repeat — now I have copied that pretty exactly, but I don't have any idea if this is going to work. I think this is just another approximation, so I'm gonna tell it to stop."
    Writes: repeat with (num becomes (sub1 num))

The other subjects in this group showed the same kind of planning behavior, with decreasing reliance on the example. Some of the subjects actually committed syntactic mistakes because they did not check the example for the right application of such statements as **REPEAT WITH . . .** or **ANSWER BECOMES . . . .**

There is some evidence that subjects carried over their problem-solving strategy into the transfer phase. The subjects in this condition seemed to use planning instead of means–ends transformation of the example during the transfer phase. The following quotation from S5's protocol illustrates this strategy transfer:

> We don't need a loop command here, we need an "if." We're gonna analyze from v down, we're gonna check to see if v equals 0 — yeah, you can check for v equals 0.

> Let's see, you get to something that is a science [reading the instructions]. This program is gonna end when you hit the first science ID. How do I end this program? It's gonna end when you reach either a science or 0.

> I could make a list from v to the first science. If it isn't a science then you can add it in. If it's not, you don't. I'll take a wild stab at "if v isnota?" But you need something if v is 0. What if v equals 1? No that makes sense, I think. If v equals 0, then nothing."

When making these comments, the subject had only written the header line of the function. He sketched the algorithm, and only afterwards went on coding the function. Although he did not write a correct function, his strategy carried over to subsequent problems.

As will be discussed in the next section, there is no evidence that the understanding of recursion was better for this group than for the other group. It seems that the groups distinguished themselves mainly in the strategy they were using.

4.4. Quantitative Analyses

In order to substantiate the claims made in the previous sections, we looked for more quantitative indicators in the protocols that would help support our hypotheses. There are two major claims:

1. The groups use different strategies in solving the programming problems.
2. The groups acquire essentially the same mental models of the constructs.

We characterized the different strategies as means–ends analysis involving a line-by-line mapping for the recursion-iteration group and planning for the iteration-recursion group. Apart from the anecdotal evidence in the protocols, one important indicator of this strategy difference should be the number of references subjects made to the example and the feedback (the correct functions). We would expect the recursion-iteration group to make substantially more use of these knowledge sources, because subjects did not rely on the control structure of the problems. Their mapping needed the feedback or the example as a point of departure. On the other hand, the iteration-recursion group needed the example primarily to check for syntactic errors. However, they also could use the instructions for this purpose. Furthermore, syntactic checking was not done very frequently, probably because the subjects had enough practice with the expressions they had to use. For these reasons, the recursion-iteration group should show more references to the example than the iteration-recursion group. Figure 10 shows the number of references made by both groups in the training and transfer phase. Only the first four trials in each phase have been considered because the subjects had learned the important features of the problems. An ANOVA with group as between-factor and phase and trial sequence as within-factors revealed that the only significant effect was the effect of sequence, $F(3, 18) = 10.81$, $p < .001$. Not surprisingly, most references occurred in the first trial in both phases. Although the test is not powerful enough to detect a significant difference with only four subjects in each group, $F(1, 6) = 2.16$, $p < .2$, the recursion-iteration group seemed to make more references to the example regardless of the phase. This would support our original conjectures.

Finally, we can look at one more indicator in order to find out about the subjects' representation of the control structures. This is the number of references to the control structure (loop or recursive call). As Figure 11 shows, the subjects did not distinguish themselves in the number of references over the first four trials in each phase. Again, only the trial sequence effect was significant in the ANOVA, $F(3, 18) = 7.89$, $p < .01$. This time, however, no trend is visible in the data, except for the fact that there were more references to the recursive control structure than to the iterative structure in both groups, $F(1, 6) = 3.99$, $p < .1$.

In order to understand subjects' representation of the control structure, it is not enough to consider how often they mentioned something about the structure. It is equally important to find out what exactly subjects were saying about their notion of control. Figures 12 and 13 give some sample comments from subjects in the two groups. With the iterative construct (Figure 12), all of the subjects' utterances were fairly straightforward. Subjects usually mentioned that they needed a **REPEAT** statement, and they became more confident about the loop structure as they proceeded through the experiment. There was no case in which their utterances about iteration revealed a misconception about what was going on in the program.

With the recursive construct, the picture looks different. None of the subjects volunteered a comment that unequivocally showed an understanding of recur-

Figure 10. **Number of references to the example function.**

Condition	Recursion-Iteration	Iteration-Recursion
TRAINING (n = 4 for each cell)		
Trial 1	17	8
Trial 2	10	0
Trial 3	3	0
Trial 4	3	0
Total	33	8
TRANSFER (n = 4 for each cell)		
Trial 1	13	6
Trial 2	6	1
Trial 3	5	0
Trial 4	2	0
Total	26	7

Figure 11. **Number of references to the control construct.**

Condition	Recursion-Iteration	Iteration-Recursion
TRAINING (n = 4 for each cell)		
Trial 1	6	5
Trial 2	4	1
Trial 3	4	2
Trial 4	0	0
Total	14	8
TRANSFER (n = 4 for each cell)		
Trial 1	3	6
Trial 2	1	4
Trial 3	2	1
Trial 4	1	1
Total	7	12

Figure 12. **Sample utterances about control structures: Iteration.**

Subject 1, Trial 1, Transfer:
"I have just said 'rest list.' Now, if the first list is a science, then it's at the beginning. And here I told it to stop if the first is not a science. So, now I want it to iterate, repeat with—"
Subject 1, Trial 4, Transfer:
"And then we have our repeat . . . Alright, that tells it to continue . . ."
Subject 4, Trial 2, Transfer:
"If I do an 'if' and then an 'else' and then another 'then,' is it going to include all—oh wait, there's also a 'repeat with.' "
Subject 5, Trial 3, Transfer:
"I have to reassign the answer, and 'x becomes' will be in the repeat loop. I'm gonna do repeat to chop it off."

Figure 13. **Sample utterances about control structures: Recursion.**

Subject 1, Trial 1, Training:
"Now, the trouble with 'rest list' — wait a minute, 'rest list' says it also gives the rest of the list. So maybe I don't want that there. I have to have that there, otherwise it will stop, it won't be recursive. 'Pre first list' — I wonder if what I want is just 'pre func rest list.' I never did understand what that meant."

Subject 1, Trial 3, Training:
"I want it to list the isnota's. Take a look at the rest of the list, exercise function, and put this at the beginning, so . . ."
Writes: **then ((first list) pre (func (rest list)))**,
"else — now, if the first thing is not, is a science, then — if the first item in the list is not a science, put it first; however, if it is a science, I don't want that 'post,' what I want is exercise your function on the rest of the list. . . . So, do I want 'func rest list?' If the first line is not a science, then take it out, look at the rest of the list, exercise your function, and put this at the beginning. If it is a science, then look at the rest of the list and exercise your function. You don't want 'post,' no, no, no, so I think it's just . . ."
Writes: **else (func (rest list))**.

Subject 2, Trial 1, Training:
(looking at the example function "sort")
"I thought sort was a function in the language. Is sort already in there?"

Subject 2, Trial 2, Training:
"I need to use the function that I declared in the problem somewhere."

Subject 4, Trial 1, Training:
"If it's a science, then I'm gonna do like the example, put it in front and then continue 'funcing' it with the rest of the list."

Subject 5, Trial 1, Transfer:
"Wait, this is supposed to be recursive, I should have 'function v' in there somewhere. . . . I need to recur in there somewhere, I'm not gonna use 'answer becomes.' "

Subject 6, Trial 1, Transfer:
"Okay, then I put x before 'function sub1 x' — but is that gonna put me back up where 'sort x' is?"

Subject 8, Trial 2, Transfer:
"If 'num isnota? science,' it would take 'pre func sub1 num,' so it would go one lower, and go through the function again, and put that not-a-science before. I think that's the basic idea, but I'm not sure if it's gonna work."

---

sion. As Figure 13 demonstrates, the majority of utterances about recursion showed only a superficial level of understanding or a complete misconception. All comments were made by the subjects in the course of their problem solving. The subjects usually did not reflect on their understanding of the construct and were not asked about it. One subject (S1), however, volunteered the following statement about her understanding of recursion after she had correctly solved all problems in the training phase:

```
Code: func list is
      ......,
      if (first list) isa? science then [],
      else ((first list) pre (func (rest list))).
```

I never did understand recursion. . . . If it's not a science, take it out, look at the rest of the list, and then I would think it would see this word, func, and it would say, "hey, you never told me what func is — you mentioned it up here in Line 1, but you never have spelled anything out."

Taken together, the evidence shows that subjects do not develop a correct representation of recursion. However, over the course of solving the problems, they can develop a working model that incorporates the notion of repeating some action over and over. This, of course, is the misrepresentation of recursion as a loop structure that was observed by Kahney and Eisenstadt (1982) and Kurland and Pea (1983).

5. GENERAL DISCUSSION

In this study, we established that there is asymmetric transfer between the acquisition of recursive and iterative control structures. Although there is positive transfer from iteration to recursion, there is no transfer from recursion to iteration. The protocol studies pointed out that this asymmetry may be due to differences in the solution strategies between subjects in the iteration-recursion and recursion-iteration conditions. Our subjects had further difficulties with the skip/eject dimension which also is closely related to flow of control.

With the following account of the differences in the solution processes between the two groups, we try to provide an explanation for the observed differences in solution times. The iteration-recursion group was able to extract the idea of a general notion of control in the training phase. When subjects went into the transfer phase, they were able to accommodate the recursive function to the representation of flow of control they had developed. Their previous experience with the task dimensions made it easier to distinguish the parts of recursive code responsible for the different actions to be taken. In particular, they were able to recognize the recursive call as a type of repeat statement. This account by no means presupposes that the subjects actually understood recursion. However, looking at a function in terms of flow of control enabled subjects to plan a solution. This strategy proved more effective than the one the recursion-iteration subjects settled on.

The recursion-iteration group started out by solving the problems using means–ends analysis. Subjects took the example and tried to match it line-by-line to the problem specification. With the constant feedback given after incorrect solutions, this amounted in the end to a memory task. If the relevant pieces of code could be remembered correctly, these subjects were guaranteed a solution. Subjects never needed to look at the function as a whole; they could concentrate on the small differences between the skip/eject or success/failure dimensions. And even if they took the whole function into account, it was unlikely that they followed the flow of control through the recursive function. When entering the transfer phase, these subjects continued to use this strategy. They were not able to plan their functions on the level of the algorithm, because they had not acquired any representation of flow of control. Rather, they relied on the means–ends analysis method for local fixes. Because the surface form of the iterative code was sufficiently different from the recursive code, there was not much opportunity for transfer. Therefore, subjects had to learn how to deal with the new construct both without benefiting from their previous problem solving and with an inappropriate learning strategy.

Clearly, subjects do have difficulty with concepts involving flow of control. In either iteration or recursion, in training or transfer, subjects had difficulty mastering the skip/eject dimension. These results reinforce the importance of having adequate mental models of programs and, in particular, flow of control for mastering programming. Having a model of iteration enabled subjects to see how to transfer their training knowledge to recursion. In contrast, subjects studying recursive programs without the aid of such models were overwhelmed by the surface differences between iteration and recursion.

In general, we speculate it is good to teach iterative programming before recursive programming for students who have had no prior programming experience with either construct. Students can develop mental models of iterative procedures relatively easily. These mental models can serve as the basis for understanding recursive procedures — although not in the simple way our subjects did. Rather, recursive procedures can be understood in terms of a procedure looping over a stack of function calls. This is the copy model advanced by Kahney and Eisenstadt (1982).

It is informative to compare the results of our experiments with other studies of how people learn to program (Anderson et al., 1984; Pirolli & Anderson, 1985). All accounts emphasize the importance of analogical reasoning as a basis for learning to program. We characterized this process as a complex mapping procedure which goes beyond mere copying of an example. Although it has not been the purpose of this article to discuss analogical reasoning as a basic mechanism of skill acquisition (see Carbonnell, 1983; Gentner, 1983; Gick & Holyoak, 1980, 1983; Rumelhart & Norman, 1981), it should be noted that our experiments demonstrated the benefits as well as the limitations of the use of analogies. The benefits were clear in cases in which the subjects had developed an adequate, if sometimes incorrect, mental model of the programming construct. Here, subjects could make use of the example to write syntactically correct code. In accordance with previous studies, these subjects also demonstrated great savings in solution time when going from the first problem to the second. In addition, these subjects showed less reliance on the example in subsequent problems. On the other hand, the subjects who did not develop an adequate mental model of the programming construct used a mapping strategy that depended heavily on the surface features of the example through both phases of the experiment. As we have shown, this second group of subjects showed no benefit of training in the transfer condition, although the first group did. This extends the observations of Pirolli and Anderson (1985), who showed that successful learning of recursion depended on an adequate mental model. We now know that possessing an adequate mental model is also critical to the transfer of learning between recursion and iteration.

In conclusion, the reason for programming novices' difficulty in understanding flow of control lies in their inability to develop adequate mental models of the task. The importance of mental models for the understanding of human skill acquisition is currently a well-represented research topic in cognitive science (see Gentner & Stevens, 1983). The preceding account tried to illustrate some of the cognitive processes underlying the formation of mental models of flow of control in programming, especially in relationship to the control dimensions of our tasks, recursion and iteration. We could demonstrate that these task variables influenced the development of mental models of our subjects.

Acknowledgments. We thank Peter Pirolli for his help in designing the programming tasks and for making his instructions on recursion and iteration available to us.

Support. This research is supported by contract N00014-84-K-0064 from the Office of Naval Research.

REFERENCES

Anderson, J. R., Farrell, R., & Sauers, R. (1984). Learning to program in LISP. *Cognitive Science, 8,* 87–129.

Anzai, Y., & Uesato, Y. (1982). Learning recursive procedures by middleschool children. *Proceedings of the Fourth Annual Conference of the Cognitive Science Society,* 100–102.

Carbonnell, J. G. (1983). Learning by analogy: Formulating and generalizing plans from past experience. In R. S. Michalski, J. G. Carbonnell, & T. M. Mitchell (Eds.), *Machine learning — An artificial intelligence approach* (pp. 137–162). Palo Alto, CA: Tioga Publishing.

Gentner, D. (1983). Structure-mapping: A theoretical framework for analogy. *Cognitive Science, 7,* 155–170.

Gentner, D., & Stevens, A. L. (Eds.). (1983). *Mental models.* Hillsdale, NJ: Lawrence Erlbaum Associates, Inc.

Gick, M. L., & Holyoak, K. J. (1980). Analogical problem solving. *Cognitive Psychology, 12,* 306–355.

Gick, M. L., & Holyoak, K. J. (1983). Schema induction and analogical transfer. *Cognitive Psychology, 15,* 1–38.

Kahney, H., & Eisenstadt, M. (1982). Programmers' mental models of their programming tasks: The interaction of real world knowledge and programming knowledge. *Proceedings of the Fourth Annual Conference of the Cognitive Science Society,* 143–145.

Kurland, D. M., & Pea, R. D. (1983). Children's mental models of recursive LOGO programs. *Proceedings of the Fifth Annual Conference of the Cognitive Science Society,* 1–5.

Pirolli, P., & Anderson, J. R. (1985). The role of learning from examples in the acquisition of recursive programming skills. *Canadian Journal of Psychology, 39,* 240–272.

Rumelhart, D. E., & Norman, D. A. (1981). Analogical processes in learning. In J. R. Anderson (Ed.), *Cognitive skills and their acquisition* (pp. 335–360). Hillsdale, NJ: Lawrence Erlbaum Associates, Inc.

Shrager, J., & Pirolli, P. L. (1983). *SIMPLE: A simple language for research in programmer psychology* [Computer program]. Pittsburgh, PA: Carnegie-Mellon University, Department of Psychology.

13
CONDITIONS OF LEARNING
IN NOVICE PROGRAMMERS*

D. N. PERKINS
CHRIS HANCOCK
RENEE HOBBS
FAY MARTIN
REBECCA SIMMONS
Educational Technology Center
Harvard University

ABSTRACT

Under normal instructional circumstances, some youngsters learn programming in BASIC or LOGO much better than others. Clinical investigations of novice programmers suggest that this happens in part because different students bring different patterns of learning to the programming context. Many students disengage from the task whenever trouble occurs, neglect to track closely what their programs do by reading back the code as they write it, try to repair buggy programs by haphazardly tinkering with the code, or have difficulty breaking problems down into parts suitable for separate chunks of code. Such problems interfere with students making the best of their own learning capabilities: students often invent programming plans that go beyond what they have been taught directly. Instruction designed to foster better learning practices could help students to acquire a repertoire of programming skills, perhaps with spinoffs having to do with "learning to learn."

Learning to program with some competence in languages like BASIC or LOGO poses a daunting challenge to many youngsters. Teachers of programming in primary and secondary schools frequently comment on the startlingly different rates at which children progress. "Johnny can do anything, but Ralph just can't seem to get the hang of it." A series of clinical studies of young programmers conducted in association with the Educational Technology Center at the Harvard

* The research reported here was conducted at the Educational Technology Center, based at the Harvard Graduate School of Education, and operating with support from the National Institute of Education. The ideas expressed here do not necessarily represent the opinions or policies of the supporting agency.

Graduate School of Education confirms this picture. The range of competence is indeed striking, the natural question is, "Why?"

Several factors may contribute to this phenomenon, including the limited instruction that students receive. In schools with only a few computers, students commonly use a machine for only one or two hours a week. Furthermore, many teachers of programming in primary and secondary school are new to the enterprise, and are having to find their own way in a difficult, and sometimes unwelcome, new field. Finally, programming as a recent subject area has a relatively undeveloped pedagogy, especially at the primary and secondary levels. In such circumstances, student achievement naturally sprawls across a wide range depending on such variables as intelligence, flair for computing specifically, presence of a computer in the home that allows more "hands on" learning, and so on.

Although these factors are important, they do not penetrate very deeply into the learning processes of young programmers. The issue is to identify what the most successful learners do that helps them to learn, in contrast to those who lag behind. Definitive answers to this question would require a massive program of research. However, our clinical studies allow some tentative conclusions about patterns in the behavior and attitudes of novice programmers that favor progress. Not only do these patterns help in understanding why some learn more than others but they also offer a guide to remaking instruction. The attitudes and behaviors that help students to learn might be directly encouraged by the teacher and the instructional program. We will return to this point.

A NOTE ON METHODOLOGY

Although the aim of this article is not to present a technical account of our research, we offer this brief note on our subjects and methods. Observations of two subject populations inform the perspective presented here. At one high school, we have been observing students from mixed-grade introductory BASIC classes that meet for one period per day. The period is devoted both to classroom discussion and to hands-on programming work. At an elementary school we have been working with LOGO students from the fourth, fifth, and sixth grades. These students learn LOGO less formally than the high-school BASIC students. There are two computers at the back of the classroom, and groups of two or three youngsters work at each computer while the rest of the class carries on with other subjects. At both of these sites, there was an initial stage in which we observed students as they worked in the classroom, after which we began to see students individually outside the classroom setting. In this latter stage we have observed approximately thirty BASIC students and twenty-five LOGO students.

The method of observation is a structured clinical one. An experimenter sits with a student and presents a programming problem. The experimenter observes as the student attempts to solve the problem, probing occasionally for explanations of the student's ideas and intentions. When the student encounters substantial difficulty, the experimenter intervenes with prompts designed both to help the student and to disclose the nature of the difficulty. Working within general guidelines, the experimenter tries to devise a revealing probe, responsive to the student's particular situation. The experimenter takes notes on what the student says and types and how the computer responds; in addition the session is audio tape-recorded. Later, a rough transcription is prepared, reflecting both the notes and the tape. The transcription is examined to track the thinking of the student and interpret the nature of the difficulties the student encountered.

For a simple example of a probe, suppose a student has already described a dilemma in a way that clearly calls for a FOR loop, but the student has not retrieved that construct. The experimenter might ask, "Can you think of any instruction you know that might help with that?" If this yields nothing, the experimenter might go on to suggest, "Why don't you try a FOR loop?" Suppose the student then proceeds to apply a FOR loop correctly: in that case one has learned that the student has some ability to use the FOR loop construct but a problem with retrieving it on appropriate occasions. From a number of such clinical interviews, a map of typical difficulties is emerging.

Initially, the probes were limited to high-level problem-solving advice, such as "What do you think the problem is right now," "If you don't see how to do the whole thing, is there a part of it you can do," or "Can you read through the program and tell me exactly what it does?" The hypothesis was that many students had difficulty with programming in large part for lack of good high-level problem management skills. Gradually, however, a much more complex situation emerged, leading to the occasional use of more directive probes such as, "Why don't you try a FOR loop?" One discovery was this: far from being haphazard and unpatterned, many students' management of the task showed strong patterns that interfered both with the immediate programming problem and with learning. The present article focuses on certain of these patterns and explores their import for the pedagogy of programming. Later articles will examine other results from these clinical studies.

THE POSSIBILITY OF LEARNING

It is important to appreciate the challenge that beginning programmers face. Seemingly straightforward problems can present appalling difficulties to the novice. For example, consider one problem sometimes used in our clinical research. The problem directs the student to write a BASIC program that will print a square of stars, where the number of stars on each side is to be specified by the user. For instance, if one enters a five in response to the program's prompt, the program will type back:

```
* * * *
*       *
*       *
*       *
* * * *
```

Although this problem is easy enough for an experienced programmer, it challenges the beginner in a number of ways. For instance, many of the students we work with have never encountered a problem that requires a variable, much less an algebraic expression, for the upper limit of a FOR loop. Our square problem calls for upper limits of S and S-2, where S is the number of stars per side. Moreover, the students have never encountered a loop that iterates across a single line of output, as in the top and bottom rows, nor a circumstance requiring nested loops, as the middle rows of the square demand. They have rarely considered problems that must be solved in parts, each segment of the program producing one section of an output that looks like a seamless whole.

We use this problem because it demands of many students that they employ the primitives they know in new ways: in other words, that they invent. When this happens, they are "going beyond the information given," in Jerome Bruner's felicitous phrase. To put it another way, they are lifting themselves up by their own intellectual bootstraps. Such learning by discovery is entirely appropriate considering the open-ended character of programming problems. When we say that someone knows how to program, we are implying that that person can solve programming problems that are more than trivially different from problems he or she has encountered before.

Of course, it is also possible to prepare students more explicitly for the range of problems they will encounter. Skilled programming appears to depend on a repertoire of well-practiced schemas, as do other complex intellectual performances such as problem solving in mathematics and physics, and chess play [1-5]. Such schemata and accompanying reasoning tactics might be taught to students directly, rather than leaving students to figure them out for themselves as more typically happens. Soloway is investigating this approach in the teaching of Pascal [5, 6], while Anderson and his colleagues are conducting a somewhat similar experiment, involving a computerized tutor, at the college level with the LISP programming language [7]. There is every reason to think that these schema-based approaches to instruction will result in more efficient learning.

The point remains that, even without carefully designed instruction based on cognitive science and in-depth study of the particular domain, some students learn. What might be called "bootstrap learning," where students go significantly beyond what they have been taught, does occur. Not only is this apparent from the occasional student with a flair for programming, but our clinical inquiries teach us that even students who are not doing that well overall can occasionally invent programming tactics for themselves. Consider these examples.

Sandra was working on some simpler problems in preparation for the square-of-stars task. First, she was asked to print a vertical row of ten stars. This posed no difficulty. Then she was asked to write a program that would accept a number from the keyboard and print that number of stars. Sandra puzzled for a moment and then said she thought she saw how to do it. Sandra read the number into a variable with an INPUT statement and used the variable as the upper limit of a loop. This would be completely unremarkable except for the fact that Sandra had never needed to employ a variable as the limit of a FOR loop in any previous work.

George, working on the square-of-stars problem itself, realized that he needed a loop to generate the middle lines of the square. Recognizing that there were S-2 lines, George asked, "Can I use something like S-2 in the loop?" Unremarkable again, except that George had never before used an expression in a FOR statement.

In LOGO, we often ask learners to write a program that will draw three identical rectangles in a stack, with some space between. Beverly had written code for the first of three rectangles. She was asked how she could use that code to create the subsequent two rectangles. Beverly employed the immediate mode to explore what would happen if she executed the procedure she had just written with positioning moves to place the turtle in different locations on the screen. She asked the researcher, "Can I put this into a procedure?"—referring to her work using three repetitions of the procedure she had already written. This is just what students are supposed to do in LOGO, of course, However, this student had never written programs involving embedded procedures, nor had she even been exposed to them as far as we could tell.

The students discussed here are just beginning to learn programming. Nonetheless, they display significant powers of invention. In our observations, many students can be seen inventing ways of tackling the particular problems they encounter. The difficulty is that a number of pitfalls in the process of programming can interfere with their making the best use of the problem-solving abilities to bootstrap themselves toward a reasonable level of competence. It seems likely that only the students who both invent solutions as illustrated here and avoid the pitfalls make steady progress. We now examine what some of these pitfalls are.

STOPPERS AND MOVERS

When novice programmers see fairly quickly how to proceed, naturally they do so. When, however, a clear course of action does not present itself, the young programmer faces a crucial branch point: what to do next? Try to break the problem down, look in the text for an idea, attempt something by trial and error?

Some students quite consistently adopt the simplest expedient and just stop. They appear to abandon all hope of solving the problem on their own. A dialogue like this is typical:

Student: I'm stuck.
Observer: What do you think the problem is?
Student: I don't know how to program it.
Observer: What ideas do you have?
Student: I don't know.

Lacking a ready answer to the difficulty, the student not only feels at a complete loss, but is unwilling to explore the problem any further. We label learners who display this type of behavior "stoppers."

Other students consistently try one idea after another, writing or modifying their code and testing it, never stopping long enough to appear stuck. We call them "movers." Sometimes movers do well, making progress on a problem and carrying it through to a successful completion. Extreme movers, however, move too fast, trying to repair code in ways that, with a moment's reflection, clearly will not work. This approach sometimes leads students to abandon prematurely quite promising ideas because they don't work the first time. Moreover, the extreme mover often does not appear to draw any lessons from ideas that do not work. There is no sense of "homing in" on a solution. Indeed, the student may even go round in circles, retrying approaches that have already proven unworkable.

Stoppers and extreme movers can be viewed as being at endpoints of a continuum based on the ratio of time spent thinking (or time spent sitting in front of a terminal and not typing) to time spent entering and testing code. But this image of a continuum is in a way misleading. It suggests a distribution with most students in the middle while extreme stoppers and movers occupy the statistically rare tails. On the contrary, the descriptions of stoppers and movers are not caricatures of the norm. Extreme stoppers or movers are common.

Although movers have their problems, at least they are in motion, with some hope of wresting a solution out of their venturing. Stoppers, on the other hand, have no chance of making progress, because they have given up. Stoppers represent the most obvious sign of the powerful affective factors we constantly see at work in novice programmers. Cindy, for example, had ground to a halt working on the square-of-stars problem. Asked if she had any ideas about the problem, she replied that she didn't. She was clearly waiting for the researcher to give her the answer. The researcher posed a question designed to relieve Cindy of immediate pressure, and also to dodge the request for help: "Suppose you were working on this problem in a room by yourself, with no one to help. What would you try next?" Cindy replied in frustration that if she were by herself, and could do what she wanted, she wouldn't be working on a computer.

One would expect the affective element to have its greatest negative impact with novices. Such learners are most likely to feel unsure of what they are doing, harbor fears about handling the machine, and hold in doubt their ability to make the machine do what they want it to do. Computer work can be a challenging and stimulating experience, but also it can become a threat to self-esteem and one's standing with peers and teachers.

Another factor clearly affecting many students is their attitude toward making mistakes [8]. Some novices seem to take the inevitable occurrence of bugs in stride, while others become frustrated every time they encounter a problem. The former seem to recognize that mistakes are part of the process of programming, part of the challenge. They study their bugs and try to use the information they gain. The latter students appear to view bugs more as reflecting on the value of their performance. For them, programming mistakes can be devastating because the mistakes are so obvious—they show up on the screen as incorrect output or in a program that will not run or gets stuck in the middle. We saw a striking example of this at one of our classroom observation sites. As a researcher walked by, one student hurriedly cleared his computer screen in order to conceal his program's erroneous output.

Such attitudes almost inevitably breed stoppers. Naturally, some stoppers become so disengaged that they learn very little. Surprisingly often, though, we have observed students who initially felt very reluctant to persevere in a programming task but, when encouraged, proved able to complete the task or at least a portion of it. For example, consider the case of Tom, a young student of BASIC. When the researcher first sat down with him, Tom was quick to point out that he had had no programming experience prior to this course, and that he didn't really know what he was doing. He said that the other students around him knew a lot more than he did, mentioning one student in particular who was working on a program for a game.

When Tom encountered difficulties he tended to leave the current problem and go on to the next, without making an effort to understand what was wrong. For instance, he encountered a bug when running a program that he had copied from the text. The program used array subscripts. When he ran it, he received the error message, "subscript out of range." He paused for a few seconds. Then, without a word, he began to look at the next problem. The researcher stopped him and asked what he thought the error message meant, to which Tom replied that he didn't know. When pressed for an answer, Tom thought for a little while, and then said that maybe the number in the parentheses needed to be smaller. The researcher asked him to try this idea out at the computer. Tom tried a smaller subscript value, and the program ran successfully. Without further prompting, he went on to test various values until he had established the exact range of allowable subscripts.

Cases such as Tom's are cause for optimism: it may be that, with appropriate instruction and encouragement, students can learn not to give up so easily. The result may be enhanced learning and enjoyment for many students.

If stoppers illustrate the powerful influence of negative affect on students learning to program, certain movers in a different way show such an influence too. An extreme mover is also, in his own way, disengaging from the problem.

While a successful mover is involved in the task, taking pleasure when things go right and acknowledging when they go wrong (one has to acknowledge a mistake before one can learn from it), the typical extreme mover seems emotionally more distanced from the task. The keyboard and screen are a handy distraction, allowing the student to keep busy without pausing to think about the difficulties of the problem at hand. Instead of dealing with mistakes and the information they might yield, the extreme mover seeks to avoid them by moving on.

To summarize, many novice programmers exhibit to a greater or lesser extent the "stopper" syndrome, a kind of disengagement that reinforces itself by interfering with the student's development of greater competency. Stoppers, especially those who, with encouragement prove able to do the problems posed, demonstrate by their conduct the powerful affective factors at work in the novel environment of computing. Although movers, by virtue of their motion, have at least some chance of solving a posed problem, impulsive, unreflective coding leaves some movers moving without getting anyplace.

CLOSE TRACKING OF CODE

A vital skill for any programmer is what we call "close tracking." Close tracking means reading written code to determine precisely what it does. A small incident will illustrate the value of close tracking. Anita was trying to write a program to make a horizontal line of stars, of arbitrary length. She wrote this line

```
20 print "*" x
```

and then stopped to consider whether it would work.

Anita:	Can you make it go, like x times?
Experimenter:	What do you mean by that?
Anita:	Five times this way, you know how it is.
Experimenter:	Tell me what you're doing with that statement.
Anita:	Print star and then semicolon so that x times it will print out. But that wouldn't work.
Experimenter:	Why do you think it wouldn't work?
Anita:	Because x is a number so it will just print it out. x is the variable number like 5, so . . . can I just see how it turns out?

Anita ran the program and found her suspicion confirmed: the line produced a star followed by a number, instead of the line of stars that she wanted. It is important to see how close tracking helped Anita here. By taking the computer's point of view, she was able to see how her idea for making a line of stars would not work. Our clinical observations include many cases where students tried similarly unworkable strategies, but did not track their code this closely. As a result they spent considerable time and energy trying in vain to get their programs to work. Anita, on the other hand, freed herself to go on to look for more promising ideas.

Close tracking can be useful, as in Anita's case, for filtering out bugs before testing a program. It is also important for diagnosing bugs that appear when the program is run, and sometimes gives clues to how they should be repaired. Accurate close tracking is a mentally demanding activity. It requires understanding of the primitives of the language and the rules for flow of control. In addition, as the student proceeds through the code, the student must map its effects onto changes in what might be called a "status representation," specific to the problem. For instance, in LOGO graphics problems, the turtle signals the status in large part; the student must read with precision how each piece of code alters the position and orientation of the turtle, and whether the pen is currently up or down. In BASIC, or in nongraphics LOGO problems, the status is best conceptualized as a matter of the values of variables and the appearance of accumulated output at a given point in time; the student must interpret accurately how each piece of code adds to the output or alters the value of a variable.

Although in principle close tracking is a mechanical procedure, in practice it often proves a source of difficulties. Students commonly neglect to do it when they need the information close tracking provides to untangle a problem. For example, Fred was working on the square-of-stars problem in BASIC. He had written the following code:

```
10 n$ = "*"
20 input "how many stars per side";n
30 for x = 1 to n
40 print n$;
50 print n$
60 print n$;
70 next x
```

When he ran the program he got this output:

```
**
***
***
***
*
```

He repaired the program by changing line 40 to:

```
40 print n$,
```

so that the cursor would move to the next print zone. When he ran the program again he got this output:

```
*          *
**         *
**         *
**         *
*
```

Now the program was at least *looking* more like two sides of the square and he seemed to think that he was getting closer to the solution. Close tracking might have helped Fred to realize that his approach could not possibly work in the general case, because it allowed the width of the figure to be determined by print zones instead of n, the desired width. But rather than track to see what the program was actually doing, Fred persisted in making many small repairs to lines 40, 50 and 60; he became stuck in a cycle of diagnosis and repair that could never get him closer to the correct programming solution. Through failure to track the program, students are more likely to follow a dead end path without even realizing they are doing so. Moreover, failure to track leaves them with few effective strategies for getting unstuck.

As this example shows, the problem is sometimes simply that students do not even try to track. Several factors seem to contribute to students' neglect of this strategy. First, many students do not realize that tracking is an important programming strategy. In our research, students seldom tracked their programs without prompting. This phenomenon seems akin to the widespread tendency of students not to check their work in mathematical problem solving [9-11]. Failure to track may also result from a lack of confidence in one's abilities to predict or simulate the outcome of the program. Lack of confidence may result from the belief, articulated by some young LOGO students, that you can never be sure about what the computer will do. In other cases, lack of confidence may result from realizing that you do not completely understand how the language works.

Finally, for programs that have a graphic output, students may be discouraged from tracking by their visual perception of what is going on. Fred, in the case described above, may have thought he understood what the program was doing because he could see a more or less accurate representation of the desired product. In fact, his program was much further away from being correct than the appearance of the output suggested.

Neglect of close tracking aside, when students do attempt to track what their programs are doing, they often fail. In its simplest form, this reflects an inadequate grasp of the primitives of the language, a problem that arises often. For example, Jane was making a square in LOGO using immediate mode. To create the square she successfully used the commands FD 90 RT 90. When asked to make a smaller square, she coded FD 30 RT 30. Apparently she believed that to make a square in LOGO the forward and turn inputs must be the same. Tracking the program would be unlikely to help her make an accurate repair until she acquires a correct concept of how RT 30 is different from RT 90.

For another example, in BASIC we have often observed confusion between the READ and INPUT statements for getting information into the program. Although the programs require inputs from the terminal, many students have coded READ statements, which do not get input from the terminal but rather from a data section that is coded directly into the program. When proofreading their code they seem to interpret such a statement loosely as the line that gets the numbers into the program. It has been suggested that in general people learn only the discriminations they have to in order to cope with the problem at hand [10]. Some lapses in mathematical computation and reasoning, as well as the confusion noted here, follow from this principle. Students introduced to INPUT and later to READ (or vice versa) are likely to take their cue as to which to use from whichever topic is current rather than from situational need; hence they do not at first learn how to differentiate sharply situations suited to one or the other.

In some respects tracking is similar to proofreading—reading back the code to make sure that you have recorded what you meant to write and that it is accurate in detail. As in proofreading and other contexts, errors get overlooked because one projects one's expectations on the stimulus, a marked feature of human perception generally [12]. We describe this type of failure to track accurately as projecting intentions on the code. For example, Tom was having trouble with a LOGO exercise because of the orientation of the turtle after drawing a rectangle. After the rectangle was drawn, the turtle was facing left. To complete his design, he needed the turtle to face north. Tom could not find his error and could not understand why the turtle was not facing up. He was prompted by the experimenter to track the program—to map his code onto the figure that was drawn. On successive attempts, he was simply unable to make the one-to-one correspondence, even though he clearly understood the LOGO primitives involved. He would start off tracking precisely but, as he proceeded around the edges of the square, he would pay less and less attention to the code, extrapolating impressionistically from the previous sides.

We have discussed causes of difficulties with close tracking primarily in the context of programming. It is also worth noting that these influences may be aggravated in some students because of broad cognitive style traits that they bring to the programming task. Those students who naturally approach problems methodically and reflectively may be better trackers than those who approach their work in a more trial-and-error, or impulsive, fashion [13].

In summary, we have observed how students' differential abilities and propensities to track their programs lead to more or less successful programming. Several factors may account for failure to track accurately: 1) motivational influences stemming from lack of understanding that tracking is important and lack of confidence in one's ability to track; 2) faulty understanding of how the programming language works; 3) projecting intentions onto the code so that one cannot objectively map the code as written onto the output; and 4) cognitive style differences.

TINKERING

Students often program by means of an approach we call tinkering—they try to solve a programming problem by writing some code and then making small changes in the hopes of getting it to work. In some cases this strategy can be effective, while at other times it interferes with students' progress in solving programming problems.

For a positive example, Deborah, working on the three-rectangles problem in LOGO, wrote a long, unstructured string of code to draw the rectangles. When repairing the code, Deborah did not track systematically, but diagnosed her bug as "an angle problem." She tinkered with the code by making a series of small repairs and tests. Because this student was careful to correct the tinker if she found that an earlier repair was incorrect, she was able to isolate the problem and complete her program.

On the other hand, tinkering often works out poorly. For example, Donald was also attempting the three-rectangles problem. He wrote a line of code to draw all three rectangles: REPEAT 3 [REC MOVE REC MOVE REC MOVE], where REC and MOVE were procedures he had defined earlier. The REC procedure drew a single rectangle and the MOVE procedure repositioned the turtle. The output drew nine rectangles instead of the desired three. Instead of re-thinking the problem, and questioning his understanding of how REPEAT works, he assumed that only some minor change was required, and so made repeated efforts to repair his code by rearranging the order of the procedures within the brackets.

The phenomenon of tinkering relates both to the theme of stoppers and movers and to the theme of close tracking. Tinkerers are by definition "movers," that is, they are not easily frustrated when a program fails the first time. In addition, tinkerers like to experiment with the code, so that they are not afraid of making changes. Finally, tinkerers hold the belief that the problem is solvable, and that they may be able, with their strategy, to find the solution. These important attitudes help a student to use tinkering as a problem-solving strategy.

At the same time, *effective* tinkering depends to an extent on close tracking. Those rare students who track very closely indeed are not tinkering at all; they know exactly what is going on. Students who do some tracking may succeed with a tinkering strategy, because even though they do not know exactly what the problem is they have it somewhat localized. Students who track poorly or neglect to track may fall into a pattern of unrestrained and haphazard tinkering.

Students who tinker unsystematically often make their problems worse. For example, Adele, working on the three-rectangles problem in LOGO, tinkered with the code in a peculiar way. She made small changes in the code, and subsequently did not test to see the results. With no monitoring of the impact of her repairs, the program got worse and worse. Eventually, Adele wisely abandoned the procedure and started from scratch.

Tinkering is a particularly tempting trap when the program seems as though it is behaving nearly as desired. Fred's work on the square-of-stars problem, described in the previous section, is a case in point. Encouraged because his output resembled the target, Fred fell to tinkering with the program to try to achieve a complete match. Unfortunately, a completely different approach was needed. Fred was operating at the wrong level. In information processing terms, he was employing a hill-climbing strategy that encountered a local maximum: Fred could never make his output much better than it was by minor modifications. He needed to find a different hill to climb. As a generalization, tinkering may be helpful so long as the tinkerer is climbing the right hill—has the right general approach—and tinkers systematically, removing unsuccessful repairs so that the program does not become a tangle.

In summary, for novice programmers tinkering has both positive and negative features. On the positive side, it is a symptom of a mover rather than a stopper: the tinkerer is engaged in the problem and has some hope of solving it. With sufficient tracking to localize the problem accurately and some systematicity to avoid compounding errors, tinkering may lead to a correct program. On the negative side, students often attempt to tinker without sufficient tracking, so that they have little grasp of why the program is behaving as it is. They assume that minor changes will help, when in fact the problem demands a change in approach. Finally, some students allow tinkers to accumulate untested or leave them in place even after they have failed, adding yet more tinkers until the program becomes virtually incomprehensible.

BREAKING PROBLEMS DOWN

Breaking a programming task down into subproblems is a crucial skill for the able programmer. There are few significant programming problems that can be solved by a single loop or one round of input, conditional branching, and output. Problems of any complexity call for partitioning the problem into parts, each one of those parts corresponding to a distinct segment of code and often to a separate syntactic unit in the program, such as a FOR loop, a REPEAT statement, or a subroutine call. The importance of breaking problems down is, of course, not limited to programming. It is one of the basic "weak strategies" of problem solving in general [14-16], and figures prominently in, for instance, heuristic approaches to mathematical problem solving [11, 17-19].

Ways of breaking problems into parts depend on the programming environment and the nature of the programming language, quite apart from the student's own intellectual skills. Students often program in LOGO by composing code in the immediate mode exclusively, so that their work more closely resembles a videogame-like maneuvering on a two-dimensional screen than programming. They then rewrite their code, often complete with false moves, backups and erasures, into one long procedure.

LOGO permits students to produce rather complex output without the use of high level programming concepts. Many turtle graphics problems are susceptible to a trivial kind of breaking down: the components are the segments of a target figure and the turtle need only trace them out, one by one. Neither BASIC problems nor non-graphics LOGO problems typically break down in this easy way. This property of LOGO is, of course, distinctly double-edged; it makes programming accessible even to rather young children, but does so through a simple linear pattern of thinking that does not generalize well to more sophisticated problems. Pea and Kurland suggest that such programming is not cognitively demanding, but requires mainly stamina and determination [20, 21].

When students do have to break down problems in nontrivial ways, they often falter. Some appear not to recognize the need to factor a programming problem into parts. Dorothy, for example, had solved a couple of easy problems in BASIC that demanded only a single organizational unit, a FOR loop with a preceding input statement. Then the experimenter posed the square of stars problem. After some moments of puzzlement, Dorothy announced that she had no idea how to proceed with the problem. When the experimenter prompted her to break the problem down into parts, she showed some ability to do so; yet this strategy had not occurred to her at the outset.

When students do break a problem down, they often do not identify appropriate or workable chunks. They may factor the problem into subgoals that are not suited to the language or the task. Sometimes the natural perceptual characteristics of the programming goal lead students to formulate chunks that make the programming task more difficult or even impossible to solve.

For example, students addressing the square-of-stars problem in BASIC often break the problem down according to its visual components, without taking into account the constraints exercised by the primitives at their disposal. In a typical case, one student successfully coded the top row of stars, but then identified the left side of the square as the second subgoal, without recognizing that, because of the way the PRINT statement works in BASIC, both the left and right sides must be dealt with in the same chunk (unless one uses the LOCATE primitive, which can move the cursor to any position on the screen. LOCATE is not commonly taught to beginning BASIC students). This pitfall reflects the gestalt pull of the square of stars, with its natural decomposition into four sides. Ironically, in LOGO one proceeds with such a problem in just the way that BASIC students mistakenly lean towards—one side at a time. In addition, the pitfall reflects an insufficient mental model of the way PRINT prints—line by line—or at least a failure to bring that knowledge to bear in factoring the problem. Broadly speaking, students need to break problems down according to the sorts of operations the language affords rather than according to superficial features of the output.

Our observations of LOGO students suggest that students frequently approach a programming task without thinking out in advance the necessary components of the project. The strategy of planning as one codes may be feasible for expert programmers because they have at their disposal a well-developed repertoire of programming "plans" for different chunks of the programming task. But for novices with a scanty repertoire of programming plans, this often leads to an unworkable breakdown of the problem.

For example, Rodney, working on the three-rectangles problem, wrote a program named RECTANGLE which included, along with the rectangle itself, the positioning moves to place the cursor at the top of the screen. He encountered repeated difficulties using this procedure to make the other two rectangles. Because Rodney had decided somewhat arbitrarily, as he went along, where to chunk the problem, he ran into a series of troubling debugging problems that eventually led him to abandon the procedure and start afresh.

To summarize, several factors influence whether and how well students break problems down. The programming language affects the extent to which students can solve problems without the use of modular programming. Students do not always recognize that breaking problems down will aid in the solution of programming problems. Students often face trouble in attempting to break complex problems into subgoals because their expectations intefere with planning: they use inappropriate analogies to drawing or other activities and fall under the influence of perceptual components of the programming goal. Lacking an accurate mental model of the language, its primitives, and the sorts of programming plans that can be built out of those primitives, students cannot easily discriminate inappropriate decompositions of problems. Finally, students face trouble in breaking problems down because they often try to deal with decomposition issues in the middle of coding, instead of planning deliberately in advance. Instructional intervention which encourages pre-planning might help.

CONDITIONS OF LEARNING
VERSUS COMPONENTS OF EXPERTISE

The foregoing sections provide a broad-stroke description of some of the challenges novice programmers face. It was emphasized that beginners sometimes evince "bootstrap learning," inventing ways of handling particular programming problems, rather than applying only what they have learned in a narrow manner. At the same time, numerous factors interfere with their achieving such insights and making the best use of them to carry problems to completion. In particular, the affective and attitudinal profile of "stoppers" prevents them from exploring the problem situation. Neglect of close tracking or inability to track deprives students of crucial information about the behavior of their programs in progress.

Tinkering at its worst mires learners deeper in mistaken approaches to a programming problem. Difficulties in breaking a problem down bar programmers from proceeding with problems that involve much complexity.

These factors relate both to general problems of learning and to problems specific to programming. On the side of generality, it is clear that being a "stopper" inhibits progress in any domain, as does undirected tinkering. Attempting to break a problem down is a general problem-solving strategy. Close tracking reminds one of the difficulties many students encounter with any problem that requires high precision, as in arithmetic, for instance. At the same time, many aspects of the phenomena discussed seem specific to programming. The importance of close tracking relates to the activity of running a program and explaining its behavior, right or wrong, by examining the instructions one has written; in most other precision-demanding activities, such as arithmetic, one cannot "run" anything to test the adequacy of one's work. While breaking problems down is a general problem-solving strategy, good *ways* to break a problem down are of course conditioned by the nature of the programming environment; it was emphasized earlier, for instance, that BASIC and LOGO lead to somewhat different difficulties here.

It appears likely that proper instruction might alleviate many of the problems identified. For instance, instruction could simply emphasize the value of certain practices: being a mover rather than a stopper, tracking closely, seeking ways to break problems down. This follows from our observation that, quite apart from ability, simple neglect of such strategies is often a difficulty. In addition, instruction might enable students to carry out key activities much better than they typically do. For example, teaching a mental model of the machine in relation to the particular programming language, treating it as a "glass box" instead of a black one [22], should help students both with close tracking and with decomposing problems in ways fitting the language's capacities. Research by Mayer testifies that teaching such a model can improve programming performance [23]. For another example, students could be taught explicitly the pitfalls of tinkering, and could be encouraged in such practices as removing failed repairs and considering, if several tinkers fail, whether a completely different approach needs to be taken.

These implications for teaching complement in an interesting way contemporary approaches to programming instruction based on studies of expertise. As noted earlier, expert performance in any domain appears to depend on a sizable repertoire of schemata that skilled individuals marshal in dealing with particular tasks. Soloway, developing this approach for teaching Pascal, discusses such "programming plans" as a counter variable, where a statement like N=N+1 serves to increment a variable and thereby keep count of items or events, or an accumulator variable, where a statement like A=A+MORE serves to keep a running total of numbers [6]. As these examples suggest, such programming plans go considerably beyond the primitives of the language in question. They constitute purposeful units of code that serve particular functions. A programming problem can be analyzed in terms of the functions needed and appropriate programming plans retrieved from one's repertoire to implement a program. Soloway's approach to instruction involves teaching such plans and their use directly.

Anderson and his colleagues are pursuing a related line of research aimed at developing a computer tutor for the programming language LISP. They analyze expertise in LISP programming as a production system [15] in which, roughly speaking, particular problem characteristics trigger the installation of particular programming plans [7]. The computer tutor incorporates certain principles of tutoring, based on Anderson's ACT theory and the general literature on learning, to equip students with a repertoire of productions that enables them to program.

Both Soloway's and Anderson's approaches seek to supply students rather directly with the schemata that, in normal instruction, a few students work out for themselves. The question remains why some students do and others do not. We have argued here that certain broad attitudes and conducts interfere with students discovering their own programming plans, behaviors such as stopping, neglect of close tracking, casual tinkering, and neglect of or systematic errors in breaking problems down. If instruction were to address these problems, more students might build their own schematic repertoires without elaborately choreographed instruction in the component schemata of expertise.

Each approach has its merits. The "expertise" approach almost certainly promises faster learning and greater competence for the sorts of programming tasks being addressed. On the other hand, instruction closely targeted on a particular performance tends not to transfer as well to related performances [24]; with reference to programming, see Mayer [23].

Instruction designed to foster bootstrap learning but not providing an explicit schematic repertoire might produce competent and flexible programmers, and might yield the broad cognitive ripple effects some advocates of programming instruction have hoped for. Certainly Seymour Papert's ambitions for LOGO reflect such a hope [25]. Recent findings on the efficacy of LOGO suggest that students typically do not develop much mastery of the language nor the associated metacognitive skills [20, 21]. However, some of the factors behind this shortfall have been discussed here, and other results also suggest that a strongly mediated style of instruction should do better [26, 27]. On the other hand, any instructional approach that depends on bootstrap learning probably will prepare students somewhat less efficiently in the content directly addressed.

In summary, the relatively undeveloped pedagogy of computer programming instruction falls short on two fronts. It does not teach directly the sorts of schemata a skilled programmer needs. Moreover, it does not guide students in ways that foster bootstrap learning of those schemata. In consequence, youngsters vary widely in their progress, succeeding only to the extent that they happen to bring with them characteristics that make them good bootstrap learners in the programming context. Advances in either direction (or, better yet, in both directions simultaneously) should do better by young students of programming.

REFERENCES

1. M. Chi, P. Feltovich, and R. Glaser, Categorization and Representation of Physics Problems by Experts and Novices, *Cognitive Science, 5*, pp. 121-152, 1981.
2. W. C. Chase and H. A. Simon, Perception in Chess, *Cognitive Psychology, 4*, pp. 55-81, 1973.
3. J. H. Larkin, J. McDermott, D. P. Simon, and H. A. Simon, Modes of Competence in Solving Physics Problems, *Cognitive Science, 4*, pp. 317-345, 1980.
4. A. H. Schoenfeld and D. J. Herrman, Problem Perception and Knowledge Structure in Expert and Novice Mathematical Problem Solvers, *Journal of Experimental Psychology: Learning, Memory, and Cognition, 8*, pp. 484-494, 1982.
5. E. Soloway and K. Ehrlich, Empirical Studies of Programming Knowledge, *IEEE Transactions on Software Engineering, SE-10*:5, pp. 595-609, 1984.
6. E. Soloway, Presentation at Harvard University, February 12, 1985.
7. J. R. Anderson and B. J. Reiser, The LISP Tutor, *Byte, 10*:4, pp. 159-175, 1985.
8. C. S. Dweck and B. G. Licht, Learned Helplessness and Intellectual Achievement, in *Human Helplessness*, J. Garbar and M. Seligman (eds.), Academic Press, New York, 1980.
9. G. Polya, *How to Solve It: A New Aspect of Mathematical Method* (2nd edition), Doubleday, Garden City, New York, 1957.
10. R. B. Davis, *Learning Mathematics: The Cognitive Science Approach to Mathematics Education*, Ablex, Norwood, New Jersey, 1984.
11. A. H. Schoenfeld, Teaching Problem-solving Skills, *American Mathematical Monthly, 87*:10, pp. 794-805, 1980.
12. U. Neisser, *Cognitive Psychology*, Appleton-Century-Crofts, New York, 1967.
13. J. Kagan and N. Kogan, Individuality and Cognitive Performance, in *Carmichael's Manual of Child Psychology*, Vol. 1, P. Mussen (ed.), Wiley, New York, 1970.
14. S. Amarel, Problems of Representation in Heuristic Problem Solving: Related Issues in the Development of Expert Systems, in *Methods of Heuristics*, R. Groner, M. Groner, and W. F. Bischof (eds.), Erlbaum, Hillsdale, New Jersey, 1983.
15. A. Newell and H. Simon, *Human Problem Solving*, Prentice-Hall, Inc., Englewood Cliffs, New Jersey, 1972.
16. D. B. Lenat, Toward a Theory of Heuristics, in *Methods of Heuristics*, R. Groner, M. Groner, and W. F. Bischof (eds.), Erlbaum, Hillsdale, New Jersey, 1983.
17. G. Polya, *Mathematics and Plausible Reasoning* (2 vols.), Princeton University Press, Princeton, New Jersey, 1954.

18. A. H. Schoenfeld, Measures of Problem-solving Performance and of Problem-solving Instruction, *Journal for Research in Mathematics Education, 13*:1, pp. 31-49, 1982.
19. W. A. Wickelgren, *How to Solve Problems: Elements of a Theory of Problems and Problem Solving*, W. H. Freeman and Co., San Francisco, 1974.
20. R. D. Pea and M. D. Kurland, Logo Programming and the Development of Planning Skills, paper presented at the Conference on Thinking, Harvard Graduate School of Education, Cambridge, Massachusetts, August, 1984.
21. R. D. Pea and M. D. Kurland, On the Cognitive Effects of Learning Computer Programming, *New Ideas in Psychology, 2*:2, pp. 137-168, 1984.
22. B. DuBoulay, T. O'Shea, and J. Monk, The Black Box Inside the Glass Box: Presenting Computing Concepts to Novices, *International Journal of Man-Machine Studies, 14*, pp. 237-249, 1981.
23. R. E. Mayer, The Psychology of How Novices Learn Computer Programming, *Computing Surveys, 13*:1, pp. 121-141, 1981.
24. G. Salomon and D. N. Perkins, Rocky Roads to Transfer: Rethinking Mechanisms of a Neglected Phenomenon, paper presented at the Conference on Thinking, Harvard Graduate School of Education, Cambridge, Massachusetts, August, 1984.
25. S. Papert, *Mindstorms: Children, Computers, and Powerful Ideas*, Basic Books, New York, 1980.
26. D. H. Clement and D. F. Gullo, Effects of Computer Programming on Young Children's Cognition, *Journal of Educational Psychology, 76*:6, pp. 1051-1058, 1984.
27. V. R. Delclos, J. Littlefield, and J. D. Bransford, Teaching Thinking Through LOGO: The Importance of Method, *Roeper Review, 7*:3, pp. 153-156, 1985.

SECTION IV:
DIFFICULTIES, MISCONCEPTIONS,
AND BUGS

What sorts of difficulties do novices encounter when they are learning to program and what sorts of bugs are novices therefore prone to make? The papers in this section approach this question in several different ways, and employ diverse terminology to discuss some of the same concepts. Each term (e.g., difficulties, mistakes, errors, misconceptions, surface error, deep error, bug cause, etc.) has a particular technical meaning that may vary from paper to paper. Below some of the important distinctions are clarified to help put these papers in perspective.

The first important distinction to make is the difference between comprehension (or interpretation, analysis) tasks and generation (or production, synthesis) tasks. In a comprehension task, a novice is given a program or program fragment and asked to explain what the resulting behavior of the program would be. Whereas in a generation task, a novice is given a problem specification describing a desired behavior and asked to write a program that performs the desired function. Kurland and Pea's study used comprehension tasks to get at the nature of students' misconceptions about recursive Logo programs. The papers co-authored with Soloway focus on generation tasks — students writing Pascal programs. The Putnam, Sleeman, Baxter, and Kuspa study employed both types of tasks — a generation task in a screening phase, and comprehension tasks in the main study.

The second important distinction to make is between a bug (or mistake, surface error) and its underlying misconception (or cause, deep error). Identifying a bug answers a *what question* — what did the student do wrong? Identifying a misconception answers a *why question* — why did the student make the bug? The Spohrer, Soloway, and Pope paper categorizes the space of bugs in introductory Pascal program in terms of the goal and plan structure of programs — missing initialization, malformed calculation, misplaced output. While in his paper, du Boulay categorizes bugs in terms of three main misconceptions: misapplication of analogy, overgeneralization, and mishandling interactions. Kurland and Pea also focus on misconceptions that lead to recursion comprehension errors: decontextualized interpretation, misassignment of intentionality, misassignment of conversiveness, overgeneralization from natural language, overextension from mathematics, and inappropriate mental models.

The third distinction is between descriptive theories and process theories. Only the Bonar and Soloway papers present a process theory that explains in detail how the bugs are generated. A process theory goes a step beyond simply describing bugs and their underlying misconceptions, and provides a mechanism (in their case, an impasse-repair mechanism) that can explain the generation of the bugs. All the other papers provide descriptive theories of comprehension/generation bugs/misconceptions.

Finally, the fourth distinction is between qualitative analyses and quantitative analyses. The paper by du Boulay focuses on identifying the types of misconception novices possess, without providing details of how prevalent each of the specific misconceptions is. Alternatively, the papers by Putnam, Bonar, and Spohrer attempt to provide quantitative analyses of how wide-spread the bugs/misconceptions they studied are. In both of the Spohrer papers, quantitative analyses are essential for focusing attention on the high frequency bugs novices make.

As one reads these papers, bearing in mind the four distinctions — comprehension/generation, bug/misconception, descriptive/process, qualitative/quantitative — one should also consider what academic level the subjects were at (e.g., elementary, high school, college), what programming language was being used (e.g., Logo, Pascal, Basic), and what type of data was employed. Some studies used on-line protocols (student generated programs), others used thinking-aloud protocols (verbal reports of students engaged in problem solving), while others responses from questionnaires. Once again we think the reader will find the papers are interesting not only for their empirical results, but for the diverse research methods they illustrate.

14

SOME DIFFICULTIES OF LEARNING TO PROGRAM

BENEDICT DU BOULAY
University of Sussex, England

ABSTRACT

This article is a brief introduction to some of the issues that teachers of programming may find helpful. It starts by presenting a fairly idiosyncratic view of teaching programming which makes use of mechanistic analogies and points out some of the pitfalls. The article goes on to examine certain errors based on the misapplication of analogies as well as certain interaction errors. The main emphasis is on the notional machine both at the general level of understanding (and misunderstanding) the relationship of the terminal to the computer as such, as well as at the more specific level of understanding assignment. Notation and mistakes that poorly-designed languages can induce novices to commit are discussed.

AREAS OF DIFFICULTY

Learning to program is not easy. The difficulties can be separated into five areas with a certain degree of overlap. First there is the general problem of *orientation*, finding out what programming is for, what kinds of problem can be tackled and what the eventual advantages might be of expending effort in learning the skill. Second, there are difficulties associated with understanding the general properties of the machine that one is learning to control, *the notional machine*, and realizing how the behavior of the physical machine relates to this notional machine. For example, it is often unclear to a new user whether the information on the terminal screen is a record of prior interactions between the user and the computer or a window onto some part of the machine's innards. Third, there are problems associated with the *notation* of the various formal languages that have to be learned, both mastering the syntax and the underlying semantics. The semantics may be viewed as an elaboration of the properties and behavior of the notional machine, crudely sketched above. Fourth, associated with notation are the difficulties of acquiring standard *structures*, cliches or plans [1] that can be used to achieve small-scale goals, such as computing a sum using a loop. Finally, there is the issue of mastering the *pragmatics* of programming, where a student needs to learn the skill of how to specify, develop, test, and debug a program using whatever tools are available. None of these issues are entirely separable from the others and much of the "shock" [2] of the first few encounters between the learner and the system are compounded by the student's attempt to deal with all these different kinds of difficulty at once.

KINDS OF MISTAKES

Orthogonal to the areas of difficulty noted above are the kinds of mistakes that novices make about ideas in each of these areas. There seem to be three important types that teachers of programming should look out for. First there are errors due to the *misapplication of analogy*. These are errors that arise when the learner tries to extract more structure or relationships from an analogy than are warranted. For example, students often believe that since a variable is like a "box" it can hold more than a single value [3]. A second kind of error is concerned with *overgeneralizations* without any sense of misapplying an analogy. An example here might be the student surrounding the text following a REM statement in Basic with quotes because the text following a PRINT statement is quoted, or separating the actual parameters in a Pascal procedure call with semicolons because the formal parameters can be so separated in the procedure definition (such errors need not be limited to syntactic overgeneralizations). A third sort of error arises through inexpert handling of complexity in general, and *interactions* in particular. Thus we find different sub-parts of a program improperly interleaved [4], or the perceptual shape of the program on the screen interfering with a correct appreciation of what its text actually denotes.

This article is a brief introduction to some of the issues that teachers of programming may find helpful. It starts by presenting a fairly idiosyncratic view of teaching programming which makes use of mechanistic analogies and points out some of the pitfalls. The article goes on to examine certain errors based on the misapplication of analogies as well as certain interaction errors. The main emphasis is on the notional machine both at the general level of, say, understanding (and misunderstanding) the relationship of the terminal to the computer as such, as well as at the more specific level of, for example, understanding assignment. There is also some discussion of notation and of the sorts of mistakes that poorly-designed languages can induce novices to commit.

THE NOTIONAL MACHINE
An Engineering Analogy for Computing

Learning to program is like learning to use a toy construction set, such as a Meccano, to build mechanisms, but as if inside a darkened room with only very limited ways of seeing the innards of one's creation working. To someone unfamiliar with engineering many of the pieces inside such a set look very odd, and while the learner may have some general idea what the set as a whole is for—to build cars and cranes etc.—she or he may not realize how apparently dissimilar mechanisms can be decomposed into similar small chunks and how the shapes of the pieces in the set are suited to the construction of such standard chunks.

A running program is a kind of mechanism and it takes quite a long time to learn the relation between a program on the page and the mechanism it describes. It's just as hard as trying to understand how a car engine works from a diagram in a text book. Only some familiarity with wheels, cranks, gears, bearings, etc. and "getting one's hands grubby," gives the power to imagine the working mechanism described by the diagram and crucially, to relate a broken engine's failure to work to malfunctions in its unseen innards.

Even after becoming familiar with some of the pieces that make up a program, e.g., PRINT or IF, the novice may not see a program as a working mechanism in the same way as an experienced programmer [5]. This ability to see a program as a whole, understand its main parts and their relation is a skill which grows only gradually. Two comparisons are often made. One is to foreign language learning with its halting progression from disconnected words and small phrases to fluent speech. The other is to the way an experienced chess player can "read" a chessboard, where a novice sees only a jumble of individual chessmen.

A Tool-Building Tool

The computer plus its programming system is also a mechanism, but a mechanism which can be used to build other mechanisms (i.e., programs). Even if no effort is made to present a view of what is going on "inside" the learners will form their own. Without help, this view may be rather impoverished, relying on coincidence, and may be insufficient to explain much of the observed behavior. When things are going well, this may not matter, but understanding errors often requires knowledge of the sort "the machine was trying to do this . . . but came across that . . . and so did not know how to continue."

This view of the computer system as a machine has to develop at the right level of detail. Some learners are given instruction in the binary system, gates, the central processor unit, and other low-level detail, which they find impossible to relate to the machine they have contact with. The learner needs a very unsophisticated explanation of what is inside, but she or he does need some explanation. Teaching schemes based on "match box" computers and their like seem quite successful, especially in equipping the novice to solve novel problems, even if they make little difference to their ability to solve stock exercises [6, 7].

What Does the Screen Show?

Pressing ENTER or RETURN is an issue which causes difficulty at first but which soon becomes second nature to the students. However underlying it is the question of whether what one sees on the screen is a record of what one has typed, a place to display the effects of certain commands, or a kind of window into the "inside" of the computer. An advantage of certain simple systems, such as the Sinclair Spectrum, which display only the current command line is that pressing RETURN has an obvious effect on what one has typed. It disappears, in a sense "into" the machine, and some effect is produced. The notion that one can change the line, using character deleting keys or whatever, up until one presses ENTER makes sense where executing a command causes it to disappear from the screen. However there are disadvantages in that, if each command is issued for immediate execution, there is no visual record of previous commands, so one cannot point out the one-to-one correspondence between objects drawn on the screen and commands previously typed.

Typing and other mistakes will occur when entering single commands. At first the novice will be unsure of how to respond to the subsequent error message. The beginner will wonder whether the command has been partially understood and partially carried out so that the sensible response would be to rephrase that part of the command that seems to have caused the error. Should the command be completely reformulated? Has some irrevocable internal change been produced?

More often than not the system will simply disregard the command which it could not interpret and issue a new prompt inviting the user to try again. Learning to treat errors as producing no internal change of state has its dangers later. It reduces the chance that the novice will spot when a real change of state has occurred, perhaps by accident, as when pressing an ESCAPE key rather than RETURN or ENTER. One can tell the novice that observing the type of prompt helps, but attention can easily be distracted from this small signal of internal state.

Modern bit-mapped graphic display screens may make life easier for the novice because different areas of the screen have quite different relationships with the underlying notional machine. One part may be a record of what has been done, another shows a file, yet another displays the results of some running program and so on. These different roles may more easily be contrasted since they can be shown in parallel.

Managing the Notional Machine

There is a crucial distinction between the different roles a computer can play which is often missed by the learner. One is as a machine which is executing one of the learner's programs. In this mode the computer effectively becomes the mechanism described by the program. Pressing the RUN button, or otherwise making the program run, turns the computer into a machine executing the given stored program.

In its other mode, the computer is used as a kind of "manager" of programs— to do the reading in, storing, and editing. In this mode, input from the keyboard will be concerned to do something to a program, e.g., add a line to it, make some change, print it out, store it on disk, or delete it. The conventions or rules for how one tells the computer to carry out these actions will be fixed by command language of the system in question (and with modern systems they may even be iconic).

Confusing the issue further, there are other conventions which make up the rules of the programming language, such as Basic, in which one describes programs. These latter conventions are usually different from those used to type to the machine in its managerial role. For example, few languages allow us to include an edit command as part of a program.

It is important not to underestimate the problems which arise from the above, namely misunderstandings about "who" is being addressed and which set of conventions (i.e., which language) is appropriate. Learning a programming language involves not only learning that language, but also the language for managing programs as well as the language for editing programs, e.g., use of the cursor keys in a screen editor.

It is common for programmers at all levels of skill to forget who they are addressing and issue the wrong kind of command. Students often find it hard to escape from the muddle that this causes, partly because they take longer to recognize that something silly is going on, partly because they may have expectations that the system will do what they mean rather than what they say, and finally because they may not be familiar with the various methods providing for escaping from such situations, such as BREAK, ESCAPE, or control characters.

Beginners sometimes take over-drastic action to restore the computer to a standard state, e.g., switching it off and on again, or deleting a complete program where only some part of it is wrong. Some people give up the attempt to learn programming because they fail to master the use of the computer in its managerial role rather than because they cannot write programs.

Once the student starts making programs there will be the need to make a further distinction, i.e., between typing in the text of a program, editing that text, listing the program on the screen, or some other output device and running the program. Novices are sometimes directed to make their initial programs out of sequences of PRINT statements. This can cause confusion because the effect of listing the program containing the PRINT commands is not all that different from the effect of that program when it is run. So listing the program and running it produce very nearly the same kind of output, thus blurring the distinction between these two ideas.

The notion of the system making sense of the program according to its own very rigid rules is a crucial idea for the learner to grasp. Both our own use, as teachers, of anthropomorphic language, e.g., "it was trying to . . . ," "it thought you meant . . . ," and the use of English words and names (e.g., PRINT) in programming languages can mislead. These can suggest that the system has the normal human ability of being able to infer what is meant from what is said.

Early teaching examples of simple programs based on sequences of instructions for human execution (e.g., how to boil an egg) can also give the wrong impression in two ways. First, the language for the instructions is usually unconstrained and, secondly, the instructions usually gloss many issues which it is perfectly reasonable to leave implicit. Novices are often surprised at the level of detail in which tasks need to be programmed.

I do not wish to suggest that anthropomorphic terms are a bad thing. Treating the computer as a highly limited rational entity is a perfectly reasonable way to proceed. Indeed enlisting the students' tolerant pity for the impoverished intellect of the object can be a good strategy for dispelling any fears. Where the system produces good error messages it is often beneficial to get the learner to make errors deliberately so that she can see how the system works.

The Analogy with English

The use of English words in programming languages can mislead in further ways than just suggesting more intelligence than the system possesses. The English word is usually chosen precisely because it suggests something about its effect. The hope is that using words like PRINT, READ, or INPUT makes things easy. This is often far from the case. First of all such words have often come to have a very specialized meaning within computing which is far removed from their everyday connotation. Secondly, many of these words have several meanings in English and the learner can easily latch onto the wrong one. For example, people sometimes use "then" in the sense of what next: "I went to the shop and then I bought a paper." The boolean operator "and" is sometimes used in this sense as well, as a way of joining a sequence of actions together: "Wash your hands and set the table." "Repeat" misleads beginners who expect that there must be something already in existence to be repeated, and so on. Exasperation with a programming system can occasionally be caused by the mismatch between the designer's and the user's understanding of what is implied by a particular name.

Where Is the Program?

Typing in a program brings with it the idea of a program being some kind of object and of it being somewhere. The Sinclair Spectrum, for example, provides physical analogy in that, on pressing the ENTER button, the line just typed pops up to the top half of the screen where the program being built is shown. This uses the top half of the screen as a kind of window into the memory of the computer.

In more complex systems the notion of a place for holding code before it is placed in main memory is usually extended from the single line of the Spectrum to a buffer of arbitrary size. Editing an existing program means that there are likely to be three different versions of a similar object. One will be the program actually in memory, the other will be a copy of it in the edit buffer incorporating whatever changes have been made, and the third will be the version held in a permanent file (this is likely to be the source of the version in memory). Most editors provide two methods of exit. One simply abandons the contents of the edit buffer and leaves the contents of memory or filing system unaffected. The other overwrites memory or the original file with the contents of the edit buffer. A problem for beginners is that although entry to an editor, and the consequent change of state of the machine, is usually well signalled by a change of prompt or a visual representation of the buffer, exit from the editor is a much quieter business. The large difference between the two exit routes is not usually marked in any visually distinctive manner. This is a manifestation of a very general problem in learning to program: the fact that many important internal changes of state of the machine are not externally signalled in a clear way.

Compiled Languages

The problems mentioned in the previous section, namely use of editors and keeping up with the system's changes of state are compounded when the novice's first language is compiled, such as Pascal, rather than interpreted.

Much technical detail has to be mastered, both to do with the language itself and the system for managing programs before even a simple first program can be run. In general only complete programs can be run, making it impossible to find out easily what a single command, procedure, or function will do on its own. This makes it hard for the novice to learn how to build programs out of smaller parts that he has become familiar with. One partial way around this problem is to provide program templates in which the novice is asked to insert or adjust some small segment.

Novices can be confused about the status of the compiled version of the program and expect that this will automatically keep in step with changes in the source code. A related error is believing that the source code has to be re-compiled each time the program is run, rather than just re-executing an existing compiled version of the program (if one does exist). Use of compiled languages brings other problems for the novice, especially in the diagnosis of errors, since there are usually few debugging aids and the run-time system often has little access to the source code to help construct meaningful error messages.

INAPPROPRIATE ANALOGIES FOR ASSIGNMENT, VARIABLES AND ARRAYS

This section looks at assignment as one small aspect of the notional machine and describes some of the ways that people misapply analogies as well as deal badly with interactions, such as the sequencing between commands. Many of the errors are taken from the work of Soloway and his colleagues at Yale [1, 3, 4, 8].

In the first place, assignment often has a kind of mathematical flavor derived from the names of variables, e.g., A or X, from the quantities assigned, e.g., 3 + B, and from the symbol used to denote assignment, e.g., =, := or −>. The mathematical flavor on its own may be enough to evoke negative reactions.

There is an asymmetry in assignment which confuses some learners. Thus in BASIC we can say

    LET A = 2

but not

    LET 2 = A

which looks entirely plausible.

A common exercise for beginners in Pascal is to interchange the values of two variables. This requires the use of a third, temporary variable, so

    TEMP := A;
      A := B;
      B := TEMP;

Many students get these assignments in the wrong order and express individual assignments back to front. Difficulty in expressing the overall order of the assignments may be due to a lack of regard for the sequential nature of the three commands. They look a little like three equations which are simultaneous statements about the properties of A, B, and TEMP rather than a recipe for achieving a certain internal state (certain programming languages, not considered here, do indeed, make it possible to write equations which may be considered to operate in parallel).

Beginners are often puzzled by such assignments as:

    LET A = A + 1

precisely because they have not understood the asymmetry and the sequential nature of the execution of even this single assignment. The "A"s on each side of the "=" sign are not being treated in the same way. One stands for a location and the other for a value. This difficulty is bound up with lack of understanding both of exactly what a variable is and of the rules for interpretation of statements in the language. Some people get round the difficulty in such statements as:

    LET A = A + 1

by employing a second variable:

```
LET B = A + 1
LET A = B
```

The most common analogy for a variable is to some kind of box or drawer with a label on it. Without further explanation this can be confusing. In particular it is important to stress that each box can hold only one item at a time. An alternative analogy which underlines this idea is that of a slate on which the value is written. Unless this idea is stressed some beginners may not realize that assignment overwrites the existing value. They may think of a variable as either a little self-contained stack or a self-contained list which has the ability to "remember" the history of assignments made to it. After all, most boxes hold more than one thing. They expect that the value overwritten is still available somewhere and can be retrieved.

Another misconception concerns the after-effects of assigning one variable to another:

```
LET A = B
```

Some novices see this as linking "A" and "B" together in some way so that whatever happens to "A" in future also happens to "B." For those who continue in programming there are, of course, situations like this, so the idea is not entirely fanciful. For instance, one of the difficulties when advanced students learn about pointers is understanding that side effects can be produced. So if A and B are pointers and one is assigned to the other (in Pascal)

```
A := B;
```

following down the pointer "B" and changing some part of the structure pointed at also changes the (identical) structure pointed at by "A." This conflicts with what they will have learned to be the case when "A" and "B" hold other kind of data.

The above is an example of a hard issue that occurs in many places when teaching computing, namely the difference between identity and equality. In other words knowing when two objects are in reality the same object as distinct from merely having correspondingly similar parts. A related issue,which is equally hard to grasp concerns objects which look identical on the terminal screen, or printed on paper, but which are really quite different objects. A favorite example is a string of characters such as 456 and the corresponding number.

A third misconception about assignment concerns temporal scope: the fact that the value does not fade away and hangs around until either explicitly changed, the contents of memory are erased or the machine switched off. This may be linked to the idea of a variable remembering its previous values.

A common mistake, when using a variable to keep a running total, is to forget to initialize the total to zero. This omission is reasonable when following the box analogy. After all, if one has not put anything into a box, it's empty, which is sort of like zero. So adding the first item is like adding it to zero. Some systems exacerbate this misunderstanding by assigning default values to unassigned variables.

A further misunderstanding concerns the assignment of values derived from an expression

LET A = 7 + 4

A student may understand "A" to hold 7 + 4 as an unevaluated expression rather than 11. In some Basics "A" is only allowed to hold numbers, so this misunderstanding can be tackled by stressing the idea that a variable can hold only one number.

A very common idea is that assigning from one variable to another involves removing the contents of one box and placing it in the other. Thus the end result of

LET A = 2
LET B = A

is seen as "A" empty and "B" containing 2. Underlying many computer operations is the notion of making a copy and there then being two objects with independent existences. One of the problems for the learner is distinguishing an operation which implies copying, and so independence, from one of sharing and so dependence.

Names are another source of trouble in assignment and in learning to program in general. The policy of using meaningful (to the human) variable names can suggest that the names are meaningful to the computer as well and that there is some link between the human meaning of a name and its corresponding value.

It is a useful teaching strategy to occasionally introduce the use of nonsense names for variables and other entities. This helps to dispel expectations that the machine understands English. However, it may prove surprising to someone who has only understood the system by thinking that it "understood" the appropriate words, so it is as well to be prepared for the resulting confusion.

Arrays

Many of the difficulties concerning assignment of numerical values carry across to assignments involving arrays. In addition, arrays themselves introduce their own problems. Beginners muddle up the array as a whole with a single cell within that array. They also often confuse the subscript which denotes one of the cells with the value stored in that cell.

Arrays are often illustrated as sets of contiguous boxes. Sometimes these are shown in a horizontal line, sometimes as a vertical line. While it does not particularly matter when dealing with one-dimensional arrays, drawing one-dimensional arrays horizontally can cause problems when later dealing with two or more dimensions. This is because it may conflict with standard conventions and so make it harder for the beginner to grasp which subscript deals with which dimension. As it is, students often find it hard to distinguish rows and columns and which subscript should be varied and which held constant in order to progress along a row or down a column.

The confusion between the subscript of an array cell and the value stored there can be deepened by the more general problem of understanding assignment and that symbols on the left of the assignment refer to locations and those on the right to values. See, for example, the following which uses square brackets to enclose array subscripts:

```
A[3] := A[4] + A[2] ;
```

and more difficult:

```
A[3] := A[3] + 5;
```

This last case is hard for all the same reasons that understanding

```
a := a + 5;
```

is hard with the added complication that the beginner may wonder whether it is the subscript which is being added, rather than the value at $A[5]$. Luckily many of these early difficulties do not prove intractable, but "arrays" do represent a real hurdle for the novice programmer. At a later stage further problems arise because of the way that arrays are used to refer to data indirectly, e.g., arrays holding subscripts as their values. This in its turn is an example of a generally hard problem which programmers at all levels find difficult, namely issues concerned with "indirection," i.e., use of pointers, etc.

Beginners get confused by the kind of language used to talk about arrays, for example, the words "read" and "write." We often talk about reading data in and out of arrays both when we mean simply assigning to, or copying from, as well when true input/output is involved.

A stumbling block for many beginners is building a program to input ten values, insert them in sequence into an array, process the array in some way, and then print out a result. Coordinating the necessary loop, array indexing and input/outout and array assignments often proves surprisingly difficult.

There is an interesting input error related to misunderstanding subscription and variables. Some learners write for example (in Pascal) [8]:

```
read(x);
while x < 999 do
begin
    sum := sum + x;
    x := x + 1
end;
```

Here incrementing in the penultimate line (x := x + 1) is understood as meaning read the next value of "x"—as if the values for it already existed in an array and the code meant that it takes on the next value in that array.

INTERACTION ERRORS

Flow of Control

Most students soon learn that a program designates a sequence of events and that these events usually take place on the same order as the instructions are set out in the program. What sometimes gets forgotten is that each instruction operates in the environment created by the previous instructions. Some beginners seem to imagine that the effects of each instruction are somehow saved up until the end of the program, at which point they all happen. Others fail to appreciate the ubiquity of the default rule about flow of control—namely that the next instruction is always executed unless the program instructs otherwise. Some seem to have fond hope that the system will of itself jump around and ignore sections of code which are not wanted under some circumstances. For example, consider the following program designed to print tables for an input number greater than 0.

```
20    INPUT I
30    IF I < 1 THEN GOTO 70
40    FOR J = 1 TO 10
50    PRINT J, "TIMES", I, "IS", J x I
60    NEXT J
70    PRINT "YOUR NUMBER IS TOO SMALL"
```

Here line 70 gets executed whatever the value of I. It's as if mentioning line 70 in the GOTO is thought of as "insulating" this line from entry except via that GOTO.

This kind of "drop through" error is quite common but can be helped by having the student single-step the program if the system supports this. The error can be viewed as an example of a more general and very common difficulty, namely dealing with a programming problem by subdividing it into subproblems and then not taking enough account of the consequent interactions between the subproblems. In the example, the subproblems are "deal with numbers under 1" and "deal with all the other numbers."

There has been a great deal of discussion of the GOTO in the computer literature. Some maintain that like sugar it should be banished from the scene entirely, others suggest that it does not harm in small doses, and others again cheerfully sprinkle their code with it. There is some evidence that they make programs harder to debug (because it is harder to find one's way back through a program, against the stream of the GOTO's as it were) [9]. It is also rather harder to use indenting to help emphasize the structure of a program when using IF . . . GOTO as opposed to IF . . . THEN . . . ELSE.

Novices have trouble with IF . . . THEN and with IF . . . THEN . . . ELSE as they do with IF . . . GOTO (or syntactic variants). They forget that action 2 in

```
IF <boolean expression> THEN <action 1>;
<action 2>
```

in the above is executed whether or not action 1 is: again the same "drop through" error.

Loops cause beginners all kinds of trouble. FOR loops are troublesome because beginners often fail to understand that behind the scenes the loop control variable is being incremented on each cycle of the loop. This is another example of that ubiquitous issue of hidden, internal changes causing problems. Learners also fail to see that an expression involving the control variable will have a different value on each cycle of the loop.

Soloway and his colleagues have collected many examples of undergraduates' difficulties with WHILE and REPEAT loops in Pascal. Many of these center around a program to read in a sequence of values terminated by 99999 and compute the average of the values, not including the 99999. Some of the difficulties concerned the interaction between reading data and looping. For example, a solution might be produced where the first item of data is read outside the loop and so is not included in the total. Many of the problems concerned the ordering of statements inside the loop so that it either did not start or terminate correctly, e.g., by including the 99999 in the average.

Finally, some students treated the WHILE loop as if it generated some kind of interrupt. They expected that the loop could terminate at the very instant that the controlling condition changed value (imagining incorrectly, but reasonably, that the system constantly keeps a check on that value) rather than the next time it was evaluated as the loop cycled.

Some people find it very hard to grasp the idea of what goes on when a program reads in data, say from the keyboard (i.e., INPUT in Basic). In most languages the syntax disguises that a kind of assignment is involved and that the variable mentioned in the statement has its value changed (or initialized) by the statement. Beginners' programs sometimes contain redundant READ or INPUT statements as if they acted as a declaration of intent to the use of the variable named later on. They do not appreciate that execution of the READ stops further execution of the program at that point and that it cannot continue until something is typed in by the user. They do not understand how this statement transfers responsibility from the system to the person at the keyboard to ensure that something happens. I have seen many beginners getting puzzled and complaining that nothing is happening—even eventually breaking out of the program altogether—because they have not understood that the system was waiting for them rather than vice versa.

Perceptual Interactions Between Form and Content

Many syntactic errors in Pascal are associated with the semicolon [10]. Beginners misuse the semicolon in various ways, by omitting it when it should be included, by inserting it when it should be omitted and by muddling up its use with that of the comma.

Semicolons are often omitted in places where the layout of the program appears to make them perceptually redundant, e.g., in the positions surrounded by | | symbols in the following examples.

```
program myprog |;|
var x, y : integer;

functions double(i : integer) : integer;
begin
    ~~~~~~~~
    ~~~~~~~~
end |;|

begin {main program}
    ~~~~~~~~
    ~~~~~~~~
end.
```

In some ways the better the program is laid out, the less need there seems for some of the semicolons. A similar effect seems to apply to the BEGIN at the beginning of the main program which is also often omitted, especially when no procedures or functions are declared.

Redundant, but harmless, semicolons are often placed just prior to an "end" or an "until":

```
begin
    x := 3;
    y := 5;
end
```

Some teachers argue that putting a semicolon in at this position is good practice in that otherwise if an extra line is subsequently inserted before the "end," it is easy to forget to include the terminating semicolon on the previous line.

Extra semicolons in certain positions can disrupt the logic of a program to cause either compile errors or peculiar (and often hard to understand) run time behavior. A favorite position for an extra semicolon is between the "then" part of a conditional and the "else" part:

```
If x > 4
then writeln('x is greater than 4') |;|
else writeln('x is less than or equal to 4');
```

The semicolon surrounded by | | symbols looks perfectly harmless sitting at the end of a line just like other semicolons. The compiler however treats it as the terminator for the "if" statement and then wonders what to do with a new statement starting with "else." Often the error message is not very explicit about what the novice has done wrong.

As mentioned earlier, careful layout of a program can hide misplaced semicolons, whether they be omitted or inserted. As an example of the latter, consider the following program extract:

```
for i := 1 to 10 do |;|
begin
    myarray1[i] := 0;
    myarray2[i] := 0;
end;
```

Perceptually the scope of the FOR loop includes the compound statement from BEGIN down to END. The intention of the loop is to initialize ten elements of two arrays to zero. Because of the extra semicolon, marked, the effect is to execute the FOR loop ten times doing nothing at all and then execute the compound statement once, using whatever value i has (usually ten) once the loop has terminated. This is the kind of behavior that makes novices despair of ever learning to communicate with the computer.

CONCLUSIONS

Programming is a complex skill to learn where even languages designed for the novice such as Basic and Pascal contain many traps for the unwary. Two issues stand out in the examples I have cited. First is the need to present the beginner with some model or description of the machine she or he is learning to operate via the given programming language. It is then possible to relate some of the troublesome hidden side-effects to events happening in this model, as it is these hidden, and visually unmarked, actions which often cause trouble for beginners. However, inventing a consistent story that describes events at the right level of detail is not easy. Very often an analogy introduced at one point does not fit later on, so producing extra confusion in addition to any misapplication of the analogy at the point where it was appropriate.

Occasionally teachers have complete control, not only over the content of the teaching syllabus, but also over both the syntax and semantics of the programming language, as well as over the associated command language.When this is the case it is possible to ensure that the system behaves in a way which is both self-consistent as well as consistent with what the learners are being told by their teaching notes. Most teachers are not in this fortunate position and have to put up with, for example, terrible error messages from their computer whose content, if not impossible to understand, may well be at odds with the story about the machine that they have told the students.

The second important issue concerns the way that learners form a view of how the programming language works and what is going on inside the computer. Very often they form quite reasonable theories of how the system works, given their limited experience, except that their theories are incorrect. They may derive from chance associations with the meaning of English words used in the programming or command language, from overgeneralizations from one part of the language to another, or from the application of inappropriate anlogies. I have often been surprised at the bizarre theories about how the computer executes programs held even by students who have successfully "learned to program."

ACKNOWLEDGMENTS

This article is an abridged version of a longer work commissioned by the Scottish Microelectronic Development Programme. I thank my colleagues, Peter Gray, Roly Lishman, and Josie Taylor for helpful comments and the anonymous referee for convincing me that abridging the original was a worthwhile task.

This chapter has been reprinted by permission of Baywood Publishing Co.

REFERENCES

1. E. Soloway and K. Ehrlich, Empirical Studies of Programming Knowledge, *IEEE Transactions on Software Engineering, SE-10*:5, pp. 595-609, 1984.
2. C. B. Kreitsberg and L. Swanson, A Cognitive Model for Structuring an Introductory Programming Curriculum, *AFIPS Conference Proceedings, 43*, pp. 307-311, 1974.
3. M. H. Burstein, "Learning by Reasoning," unpublished doctoral thesis, Department of Computer Science, Yale University, New Haven, CT, 1985.
4. J. C. Spohrer, E. Soloway, and E. Pope, Where the Bugs Are, *CHI-85 Conference Proceedings*, San Francisco, 1985.
5. B. Shneiderman, Measuring Computer Program Quality and Comprehension, *International Journal of Man-Machine Studies, 9*, pp. 465-478, 1977.

6. R. E. Mayer, Comprehension as Affected by Structure of Problem Representation, *Memory and Cognition*, *4*, pp. 249-255, 1976.

7. J. Statz and L. Miller, The Egg Series: Using Simple Computer Models, *The Mathematics Teacher*, *71*, pp. 459-467, 1978.

8. E. Soloway, E. Rubin, B. Woolf, and J. Bonar, MENO-II: An AI-Based Programming Tutor, *Journal of Computer-based Instruction*, *10*, pp. 20-34, 1983.

9. M. E. Sime, A. T. Arblaster, and T. R. G. Green, Structuring the Programmer's Task, *Journal of Occupational Psychology*, *50*, pp. 205-216, 1977.

10. G. D. Ripley and F. C. Druseikis, A Statistical Analysis of Syntax Errors, *Computer Languages*, *3*, pp. 227-240, 1978.

15

A SUMMARY OF MISCONCEPTIONS
OF HIGH SCHOOL BASIC PROGRAMMERS

RALPH T. PUTNAM
University of Pittsburgh

D. SLEEMAN
JULIET A. BAXTER
LAIANI K. KUSPA
Stanford University

ABSTRACT

This study examined high school students' knowledge about constructs in the BASIC programming language. A screening test was administered to ninety-six students, fifty-six of whom were interviewed. Students were asked to trace simple programs and predict their output. Errors in virtually all BASIC constructs we examined were observed, with many of the misconceptions arising from the application of knowledge and reasoning from informal domains to programming. It is argued that a lack of knowledge of basic features of programming language will prevent students from developing the higher-level cognitive skills that much programming instruction is intended to foster.

Computer programming courses are often offered by high schools on the grounds that learning programming is a powerful way to develop problem solving and reasoning skills. Linn has suggested that such problem solving skills are the culmination of a chain of cognitive consequences of programming instruction [1]. This chain includes competence with specific features of the programming language being learned, skills for designing programs within the language, and general problem solving skills applicable to other formal systems. While knowledge of specific features of the language being studied is only the first link in this chain, it is a prerequisite to the learning of more general design and problem solving skills. For students to engage in tasks such as debugging programs or designing algorithms by analyzing complex tasks, they must have a certain amount of knowledge about the syntax and semantics of a programming language. A student cannot successfully design or debug a program using IF statements, for example, if he or she does not know how these statements operate. Indeed, a major component of learning to program is learning enough about the specific constructs in a language (e.g., IF, PRINT, GOTO, and READ statements in BASIC) to gain an understanding of the "virtual machine" [2], or "conceptual machine" [3], underlying a programming language—a working model of how various constructs in the language function.

In the study reported here, we examined high school students' misunderstandings of the conceptual machine of the BASIC programming language. We used a screening test and structured interviews to determine students' understanding of fundamental constructs such as variables, assignment, and loops. The work parallels research on students' understanding of the Pascal language reported elsewhere [4].[1] By describing the students' misunderstandings we hope to provide data for improving instruction in programming as well as helping us understand the kinds of thinking that learning to program can foster.

METHOD

Subjects

Students from five high school classes participated in the study. The first class (9 students) was designed to teach mathematical concepts by using BASIC programming. Because students were expected to have completed a beginning programming course, little emphasis was placed on developing programming style and competence. Three classes (64 students) were second semester courses in BASIC programming. Students in these classes were interviewed near the beginning of the school term; all had completed an introductory BASIC programming course. The fourth class (23 students) was a first course in BASIC programming; students in this class were interviewed near the *end* of the school term. Of the total of ninety-six students who took the screening test (described below), fifty-six were interviewed.

Screening Test

A test of BASIC programming concepts was developed for the study. The test was devised after examining programs written by students and probing students about programs they had written. The purpose of the test was to detect possible problems in fundamental constructs such as reading data, branching, and looping. Four items required writing the output produced by short (four- to ten-line) programs, each designed to highlight a single concept. In two pairs of items the student was to determine the output to slight variants of programs. The task for two items was to debug a slightly more complex program for which a written description of the intent of the program was provided.

---

[1] This article gives a broader literature review and background for *both* the Pascal and BASIC studies.

Procedure

The screening test was given to volunteer students in the first class and to all students in the other four classes. Most students who made errors on the test were interviewed. (Students who had minor or no difficulties were not interviewed.) The interviews were clinical in nature, with interviewers using questions and short programs prepared in advance, but also following up with various probes and programs composed on the spot. The goal was to clarify as much as possible the nature and extent of the students' misconceptions about BASIC constructs. Students were asked to say what output would be produced by various programs, to trace programs and explain how they worked, and to debug short programs. In several cases, students were asked to trace identical programs with different sets of input data. The questions generally continued until the researcher was able to decide: 1) the nature of the student's error, 2) that the student had a variety of possible ways of interpreting a construct, or 3) that the student had little knowledge of a particular construct. Many of the programs and program fragments used in the interviews are presented in the discussion that follows. A complete set of the materials used will be furnished upon request.

Tape recordings, written notes, and responses generated during the interviews were perused for patterns of errors and misconceptions. As the study was exploratory and qualitative in nature, no quantitative analysis techniques were used. Findings are discussed in the following section.

DESCRIPTION OF
MISCONCEPTIONS ENCOUNTERED

The students we interviewed made errors involving virtually all of the BASIC constructs included in the screening test and interviews. Some of these errors were at a *surface* level, involving faulty knowledge of syntactical features of BASIC (e.g., interpreting the statement LET A = B as assigning the value of A to B rather than the value of B to A). As pointed out in our previous discussion of errors in Pascal [4], these surface errors are analogous to *manipulative* errors in algebra [5] and should be rather easily corrected. *Deep* errors on the other hand, reflect misconceptions involving more fundamental constructs in the programming language. Such errors might imply, for example, a lack of understanding of variables or of flow of control in a program. These misconceptions are presumably more difficult to correct than those involving only surface features of the language.

Errors

The errors (both surface and deep) described below clearly reflect an absence of correct knowledge about various BASIC constructs. In addition, many of the errors reflect the inappropriate imposition of reasoning and knowledge from more informal domains to the formal domain of programming. When confronted with the task of interpreting a piece of programming code involving constructs that they do not understand, students often appear to fill in or *repair* the gaps in their knowledge [6] by giving natural language interpretations to BASIC statements or by attributing to the machine the reasoning power of an average human. If, for example, a student is not sure what a FOR statement does in a BASIC program, he or she may use knowledge about what *for* means in English to make reasonable (but likely incorrect) inferences about how the word functions in the program. Or, a student may assume that the computer will act *reasonably* upon the code in a program, carrying out its instructions as a human would. This student might believe that if a data value is to be read into a variable called SMALLEST, the computer will select the smallest value from a list of values in a DATA statement. (The computer is not this smart; it would actually read the *next* value in the DATA statement, without regard to its value.) Bonar and Soloway have similarly found that in *writing* programs, novices fill in gaps in their programming knowledge by inappropriate use of informal natural language procedures [7].

A comment on the frequency of errors – Our primary purpose in this research was to describe the *nature* of misconceptions of students learning BASIC programming; the *frequency* with which various errors occurred was of secondary concern. Because of the clinical and flexible nature of our interviews it was impossible to assign precise frequencies to the particular misconceptions described below. We shall therefore refer to the frequency of misconceptions only in general terms. As noted above, the screening test was given to ninety-six students of whom fifty-six were subsequently interviewed. We shall refer to a misconception as being *frequent* with this population if it occurred with 25 percent or more of the *interview* population (i.e., 14 or more students), *fairly frequent* if it occurred with six to thirteen students, and *occasional* if it occurred less frequently (i.e., with 1 to 5 students). These figures do not reflect the frequency or the consistency with which each misconception was used by individual students.

Assignment Statements

Two errors with assignment statements occurred. The most common, an occasional error, was the surface level *reversal* of an assignment statement. For example, the statement LET A = B was thought to assign the value of A to B rather than the value of B to A. Students making this error generally interpreted statements such as LET A = B + C correctly.

One student had a somewhat deeper misconception involving the use of an assignment statement as a counter. He declared that the statement LET C = C + 1 was impossible. He had previously assigned the value of 0 to C and interpreted the statement as "Let 0 equal 0 + 1." He said this did not make sense and seemed to think that the statement was an error. Even when the interviewer had the student work through a program containing the statement LET W = A + 1, which the student interpreted correctly, the student could not make sense of LET C = C + 1. This student's misconception appears to be the result of inappropriately bringing knowledge from another domain—algebra—to programming.

PRINT Statements

Students made several different erroneous predictions about output from PRINT statements. The errors demonstrate the variety of interpretations that students can give in the absence of correct knowledge about language features.

Quotation marks – Three students misinterpreted quotation marks in PRINT statements such as PRINT "Q:"; Q. One student simply ignored the text within the quotation marks, printing the value of Q once. Another student thought the quotation marks caused the value of the variable to be printed, saying that the statement would print 4:4. A third student thought that the quotation marks would cause the first value assigned to the enclosed variable during program execution to be printed, resulting in the output 0:4 for the statement PRINT "Q:"; Q. (LET Q = 0 was the first statement in the program.) This last error was the only one of the three that suggested a deeper misconception that a variable could "remember" its original value.

Repeated print – One student, who had major programming difficulties, thought that the statement PRINT X would cause the value of X to be printed several times—enough times to fill up about half a line on the screen. The student gave similar outputs for seven different programs. Although he was not entirely consistent, he generally said the value would be printed only once if there were more data items to be read by the program, several times if there were not more values to be read.

Multiple-value print – Some students thought that when a variable was printed, *all* the values that had been contained in that variable were printed. This occasional misconception is related to *multiple-valued variables* and will be discussed below.

READ Statements

More of the students we interviewed had difficulties with READ statements than with any other aspect of the BASIC language. These difficulties were evidenced both by the large number of students for whom they occurred and the large number of different errors made. All of the students interviewed had seen and used READ statements, although many of them made heavier use of other constructs for inputting data (i.e., INPUT statements). Nevertheless, reading data seemed to be a difficult concept for these students.

Feature-dependent reads – Several of the errors with READ statements involved the belief that the program can select values from the DATA statement on the basis of features of those values (the values are actually read sequentially). All of these errors are examples of the *reasonably human* error class, in which students ascribe too much interpretive ability to the computer.

We call the most common of these feature-dependent reads *semantic read*. Students with this frequent misconception believed that a READ statement used with a meaningful variable name caused the program to select a value based on the name's meaning from the list of values in the DATA statement instead of reading the next value in sequence. For example, students were given the following program fragment:

```
40 READ SMALLEST
50 READ FIRST
60 READ SECOND
70 READ THIRD
80 READ FIRST
200 DATA 99, 2, −3, −100, 6, 29
```

Some students said that −100 would be read into SMALLEST, 99 into FIRST, 2 into SECOND, −3 into THIRD, and then 99 into FIRST. These students thought that semantic constraints created by the meaningful variable names determined which values were read from the line of data. Most of the students with this misconception were consistent, incorrectly assigning semantically constrained values to all meaningful variable names encountered.

In a variant of the semantic read misconception, three students at first appeared to be using variable names as constraints. Probing revealed, however, that they believed the meaningful variable names functioned as subroutine calls or branches to other parts of the programs. One of these students realized later in the interview that he was indeed dealing with variables and subsequently interpreted the READ statements correctly.

Some of the students with the semantic read misconception also tried to impose meaning on single-letter variable names in READ statements. In an occasional misconception, some students thought the position of the letter in alphabetical order determined the position of the value in the data line to be read. The following program was involved:

```
40 READ A
50 READ B
60 READ N
200 DATA 9, 38, −100, 5, 12
```

These students said 9 would be assigned to A (because 9 is the first value in the DATA statement), 38 (the second number) would be assigned to B, and 12 would be assigned to N (because N is near the end of the alphabet and 12 is the last number in the list of data). In another program, in which N was the only variable used, one student used the same reasoning to predict that N would be assigned the last value in the DATA statement. She said this value was assigned to N in *each* of the three READ N statements.

Some students thought that values assigned to single-letter variable names were constrained by other statements in the program. For example, when confronted with the preceding program, one student stated that he could not say what values would be read into variables A, B, and N because he did not know what values the variables were supposed to have. The interviewer then added lines to make the program read as follows:

```
10 LET A = 5
20 LET B = 38
30 LET N = 9
40 READ A
50 READ B
60 READ N
200 DATA 9, 38, −100, 5, 12
```

The student then said that at line 40 the 5 from the DATA statement would be read into A, at line 50 the 38 would be read into B, and at line 60 the 9 would be read into N.

Another student believed that IF statements exerted similar control over READ statements elsewhere in the program. He said that at line 10 of the following program, N would "pick" 0 from the data line because of the condition in line 30:

```
10 READ N
20 PRINT N
30 IF N ≤ 0 THEN GOTO 20
40 DATA 34, 3, 16, 10, 0
50 END
```

Multiple-value read – In a frequently occurring misconception, students thought that a READ statement could cause more than one value to be assigned to a variable, reflecting fundamental misunderstandings about the nature of variables as well as the function of READ statements in programs. *Multiple-value* read errors often occurred in conjunction with *semantic read* as in this program:

```
40 READ EVEN
50 READ ODD
60 READ POSITIVE
70 READ NEGATIVE
200 DATA 9, 38, −100, 5, 12
```

Some students said that the values 38, −100 *and* 12 would be read into EVEN, 9 *and* 55 into ODD, and so forth.

Other students thought that *all* the values in the DATA statement were read into a variable, as in the following program:

```
10 READ X
20 READ Y
30 IF X = 0 THEN GOTO 80
40 IF X = 1 THEN GOTO 60
50 PRINT X
60 PRINT Y
70 GOTO 10
80 END
90 DATA 2, 3, 1, 2, −5, −9, 0
```

These students said that all the values would be read into X and into Y. One student subsequently had difficulty interpreting the IF statement in line 30. As this statement required evaluating only one value and X contained several, the student was unable to predict what the program would do.

In a final variant of *multiple-value read*, some students thought that the number of characters in the variable name determined the number of values read, with one value being read into each character.

Read control − A variety of misconceptions of the READ construct involved the way in which the assignment of values to variables is controlled or ordered. In the first of these misconceptions, the use of more than one READ statement containing the same variable repeatedly accessed the same value in the line of data. Given the following program students with this fairly frequent misconception said that 3 would be assigned to N by each of the READ statements:

```
40 READ N
50 READ N
60 READ N
200 DATA 3, 6, 9, 12
```

Other *read control* misconceptions included different variables reading the data line independently and the requirement of a separate DATA statement for each READ statement. One student thought that a READ statement caused the data value to be *added* to the original value in the variable, the variable thus holding a running total of all values read.

Some students had correct knowledge about how READ statements sequentially access values in the DATA statement but were unsure about what happens when the last of the values is encountered. (In most versions of BASIC, an error message will occur if a READ is attempted after all data values have been read.)

These students gave the following reasonable, but incorrect, predictions about what would happen when READ statements were executed after all values in the DATA statement had been read: 1) subsequent READ statements continue to access the last value in the DATA statement; 2) subsequent READ statements cause the value 0 to be assigned to variables; and 3) subsequent READ statements go back to the beginning of the list of values in the DATA statement.

Variables

The most significant misconception involving variables was that a variable can contain more than one value.[2] These multiple values occurred in a variety of ways. As discussed earlier, some students believed that several values could be assigned to a single variable by a READ statement (*multiple-value read*). Other students knew that values were read one at a time but thought that the values were collected in the variable as they were read or assigned.[3] A PRINT statement would then cause all of the values in the variable to be printed.

Additional difficulties involving variables included confusing two variables in a program and repeatedly using the initial value of a variable rather than updating it. Both of these errors appeared to be instances of a general difficulty in keeping up with the values of variables when tracing programs.

Loop Construction

Several errors in predicting output arose in programs with loop constructions. In one fairly frequent error, a PRINT statement following a loop was repeated as though it were inside the loop, as in this program:

```
10 LET Q = 0
20 READ P
30 IF P = 0 THEN GOTO 70
40 IF P < 0 THEN GOTO 60
50 LET Q = Q + 1
60 GOTO 20
70 PRINT "Q:"; Q
80 DATA 1, -1, 2, 5, -4, -6, 10, -3, 0
90 END
```

Some students said the value of Q would be printed each time the loop was executed.

---

[2] A BASIC variable holds only one value, which is replaced when a new value for that variable is read or assigned.

[3] Similar to the stack construct in computer science.

In an occasional error, which we call *data-driven looping*, loop iterations were thought to continue as long as there were data to be read. For example, students were presented with the following program:

```
10 FOR I = 1 TO 5
20 READ X
30 PRINT X
40 NEXT I
50 DATA 5, 8, 6, 3, 10, 11, 1, 25, 2
```

The following output was predicted:

5   8   6   3   10   11   1   25   2

In both of these errors, students apparently inferred what the program *should* do, incorrectly supplementing their faulty knowledge of the constructs used in the programs with this inference.

Misconceptions specific to FOR/NEXT loops – Three misconceptions occurred only in the context of FOR/NEXT loops. In the first of these misconceptions, the FOR statement acts as a *constraint* on READ statements within the loop rather than determining the number of times the loop body is repeated. This fairly frequent misconception is illustrated in the following program:

```
10 FOR I = 1 TO 5
20 READ X
30 PRINT X
40 NEXT I
50 DATA 5, 8, 6, 3, 10, 11, 1, 25, 2
```

Some students said that only the values between 1 and 5 would be read and printed, resulting in the following output: 5 3 1 2. Other students predicted similar outputs, but with different orderings and repetitions of the values. These errors are examples of students giving incorrect natural language interpretations to BASIC statements; their predictions were reasonable, but incorrect.

In a second misconception involving the above FOR/NEXT loop, one student thought that the FOR statement specified the number of times a variable's value should be printed when it actually determined how many values are read and printed. This student predicted that each of the seven numbers in the data statement would be printed five times (when the program would actually print the first five numbers once).

Finally, some students did not realize that the counter variable in a FOR statement is a variable that is incremented with each iteration of the loop. These students thought that it was acceptable to change the value of the counter variable within the loop body.

IF Statements

Three occasional misconceptions involving IF statements were noted. In all of these misconceptions, students appeared to understand the basic concept of a conditional. They had incorrect knowledge, however, about program actions or flow of control after execution of an IF statement: 1) When the condition of an IF statement is false, execution of the entire program terminates; 2) when the condition of an IF statement is false, control is passed to the beginning of the program; and 3) when an IF statement results in a branch to a PRINT statement, both the variable to be printed *and* the value in the conditional expression are printed. The following lines of a program were involved in one instance of this last misconception (where the value of SMALLEST was 1):

```
30 IF N = 0 THEN GOTO 60
. . .
60 PRINT SMALLEST
```

The student said the output would be:

```
1  0
```

When the conditional in line 30 was changed to N = −99, the student said the output would be:

```
1  −99
```

The student predicted similar output for other programs.

Other Flow of Control Difficulties

In addition to the difficulties involving loops and IF statements, we observed at least two occasional difficulties with the flow of control in programs. The first misconception was that all PRINT statements in a program are executed (even if they should be skipped because of a branching statement). The second was that *all* statements in a program must be executed at least once, even statements that might be skipped because of branches in the program. One student, for example, was asked to trace the following program:

```
10 LET X = 1
20 LET Y = 2
30 IF X = 1 THEN GOTO 50
40 PRINT X
50 PRINT Y
60 END
```

The student traced the program correctly through line 30 and said correctly that 2 would be printed at line 50. At that point, however, the actual end of execution, she said that because line 40 was missed, the computer would go back to line 40 and print X, then continue to line 50 and print Y a second time. She said that execution now ended "because all the statements had been visited." These misconceptions involving the execution of all statements suggest a belief that if something is in a program, it should be used.

Tracing and Debugging

In addition to the particular misconceptions or bugs we have described, many students had general difficulties tracing and debugging programs. Most students were asked to trace programs during the interviews and some were given a program to debug. Students had the following three general difficulties. First, students inferred the function of a program from a few statements. They would trace or predict output, ignoring or misinterpreting statements that did not fit with what they *thought* the program should do. Second, students concentrated on small segments of the program when debugging, making assumptions about what other parts of the program did. In both of these cases, students seemed to be assuming that the computer would be *reasonably human* in its interpretation of programs. Third, students had difficulty keeping track of the values of variables when tracing programs (reflected in an error described earlier in the section on variables).

SUMMARY ASSESSMENTS

After interviewing each student, we rated his or her overall performance on the programming tasks. Twelve (24%) of the students were classified as having essentially no difficulties, nineteen (38%) as having minor difficulties, and nineteen (38%) as having major difficulties.[4] The twelve students who had no difficulties in the interview had made errors on the screening test. In most cases these students made careless errors or rushed through the test.

DISCUSSION

As can be seen, the high school students we interviewed exhibited numerous misconceptions about various constructs in BASIC. We saw errors in virtually every construct in our test and interviews. The students' apparent attributing of human reasoning ability to the computer gave rise to a wide variety of misconceptions. As in our work with Pascal [4], students with a semester or more of experience with BASIC had very fuzzy knowledge of language features and the conceptual machine underlying BASIC.

[4] Summary assessments were missing for six students.

The considerable amount of difficulty students had in predicting the output from and tracing simple programs raises serious questions about the level of understanding high school students are gaining from programming classes. This low level of understanding of the language features and basic constructs of the programming language surely impedes productive engagement in higher level problem solving skills such as planning and debugging. If the goal of programming courses is to develop higher level cognitive skills, it is important that they also provide knowledge in the fundamental programming constructs to which these higher level skills will be applied.

One possible cause for the high levels of misunderstanding may be the students' writing of programs essentially by trial and error, without careful evaluation of results. We have found in our observations of high school programming classes that the focus of assignments is frequently on getting a program to complete a particular task correctly (e.g., adding a list of prices) rather than on aspects of the program that will generalize to other situations (e.g., the structure of a loop for searching through a list).

Joni and Soloway have argued that such a focus solely on correctness often leads to poorly written programs—programs that are difficult to debug, modify, and understand [8]. In addition, this focus seems less than ideal either for gaining the necessary command of programming language features or for developing the more generalizable competencies in Linn's chain of cognitive consequences of programming [1].

ACKNOWLEDGMENTS

We wish to thank the teachers and students who participated in this study. Haym Hirsh and Alan Char helped with the interviewing. Marcia Linn provided an earlier test of BASIC programming. We also thank the Study of Stanford and the Schools for providing funding for the study.

REFERENCES

1. M. C. Linn, The Cognitive Consequences of Programming Instruction in Classrooms, *Educational Researcher, 14*:5, pp. 14-16, 25-29, 1985.
2. P. Wegner, *Programming Languages: Information Structures and Machine Organization*, McGraw-Hill, New York, pp. 84-91, 1968.
3. B. DuBoulay and T. O'Shea, Teaching Novices Programming, in *Computing Skills and the User Interface*, M. Coombs and G. Alty (eds.), Academic Press, London, pp. 147-200, 1981.
4. D. Sleeman, R. T. Putnam, J. A. Baxter, and L. K. Kuspa, Pascal and High School Students: A Study of Errors, *Journal of Educational Computing Research, 2*:1, pp. 5-24, 1986.
5. D. Sleeman, An Attempt to Understand Students' Understanding of BASIC Algebra, *Cognitive Science, 8*, pp. 387-412, 1984.

6. K. VanLehn, On the Representation of Procedures in Repair Theory, in *The Development of Mathematical Thinking*, H. P. Ginsburg (ed.), Academic Press, New York, pp. 201-252, 1983.
7. J. Bonar and E. Soloway, Pre-Programming Knowledge: A Major Source of Misconceptions in Novice Programmers, *Human-Computer Interaction*, 1:2, pp. 133-161, 1985.
8. S. A. Joni and E. Soloway, But My Program Runs! Discourse Rules for Novice Programmers, *Journal of Educational Computing Research*, 2:1, pp. 95-128, 1986.

16
CHILDREN'S MENTAL MODELS
OF RECURSIVE LOGO PROGRAMS*

D. MIDIAN KURLAND
ROY D. PEA
Center for Children and Technology
Bank Street College of Education, New York

ABSTRACT

Children who had a year of Logo programming experience were asked to think-aloud about what brief Logo recursive programs will do, and then to predict with a hand-simulation of the programs what the Logo graphics turtle will draw when the program is executed. If discrepancies arose in this last phase, children were asked to explain them. A prevalent but misguided "looping" interpretation of Logo recursion was identified, and this robust mental model persisted even in the face of contradiction between what the program did when executed and the child's predictions for what it would do.

The power and elegance of recursion as a development in the history of programming languages (such as LISP, the lingua franca of artificial intelligence, and Logo) and its conceptual importance in mathematics, music, art and cognition generally is widely acknowledged [1]. Far less attention has been given, however, to the fundamental *developmental* problem of how people learn to use the powers of recursive thought and recursive programming procedures. Our approach to this research question has been influenced by several findings basic to a developmental cognitive science, specifically, the role of mental models in guiding learning and problem solving, and the widespread use of systematic, rule-guided approaches to problem solution by children, not only adults [2]. Understanding recursive functions in programming involves (programming language) notational and conceptual problems, the latter including problems with understanding flow of control. In programming, the novice is guided by a mental model of how program code controls the computer's operations. For novices, this model is adapted

* This work was supported by a grant from the Spencer Foundation.

over time as the result of both direct instruction and feedback from their own programming and debugging experiences, in which conflicts between their current theory and the behavior of the program is reflected upon.

A widespread belief among computer educators of precollege age populations is that young children can "discover" many of the powerful ideas formally present in programming simply through experimenting within a rich programming environment, as if unconstrained by prior understandings. This belief has been largely due to Papert's popularization of Logo [3], a LISP-like language designed for use by children to allow them to develop powerful ideas, such as recursion, in "mind sized bites." Papert and others assume that children can learn recursion through self-guided explorations of programming concepts in the Logo language. However, our observations of eight- to twelve-year-olds who have had a year of experience programming in Logo indicates that most avoid all but simple iterative programs, which do not require the deep understanding of control structure prerequisite for an understanding of recursion.

In a study examining children's ability to develop recursive descriptions of problems, Anzai and Uesato have shown how adolescents' understandings of recursive formulations of the factorial function is facilitated by a prior understanding of iteration [4]. They demonstrate that for mathematics, recursion can be learned via a discovery process by most children, particularly if they have first experimented with iterative functions. Of their subjects who correctly identified the iterative structure in a set of problems, 64 percent were also able to work out recursive solutions to a second set of problems. However, only 33 percent of the subjects who did not have prior experience with iteration were able to work out the recursive functions. Anzai and Uesato conclude that understanding recursion is aided by an understanding of iteration, but that "we should be cautious when we try to extend the consideration to more complex domains such as computer programming . . . [since] a complex task necessarily involves many different cognitive subprocesses, and it is not always easy to extract from them only the part played by recursion." [4, p. 102]

While Anzai and Uesato focus on the insight necessary to generate a recursive description of a math function, in programming one must acquire that insight *and* be able to implement it in specific programming formalisms [4]. In addition to an understanding of recursion, the child requires an understanding of the logic and terminology governing the control structure of the language. Adult novices have trouble with both. Learning to program they have great difficulties in thinking through flow of control concepts such as Pascal's *while* loop construction [5], and tail recursion in SOLO, a Logo-like language [6], even following extensive instruction. Furthermore, Bonar has found that prior natural language understandings of programming terms misleads novice programmers in their attempts at explaining how a program works [7]. Prior meaning is brought to the task of constructing meaning from lines of programming code. We expect children will also be guided in their interpretation of programming language constructs by their natural language meanings, and by faulty mental models of flow of control structure. Indeed, a widespread experience among programming instructors is that novices have great trouble acquiring the concept of recursion and the ability to use recursive formalisms in their programs.

HOW RECURSION WORKS IN LOGO: A USER'S PERSPECTIVE

In this study, children worked with recursive programs composed of procedures written in Logo. When a Logo program is run, if a procedure references itself, execution of that procedure is temporarily suspended, and control is passed to a *copy* of the named procedure. Passing of control is *active* in the sense that the programmer is explicitly directing the program to execute a specific procedure. However, when the execution of this instantiation of the procedure is finished, control automatically is passed back to the suspended procedure, and execution resumes at the point where it left off. Passing of control in this case is *passive* since the programmer did not need to specify where control should be passed in the program.

To understand how recursive procedures work in Logo one must know:

1. The rule that execution in Logo programs proceeds line by line. However, when a procedure calls another procedure *or* itself, this acts to insert all lines of the named procedure into the executing program at the point where the call occurred. Control then proceeds through each of these new lines before carrying on with the remaining lines of the program. Thus control is *passed forward* to the called procedure, and then is *passed back* to the calling procedure.
2. That when a procedure is executed, if there are no further calls to other procedures or to itself, execution proceeds line by line to the end of the procedure. The last command of all procedures is the END command. END signifies that execution of the current procedure has been completed *and* that control is now passed back to the procedure from which the current one was called. END thus 1) signals the completion of the execution of one logical unit in the program, and 2) directs the flow of control back to the calling procedure so the program can carry on.
3. That there are several exceptions to the line by line execution rule. An important one for recursion is the STOP command. STOP causes the execution of the current procedure to be halted and control to be passed back to the procedure from which the currently executing one was called. Functionally, then, STOP means to branch immediately to the nearest END statement.

How well novice programmers' mental models of the workings of recursive procedures took into account these three central points was our research focus.

CENTRAL POINTS

Subjects

Seven children (two girls and five boys, eleven- to twelve-years-old) in their second year of Logo programming participated in the study. The children were highly motivated to learn Logo programming, and had averaged over fifty hours of classroom programming time under the supervision of experienced classroom teachers knowledgeable in the Logo language, who followed the "discovery" logo pedagogy set out by Papert [3]. All seven children had received instruction in iteration and recursion, and had demonstrated in their classroom programming that they could use iteration and recursion in some contexts.

Materials

Short Logo programs were constructed of procedures which reflected four distinct levels of complexity: 1) procedures involving only direct commands to move the turtle; 2) procedures using the iterative REPEAT command; 3) tail recursive procedures; and 4) embedded recursion procedures. This article focuses on the revealing features of children's performance at levels 3 and 4. Examples of programs at levels 3 and 4 are:

Level 3: tail recursion program (:SIDE = 80)

```
TO SHAPEB :SIDE
    IF :SIDE = 20 STOP
    REPEAT 4 [FORWARD :SIDE RIGHT 90]
    RIGHT 90 FORWARD :SIDE LEFT 90
    SHAPEB :SIDE/2
END
```

Level 4: embedded recursion program (:SIDE = 80)

```
TO SHAPEC :SIDE
    IF :SIDE = 10 STOP
    SHAPEC :SIDE/2
    REPEAT 4 [FORWARD :SIDE RIGHT 90]
    RIGHT 90 FORWARD :SIDE LEFT 90
END
```

Experimental Procedures

Our choice of a method was guided by comprehension studies which utilize "runnable mental models" or simulations of operations of world beliefs in response to specific program inputs [8]. Children were asked to give a verbal account of how a Logo procedure would work, then to hand simulate the running of the program line by line by using a graphic turtle "pen" on paper. Then they were shown the consequences of running the program they had just explained, and if their simulation mismatched the turtle's actions during drawing, they were asked to explain the discrepancies, and one additional problem at that level was presented, with the same procedure.

RESULTS

All seven children made accurate predictions for programs at the first two complexity levels with only minor difficulties. They expressed no problems with the recursive call of the tail recursive programs of level 3; however, two children treated the IF statement as an *action* command to the turtle, and another assumed that since *she* did not understand the IF statement the computer would ignore it. No child made accurate predictions for either embedded recursion program at level 4. The children's problems with explaining embedded recursion may be traced to two related sources. The first involves general bugs in their mental model for how lines of programming code dictate the computer's operations when the program is executed, while the second concerns the particular control structure of embedded recursive procedures.

General Bugs in Program Interpretation

Decontextualized interpretation of commands – Children carried out "surface readings" of programs during their simulations. They attempted to understand each line of programming code individually, ignoring the context provided by previous program lines. They stated the definition of each command, rather than treating program lines as parts of a functional structure in which the purpose of particular lines is context-sensitive and sequence-dependent. This caused particular trouble during their simulations in keeping track of the current value of the variable SIDE, and in determining the actual order in which lines of code would be executed. Understanding recursion is impossible without this knowledge about sequential execution. The child must learn to ask: "How does the line I'm reading relate to what has already happened and affect the lines to follow?" The two bugs which follow concern an opposite tendency, an overrich search for meaning in other program lines.

Assignment of intentionality to program code – The children often did not differentiate the meaning of a command line they were simulating from the meaning of lines of commands they *expected* to follow (e.g., lines that if executed would draw a BOX). For example, in the program SHAPEC, one child came to the IF statement and said: "If :SIDE equals 100 stop. O.K., I think this will make a box that has a hundred side." Another child at the same point in that procedure, simply said: "this makes it draw a square."

Treating programs as conversation-like – As in understanding conversation, and in the problems non-schooled people encounter in formal reasoning (where beliefs about the truth of an argument's premises are focused on rather than the validity of its form [9, 10], children appropriate for problem solving any knowledge they believe will help them understand. In the case of Logo program comprehension, this empirical strategy has the consequence of "going beyond the information given" to comprehend the meaning of lines of code, such as deriving implications from one line of code (e.g., an IF statement) about the meaning of another line. For example, one child interpreted the recursive statement in SHAPEC as having the intention of drawing a square, predicting that the turtle would immediately draw a square before proceeding to the next command.

Overgeneralization of natural language semantics – Children interpreted the Logo commands END and STOP by analogy to their natural language meanings, which led them to believe that when they appear the program comes to a complete halt. Several children thus concluded that procedure SHAPEC would not draw at all, since when :SIDE reaches the value of 10, the program "stops, it doesn't draw anything." In fact, STOP and END each passively return control back to the most recently active procedure.

Overextension of mathematical operators – Children expressed confusion about the functions of numbers as inputs, and in arithmetic functions such as dividing the variable value, or addition of a constant to it, during successive procedure calls.For example, one child explained SHAPEC this way:

> . . . if SIDE equals 10 then stop. See, instead of going all forward 80, you just go forward 10. Then you're gonna stop. Then you're gonna go. Then (line 3) I guess what you're gonna do is keep on repeating that two times, so it'd be forward about 20 instead of forward 10, forward 20 (line 4), and you're gonna repeat 4, so it'd be forward 80 because it says repeat 4 forward side . . .

Numbers were also often pointed to as the mysterious source of discrepancies between the child's predictions and the results of program execution.

Mental model of embedded recursion as looping – The children were fundamentally misled by thinking of recursion as looping. While this mental model is adequate for *active* tail recursion, it will not do for embedded recursion, which requires an understanding of both *active* and *passive* flow of control. *The most pervasive problem for all children was this tendency to view all forms of recursion as iteration.* For example, one child explained the recursive call in program SHAPEB in the following manner:

> [the child explained what the first four lines did, then said]: "line 5 tells it to *go back up* to SHAPE, tells it to *go back up* and do the process called SHAPEB, this is the process [points to lines 2–4]. It *loops back up*, and it divides SIDE by 2 so then SIDE becomes 40 . . . [carries on explaining correctly that the procedure will draw two squares]"

In this example, the child clearly views tail recursion as a form of looping, rather than as a command to suspend execution of the currently executing procedure and pass control over to a new version of SHAPEB. However, in this case his wrong model leads to the right prediction, so he is not compelled to probe deeper into what the procedure is actually doing. This same child explained that SHAPEC:

"... checks to see if SIDE 80 equals 10. If it does, end the program. Next, line 3 [the recursive call] tells it to *go back to the beginning* except to divide SIDE by 2 which ends up with 40. Then it goes down there (line 2) checks to see if SIDE is 10 ... [then] *back to the beginning* ... [continues to loop back until SIDE equals 10 then] checks to see if it equals 10, it does, stops. OK, a little extra writing there (points to lines 4 and 5). [Draws a dot in the paper to indicate his prediction of what the procedure will do and comments] and that is about as far as it goes because it never gets past this SHAPE (line 3). *It is in a loop* which means it cannot get past 'cause every time it gets down there (line 3), *it loops back up.*"

This time the child's explanation and prediction were incorrect since the SHAPEC program makes the turtle draw a series of three squares in a line, each twice as big as the previous one. The child expressed complete bewilderment when the procedure was executed, and could offer no explanation to account for the discrepancies. On the second program of this type, which makes the turtle draw three squares of different sizes inside one another, the child worked down to the recursive call and then said:

"um. Wait a minute. I don't understand this. Well anyway, from past experience, like just now, I guess *it's not going to listen to that command* (points to the recursive call) and *it's going to go past it*, and it's going to [draw a square] and I guess *it's going to end then.*"

Again, when the procedure was run and the child saw he was wrong he expressed confusion, but instead of trying to explain what might cause the procedure to behave as it did he instead asked:

"Is this the same language we used last year? Because last year if you said SHAPE, if you named the program in the middle of the program, *it would go to that program.* We did that plenty of times, but it's not doing that here. I don't know why."

The child blamed the language for not conforming to his expectations, but in doing so he indicated that at *some* level he knew the correct meaning of a recursive call: "It would go to that program." However, though he seemed to know the rule, when he worked through a program, his simpler, and in many cases successful, looping model prevailed.

DISCUSSION AND CONCLUSIONS

We believe these findings are important because they reveal that the children's conceptual bugs in thinking about the functioning of recursive computer programs are *systematic* in nature, and the result of weaker theories that do not correspond to procedural computation in Logo.

These findings also imply that, just as in the case of previous work with adults, programming constructs often do not allow mapping between meanings of natural language terms and programming language uses of those terms. Neither STOP or END stop or end, but pass control back. The reason that this is important for the Logo novice is that when their mental model of recursion as looping fails, they have no way of inferring from the syntax of recursion in Logo how flow of control does work. So they keep their inadequate looping theory, based on their successful experience with it for tail recursion, or blame discrepancies between their predictions and the program's outcomes on mysterious entities such as numbers, or the "demon" inside the language itself. An important issue of a development theory of programming then is: How do inadequate mental models get transformed to better ones?

For a developmental psychology of programming, we require an account of the various factors that contribute to learning central computational concepts. So far efforts to help novices learn programming languages through utilizing programming tutors or assistants have bypassed what we consider to be some of the key factors contributing to novice's difficulties working with computational formalisms. Beyond mistaken mental models about recursion, we have found these to involve atomistic thinking about how programs work, assigning intentionality and negotiability of meaning as in the case of human conversations to lines of programming code, and application of natural language semantics to programming commands. In studies underway, it appears that none of these sources of confusion will be intractable to instruction, although their pervasiveness in the *absence* of instruction, contrary to Papert's idealistic individual "Piagetian learning," suggests that self-guided discovery needs to be mediated within an instructional context.

ACKNOWLEDGMENTS

We wish to thank the participants of a workshop at MIT's Division for Studies and Research in Education, from Geneva and Cambridge, for provocative discussions of these issues. Sally MacKain provided invaluable assistance in running the studies, and providing transcripts.

REFERENCES

1. D. R. Hofstadter, *Godel, Escher and Bach: An Eternal Golden Braid*, Vintage Books, New York, 1979.

2. R. S. Siegler, Developmental Sequences Within and Between Concepts, *Monographs of the Society for Research in Child Development*, *46*, (Serial No. 189), 1981.
3. S. Papert, *Mindstorms*, Basic Books, New York, 1980.
4. Y. Anzai and Y. Uesato, *Learning Recursive Procedures by Middleschool Children*, Proceedings of the Fourth Annual Conference of the Cognitive Science Society, Ann Arbor, Michigan, August 1982.
5. E. Soloway, J. Bonar, and K. Ehrlich, Cognitive Strategies and Looping Constructs: An Empirical Study, (Technical Report No. 242), Yale University Press, New Haven, Connecticut, 1982.
6. H. Kahney and M. Eisenstadt, *Programmers' Mental Models of Their Programming Tasks: The Interaction of Real-World Knowledge and Programming Knowledge*, Proceedings of the Fourth Annual Conference of the Cognitive Science Society, Ann Arbor, Michigan, August 1982.
7. J. Bonar, *Natural Problem Solving Strategies and Programming Language Constructs*, Proceedings of the Fourth Annual Conference of the Cognitive Sciences Society, Ann Arbor, Mighican, August 1982.
8. A. Collins and D. Gentner, *Constructing Runnable Mental Models*, Proceedings of the Fourth Annual Conference of the Cognitive Science Society, Ann Arbor, Michigan, August 1982.
9. A. R. Luria, *Cognitive Development*, Harvard University Press, Cambridge, Massachusetts, 1976.
10. S. Scribner, Modes of Thinking and Ways of Speaking: Culture and Logic Reconsidered, in *Thinking*, P. N. Johnson-Laird and P. C. Wason (eds.), Cambridge University Press, Cambridge, 1977.

17
Preprogramming Knowledge: A Major Source of Misconceptions in Novice Programmers

Jeffrey Bonar
University of Pittsburgh

Elliot Soloway
University of Michigan

ABSTRACT

We present a process model to explain bugs produced by novices early in a programming course. The model was motivated by interviews with novice programmers solving simple programming problems. Our key idea is that many programming bugs can be explained by novices inappropriately using their knowledge of step-by-step procedural specifications in natural language. We view programming bugs as patches generated in response to an impasse reached by the novice while developing a program. We call such patching strategies *bug generators*. Several of our bug generators describe how natural language preprogramming knowledge is used by novices to create patches. Other kinds of bug generators are also discussed. We describe a representation both for novice natural language preprogramming knowledge and novice fragmentary programming knowledge. Using these representations and the bug generators, we evaluate the model by analyzing four interviews with novice programmers.

This paper is based on Jeffrey Bonar's doctoral dissertation.

Authors' present addresses: Jeffrey Bonar, Intelligent Tutoring Systems Group, Learning Research and Development Center, University of Pittsburgh, Pittsburgh, PA 15260; Elliot Soloway, Cognition and Programming Project, Computer Science Department, Yale University, New Haven, CT 06520.

CONTENTS

1. INTRODUCTION

There is a growing literature about bugs[1] in novice programming (Anderson, Farrell, & Sauers, 1984; Johnson, Draper, & Soloway, 1982; Kahney & Eisenstadt, 1982; Shneiderman, 1976; Soloway & Ehrlich, 1984). In this article, we propose a process model to explain bugs produced in early phases of an introductory course. We are concerned with the difficulties a novice has in using basic programming constructs in short programs. In particular, we focus on the knowledge that novice programmers bring to these early programming problems. Our key idea is that many novice programming bugs can be explained as inappropriate use of the knowledge used in writing step-by-step procedural specifications in natural language.[2]

---

[1]There are two usages for the term *bug*. We are using it to refer to an error in a person's behavior, particularly an error in a computer program he or she has written. Often, though, bug is used to refer to perturbations in a person's mental procedure for some task. In this usage, systematic errors in behavior are explained by the bugs in mental procedures. This second meaning is used by Brown and VanLehn (1980) and Resnick (1982) when discussing children's problems with multicolumn subtraction.

[2]Throughout, the term *natural language* will be used to refer to the language in which step-by-step procedures are written. *English,* the other obvious choice, was not used because it unnecessarily implied that the novice programming phenomena discussed here were limited to English.

Our model is motivated by patterns of behavior we repeatedly observed in video-taped interviews of novice programmers solving programming problems (see Bonar, 1985, for a complete discussion). In particular, we characterize what happens when a novice produces a bug:

While solving a programming problem (writing a program), novices will encounter some aspect of the problem they don't understand (an impasse).

In order to move beyond the impasse, novices cast about for a way to resolve the aspect of the problem they don't understand (a patch). Frequently, that resolution involves an appeal to their knowledge of natural language step-by-step procedures that would be applicable in a similar situation.

In implementing the patch, a bug is introduced.

Consider an example from one of our interviews. Subject 13 is working on the averaging problem (Figure 1). This problem requires the student to read in a series of numbers, watching for an ending value of 99999 and producing the average of the numbers read in before the 99999. Producing the average requires the student to accumulate both a sum and count of the numbers read. In the excerpt of Figure 2, he has just specified the test for a **repeat until** loop and is considering how to implement the step after the loop. (Note that the most straightforward solution to this problem would use a **while** loop rather than the **repeat until** loop. We do not focus on that issue here, but see Soloway, Bonar, & Ehrlich, 1983.) At this point (beginning of Segment 143), we see the subject stumbling and apparently searching around. We call this commonly observed behavior an impasse. At the end of Segment 143, he proposes **then** as a connective between the loop test and the average computation after the loop. Note that he is unsure whether this is a correct approach (Segment 144). We describe this proposed **then** as a patch to the impasse. He tests this usage by sounding the phrase to himself (Segment 146), reasoning from Pascal's **if then** statement. Finally, in Segment 148, he uses phrasing from natural language to justify his usage of the buggy **repeat . . . until then . . . .** At this point, he has written the **then** and committed the bug.

Our model draws on the repair theory work of Brown and VanLehn (1980). They studied impasses in children's subtraction algorithms and developed a detailed theory and process model for how bugs arise and are patched (in their work, they refer to repairs instead of patches). In the more complex domain of programming, we have developed a model with two important components:

1. We characterize the knowledge that allows a novice to form a bridge between programming language syntax and semantics and higher level design

Figure 1.   **The averaging problem.**

Write a program which repeatedly reads in integers until it reads the integer 99999. After seeing 99999, it should print out the CORRECT AVERAGE without counting the final 99999. Remember, the average of a series of numbers is the sum of those numbers divided by how many numbers there are in the series.

---

concerns. This is information about how the language constructs are used to accomplish standard programming tasks. We represent this information as schemalike structures called *programming plans*. We discuss the programming plans for both the introductory programming language Pascal and natural language step-by-step procedures.

2. We characterize impasses arising from missing or misapplied programming plans needed in the course of developing a program. We propose that many bugs arise out of novice strategies for patching an impasse and continuing a problem solution. We call these strategies *bug generators*. We focus on the bug generators that patch an impasse by using the knowledge of how the problem would be solved with natural language step-by-step procedures. This knowledge is used to to supply missing programming language knowledge.

The paper is organized as follows. In Section 2, we discuss programming plans as a representation to describe both the knowledge used to write step-by-step natural language procedures and the knowledge used to write Pascal programs. We also describe the relationship between natural language procedure knowledge and Pascal programming knowledge. Section 3 discusses the process of novices resolving impasses with patches characterized by our bug generators. In Section 4, we present a preliminary evaluation of the model.

2.   REPRESENTING NOVICE PROGRAMMING KNOWLEDGE

The content and structure of novice knowledge has been studied in several different domains including physics (Chi, Feltovich, & Glaser, 1981; DiSessa, 1982), geometry (Anderson, Greeno, Kline, & Neves, 1981), algebra (Lewis, 1981; Matz, 1982), and programming (Ehrlich & Soloway, 1983; Rich, 1981; Soloway, Ehrlich, Bonar, & Greenspan, 1982). A key generalization is that novices use schemalike structures we call *plans*. We propose two kinds of plan knowledge and links between them:

Novice knowledge of step-by-step natural language procedures: We refer to the set of step-by-step natural language procedure plans that a novice

Figure 2. **Excerpt of transcript for Subject 13. Up to this point, the subject has written a loop body for the ending value averaging problem. Here he is working on specifying the test for the loop and the code following the loop. Square brackets enclose comments we have added.**

Subject 13: [reading from problem] After seeing **99999**, it should print out the correct average, so until, ahhh, until I equals **99999** [he writes **until I = 99999**].

Interviewer: Okay.

Subject 13: Ahhh, and then [he pauses, reading what he's written], "repeat, until," and then I would have, then [writes **then**]. Can you have a **then** in the repeat until? No, I don't recall that.

Interviewer: Okay.

Subject 13: [mumbles] if then, while then, repeat until then [louder now], well, it makes sense. I'm not sure if that's right, I don't recall using it before.

Interviewer: How does it make sense?

Subject 13: It makes sense because you are repeating until that [points to **until** line] and *then* [his emphasis] what do you do? Well, *then* take the average. ... [after the **then** he writes **Average : = Sum/N**]

---

brings to a programming course as *SSK* (step-by-step natural language programming knowledge).

Novice knowledge of the programming language under study: We refer to these plans as *PK* (Pascal programming knowledge).

Functional and surface links between the SSK and PK: These links allow a novice to traverse between the two different sets of knowledge structures.

In what follows, we describe each of these components in turn.

2.1. SSK: Preprogramming Knowledge

Novices bring a knowledge of standard tasks in step-by-step natural language procedures to their introductory programming course. Examples of such tasks include looping, making choices, and specifying sequences of actions. We have studied this preprogramming knowledge with problems like the factory gate problem shown in Figure 3. The problem asks the subject to write a

Figure 3.   **The factory gate problem.**

Please write a set of explicit instructions to help a junior clerk collect payroll information for a factory. At the end of the next payday, the clerk will be sitting in front of the factory gates and has permission to look at employee pay checks. The clerk is to produce the average salary for the workers who come out of the door. This average should include only those workers who come out before the first supervisor comes out, and should not include the supervisor's salary.

---

step-by-step natural language procedure for a junior clerk to collect payroll information from workers coming out of a factory gate. The clerk needs to report on the average salary for all the workers who leave the gate before the first supervisor leaves the gate. This problem was designed to parallel the averaging problem.

Figure 4 shows a sample solution to the factory gate problem. This solution is from one of our subjects before he had taken a programming course, and it illustrates several features of step-by-step natural language procedures. Step 5, for example, specifies counting with the phrase "add number of"; Step 6 specifies a total with the phrase "add all." The overall structure of the loop (Steps 1 to 4) is specified by illustrating how to do the task for the first two workers followed by the phrase "and so on" (Step 3). Finally, step 4 specifies the stopping condition for the loop. This condition is phrased as a continuously active test, always watching the action of the loop for the exit condition to become true. (This is sometimes referred to as a *demon* control structure.) In general, the novice seems to be using plans for standard tasks such as adding up numbers, stopping the loop, and so forth.

When coming into a programming course, novices will have a fairly complete SSK. This is to be expected because SSK is regularly used by most people to specify simple step-by-step procedures (Bonar, 1985, discusses SSK plans in detail; see Miller, 1981, for an earlier discussion of some standard features in step-by-step natural language procedures).

2.2. PK: Fragments of Programming Knowledge

PK represents the knowledge that allows novices to write some parts of a program correctly. Besides the obvious information about syntax and semantics, PK plans also capture the goals and tactics critical to implementing some task as a program. Our plans contain several different pieces of information. Consider, for example, the counter variable plan shown in Figure 5 and its components:

Plans are linked together in a general/specific hierarchy. The counter variable plan, for example, is a specialization of the running total variable plan.

Figure 4.   **Typical answer for the factory gate problem. This procedure was written by Subject 11 before studying Pascal.**

---

1. Identify worker, check name on list, check wages
2. Write it down
3. Wait for next worker, identify next, check name, and so on
4. When super comes out, stop
5. Add numbers of workers you've written down
6. Add all the wages
7. Divide the wages by the number of workers

Plans contain information about the key roles and aspects of the plan. In the counter variable plan, we represent this information as slots describing the plan, its initialization, its update, how it is used, and the type of the variable.

Plans contain knowledge needed to actually implement a plan in a specific programming language. With the counter variable plan, there is specific information about how a counter is implemented in Pascal.

Although a novice's SSK is relatively complete, his or her PK is fragmentary. This is to be expected; the novice is just learning about PK. Not only does a novice have fewer PK plans than would an expert, but the connections between the PK plans are not as rich.

2.3. Functional and Surface Links Between SSK and PK

Although we have discussed SSK and PK separately, they have many similarities. There are two in particular:

1. Functional similarities exist because both SSK and PK are concerned with repeated actions, choice between conditions, counting, and so on.

2. Surface similarities exist because the programming language Pascal (like most others) shares many words with natural language. There are many common lexical entities in the two plan sets, irrespective of functional similarity of the plans connected.

We capture these similarities as functional and surface links between the SSK and PK plan sets. Although we distinguish between these two kinds of links, novices often do not. For example, the bug in the protocol of Figure 2 shows a confusion between surface and functional links. We see that the subject is confused about the relationship between the natural language *then* (indicating a following step) and the **then** of Pascal's **if-then-else** construct. We say that he is

Figure 5.   Counter variable plan. The double right arrow (a) indicates a link to another (more general) plan. The boxes (□) indicate slots of the plan.

Counter Variable Plan

SPECIALIZATION OF ⇒ Running Total Variable Plan

□ *Description:* Counts the occurrences of some specific action.
□ *Initialization:* Set to zero.
□ *Update:* Adds one to the current value.
□ *How used?* Always found within a piece of code that is executed repeatedly.
□ *Type:* Integer values.

Pascal Implementation of Counter Variable Plan

□ *Initialization:* CV := 0
□ *Update:* CV := CV + 1
□ *How used?* Usually found within a **while** or **repeat** loop. Counts are created by successive increments as the events to be counted occur.
□ *Type:* **integer**

---

using the surface (lexical) link between *then* and **then**. Based on this surface link, he is assuming a functional link that allows him to use **then** with a natural language meaning.

Another example from the protocols illustrates confusion between surface and functional links associated with the word *while*. In natural language, *while* is typically used as a continuously active test, as in: *"while* the highway stays along the coast, keep following it north." This kind of control structure is unusual in a programming language. More typical is a construct in which the loop condition gets tested once per loop iteration (e.g., the **while** loop in Pascal). The surface link between the two kinds of "while" allows a novice to infer similar semantics. One of our subjects even inferred a semantics for a continuously active test in the Pascal **while** loop: "every time [the variable tested in the **while** condition] is assigned a new value, the machine needs to check that value. . . ."

3.   THE PROCESS OF GENERATING A BUG

Because novice programming knowledge is fragmentary, by definition there must be gaps in that knowledge. Thus, in writing a program, a novice will encounter such a gap and be at what we have called an impasse. In order to bridge these gaps, the novice uses patches. By their very nature, these patches are likely to be incorrect. For this reason, we call the processes that create these patches bug generators. We argue that the bug generators draw on inappropriate or incorrect knowledge, such as from SSK.

Consider a detailed example of some bug generators. Subject 13 wrote Sum : = 0 + I as part of a running total update inside a loop body for the averaging problem (see his code in Figure 6). He has identified I as the variable to receive new values, entered by the user. He has also identified Sum as the variable to hold the running total. Although there are a number of problems with this code, we focus on a single bug. (In the Appendix we show a detailed excerpt from Subject 13's protocol. That excerpt shows Subject 13 actually writing this code and attempts to analyze all the bugs that appear there.) In the protocol, Subject 13 points to this line and says "it reads the sum." The only Read statement Subject 13 has used has no arguments and is above the loop along with a Readln. What, then, does the subject mean by "reading the sum"? Our bug analysis describes several relevant bug generators and is shown in Figure 7.

The impasse in this case is that Subject 13 did not know how to implement a read operation for an input new value variable in Pascal. A correct Pascal implementation uses an explicit Read(I) in each iteration of the loop. Three plausible explanations, each based on a different bug generator and one based on a slip interpretation, are shown for the bug. (The reason for multiple explanations is discussed later.)

The first bug generator plausibly explaining this bug is the *programming language used as it if were natural language (PL used as NL)* bug generator. This bug generator operates on a specific plan or plans, using surface links between SSK and PK versions of the plan. Even though they are surface links, the novice treats them as functional links, assuming that the natural language semantics can be used for programming language constructs. The programming language construct is given similar semantics to the parallel natural language construct. In the example with Subject 13, the PL used as NL bug generator operates on the input new value variable plan. Getting a new value for the input new value variable has been implemented implicitly, which we claim is typical of the natural language implementation.

This claim about natural language implementation derives from our studies of SSK using problems like the factory gate problem of Figure 3. In those studies, we found that getting data was often implemented implicitly. For example, in Line 1 of Subject 11's answer to the factory gate problem (Figure 4), he says: "1. Identify worker, check name on list, check wages." Here, we claim, getting the input value (the worker) has been done implicitly. Note that this operation is not always implicit. In Line 3 of the same factory gate procedure, for example, the subject says: "3. Wait for next worker, identify next, check name, and so on." In this case, we say that getting the input value has been done explicitly with the phrase: "Wait for next worker . . . ."

The second explanation for the bug in Figure 7 uses the *programming language interpreted as natural language (PL interpreted as NL)* bug generator operating on the

Figure 6.   Subject 13's first attempt at the loop for the averaging problem. Line numbers are referred to in the protocol shown in the Appendix. N is the counter variable, Sum is the running total variable, and I is the input new value variable.

```
N := 0;                              (1)
Sum := 0;                            (2)
repeat                               (3)
    Sum := 0 + I                     (4)
    N := 1                           (5)
    Sum := I + I                     (6)
    N := 2                           (7)
until                                (8)
```

Read statement written above the loop. In this case, the subject is seen to be interpreting the Read as if it were a declaration statement. (There is support for this explanation in that the subject discussed the Read statement while discussing other declarations.) The patch was to interpret the Read as if it were natural language. We claim that in natural language one can declare that reading will be done and have that reading be implicit in the rest of the step-by-step procedure.

This claim about natural language again derives from our studies of SSK. This notion of an input declaration comes from a natural language implementation strategy where the subject uses an early step in the procedure to describe how new data values are retrieved. In later steps, new input values are referred to implicitly. For example, one of our subjects working on the factory gate problem used the lines: "Each worker will be coming out of the gate in turn. Write down the value of each paycheck . . . ."

Note that the distinction between the PL used as NL bug generator and the PL interpreted as NL bug generator is fine. In the PL interpreted as NL bug generator, the novice uses a programming language construct to implement a natural language plan: a Read used as a declaration that reading will occur into a certain variable. In the PL used as NL bug generator, on the other hand, the novice uses programming language constructs as if they had their natural language meanings or omits programming language constructs that would not be needed in natural language: the implicit Read(I) every time a data value is needed.

The third explanation for the bug in Figure 7 uses the *one variable assumed to have multiple roles (multirole variable)* bug generator. In this interpretation, the subject patches an impasse about getting new values in the loop by collapsing the purpose for two different variables. In particular, he has collapsed the running total to be accumulated with the new value to be read from a user. In this interpretation, he thinks that the running total happens automatically when a new value is read from the user. The subject understands the statement Sum

Figure 7. **Bug analysis showing the operation of bug generators. The hands pointing right (🖝) indicate each different plausible bug generator explanation for the bug.**

BUG: "It reads the sum": Sum : = 0 + I

The subject should be saying something like "it reads in a value which is added into the sum."

🖝 *PL used as NL* **on input new value variable**

The read operation is done implicitly whenever a value is needed.

🖝 *PL interpreted as NL* **on Pascal — Read/Readln**

Here the subject is treating **Read; Readln** pair as if it was declaring that reading is to be done, and the results of the read will be used with sum.

🖝 *Multirole variable* **on running total variable, input new value variable**

The subject is using the variable sum as if it will automatically get a new value added in whenever that new value is read.

🖝 *Slip*

Just slipped and forgot to say ". . . a value which is added. . . ."

: = 0 + I to mean that the variable **Sum** gets the value of I added in every time a new value of I gets **Read**. This bug generator derives from the flexibility of a natural language noun phrase. A noun phrase can have several different aspects, normally disambiguated by context. In the multirole variable interpretation of our example, the noun phrase "the sum" has the two aspects accumulated so far and made up of values read. Rosnick (1982) has found a similar collapsing of variable roles in algebra students solving word problems.

The fourth explanation is a slip bug generator explanation. It says that the subject simply spoke sloppily and clearly understands that a **Read(I)** statement must appear elsewhere.

From the example in Figure 7, we see that it is possible to produce plausible explanations for a bug based on patches from two or more bug generators. If several different patches produce the same result, there is no systematic way to choose between the different possible bug generators. In fact, it is reasonable that novices can construct a patch using several bug generators that suggest similar approaches. Given the current methodology, however, we have no way to relate the novice programmer's behavior to possible interactions between plausible bug generator explanations.

Notice that we describe each bug generator in the example in terms of the plans active at the time of the impasse. We view bug generators as procedures that use one or more active plans to create a patch. We have categorized the bug generators based on how they use the active plans. We describe each of these three categories, with examples of each.

SSK Confounds PK. With these bug generators, the novice uses an SSK version of an active plan to confound the PK version of that plan.

PL used as NL (programming language used as natural language) bug generators use a programming language construct because it has the same words as a phrase used in the natural language implementation of an active plan. For example, in Figure 7, Subject 13 may have used the programming construct read as implying an implicit read operation to be executed whenever needed. In natural language, data are often retrieved in this way.

PL interpreted as NL (programming language interpreted as natural language) bug generators interpret a programming language construct as if it were a phrase used in a natural language implementation of the plan on which it is operating. In Figure 2, for example, Subject 13 seems to have interpreted then from Pascal as the phrase *then* in natural language.

Multirole variable (multiple roles for a variable) bug generators use a single variable for multiple roles from current active plans. This bug is designed to capture that aspect of natural language where a single noun phrase can have several different referents depending on context. For example, in natural language we can talk about "the sum of the wages" and "the count of the wages." Similarly, one of our subjects seems to have used the same variable to stand for both a running total variable (summing input values) and the counter variable (counting those input values). (In the excerpt, I is the variable that holds the input values and N is the multirole counter variable and running total variable: "I want to get a statement that is going to be clear that we're going to add the numbers, each number entered, we'll have the tally of the, number of integers entered . . . ahhh, N equals, ahmmm integer." [Writes: N := I].)

NL construct (new programming language construct from natural language) bug generators invent a new programming construct based on a natural language implementation of the parameter plan. For example, one of our subjects wrote the following line: New := next New; to indicate that the next value is needed for the new value variable.

Generic name (variables named generically) bug generators use generic names for parts of the program or variables. These names are based on common programming language implementation strategies. Program elements are named on the basis of how we talk about them when describing the program. For example, our subjects would talk about the input new value variable as "the variable holding the integers read in" and give that variable the name integer.

Intra-PK. These bug generators use incorrect or incomplete PK versions of the active plan to patch an impasse. Patching occurs by using knowledge within PK.

Trace (statements ordered in execution order) bug generators order the program as if it is an execution trace. For example, one of our subjects produced the following code for the body of the averaging problem (Sum is the running total variable, I is the new value variable, and N is the counter variable):

```
Sum : = 0 + I
N : = 1
Sum : = I + I
N : = 2
```

Overgeneralize (programminng language overgeneralization) bug generators allow a subject to overgeneralize from one Pascal implementation plan to
another. For example, subjects often will initialize all variables whether this is
needed or not.

In tactically similar (tactical similarity) bug generators, the subject fails to
distinguish between plans that do similar things but are implemented differently. For example, subjects will use the assignment operator to give a value to
Pascal constants or in association with a **read** statement.

Other Confounds PK. With these bug generators, the novice uses knowledge
from other (i.e., not SSK or PK) domains to confound the PK version of the active plan.

Other domain (knowledge from other domains) bug generators use an understanding from a domain such as mathematics. For example, one of our subjects assumed that the variable I will always increment implicitly, much like
the i used in mathematical notation for a series.

OS confound (operating system confound) bug generators confound a command or operation from the operating system with a programming language
construct. For example, one of our subjects used an editor command within his
program.

Our bug descriptions also include a *slip* as a plausible explanation. A slip refers to a random error produced while the novice is distracted, a speech slip, or
a typographical error.

4.   EVALUATING THE MODEL

This section presents a preliminary evaluation of our model. In particular,
we present evidence that a significant portion of novice bugs can be explained
by the SSK confounds PK bug generators. Our data are taken from a detailed
analysis of four protocols selected from a body of interviews originally conducted to explore novice programming cognition. In the selected protocols, we
present the same introductory programming problem to four different novice
programmers, all in the fourth to sixth week of an introductory programming
course.

4.1.   Methodology

In our interviews, we present introductory programming students with a
Pascal programming problem. Subjects are instructed to think aloud as they
develop a solution to this problem. Protocols of these sessions were then ana-

lyzed with standard techniques used to study novice understanding of physics (Chi et al., 1981), algebra (Clement, 1982), children's arithmetic (Resnick, 1982), and other domains. We have also drawn on methodologies developed by Newell and Simon (1972) and discussions of methodological issues arising from the use of verbal reports as data (Ericsson & Simon, 1980; Ginsberg, Kossan, Schwartz, & Swanson, 1981).

Our analysis of the protocols has two steps: the plan analysis and the bug analysis. In the plan analysis, we relate the relatively abstract plan descriptions to the actual utterances and programs produced by the novice. In addition, because our claim is that novices use both SSK and PK while programming, we need to know whether the novice has used an SSK or PK implementation of each plan. In order to make the distinctions between SSK and PK versions of each plan, we have developed a series of criteria for each. The criteria specify those subject utterances we use to justify a claim that a certain plan is in use.

The criteria for SSK plans are based on our analysis of a study in which 34 subjects were given problems like the factory gate problem (Figure 3). Each of these problems required the use of specific plans. A subject's response required some implementation for each of these plans. Each plan implementation found (including the case of not explicitly using the plan) is represented on the list of criteria for that plan. These lists of criteria represent the strategies we know to be used in implementing each plan. The criteria for PK plans are based on our own introspection about the implementation strategies for PK plans.

Consider the example of plan analysis and use of criteria in Figure 8. In that plan analysis, we claim that Subject 6 has used both an SSK and PK version of the results variable plan. In Segment 173, she is discussing her implementation of the results variable. In the first part of the segment, she describes the implementation without any reference to how the count and sum are accumulated. This satisfies a criterion for an SSK version of the plan. Later in the segment, she goes into detail about the accumulation of the count and sum, satisfying a criterion for a PK version of the plan. We call each such piece of evidence (i.e., satisfaction of a criterion) an *evidence item*.

An example in Figure 9 illustrates how subtle the plan analysis can get. In the plan analysis, we claim that Subject 11 has used both an SSK and PK version of the counter variable plan in a single sentence (Segment 112). Evidence for the SSK version is the phrase "counting the numbers of integers that come through." Evidence for the PK version is the phrase "implementing by ones." These evidence items suggest that the novice is using both the SSK and PK versions of the plan within the same sentence. The difference is based on how the counting operation is viewed. "Counting the number of integers that come through" indicates that the subject intends an operation that counts the elements of a set that has been completely acquired before the count starts. On the other hand, "incrementing by ones" both uses programming jargon ("incrementing") and indicates an operation that counts each element, one at a time.

Figure 8.   **Protocol segment with claimed use of both an SSK and PK version of the results variable plan.**

Subject 6: . . . what I'll want to be doing at the end is dividing the sum by the total of numbers to find an average, so I'll always have to keep track of both. So, after each number is read in, I will have, I will be keeping track at that same time as the calculation is made of the count and of the sum, so at any one point where the sentinel's read in, I will have both figures available to read in an average.

PLAN: Result variable
Evidence: Natural language
". . . dividing the sum by the total of numbers to find an average, . . ."
Evidence: Pascal
"after each number is read in, . . . I will be keeping track . . . of the count and of the sum . . ."

Counts of evidence items are used in our quantitative summaries (presented later) to represent overall plan activity. Note that a plan instance with several evidence items actually counts once for each evidence item. We would count two evidence items in our example of Figure 9, one for an SSK version of the plan and one for a PK version.

In the bug analysis, we show how errors made by a novice can be plausibly explained as bug generators operating on currently active plans. We analyze each piece of buggy behavior in a separate bug annotation. In Figure 7, we showed an example of such an annotation. After briefly describing the bug, the annotation describes the bug generators and plans that plausibly explain the bugs.

The bug generator set used in our bug analysis was developed after an examination of the first protocol presented here. That bug generator set was then used to analyze the other three protocols. In this way, we provide a minimal test of the explanatory power of a chosen set.

4.2. Overview of Protocols Analyzed

Before presenting a detailed analysis of the subjects' performance, we present an overview of each subject's work on the averaging problem. These programs and descriptions provide a context for the data that follow.

Interview 1. Subject 13's final program is shown in Figure 10. There are a number of things wrong with this program, but most critical is his peculiar loop body. Notice that within the loop body, **Sum** (the running total variable) is first set to **0** (Line 1) and then to **I + Next I** (**I** is the input new value variable) (Line 2), while **N** (the counter variable) is set to **1** (Line 3) and then **2** (Line 4).

Figure 9.   **Protocol segment with claimed use of both an SSK and PK version of the counter variable plan.**

Subject 11: . . . I want it simply incrementing by ones, it's counting the number of integers that come through, . . .

> **PLAN: Counter**
>   Evidence: Natural language
>   "counting the number of integers . . ."
>   Evidence: Pascal
>   "incrementing by ones"

The subject seems to be implementing the loop with the following natural language strategy: Show an example of the first few steps and assume that the other iterations will happen correctly (he actually shows the first two steps). In the Appendix, we show an analyzed excerpt from Protocol 1.

Interview 2. Subject 6's final program is shown in Figure 11. It is almost correct. His problem is that there is no **READ** inside the loop. In the protocol, he convinces himself that he needs a **READ** above the loop (Line 1) to make the **WHILE** test make sense (Line 2), but never thinks to put a second **READ** inside the loop also. At one point, he uneasily states that each test of **NEWNUM** in the **WHILE** statement (Line 2) will know to read a new value for that iteration.

Interview 3. Subject 11's final program is shown in Figure 12. Her program is almost completely correct. Like Subject 6, her bugs are related to reading new values inside the loop. She recognized that some sort of **Read** was required inside the loop and even realized that it had to come after the **Count** increment (Line 1) and **Total** update (Line 2). The **Read (I)** below the loop (Line 3) was originally, and correctly, put at the bottom of the loop body. In the protocol, she argues that leaving it there would cause the program to read a new value before the previous value read is processed. She uneasily moved **Read (I)** out to its current position outside the loop (Line 3) and settled on **Readln** (Line 4) at the bottom of the loop to express, as she put it, "the right amount of reading."

Interview 4. Subject 12's final program is shown in Figure 13. This program is almost correct. Its bug involves the first value **READ** (before the start of the loop) (Line 1). She reads in a starting value, but then sets **NUM** (the input new value variable) to **0** (Line 2), losing that starting value. From the protocol, it seems that she does this because she wanted to initialize all variables used inside the loop to **0**.

Figure 14 contains overview statistics for the four protocols analyzed. Interviews lasted between 23 and 45 min. It is not clear why Subjects 2 and 4 took nearly twice as long as did Subjects 1 and 3. Time spent on the problem does not correlate with plan usage or with number of bugs.

Figure 10. Final program for Subject 13 working on the averaging problem. Numbers on the right mark lines discussed in the text.

```
Program Average (Input/, Output);
Var
   N, Sum : Integers
   Average : Real;
Const : Sentinel
Begin (* Average of the integers entered *)
   Writeln ('Enter series of integers to be averaged');
   Writeln (Integers will be Averaged when you
                          enter the Integer 99999);
   Read;
   Readln;
   Sentinel := 99999;
   N := 0;
   Sum := 0;
Repeat
   Read;
   Readln;
   Sum := 0                                              (1)
   N := 1                                                (3)
   Sum := I + Next I                                     (2)
   N := 2                                                (4)
   until I = 99999
   then Average = Sum/N
Writeln ('Average':= 0);
END.
```

Figure 11. Final program for Subject 6 working on the averaging problem. Numbers on the right mark lines discussed in the text.

```
PROGRAM AVERAGE (INPUT/, OUTPUT);
CONST
   SENT = 99999;
VAR
   NEWNUM, COUNT, SUM, AVE : INTEGER;
BEGIN
   COUNT := 0;
   SUM := 0;
   READLN;
   READ (NEWNUM);                                        (1)
   WHILE NEWNUM <> SENT                                  (2)
     DO BEGIN
         SUM := NEWNUM + SUM;
         COUNT := COUNT + 1;
         END;
   IF COUNT <> 0
     THEN AVE := SUM DIV COUNT
   WRITELN ('AVERAGE = '), AVE:8:2;
END.
```

Figure 12. Final program for Subject 11 working on the averaging problem. Numbers on the right mark lines discussed in the text.

```
Const
    Sentinel = 99999;
Var
    I, Count, total, AVG : Integers;
Begin
    Count := 0;
    Total := 0;
    Writeln ('Enter integer');
    Readln;
    Read (integer);
    While I <> 99999 Do
        Begin
            Count := Count + 1;              (1)
            Total := Total + I;              (2)
            Readln                           (4)
        End
    Read (I)                                 (3)
    Avg := Total Div Count
    Writeln ('Avg is ', Avg:0)
```

Figure 13. Final program for Subject 12 working on the averaging problem. Numbers on the right mark lines discussed in the text.

```
PROGRAM SUMUP (INPUT/,OUTPUT);
CONST
    SENTINEL = 99999
VAR
    NUM1, SUM, AVERAGE, COUNT : INTEGER;
BEGIN
    WRITELN ('READ IN AN INTEGER AND CONTINUE UNTIL');
            ('FINISHED THEN ENTER 99999 . . . ');
    READLN;
    READ (NUM);                             (1)
    COUNT := 0;
    SUM := 0;
    NUM := 0;                               (2)
    WHILE NUM <> SENTINEL DO
        BEGIN
        SUM := NUM + SUM;
        COUNT := COUNT + 1;
        READLN;
        READ (NUM)
        END;
    AVERAGE := SUM DIV COUNT;
    WRITELN ('AVERAGE IS, ' AVERAGE : 0);
END.
```

Figure 14.   Summary statistics for the four protocols analyzed. "Bugs" refers to the number of bugs found in the protocol.

	Protocol Number			
	1	2	3	4
Subject number	13	6	11	12
Duration (minutes)	32	45	23	45
Plan evidence items	159	177	104	107
SSK Plans	43	50	16	16
PK Plans	116	127	88	91
Plan evidence items/minute	5.0	3.9	4.5	2.4
Bugs	32	19	11	10

5.   RESULTS OF THE ANALYSIS

We present our analysis based on three expectations derived from our model of novice programming bugs.

5.1.   Expectation 1: Regular and Extensive Use of Plans

We have claimed that novices use both SSK and PK represented as plans. If this is the case, plan usage should be pervasive: The first expectation is that novices show a regular and pervasive use of plans. Novices should make use of both SSK and PK plans.

Figure 14 contains the statistics relevant to this expectation. There were 104 plan evidence items in the protocol with the fewest plan evidence items (Protocol 3). This protocol averaged 4.5 plan evidence items per minute. The protocol with the most evidence items had 177, averaging 3.9 plan evidence items per minute. Although there is no base line, it seem fair to say that our subjects did use plans pervasively.

In Figure 15, we show the plan evidence item counts broken down by type of plan (with SSK and PK lumped together). From this fine-grained breakdown, we see that all subjects used every type of plan. More intriguing, however, is that this breakdown permits an interesting speculation. Consider the following data about several different plans:

Figure 15.   **Plan evidence items for the analyzed protocols.**

	Protocol Number			
	1	2	3	4
Sentinel	9 (5%)	8 (4%)	4 (4%)	11 (10%)
Loop	20 (13%)	13 (7%)	9 (9%)	1 (1%)
Counter	29 (18%)	21 (12%)	18 (17%)	12 (11%)
Arithmetic sum	21 (13%)	38 (21%)	13 (13%)	15 (14%)
Result	23 (14%)	18 (10%)	9 (9%)	12 (11%)
New value	11 (7%)	13 (7%)	16 (15%)	16 (15%)
Input	18 (11%)	21 (12%)	15 (14%)	8 (7%)
New value loop	9 (6%)	35 (19%)	14 (13%)	23 (21%)
Result output	10 (6%)	6 (3%)	0 (0%)	1 (1%)
Instructional output	7 (4%)	0 (0%)	3 (3%)	0 (0%)
Prompt output	2 (1%)	1 (1%)	3 (3%)	8 (7%)
Illegal filter	0 (0%)	3 (2%)	0 (0%)	0 (0%)
Total	159 (100%)	177 (100%)	104 (100%)	107 (100%)

New value controlled loop plan: In Protocol 1, where the subject's loop was very far from correct, the count is quite low, accounting for only 6% of the plan evidence items. Other subjects, whose loops were fairly close to correct, had higher counts, ranging between 13% and 21% of all plan evidence items.

Sentinel variable plan: All subjects had little trouble with this plan and all had relatively low plan evidence item counts, ranging between 4% and 10% of all plan evidence items.

Input new value variable plan and input plan: These plans gave all subjects a great deal of trouble. Plan evidence items counts (for the two together) range between 18% and 33% of all plan evidence items.

From these and similar observations, it appears that plan activity is highest on those plans that a novice almost knows (i.e., those plans where the novice has a fairly good idea of what is needed, but does not have all aspects correct).

Figure 16. Bug generator statistics for the analyzed protocols. "Bugs explained" refers to the number of bugs that can be explained by one or more bug generators developed from the analysis of Protocol 1. "Total explanations" refers to the number of plausible, nonslip bug generator explanations. "Explanations/bug" refers to the average number of plausible, nonslip explanations per bug.

	Protocol Number			
	1	2	3	4
Bugs found	32	19	11	10
Bugs explained	—	19	11	10
Total explanations	55	27	15	15
Explanations/bug	1.7	1.4	1.4	1.5

5.2. Expectation 2: Bug Generators Plausibly Explain the Bugs

The second expectation is that the bug generator set presented here can plausibly explain most errors found in the protocols. The data relevant to this expectation appear in the bugs explained line of Figure 16. As discussed earlier, the bug generator set was developed based on the analysis of Protocol 1. The data indicate that one or more bug generators from that set can plausibly explain each of the bugs found in Protocols 2, 3, and 4.

It is important that the bug generators actually do discriminate between the bugs. In our data, this would mean that there are relatively few plausible explanations per bug. Figure 16 shows the total number of plausible explanations in each protocol and the mean number of plausible explanations per bug. These data indicate that although multiple bug generators may be responsible for some bugs, on the average less than two bug generators can plausibly explain each bug.

The plausible bug generator explanations summarized in Figure 16 do not include cases where the bug was plausibly explained as a slip. These data are summarized in Figure 17. First, notice that all but two bugs had a plausible nonslip explanation. That is, almost every bug detected in the analysis can be plausibly explained as a bug generator operating on plans. Second, notice that slips can plausibly explain between 34% and 58% of the bugs (depending on the protocol). Most likely, a much smaller percentage are actually slips. Though there are many bugs that can plausibly be interpreted as slips, many of these slip interpretations become less likely when the bug is examined in the context of the whole protocol. That is, subjects often return to a bug and explicitly discuss it. It is unlikely that a slip would stand up to such repeat scrutiny.

Figure 17.   **Slip versus nonslip bug generator statistics.**

	Protocol Number			
	1	2	3	4
Bugs plausibly explained by nonslip bug generators	32 (100%)	18 (95%)	10 (91%)	10 (100%)
Bugs plausibly explained by slip bug generators	11 (34%)	11 (58%)	5 (45%)	5 (50%)

5.3. Expectation 3: SSK/PK Bug Generators Are Critical

In our model, we propose that the intrusion of SSK plays an important role in novice programming bugs. The third expectation is that when novices encounter an impasse in a developing programming solution, they usually use SSK confounds PK bug generators to patch and continue. The analysis presented here contains two kinds of evidence for this expectation.

First, SSK confounds PK bug generators embody the process whereby novices use SSK knowledge to reason about their programs. As can be seen in the SSK/PK total line of Figure 18, SSK confounds PK bug generators plausibly explained 60%, 67%, 67%, and 47% of the bugs found in Protocols 1 to 4, respectively. That is, for Protocols 1 to 3, SSK confounds PK bug generators can explain 60% or more of the bugs. Protocol 4 had the lowest (47%) coverage by SSK confounds PK bug generators but also had the least buggy protocol.

Second, the subjects had between 10 and 32 bugs. Notice that in terms of bugs, there seem to be two groups in the protocols: Protocols 1 and 2 have more bugs than Protocols 3 and 4. We refer to these as the "buggy group" and the "less buggy group," respectively. Referring to Figure 19, we see that the buggy group had higher ratios of SSK to PK plan evidence items than the less buggy group. The ratios were .37 and .39 for the buggy group protocols and .18 for both protocols of the less buggy group. This is consistent with the notion that a more error prone and less advanced novice is doing more reasoning from SSK plans.

6. CONCLUDING REMARKS

In the preceding section, we presented an analysis of four protocols of novice programmers. From that analysis we provide data to support our model of novice programmer bugs. Specifically, we present evidence that:

Plans, both SSK and PK, are pervasive in the work of novice programmers.

Figure 18. The number of bugs plausibly explained by each nonslip bug generator, plus the percentage of plausible explanations by the specified bug generator out
of all possible nonslip explanations. Each bug can have several explanations. Slip
data are presented in Figure 17.

	Protocol Number			
	1	2	3	4
SSK Confounds PK:				
PL used as NL	10 (18%)	6 (22%)	1 (7%)	1 (7%)
NL interprets PL	11 (20%)	10 (37%)	7 (47%)	3 (20%)
Multirole	8 (15%)	1 (4%)	1 (7%)	3 (20%)
NL construct	2 (4%)	0 (0%)	0 (0%)	0 (0%)
Generic name	2 (4%)	1 (4%)	1 (7%)	0 (0%)
Total	33 (60%)	18 (67%)	10 (67%)	7 (47%)
Intra-PK:				
Trace	10 (18%)	5 (19%)	1 (7%)	1 (7%)
Overgeneralize	4 (7%)	1 (4%)	2 (13%)	3 (20%)
Similar	4 (7%)	1 (4%)	2 (13%)	3 (20%)
Total	18 (32%)	7 (26%)	5 (33%)	7 (47%)
Other Confounds PK:				
Other domain	3 (5%)	2 (7%)	0 (0%)	1 (7%)
OS confound	1 (2%)	0 (0%)	0 (0%)	0 (0%)
Total	4 (7%)	2 (7%)	0 (0%)	1 (7%)
Total	55 (100%)	27 (100%)	15 (100%)	15 (100%)

Our bug generator set, developed after studying only one protocol, can
plausibly explain the novice bugs observed in the other protocols.

Most important, SSK plays an important role in the bugs of novice programmers. Bug generators that describe the confounds between SSK and
PK can plausibly explain a substantial number of bugs in each of the protocols. In addition, the SSK to PK plan ratio was higher for those novices
with buggier protocols.

Figure 19. **PK to SSK plan usage ratios support the importance of SSK in understanding buggy programs.**

	Protocol Number			
	1	2	3	4
Plan Evidence Items	159	177	104	107
SSK plans	43	50	16	16
PK plans	116	127	88	91
Ratio: PK to SSK	.37	.39	.18	.18

There are several next steps planned for this work. Currently, our bug analysis does not provide data to support our specific set of bug generators, nor does it provide the ability to recognize which of the plausible bug generators actually contribute to the bug. We would like to develop the theory that makes this more specific: Are there ways to detect exactly which bug generator(s) is (are) responsible? This will require a more formal definition of each bug generator along with a more constrained set of interviews. In these interviews, subjects will be put in specific situations where bugs are very likely. For example, subjects might be given a problem statement and a skeleton program missing a key section. Such interviews would be accompanied by probes to detect the use of certain bug generators and plans. We plan to focus particularly on the input new value variable plan's use within a loop, an area of difficulty for all our subjects. In general, correctly updating within the loop seems to be difficult for our subjects and amenable to more constrained study.

We are planning to explore the use of SSK plans in better understanding the intentions of novice programmers. We are beginning the development of a curriculum organized around common programming plans. Each programming plan would be introduced by examining the SSK version. The SSK plans allow us to understand and direct the students in their basic approach to the problem solution. With the SSK plan providing a connection to something the student already knows, we then introduce the PK version of the plan and actual code. By making a clear distinction between the SSK and PK versions, we should be able to avoid many of the errors discussed in this article.

We have presented a process model of bugs for novice programmers early in a programming course. In developing our model, we have focused on the knowledge used by a novice programmer. In particular, our model is based on the role of natural language step-by-step procedural knowledge in understanding these bugs. Although our model is just a start toward understanding the source of novice bugs, it indicates how critical novice preprogramming knowledge is likely to be in a more complete theory.

Acknowledgments. The authors wish to thank the referees for their valuable comments and careful reading.

Support. This work was supported by the National Science Foundation under NSF Grant MCS-8302382. Currently, the first author is supported by the Office of Naval Research under Contract Numbers N00014-83-6-0148 and N00014-83-K-0655. Any opinions, findings, conclusions, or recommendations expressed in this report are those of the authors and do not necessarily reflect the views of the U.S. government.

REFERENCES

Anderson, J. R., Farrell, R., & Sauers, R. (1984). Learning to program in LISP. *Cognitive Science, 8,* 87-129.

Anderson, J. R., Greeno, J. G., Kline, P. J., & Neves, D. M. (1981). Acquisition of problem-solving skill. In J. R. Anderson (Ed.), *Cognitive skills and their acquisition* (pp. 191-230). Hillsdale, NJ: Lawrence Erlbaum Associates, Inc.

Bonar, J. G. (1985). *Understanding the bugs of novice programmers.* Unpublished doctoral dissertation. University of Massachusetts, Amherst.

Brown, J. S., & VanLehn, K. (1980). Repair theory: A generative theory of bugs in procedural skills. *Cognitive Science, 4,* 379-426.

Chi, M. T., Feltovich, P., & Glaser, R. (1981). Categorization and representation of physics problems by experts and novices. *Cognitive Science, 5,* 121-152.

Clement, J. (1982, January). Students' preconceptions in introductory mechanics. *American Journal of Physics, 50,* 66-71.

DiSessa, A. A. (1982). Unlearning Aristotelian physics. *Cognitive Science, 6,* 37-76.

Ehrlich, K., & Soloway, E. M. (1983). An empirical investigation of the tacit knowledge in programming. In J. Thomas & M. L. Schneider (Eds.), *Human factors in computer systems.* Norwood, NJ: Ablex.

Ericsson, K. A., & Simon, H. (1980). Verbal reports as data. *Psychological Review, 87,* 215-251.

Ginsberg, H. P., Kossan, N., Schwartz, R., & Swanson, D. (1981). Protocol methods in research on mathematical thinking. In H. P. Ginsberg (Ed.), *Development of mathematical thinking* (pp. 7-47). London: Academic.

Johnson, W. L., Draper, S., & Soloway, E. M. (1982). Classifying bugs is a tricky business. In *Proceedings of the Seventh Annual NASA/Goddard Workshop on Software Engineering.*

Kahney, H., & Eisenstadt, M. (1982). Programmers' mental models of their programming tasks: The interaction of real-world knowledge and programming knowledge. *Proceedings of the Fourth Annual Conference of the Cognitive Science Society,* pp. 143-145.

Lewis, C. (1981). Skill in algebra. In J. R. Anderson (Ed.), *Cognitive skills and their acquisition* (pp. 85-110). Hillsdale, NJ: Lawrence Erlbaum Associates, Inc.

Matz, M. (1982). Towards a process model for high school algebra errors. In D. Sleeman & J. S. Brown (Eds.), *Intelligent tutoring systems* (pp. 25-50). London: Academic.

Miller, L. A. (1981). Natural language programming: Styles, strategies, and contrasts. *IBM Systems Journal, 20,* 184-215.

Newell, A., & Simon, H. A. (1972). *Human problem solving.* Englewood Cliffs, NJ: Prentice-Hall.

Resnick, L. B. (1982). Syntax and semantics in learning to subtract. In T. Carpenter, J. Moser, & T. Romberg (Eds.), *Addition and subtraction: A cognitive perspective* (pp. 136–155). Hillsdale, NJ: Lawrence Erlbaum Associates, Inc.

Rich, C. (1981). *Inspection methods in programming* (Tech. Rep. No. AI-TR-604). Cambridge: MIT, MIT Artificial Intelligence Laboratory.

Rosnick, P. (1982). *Student conceptions of semantically laden letters in algebra.* Amherst: University of Massachusetts, Cognitive Development Project.

Shneiderman, B. (1976). Exploratory experiments in programmer behavior. *International Journal of Computer and Information Sciences, 5,* 123–143.

Soloway, E. M., Bonar, J. G., & Ehrlich, K. (1983). Cognitive strategies and looping constructs: An empirical study. *Communications of the Association for Computing Machinery, 26* (11), 853–860.

Soloway, E. M., & Ehrlich, K. (1984). Empirical studies of programming knowledge. *IEEE Transactions of Software Engineering, SE-10,* 595–609.

Soloway, E. M., Ehrlich, K., Bonar, J. G., & Greenspan, J. (1982). What do novices know about programming? In A. Badre & B. Shneiderman (Eds.), *Directions in human computer interaction* (pp. 27–54). Norwood, NJ: Ablex.

APPENDIX: A SAMPLE OF AN ANALYZED PROTOCOL

This appendix contains a short segment from a fully analyzed protocol. This segment is taken from Protocol 1 in the set of four protocols analyzed in depth and discussed in Section 5 of the text.

The subject of this segment is working on the averaging problem. At the point we pick up the protocol, he is coding the loop. The following transcript is annotated with the plan analysis and the bug analysis. In the course of the protocol, the subject will write the code shown in Figure 6. The subject's basic problem is that he does not understand how variables are used to process values inside the loop. As we see in the protocol, the subject clearly understands that the loop body must accumulate a running total in the variable Sum and a count in the variable N. He also understands that the variable I will hold new values read from the user. Explanations for the peculiar code in the loop body are presented in the bug analysis annotations with the actual transcript segment.

The transcript uses the following notational conventions:

Square brackets (e.g., [ ]) enclose explanatory comments we have added to the text.

Programming font (e.g., N : = 1) is used to indicate code that the subject actually wrote during the protocol.

Plan annotations are set off from the protocol text with horizontal lines and labeled "PLAN:". These annotations mark those places where we claim the subject has used a plan. The annotation describes our evidence for that claim. See Section 4.1 for a detailed discussion of the plan annotations.

Bug annotations are set off from the protocol text with horizontal lines and labeled "BUG:". These annotations mark those places where the subject has a bug. The annotation provides a general explanation of the bug and describes the bug generators that could plausibly explain that bug. Each plausible bug generator explanation is marked with a hand pointing right (☞). See Section 4.1 for a detailed discussion of the bug annotations.

Here is the protocol segment:

Subject 13: Ummm, ummm, well I think it's, ahh, it's [N := I, eventually changed to N := 1, eventually put on Line 5] not right I don't think, but I, I'm gonna leave it that way for the moment.

Interviewer: Okay, fine.

Subject 13: And then integer [the way the subject refers to the variable I], or rather, sum equals integer, ahm, equals zero plus integer [Writes: Sum := 0 + I, eventually put on Line 4], and the number equals the integer, ahhh.

PLAN: Arithmetic sum variable
Evidence: P3 — Running total assignment to Sum in loop.

BUG: Arithmetic sum set to current new value variable
There will be no running sum operation because the arithmetic sum, Sum, always gets the value of the current new value variable, I.
☞ *Trace* **on arithmetic sum variable**
The subject is reasoning about the execution behavior of the arithmetic sum variable. He recognizes that on the loops first iteration, Sum will be given the value 0 + I and then writes that.

Interviewer: Why don't you tell me what you are thinking?

Subject 13: Well, I'm thinking that [points to N := 1, eventually changed to N := 1 and eventually put on Line 5] should go after [points to Sum := 0 + 1, eventually put on Line 4] because the sum is going to be zero plus the integer and then the number is going to be, ahh, number equals 1.

Interviewer: Ah huh.

Subject 13: [Crosses off N : = 1] And then number equals one [Writes: **N** : = **1** on Line 5].

PLAN: Counter variable
Evidence: N7 — Counting to N done after operation.

BUG: Counter needs to go after the arithmetic sum
The increment of the counter variable, **N**, needs to be done after the update of the arithmetic sum variable, **Sum**.
☞ *PL interpreted as NL* **on counter variable**
In our study of natural language step-by-step procedures, we found that the counting operation is usually specified after the operation to be counted. Also, in one of our interviews, the subject suggested that if counting happened before the operation to be counted, there was a chance that the count would be 1 too high. Here the subject is applying that convention to Pascal.

Interviewer: Okay.

Subject 13: And then, and then sum equals integer plus integer [Writes: **Sum** : = I + I on Line 6], and number equals 1. Ahhh.

PLAN: Arithmetic sum variable
Evidence: P3 — Running total assignment to **Sum** in loop.

BUG: Arithmetic sum set to current new value variable
There will be no running sum operation because the arithmetic sum variable, **Sum**, always gets twice the value of the current new value variable I.
☞ *Trace* **on arithmetic sum variable**
The subject is reasoning about the execution behavior of the arithmetic sum variable. He recognizes that on the loops second iteration, **Sum** will be given the value I + I and then writes that.
☞ *Multirole variable* **on new value variable**
The subject is allowing the new value variable to take two roles: its "sum so far" and its next value. Note that later in the transcript, he will add *next* as a keyword in front of the second I.

Interviewer: What are you thinking now?

Subject 13: Number equals 2 [Writes: **N** : = **2** on Line 7] and it would go on, it would repeat, that, if [the loop body] continues to repeat [sweeping motions] this [points to the 2 on Line 7] will increase. I'm assuming for the moment that this is sufficient input.

PLAN: Counter variable
Evidence: P3 — Increment counter variable N inside the loop

PLAN: Indefinite Loop
Evidence: N1 — "Continues"
Evidence: N2 — "this will repeat until . . ."

BUG: Says counter variable will increase, but it won't
Says that the counter variable, N, will increase based on the N := 1 and N := 2 inside the loop.
PL interpreted as NL on Pascal — repeat, indefinite loop
The subject is expecting the loop to work like loops in natural language. There, it is common to specify a loop by giving one or two cases of the iteration and assuming that the person reading will know how to generalize. Notice below () he says that Sum := 0 + I (Line 4) is the "first format of that," referring to the action performed for each value of the new value variable.

Interviewer: Okay, "sufficient input"?

Subject 13: Input to [pause] so that the computer will know that, for each [pause] for each integer entered, you add 1, you add the integer to the sum [points to Sum := 0 + I on Line 4], and that this is the first format of that, zero plus integer, N equals 1, sum equals integer plus integer, number = 2 ["next" motion with hand], until [pause] [Writes: until].

PLAN: Indefinite loop
Evidence: N3 — "for each . . ."

PLAN: Counter variable
Evidence: P3 — Increment counter N inside the loop

PLAN: Arithmetic sum variable
Evidence: P3 — Update arithmetic sum, Sum, inside the loop

This concludes the example protocol analysis.

18
A Goal/Plan Analysis of Buggy Pascal Programs

James C. Spohrer, Elliot Soloway, and **Edgar Pope**
University of Michigan

ABSTRACT

In this paper, we present a descriptive theory of buggy novice programs and a bug categorization scheme that is based on this theory. Central to this theory is the cognitively plausible knowledge — goals and plans — that underlies programming. The bug categorization scheme makes explicit problem-dependent goal and plan knowledge at many different levels of detail. We provide several examples of how the scheme permits us to focus on bugs in a way that facilitates generating plausible accounts of why the bugs may have arisen. In particular, our approach has led us to one explanation of why some novice programs are buggier than others. A basic part of this explanation is the notion of merged goals and merged plans in which a single integrated plan is used to achieve multiple goals.

This paper is based in part on earlier articles that will appear in the proceedings of the World Conference on Computers in Education, Norfolk, VA (WCCE '85) and the proceedings of the Conference on Human Factors in Computing Systems, San Francisco, CA (CHI '85).

Authors' present address: Department of Computer Science, Cognition and Programming Project, Yale University, P.O. Box 2158 Yale Station, New Haven, CT 06520.

CONTENTS

1.   INTRODUCTION: MOTIVATION AND GOALS

Many students find learning to program a difficult task. The large number of buggy intermediate versions of a program that novice programmers generate is testament to this fact. The questions we would like to answer are: (a) What is the range of bugs that novices make? (b) What are the misconceptions that underlie the generation of these bugs? Why do students have them and how do they give rise to the observed bugs? A robust model of the novice programming process would provide answers to both of these questions. For the task domain of subtraction, such a model exists (Brown & VanLehn, 1980). Unfortunately, because programming is a much more complex problem-solving task than subtraction, such a robust theory for novice planning has not yet been proposed. In this paper, we move in that direction with a descriptive theory that tries to identify the categories of bugs that novices make. Despite the fact that a descriptive theory alone will not allow us to answer both of the foregoing questions, this kind of theory does allow us to address the first question.

Early descriptive theories of programming bugs were based on syntactic categories. For instance, Gould (1975) analyzed debugging time for bugs in assignment statements, making no distinction between assignment statements which initialize variables, or the roles of the variables and statements in the overall computation performed by the program. In fact, the debug times varied greatly depending on the different types of assignment statements.

In contrast to theories that are based on syntactic (surface) features, our descriptive theory of buggy programs is based on the cognitively plausible, deep structure knowledge that programmers have: goals and plans. Although the cognitive reality of this kind of knowledge has empirical support in the domain of text comprehension (Bartlett, 1932; Bower, Black, & Turner, 1979; Graesser, 1981; Schank & Abelson, 1977) and in the programming domain (Adelson, 1981; Bonar & Soloway, 1983, 1985; Shneiderman, 1976; Soloway & Ehrlich, 1984), we do not know how the novice uses this knowledge in generating programs. Nevertheless, a descriptive theory based on goal/plan knowledge moves us closer to a process model than the syntactic theories because the explanations for the bugs are expressed in terms of cognitively plausible knowledge components.

For example, as we see in more detail in Section 6, our analysis has uncovered one type of bug-prone coding pattern in novice programs that corresponds to merged goals and merged plans. In essence, merged code tries to achieve two or more goals with the same piece of code. A common bug that occurs when students try to achieve two goals with one piece of code is that they leave out some small, but nonetheless important, subgoal. Using our descriptive theory, identifying merged code is fairly straightforward: find sections of code which achieve multiple goals with a single integrated plan, as opposed to achieving the goals using separate plans. Describing and identifying merged code in a syntactic theory with no notion of what a particular piece of code was intended to accomplish would be much more difficult. One might suppose that some syntactic complexity measure could be useful in locating merged code based on the assumption that if a piece of code is doing two things at once, it must surely be more syntactically complex. However, merged code is in some cases an optimization which results in less syntactic complexity, not more. Although a deep description of the merged code bugs gets us closer to a process model than a syntactic description could, we still need to determine the details of the process: How was the merged code produced, and what caused the bug?

2.   GOALS AND PLANS: THE KNOWLEDGE UNDERLYING PROGRAMMING

We have been developing a theory of the knowledge that programmers use in programming. We have carried out a number of empirical studies to evaluate our theory; to date, the data we have gathered have supported our view (Soloway & Ehrlich, 1984; Soloway, Ehrlich, Bonar, & Greenspan, 1982). This theory forms the backbone of our approach to bug analysis. In this section, we describe that portion of our theory that is particularly relevant to the task of analyzing the variability in buggy novice programs.

2.1. Goals and Plans: An Example

Consider, then, the problem statement in Figure 1 that was assigned to students in an introductory Pascal programming course. We can identify four main goals that must be achieved: (a) G:LOOP: This goal corresponds to the intention of reading through many records of input data (Lines 3, 35–39, 42); (b) G:VDE: This is G:VALID-DATA-ENTRY, which corresponds to the intention of getting "good" data from the user (Lines 4–5, 9–21, 24–26); (c) G:CALC: This is G:CALCULATION, which corresponds to the intention of computing the elapsed time in this problem (Lines 6–7, 27–28); (d) G:OUTPUT: This goal corresponds to the intention of writing out the reformatted data (Lines 29–30, 40). Throughout this paper, the names of goals and plans are capitalized. Goals have the prefix "G:" and plans have the prefix "P:."

When we look at a program, we are able to find lines of code that are connected by data and control flow (as we simulate the execution of the program), but this is not the only way lines of code are connected. Code may also be connected in that it achieves a specific goal. This type of connection is illustrated in Figure 2, which shows one possible solution to the reformatting problem with blocks of code grouped together. Specifically, consider Lines 45–48 in Figure 2. These four lines are responsible for calculating the elapsed time in seconds from the start and end times; that is, they are responsible for achieving G:CALC of the reformatting problem.

The goals are also inferable from the problem statement. For instance, Lines 27–28 in the problem statement (Figure 1) indicate the need to achieve G:CALC. Thus, by analyzing the programs and the problem specification, we are able to determine a set of goals that must be achieved to solve the problem.

Figure 1.   The reformatting problem assignment.

```
01 In this problem, you will read in "raw data" collected by the
02 experimenter and entered into the computer. The objective of
03 this program is to read through the data and:
04    1. Kick out all bad data; a human typist often makes little
05       typos that need to be corrected.
06    2. "reformat" the data; convert the data into another form
07       that is more easily analyzed.
08
09 The experiment in which the following data was generated asked
10 subjects to answer a problem. The experimenter collected data
11 on how long it took the subject to solve the problem, and whether
12 or not the subject was correct. The format of the data will be as
13 follows:
14    SUBJECT_NUMBER  PROBLEM_TYPE  START_TIME  END_TIME  ACCURACY
15    1. the START_TIME and END_TIME are specified: hours minutes seconds
16       (e.g. 4 32 16, means 4 o'clock, 32 minutes, and 16 seconds).
17    2. SUBJECT_NUMBER is an integer.
18    3. PROBLEM_TYPE is a char; there are ONLY 'a', 'b', 'c' problem
19       types -- all other inputs are bad data
20    4. a correct solution for ACCURACY is represented as a '+',
21       while an incorrect solution is represented as a '-'.
22
23 The goal of your program is to:
24    1. if data is found that is "bad" then ask the user to retype
25       the data item; ASSUME that on this retyping that the user
26       will type in the data item correctly!!!!!
27    2. calculate the elapsed time IN SECONDS from the start and
28       end times.
29    3. output a new record of information that contains:
30       SUBJECT_NUMBER  PROBLEM_TYPE  ELAPSED_TIME  ACCURACY
31
32 So here is data on which your program should be tested (that is,
33 we will test your program on these data... and any other data we
34 feel will make your program cough.)
35    (1) 23 a 4 23 13 4 25 1 -      (6) 73 b 12 58 10 12 59 20 +
36    (2) 33 b 4 32 20 4 31 45 +     (7) 83 c 12 59 50 1 2 20 +
37    (3) 43 c 4 40 13 4 44 44 +     (8) 21 a 7 30 30 7 32 32 +
38    (4) 63 a 12 56 12 12 57 2 +    (9) 31 d 7 34 2 7 35 10 -
39    (5) 41 c 7 36 10 7 37 10 +
40 The output for the line (1) of data would be: 23 a 108 -
41
42 THE STOPPING CONDITION ON THE LOOP SHOULD BE A SENTINEL VALUE
```

We term the different methods for achieving a particular goal *programming plans*. A programming plan corresponds to a fragment of code that accomplishes a stereotypic action. For example, there are a number of stereotypic ways in which to achieve G:LOOP in the previous problem. Next, we list two plans that can be used to achieve G:LOOP:

1. P:RC (P:READ-SPECIAL-STOPPING-CHARACTER-FOR-SENTINEL): This plan uses a special character variable to control looping. First, the sentinel variable must get its initial value, which is then tested to see

Figure 2. A solution to the reformatting problem.

```
01   Program Reformat(input,output);
02   Var Subject_Number :Integer;
03       Start_Hour, Start_Minute, Start_Second :Integer;
04       End_Hour, End_Minute, End_Second :Integer;
05       Sentinel, Problem_Type, Accuracy: Char;
06       Start_Time, End_Time, Elapsed_Time: Integer;
07
08   Begin
09   +-------------------------------------------------------------+
10   |   writeln('Do you want to reformat some data?');            |
11   |   writeln('YES: Type a  "Y".');                             |
12   |   writeln('NO:  Type an "N" (this will STOP the program).'); |-- G:LOOP
13   |   readln(Sentinel);                                         |
14   |   while Sentinel <> 'N' do                                  |
15   |     begin                                                   |
16   +-------------------------------------------------------------+
17   |     +-------------------------------------------------------+
18   |     |writeln('Enter Subject Number, Problem Type, Start Hour,');|
19   |     |writeln('Min, Sec, End Hour, Min, Sec, and Accuracy.');|
20   |     |writeln('FOR EXAMPLE: 1 a 3 30 2 3 36 59 +');          |
21   |     |readln(Subject_Number, Problem_Type,                   |
22   |     |         Start_Hour, Start_Minute, Start_Second,       |
23   |     |         End_Hour, End_Minute, End_Second,             |
24   |     |         Accuracy);                                    |
25   |     |if ((Subject_Number <= 0) or                           |
26   |     |    ((Problem_Type <> 'a') and (Problem_Type <> 'b')   |
27   |     |                        and (Problem_Type <> 'c')) or  |
28   |     |    ((Start_Hour    < 1) or (Start_Hour   > 12)) or    |
29   |     |    ((Start_Minute < 0) or (Start_Minute > 59)) or     |-- G:VDE
30   |     |    ((Start_Second < 0) or (Start_Second > 59)) or     |
31   |     |    ((End_Hour    < 1) or (End_Hour   > 12)) or        |
32   |     |    ((End_Minute < 0) or (End_Minute > 59)) or         |
33   |     |    ((End_Second < 0) or (End_Second > 59)) or         |
34   |     |    ((Accuracy <> '+') and (Accuracy <> '-')))         |
35   |     |   then                                                |
36   |     |     begin                                             |
37   |     |      writeln('Some data bad... Try again.');          |
38   |     |      readln(Subject_Number, Problem_Type,             |
39   |     |              Start_Hour, Start_Minute, Start_Second,  |
40   |     |              End_Hour, End_Minute, End_Second,        |
41   |     |              Accuracy);                               |
42   |     |     end;                                              |
43   |     +-------------------------------------------------------+
44   |     +-------------------------------------------------------+
45   |     |Start_Time := 3600*Start_Hour+60*Start_Minute+Start_Second; |
46   |     |End_Time := 3600*End_Hour+60*End_Minute+End_Second;    |-- G:CALC
47   |     |if End_Time <= Start_Time then End_Time := End_Time+3600*12;|
48   |     |Elapsed_Time := End_Time-Start_Time;                   |
49   |     +-------------------------------------------------------+
50   |     +-------------------------------------------------------+
51   |     |writeln('Result:',Subject_Number,Problem_Type,Elapsed_Time,Accuracy);|
52   |     +-------------------------------------------------------+
53   +-------------------------------------------------------------+  |
54   |     writeln('Do you want to reformat some more data?');     |  G:OUTPUT
55   |     writeln('YES: Type a  "Y".');                           |
56   |     writeln('NO:  Type an "N" (this will STOP the program).'); |
57   |     readln(Sentinel);                                       |-- G:LOOP
58   |     end;                                                    |
59   +-------------------------------------------------------------+
50   End.
```

if it meets some termination condition. If the termination condition is met, the
loop is exited; otherwise the body of the loop is processed. The final portion of
the body of the loop must get the next value of the sentinel variable to be tested.
This plan spawns the following three subgoals:

```
G:INPUT --------> 01   writeln('Enter "N" to stop; any other to continue.');
                  02   readln(Sentinel);
G:GUARD --------> 03   while Sentinel <> 'N' do
                  04      begin
                  05      ....
G:REPEAT-INPUT -> 06      readln(Sentinel);
                  07      end;
```

2. P:RD (P:READ-INDIVIDUAL-DATA-ITEM-SENTINEL): Some-
times instead of using a special character as a sentinel variable, one of the input
data items will be used. For this particular problem, the input variable most
commonly used as the sentinel was the subject number. To achieve G:LOOP,
the plan must first read in the subject number and then test to see if it is not the
sentinel value (i.e., -1), in which case the body of the loop is executed. The final part of the body of the loop is a read statement to get the next subject number to be tested. A disadvantage of this plan compared to the previous plan for
achieving G:LOOP is that the input of the data items is split apart (instead of
being entirely within the body of the loop), and one particular data item has a
privileged status. This plan also spawns three subgoals, as follows:

```
                  01   writeln('Enter data to reformat (or -1 to Stop)');
G:INPUT --------> 02   read(Subject_Number);
G:GUARD --------> 03   while Subject_Number <> -1 do
                  04      begin
                  05      readln(Problem_Type,
                  06             Start_Hour, Start_Minute, Start_Second,
                  07             End_Hour, End_Minute, End_Second,
                  08             Accuracy);
                  09      ....
G:REPEAT-INPUT -> 10      read(Subject_Number);
                  11      end;
```

The program in Figure 2, which shows one possible solution to the
reformatting problem, employs P:RC to realize G:LOOP (see Figure 2, Lines
9–16 and 53–59). P:RC must accomplish three subgoals: G:INPUT,
G:GUARD, G:REPEAT-INPUT. In turn, there are stereotypic ways in
which to achieve these goals (i.e., there are programming plans that can be
used to realize these goals).

2.2. The GAP Tree

The relationship between programming goals and plans is that a goal can be
achieved by any one of a number of different plans and a plan may give rise to
several subgoals, which it organizes and which are all necessary for a correct
realization of the plan. We can represent the space of possible correct solutions

to the reformatting problem through the use of a goal and plan tree (GAP tree). The GAP tree for a problem encodes the goals that must be achieved to solve the problem and the many alternative plans that can be used to achieve those goals. A GAP tree not only encodes the top-level goals and their plans, but also the subgoals spawned by particular plans, their subplans, subsubgoals, and so on (see Figure 3). Decomposing a problem in terms of goals and plans is a standard approach of cognitive science. For example, Card, Moran, and Newell (1983) developed the GOMS model (Goals, Operators, Methods, and Selection rules) in analyzing the performance of expert text editor users.

When we construct a GAP tree, the goals are inferred both from the problem specification and the programs. The plans are inferred by noting all the various ways students have of implementing the same goal. There are usually many differences between the lines of code used to achieve a goal in one student's program and the lines of code used to achieve the same goal in another student's program. Some of the differences are insignificant, such as different variable names, different prompt messages, or the ordering of two statements which are not constrained by data flow, whereas other differences are significant in that they reflect a fundamentally distinct approach to the problem. Often, the significantly different methods involve differences in the number of variables, programming constructs, ordering of statements that require unusual compensations, roles for some of the variables, or the style of interaction with the rest of the program. The insignificant differences reflect surface variations of the code, whereas the significant differences reflect deep variations. Capturing the variability by cataloging the many different methods for achieving a goal is a time-consuming task which requires analyzing a large number of programs.

It is important to distinguish between two types of GAP trees:

1. Inferred Gap Tree (several plans per goal): All of the plans for achieving a goal in an inferred GAP tree are known to be cognitively plausible because they have been observed in actual human-generated programs. The inferred GAP tree for the reformatting problem is based on a detailed analysis of 46 different novices' programs (Spohrer et al., 1985). We present a simplified version of this GAP tree in Figure 3. The number of alternative plans for achieving goals in the tree is actually much larger, as is the depth of the tree.

2. Solution Subtree of a GAP Tree (one plan per goal): In analyzing novice programs, we try to identify the particular plan used to achieve each of the program's goals. Each program corresponds to a particular solution subtree of the GAP tree, which specifies the particular plan used to achieve each goal in the program.

Figure 3. The simplified goal and plan tree (GAP tree) for the reformatting prob-lem. The abbreviated plan names (e.g., P:I-A/G-A/R-A for P:INPUT-ALL/ GUARD-ALL/RETRY-ALL) are used so that the simplified GAP tree could be fit on one page. The abbreviations are used sparingly in the text.

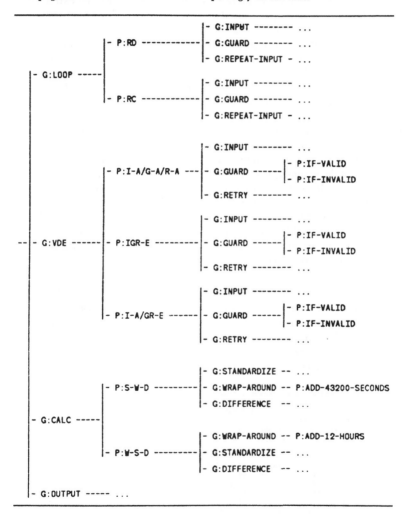

The structure of a GAP tree is that of an AND-OR tree, with goals on the AND levels and plans on the OR levels (representing alternative methods that may be selected to achieve a goal). By committing to a particular plan for achieving each goal at each OR level down the tree, a solution subtree can be extracted from the GAP tree. For every program that solves a problem, there exists a solution subtree of the GAP tree for that problem.

The simplified GAP tree in Figure 3 shows three of the possible plans for achieving G:VALID-DATA-ENTRY. The plans for achieving G:VALID-DATA-ENTRY all give rise to the same three subgoals: G:INPUT, G:GUARD, and G:RETRY. The major difference between the plans for achieving G:VDE concerns how these three subgoals are composed with the data items to be processed. For instance, the first and third plans achieve G:INPUT for all the data items before achieving any of the other subgoals. However, the second plan achieves the three subgoals for a single data item before moving on to the next data item. Space only permits a complete description of the first of these plans, P:INPUT-ALL/GUARD-ALL/RETRY-ALL (P:I-A/G-A/R-A). However, in Figure 6 a correct program fragment illustrates the second plan, P:INPUT-GUARD-RETRY-EACH (P:IGR-E). The third plan, P:INPUT-ALL/GUARD-RETRY-EACH (P:I-A/GR-E), first reads in all the data like the first plan, but then guards and retries each data variable like the second plan. The following plan is the one used in the sample solution of Figure 2 (see Lines 17-43):

P:I-A/G-A/R-A (P:INPUT-ALL/GUARD-ALL/RETRY-ALL): First, read in all the data items and then check (in one big conditional) to see if any of these data items are invalid. If any of the data items are invalid, then read them all in again. An implementation of this plan and the goals it spawns is shown below; also note that G:GUARD is achieved using P:IF-INVALID.

```
G:INPUT  --> 01 readln(Subject_Number, Problem_Type,
         02         Start_Hour, Start_Minute, Start_Second,
         03         End_Hour, End_Minute, End_Second,
         04         Accuracy);
G:GUARD  --> 05 if ((Subject_Number < 1) or
         06     ((Problem_Type <> 'a') and (Problem_Type <> 'b')
         07                         and (Problem_Type <> 'c')) or
         08     ((Start_Hour   < 1) or (Start_Hour   > 12)) or
         09     ((Start_Minute < 0) or (Start_Minute > 59)) or
         10     ((Start_Second < 0) or (Start_Second > 59)) or
         11     ((End-Hour     < 1) or (End_Hour     > 12)) or
         12     ((End_Minute   < 0) or (End_Minute   > 59)) or
         13     ((End_Second   < 0) or (End_Second   > 59)) or
         14     ((Accuracy <> '+') and (Accuracy   <> '-')))
         15 then begin
         16         writeln('Bad Data... Try Again.');
G:RETRY  --> 17         readln(Subject_Number, Problem_Type,
         18             Start_Hour, Start_Minute, Start_Second,
         19             End_Hour, End_Minute, End_Second,
         20             Accuracy);
         21     end;
```

The simplified GAP tree in Figure 3 shows two of the possible plans for achieving G:CALC. As pointed out in Lines 27–28 of the problem assignment (see Figure 1), the purpose of the calculation is to compute the elapsed time of the experiment given the start and end times. Both of the calculation plans have three subgoals, which they must organize (or combine) in order to compute the elapsed time of the experiment: (a) G:STANDARDIZE: Different time units conversion; (b) G:WRAP-AROUND: Modulo 12-hr clock period compensation; (c) G:DIFFERENCE: Subtract start time from end time.

The first of these subgoals, G:STANDARDIZE, is concerned with converting a time expressed in hours, minutes, and seconds into a time expressed only in seconds. To do this standardization, one needs to know how many seconds are in an hour and a minute, and how to mulitply and accumulate a sum. G:WRAP-AROUND is concerned with the problem that arises when, for instance, an experiment starts just before 1 o'clock (e.g., 12:58:09) and ends just after 1 o'clock (e.g., 1:02:35). In order to achieve G:WRAP-AROUND, one must first detect that wrap-around has occurred (i.e., start time is greater than end time), and then compensate by adding to the end time one full clock period (i.e., 12 hr in some units). Clearly, depending on when one attempts to do wrap-around with respect to standardization, the test and full-period add will be different. G:DIFFERENCE is concerned with the part of the calculation which just subtracts start time from end time to find the elapsed time of the experiment.

The next plan described is the one in the program shown in Figure 2 (see Lines 44–49). We include a description here of both plans because it is relevant to the discussion in a subsequent section of this paper:

P:S-W-D (P:STANDARDIZE-WRAP-AROUND-DIFFERENCE): When G:STANDARDIZE is achieved before G:WRAP-AROUND, the times are each represented as a single number in seconds; thus, achieving G:WRAP-AROUND is particularly simple given that there are 43200 sec in a 12-hr clock period, as shown below. G:CALC is achieved using P:S-W-D, and G:WRAP-AROUND is achieved using P:ADD-43200-SECONDS.

```
G:STANDARDIZE->01  Start_Time  := 3600*Start_Hour+60*Start_Minute+Start_Second;
             02  End_Time   := 3600*End_Hour+60*End_Minute+End_Second;
G:WRAP-AROUND->03  if Start_Time >= End_Time then End_Time := End_Time+43200;
G:DIFFERENCE ->04  Elapsed_Time := End_Time-Start_Time;
```

P:W-S-D (P:WRAP-AROUND-STANDARDIZE-DIFFERENCE): When G:STANDARDIZE is achieved after G:WRAP-AROUND, the plan is a bit more complex because the times are still represented in their original form as six separate variables and three different time units (i.e., hours, minutes, and seconds), as shown below. G:CALC is achieved using P:W-S-D, and G:WRAP-AROUND is achieved using P:ADD-12-HOURS.

```
G:WRAP-AROUND->01  if((Start_Hour > End_Hour) or
           02     ((Start_Hour = End_Hour) and (Start_Minute > End_Minute)) or
           03     ((Start_Hour = End_Hour) and (Start_Minute = End_Minute)
           04                            and (Start_Second >= End_Second)))
           05     then End_Hour := End_Hour+12;
G:STANDARDIZE->06  Start_Time := 3600*Start_Hour+60*Start_Minute+Start_Second;
           07  End_Time   := 3600*End_Hour+60*End_Minute+End_Second;
G:DIFFERENCE ->08  Elapsed_Time := End_Time-Start_Time;
```

In concluding this discussion of the goals and plans that comprise the reformatting problem, we emphasize that the GAP tree organizes this goal and plan knowledge allowing us to conveniently represent the incredible diversity observed in novice programs.

3.   THE SOURCE OF DATA: ON-LINE PROTOCOLS

The buggy program data analyzed in subsequent sections are actual student-generated programs. We augmented the VAX 750 operating system that the students were using and, with their permission, obtained a copy of each syntactically correct program they submitted for compilation. We call such data *on-line protocols*. We have collected this type of data from students in a number of introductory Pascal programming courses at various universities. The data reported in this paper were collected during the spring 1984 semester at Yale University in an introductory Pascal programming course specifically designed for nonscience, humanities-oriented students. The analysis reported here was based on the first syntactically correct version of the reformatting problem produced by the students. Note, however, that some of these programs are incomplete. Sometimes the student intentionally postpones achieving a goal, and other times the student leaves out the goal unintentionally; it is very difficult to ascertain whether the omission is intentional or unintentional. Nevertheless, by comparing early versions with later versions of the same program, we have been able to get some sense of the magnitude of the problem for the one type of bug count affected (i.e., missing components). Based on this comparison, we feel that the occasional missing goals that are intentional, yet counted as a bug, are not a major distortion of our data (except in one case, which we note in Subsection 5.1). We have analyzed data from other problems and from later versions (see Johnson, Soloway, Cutler, & Draper, 1983, and Spohrer et al., 1985, for a more complete analysis of these data).

4.   THE PROBLEM-INDEPENDENT SCHEME FOR BUG CATEGORIZATION

Johnson et al. (1983) developed a scheme for classifying program bugs based on differences between the buggy program and the plan that was being attempted. In this section, we review that work and point out its weaknesses; in the next sections, we propose a revised scheme for bug classification that seeks to remedy those weaknesses.

Unlike the bug categorization scheme of Ostrand and Weyuker (1982), which describes bugs as differences between the lines of code in a buggy program and a correct program, our previous scheme (Johnson et al., 1983) describes bugs as differences between the way plans are implemented by novices in their programs and the correct realization of those plans. Thus, applying this scheme requires: (a) the identification of the plan the novice intended to implement and (b) the characterization of the differences between that and the actual implementation.

A difference can usually be localized to some particular part of a plan, but occasionally the entire plan is at fault. We characterize the difference in terms of one of the following seven plan components:

1. Input: **READ** and **READLN** statements.
2. Output: **WRITE** and **WRITELN** statements, for writing out either messages or variable values.
3. Init: Initialization type assignment statements that give variables their initial value.
4. Update: Assignment statements that change variables values.
5. Guard: Conditionals, such as **IF** statements and the termination test of **WHILE, REPEAT,** and **FOR** statements.
6. Syntax: Syntactic connectives which delimit the scope of blocks of code, such as **BEGIN, END, THEN, ELSE,** and **DO.**
7. Plan: An entire plan, possibly composed of many of the foregoing microplan components.

If the difference can be localized to some part of the plan, then one of the first six plan components is used to describe the bug; otherwise, the final component is used in the bug description. Moreover, there are four ways in which a plan component can be at fault, which we call the type of difference:

1. Missing: The plan component is not present in the program.
2. Malformed: The plan component is present, but is not correctly implemented.
3. Spurious: The plan component is present, but should not be.
4. Misplaced: The plan component is present, but in the wrong place in the program.

Thus, using the plan difference approach, 28 categories of bugs are produced (seven types of plan components times four types of differences). Note that this is a problem-independent set of categories because the plan components, although general enough to handle both Pascal and Fortran, are still related closely enough to the syntactic constructs of both languages that they can be applied to any programs written in these or similar languages.

To see how this bug categorization scheme is used, consider the buggy program in Figure 4. This program is similar to the correct solution to the reformatting problem shown in Figure 2, but it contains several bugs. By counting plan component differences, we can identify four bugs in this program, which fall into the bug classes:

1. Missing plan: This bug is easiest to see; all of the code required to achieve G:LOOP is missing from the program in Figure 4.

2. Malformed guard: Spotting this bug is a little more difficult because just one of the Boolean operators in the IF statement's condition is wrong. IF statements correspond to guard plan components, so this OR-for-AND bug is classified as a malformed guard.

3. Misplaced syntax: In the THEN clause of that same IF statement, a BEGIN-END block is used, but the END comes before the retry input is done, instead of after it. Because END terms correspond to syntax plan components, this bug is classified as a misplaced syntax.

4. Spurious input: The fourth bug reflects an all too common misconception that novice programmers have about plans to achieve G:OUTPUT. Many novice programmers think that a variable must occur in a READLN statement before it can occur in a WRITELN statement. In the buggy program in Figure 4, all the variables except for the elapsed time variable have appeared in READLN statements, so the unnecessary READLN statement for elapsed time is incorporated into the program before the output. Because READLN statements correspond to input plan components, this bug is classified as a spurious input.

In Figure 5, we present a bug frequency table derived from an analysis of 46 first syntactically correct reformatting problem programs. Using this table, we can determine how many bugs occurred in each of the 28 plan component difference categories. For instance, we see in the first row and second column that there were 53 malformed input bugs in our sample.

There are several problems with this scheme of bug categorization. First, notice that almost half of the bugs are in the missing guard or malformed guard categories (265 out of 549 bugs). The fact that this scheme points out that nearly half of the bugs are guard bugs is not very satisfactory; there is simply not enough detail in that type of description. Because there are many places that a guard could have been used in the program (e.g., detecting when to stop in G:LOOP, detecting when to retry input in G:VDE, and detecting when to do wrap-around in G:CALC), it is quite reasonable to suppose that the misconception underlying the improper use of a guard in one plan of the program

Figure 4. Categorizing bugs (bottom of figure) with the problem-independent scheme.

```
01  Program Reformat(input,output);
02  Var Subject_Number :Integer;
03       Start_Hour, Start_Minute, Start_Second :Integer;
04       End_Hour, End_Minute, End_Second :Integer;
05       Problem_Type, Accuracy: Char;
06       Start_Time, End_Time, Elapsed_Time: Integer;
07
08  Begin
09  +--------------------------------------------------------------+
10  |                                                              |-- G:LOOP
11  +--------------------------------------------------------------+
12  |+-----------------------------------------------------------+
13  ||writeln('Enter Subject Number,Problem Type,Start Hour,Minute.');|
14  ||writeln('Second,End Hour,Minute,Second,and Accuracy.');    |
15  ||writeln('FOR EXAMPLE: 1 a 3 30 2 3 36 59 +');              |
16  ||readln(Subject_Number, Problem_Type,                      |
17  ||       Start_Hour, Start_Minute, Start_Second,            |
18  ||       End_Hour, End_Minute, End_Second,                  |
19  ||       Accuracy);                                          |
20  ||if ((Subject_Number <= 0) or                              |
21  ||    ((Problem_Type <> 'a') and (Problem_Type <> 'b')      |
22  ||                        and (Problem_Type <> 'c')) or     |
23  ||    ((Start_Hour   < 1) or (Start_Hour   > 12)) or        |
24  ||    ((Start_Minute < 0) or (Start_Minute > 59)) or        |
25  ||    ((Start_Second < 0) or (Start_Second > 59)) or        |
26  ||    ((End_Hour    < 1) or (End_Hour   > 12)) or           |
27  ||    ((End_Minute < 0) or (End_Minute > 59)) or            |
28  ||    ((End_Second < 0) or (End_Second > 59)) or            |-- G:VDE
29  ||    ((Accuracy <> '+') OR (Accuracy <> '-')))             |
30  ||    then                                                   |
31  ||      begin                                                |
32  ||        writeln('Some data bad... Try again.');           |
33  ||      END;                                                 |
34  ||      readln(Subject_Number, Problem_Type,                |
35  ||            Start_Hour, Start_Minute, Start_Second,       |
36  ||            End_Hour, End_Minute, End_Second,             |
37  ||            Accuracy);                                     |
38  |+-----------------------------------------------------------+
39  |+-----------------------------------------------------------+
40  ||Start_Time := 3600*Start_Hour + 60*Start_Minute + Start_Second;|
41  ||End_Time := 3600*End_Hour + 60*End_Minute + End_Second;   |-- G:CALC
42  ||if End_Time <= Start_Time then End_Time := End_Time + 3600*12; |
43  ||Elapsed_Time := End_Time - Start_Time;                    |
44  |+-----------------------------------------------------------+
45  |+-----------------------------------------------------------+
46  ||READLN(ELAPSED _ TIME);                                   |-- G:OUTPUT
47  ||writeln('Data:',Subject_Number,Problem_Type,Elapsed_Time,Accuracy);|
48  |+-----------------------------------------------------------+
49  +--------------------------------------------------------------+
50  |                                                              |-- G:LOOP
51  +--------------------------------------------------------------+
52  End.
```

- **MISSING PLAN**: There is no plan for achieving G:LOOP. Should be at about lines 9-11 and 49-51.
- **MALFORMED GUARD**: In line 29, the OR should be an AND.
- **MISPLACED SYNTAX**: In line 33, the END should come after the READLN.
- **SPURIOUS INPUT**: In line 46, the READLN for Elapsed_Time shouldn't be there.

Figure 5.   Bug frequency table — problem-independent scheme — based on an analysis of 46 novice programmers' first syntactically correct programs for the reformatting problem.

	INIT	INPUT	GUARD	UPDATE	OUTPUT	SYNTAX	PLAN	TOTAL
MALFORMED	0	53	162	19	64	0	21	319
MISPLACED	0	19	1	0	1	2	1	24
MISSING	1	22	103	0	18	11	23	178
SPURIOUS	1	1	2	0	2	22	0	28
TOTAL	2	95	268	19	85	35	45	549

is different from the misconception underlying the improper use of a guard in another plan of the program.

On the other hand, there are times when it appears that the same misconception underlies several bugs in a program; however, this bug categorization scheme does not capture the appropriate generalization. For example, in Figure 6, a buggy program fragment that attempts to achieve G:VDE of the reformatting problem is displayed. By counting plan component differences, we can identify six bugs in this program: missing guards for the six time variables (i.e., start hour, minute, second; end hour, minute, second). The bug description shown in Figure 6 is unsatisfactory. Although the bug count would say that there are six bugs in this program, it would seem that they all follow from the same conceptual bug, namely a misconception about whether to check the time data items to see if they were valid.

In other words, there are two basic weaknesses with the categorization scheme briefly outlined here and described more extensively in Johnson et al. (1983):

1. Too few distinctions made. The foregoing scheme does not, in some cases, differentiate the plans from which the plan components are missing, malformed, and so on. In effect, the scheme does not make enough distinctions (see Figure 5; almost half the bugs fall in 2 of the 28 possible categories).

2. Too many distinctions made. The foregoing scheme does not, in some cases, group bugs together that stem from a common cause. In effect, the scheme makes too many distinctions (see Figure 6; all the bugs seem to have a common cause).

The next section describes a bug categorization scheme that seeks to remedy these two weaknesses.

Figure 6. Six plan component differences in a buggy program fragment.

          Buggy Fragment

```
01    ...
02    writeln('Enter Subject Number');
03    readln(Subject_Number);
04    if Subject_Number < 1
05      then begin
06          writeln('BAD:Retry Subject Number');
07          readln(Subject_Number);
08          end;
09    writeln('Enter Problem Type');
10    readln(Problem_Type);
11    if ((Problem_Type <> 'a') and
12        (Problem_Type <> 'b') and
13        (Problem_Type <> 'c'))
14      then begin
15          writeln('BAD: Retry Problem Type');
16          readln(Problem_Type);
17          end;
18    writeln('Enter Start Hour);
19    readln(Start_Hour);
                <----------------------------- MISSING GUARD (1)
20    writeln('Enter Start Minute);
21    readln(Start_Minute);
                <----------------------------- MISSING GUARD (2)
22    writeln('Enter Start Second);
23    readln(Start_Second);
                <----------------------------- MISSING GUARD (3)
24    writeln('Enter End Hour);
25    readln(End_Hour);
                <----------------------------- MISSING GUARD (4)
26    writeln('Enter End Minute);
27    readln(End_Minute);
                <----------------------------- MISSING GUARD (5)
28    writeln('Enter End Second);
29    readln(End_Second);
                <----------------------------- MISSING GUARD (6)
30    writeln('Enter Accuracy');
31    readln(Accuracy);
32    if (Accuracy <> '+') and (Accuracy <> '-')
33      then begin
34          writeln('BAD:Retry Accuracy');
35          readln(Problem_Type);
36          end;
37    ...
```

```
FOR EXAMPLE THE FIRST MISSING GUARD SHOULD BE:

01 ...
02 if ((Start_Hour < 1) or (Start_Hour > 12))
03    then begin
04        writeln('BAD: Retry Start Hour (1-12)');
05        readln(Start_Hour);
06        end;
07 ...
```

---

5.   A PROBLEM-DEPENDENT SCHEME FOR BUG CATEGORIZATION

An analysis of the reasons for the problem-independent scheme's weaknesses leads to our current, problem-dependent scheme:

1. The problem-independent scheme only looks at plan components independent of their context. In contrast, by looking at guard plan components in the context of say, G:VDE versus G:CALC, we can generate a more fine-grained categorization scheme. For example, in Figure 7 we present a breakdown of the 28 bug categories originally descibed in Figure 5 in terms of the four top-level goals that need to be accomplished in the reformatting problem. Notice in particular that the distribution of errors in the guard component is not even with respect to the four goals. Although three of these goals had plans that required guard plans, the majority of bugs occurred in the plans for achieving G:VDE. This suggests that the students' misconceptions were more focused than simply a misunderstanding of guard plans; they seemed to have difficulty with guard plans only in a specific context.

2. Similarly, by looking at individual plan components, the problem-independent scheme can miss the common underlying generalization. Sometimes, plan components are related by the enclosing goal/plan. Thus, for example, in Figure 6 the six missing guard plan components are all the G:TIME-DATA guards. The student probably did not realize that guarding against typos for the time variables was required.

In other words, the weaknesses of the problem-independent scheme are due to its focusing only on plan components and ignoring the context in which those plan components appear. The GAP tree provides just such a context. Thus, our problem-dependent scheme includes the problem-independent scheme plus the problem-specific GAP tree.

Besides remedying the two weaknesses, the problem-dependent scheme facilitates an additional type of analysis that deals with finding the "easy" and the "hard" plans. There may be many different plans to achieve the same goal. If nearly all of the students who chose one plan were successful in implementing it and nearly all the students who chose another were unsuccessful in implementing it, this would provide a basis for collecting easy and hard plans. Again, the search for underlying misconceptions has been focused to particular plans: the hard plans. (In the final section of this paper, we present a particularly interesting class of hard plans).

Each of the following subsections acquaints the reader with a result of our new scheme (i.e., a type of analysis which the problem-dependent categorization scheme facilitates). The subsections are divided into two parts. *Description:* a bug is described in terms of the problem-dependent goals and plans

Figure 7.   Bug frequency table — problem-dependent scheme — based on an analysis of 46 novice programmers' first syntactically correct programs for the
reformatting problem. The bug counts of the problem-independent scheme have
been subdivided by problem-dependent top-level goals. (Numbers in italics are the
same as in Figure 5.)

	INIT	INPUT	GUARD	UPDATE	OUTPUT	SYNTAX	PLAN	TOTAL
MALFORMED	*0*	*53*	*162*	*19*	*64*	*0*	*21*	*319*
G:LOOP	0	0	3	1	0	0	0	**4**
G:VDE	0	53	159	9	0	0	11	232
G:CALC	0	0	0	9	0	0	10	19
G:OUTPUT	-	-	0	-	64	0	0	64
MISPLACED	*0*	*19*	*1*	*0*	*1*	*2*	*1*	*24*
G:LOOP	0	0	0	0	0	1	1	2
G:VDE	0	19	1	0	0	1	0	21
G:CALC	0	0	0	0	0	0	0	0
G:OUTPUT	-	-	0	-	1	0	0	1
MISSING	*1*	*22*	*103*	*0*	*18*	*11*	*23*	*178*
G:LOOP	1	4	0	0	6	2	9	22
G:VDE	0	18	103	0	4	9	0	134
G:CALC	0	0	0	0	0	0	12	12
G:OUTPUT	-	-	0	-	8	0	2	10
SPURIOUS	*1*	*1*	*2*	*0*	*2*	*22*	*0*	*28*
G:LOOP	1	0	0	0	1	0	0	2
G:VDE	0	1	0	0	0	18	0	19
G:CALC	0	0	2	0	0	4	0	6
G:OUTPUT	-	-	0	-	1	0	0	1
TOTAL	*2*	*95*	*268*	*19*	*85*	*35*	*45*	*549*
G:LOOP	2	4	3	1	7	3	10	30
G:VDE	0	91	263	9	4	28	11	406
G:CALC	0	0	2	9	0	4	22	37
G:OUTPUT	-	-	0	-	74	0	2	76

where it occurs. *Interpretation:* candidate explanations of the bug are examined.
Two important points that readers should bear in mind as they study these examples are: (a) How did the GAP tree influence the data analysis and focus our
attention on the particular bugs? Usually, it will be clear that disparate bug
frequencies focused our attention on a group of bugs; and (b) How did the description of the bugs in terms of the GAP tree facilitate generating plausible accounts of the bugs? The particular bug will usually be related to or distinguished from other bugs based on some feature of the goal and plan context.

5.1. Result 1: Goal and Plan Context of Bugs

Description

From Figure 7 we see that there are a total of 268 bugs related to the guard
plan components of the 46 programs analyzed for the reformatting problem.

Despite the fact that a guard plan component occurred in three of the four top-level goals for this problem, the distribution of bugs between these goals is quite uneven: All but five of the guard bugs occurred while attempting to achieve G:VDE. Now that the bug frequency information has focused our attention on this anomalous situation, we can begin to investigate the differences between the contexts supplied by the various top-level goals. In particular, we look at the role of the guard plan component and the types of conditions tested for by the guards in relation to the three relevant top-level goals in order to better identify the underlying misconceptions.

The role of the guard component is different in each of the contexts provided by the top-level goals. Referring back to Figure 2, we can identify these differences: (a) G:LOOP Context: The role of the guard in service of G:LOOP is to detect when to continue or stop the processing of data records (see Line 14 of Figure 2); (b) G:VDE Context: The role of the guard in service of G:VDE is to detect when to recover from bad data input (see Lines 25–34 of Figure 2); (c) G:CALC Context: The role of the guard in service of G:CALC is to detect when to compensate for wrap-around (see Line 47 of Figure 2).

A centrality difference exists between the role of the guard in each of these three contexts. One can ask how much of the functionality of each of the three goals remains if we remove their guards. In the case of G:LOOP, removing the guard (Line 14, Figure 2) makes both the initialization (Lines 10–13) and the reread (Lines 54–57) superfluous. The result of guard deletion would be that only one record of data could be processed at a time, leaving very little of the original functionality behind. If the guard (Lines 25–34) was removed from G:VDE, then the retry (Lines 36–42) would be superfluous, but the original input (Lines 18–24) would still be reasonable. The program would still get input to run on, but it might be bad data; assuming a careful user, a fair amount of the original functionality remains. In the case of G:CALC, removing the guard (Line 47) would not make any of the other lines of code superfluous. However, the calculation would be successful only in those cases in which wrap-around had not occurred, leaving a great deal of the original functionality, but with one major glitch. Although each of the goals requires a guard plan component to achieve full functionality, they differ in how crucial or central the guard is to the overall purpose of the goal.

A complexity difference also exists between the plans required to achieve the guard in each of these three contexts. Although each of the guards must alter the flow of control based on particular conditions, the types of conditions and their complexity, based on the number of terms in the Boolean expression, are quite varied. For instance, as shown in Figure 2, the G:LOOP guard condition is an inequality test (Line 14), whereas the G:CALC guard condition is an relative ordering test (Line 47). Another difference between the guards in the context of each of these different top-level goals is the number of terms in the Boolean expressions used to check for particular conditions. Even when

G:VDE is achieved using a plan that guards each input data item separately (e.g., P:IGR-E, as shown in Figure 6), most of the variables' guards contain multiple terms. For instance, time variables must have a term guarding the low end of the interval and a term guarding the high end of the interval, and the problem type and accuracy must have terms corresponding to each of the allowed values they can take on. These differences of type and complexity can be summarized as follows (again, line numbers refer to Figure 2):

G:LOOP Context: One variable, one type of condition, one term.
Sentinel: An inequality relationship (see Line 14).

G:VDE Context: Nine variables, three types of conditions, eighteen terms.
Subject__Number: An ordinal relationship (see Line 25).
Problem__Type: A set-member exclusion relationship (see Lines 26–27).
Start__Hour: An interval exclusion relationship (see Line 27).
Start__Minute: An interval exclusion relationship (see Line 28).
Start__Second: An interval exclusion relationship (see Line 29).
End__Hour: An interval exclusion relationship (see Line 30).
End__Minute: An interval exclusion relationship (see Line 31).
End__Second: An interval exclusion relationship (see Line 33).
Accuracy: A set-member exclusion relationship (see Line 34).

G:CALC Context: Two variables, one type of condition, one term.
End__Time and Start__Time: An ordinal relationship (see Line 47).

From the summary, it is clear that the complexity of the G:VDE guard, as measured by number of types of conditions and number of terms, is greatest.

Interpretation

In this subsection, we investigate why the bug frequencies for the guard component are so much greater for G:VDE than for G:LOOP and G:CALC. The first hypothesis might be that there are more variables to be checked in G:VDE than in the other two goals. This accounts for some of the difference (as described in the next section), but not for the bulk of the discrepancy. Another possible explanation is that some novices have a misconception that prevents them from correctly realizing guard plans with multiple terms in the condition; the G:LOOP and G:CALC guards can be realized with only a single term in the Boolean conditions. Such a misconception would explain why the Malformed Guard bug frequencies are so much higher for G:VDE (and such a misconception is proposed later), but would not explain why the Missing Guard bug frequencies are so high for G:VDE.

One explanation of the high Missing Guard bug counts in the case of G:VDE is based on a strategy that novice programmers might use to deal with the cognitive load imposed by solving complex problems. The strategy is to solve a simplified version of the problem in the first pass and, once the simplified problem is solved, to extend the functionality of the program to solve the entire problem. Because the data we analyzed were the first syntactically correct version of the students' attempted solutions, one would expect this strategy to result in the omission of certain noncentral goals or goals that are overly complex in the student's mind. Given that the role of the guard in G:VDE is less central to the functioning of the program than the guards in other contexts (input is the most important aspect of the goal) and that the guards are more complex (containing more terms), the guard(s) for G:VDE were prime candidates to be postponed for a later version of the program so that the simplified problem could be more easily solved within the particular cognitive constraints of the novice. A student could not leave out the guard of G:LOOP without leaving out the entire goal. In the case of G:CALC, leaving out the guard would mean leaving out G:WRAP-AROUND entirely. In terms of centrality to the basic functioning of the program and overall complexity, the guard component of G:VDE was a reasonably expendable part of the problem. By temporarily leaving it out, cognitive load can be reduced while still allowing considerable progress to be made. Although this explanation accounts for some of the missing guard bugs, we present another explanation in Section 5.2 which accounts for the bulk of these missing guard bugs.

In only a single case in which the users left out a goal in the first syntactically correct version does the staged development explanation probably account for the majority of what we count as bugs. In Figure 7, the Missing Plan category for G:LOOP indicates that nine students did not achieve G:LOOP at all in their first syntactically correct versions. An examination of the later versions produced by these nine students revealed that seven of the students had achieved G:LOOP in their final version. In these seven cases, students apparently attempted to correctly format one record of information before worrying about processing multiple records using a loop.

5.2. Result 2: Bug Dependencies

Description

The term bug dependencies refers to the situation in which a single underlying misconception gives rise to several bugs in a single program. A satisfactory bug categorization scheme must be able to reveal, not conceal, bug dependencies when they occur.

The table in Figure 5 shows that there were 103 missing guard bugs in the 46 novice programs analyzed. The table in Figure 7 indicates that all of those missing guard bugs occurred in the plans to achieve G:VDE. A still finer breakdown in terms of the plans to achieve the subgoals of G:VDE is also illuminating. In the table in Figure 8, we see that relatively few students were responsible for all the valid-data-entry guard bugs. Moreover, one specific bug type stands out: When a student missed a guard to check for valid timing data input (start and end time), then the student usually missed all the guards for that set of data (e.g., see Figure 6).

Viewing the data at such a fine-grained level provides several advantages. First, the count of bugs becomes more realistic: There were not 103 missing guard bugs on G:VDE. Rather, we can see that 13 students were responsible for at least 78 of those bugs. In addition, the analysis of where the student's misconception lies now becomes more focused: No longer do we tell the student that he had, say, six missing guard bugs; rather, we say that the student had a misconception about how to check for valid timing data input. This type of bug dependency analysis is precisely what was missing from the bug categorization scheme described in the previous section.

Thus, we can see that continuing to represent the bug counts at finer and finer levels of the GAP tree can provide a more effective basis for understanding how the bugs in a student's program relate to his or her misconceptions. Although removing dependencies is a standard strategy in statistical analysis, the GAP tree gives a more precise meaning to what one type of bug dependency is: bugs consistently occurring in the subgoals of a particular goal.

Taking all the bug dependencies into account, we can redo the table in Figure 7 and obtain the dependency-adjusted bug frequencies shown in Figure 9. Note that this reduces the total bug count by over half (from 549 down to 231). This reduction is important because it means that the frequencies of different groups of bugs can be more accurately compared, inasmuch as artificially inflated counts have been reduced by taking into account the bug dependency information. For instance, using the bug frequencies in Figure 7, we might have tried to focus on why most of the syntax component bugs (28 of 35) occurred in the context of G:VDE in much the way we pursued this angle in the last section for the guard component. However, the dependency-adjusted bug frequencies in Figure 9 show that this situations is not anomalous in this way after all, with a total of 11 syntax bugs distributed quite evenly between G:LOOP, G:VDE, and G:CALC.

Interpretation

The finer breakdown shown in Figure 9 also raises the question: Why would so many students (more than 25%) neglect to guard the time data, and no student omit the guards for problem type and accuracy? One explanation is that the bug arose during the interpretation phase of the program writing process, the phase in which the student is reading the assignment and forming goals. The values that the problem type and accuracy data items could take on were *explicitly* mentioned in the reformatting problem assignment (see Figure 1,

Figure 8.   Bug/subject frequency table—problem-dependent scheme—based on an analysis of 46 novice programmers' first syntactically correct programs for the reformatting problem. The missing G:VDE guard counts are further subdivided by the problem-dependent subgoals. The number of subjects who made these bugs is also shown. Note that subjects typically left out all six time variable guards as a group and rarely left out the guard for just an individual time variable.

MISSING VDE GUARD SUBGOALS	Number of Bugs	Number of Subjects
G:SUBJECT-NUMBER	23	23
G:PROBLEM-TYPE	0	0
G:TIME-DATA ---->(missing all 6)	78	13
---->(missing just a few)	2	1
G:ACCURACY	0	0
TOTAL	103	37

Lines 18–21), whereas the values that the time variables could take on were only implicitly alluded to using examples (e.g., 4 32 16, means 4 o'clock, 32 min, and 16 sec). Even though all the students probably knew the range of acceptable values for the time variables, this acceptable range was not stated explicitly in the assignment, and as a result, many students simply did not form the goal of guarding against bad time values. There may be other possible explanations, but the point is that any explanation for this bug would have to explain the absence of all and only the time variable guards.

5.3.   Result 3: Identifying the Easy and the Hard Plans

An analysis based on a GAP tree allows us to pinpoint further where the students' misconceptions might lie by identifying which goals and plans students had difficulty realizing. In what follows, we provide two examples in which just such an analysis serves to highlight troublesome goals and plans.

Achieving G:CALC: Description

Consider the section of the GAP tree shown in Figure 10. The high level goal (G:CALC) of computing the correct elapsed time can be achieved using either P:S-W-D or P:W-S-D, which basically provide two different orderings on the three subgoals of G:CALC, namely, G:STANDARDIZE, G:WRAP-AROUND, and G:DIFFERENCE. The plans available for achieving G:WRAP-AROUND are different depending on whether G:WRAP-AROUND is achieved before or after G:STANDARDIZE. If G:WRAP-AROUND is done after G:STANDARDIZE, then P:ADD-43200-SECONDS should be used; if G:WRAP-AROUND is done before G:STANDARDIZE, then P:ADD-12-HOURS should be used.

Figure 11 shows a possible implementation of the plans P:ADD-43200-SECONDS and P:ADD-12-HOURS. For each plan, a correct implementa-

Figure 9.   Dependency-adjusted bug frequency table based on an analysis of 46 novice programmers' first syntactically correct programs for the reformatting problem.

	INIT	INPUT	GUARD	UPDATE	OUTPUT	SYNTAX	PLAN	TOTAL
MALFORMED	*0*	*21*	*50*	*11*	*17*	*0*	*17*	*125*
G:LOOP	0	0	3	1	0	0	0	4
G:VDE	0	21	56	1	0	0	7	85
G:CALC	0	0	0	9	0	0	10	19
G:OUTPUT	–	–	0	–	17	0	0	17
MISPLACED	*0*	*3*	*1*	*0*	*1*	*2*	*1*	*8*
G:LOOP	0	0	0	0	0	1	1	2
G:VDE	0	3	1	0	0	1	0	5
G:CALC	0	0	0	0	0	0	0	0
G:OUTPUT	–	–	0	–	1	0	0	1
MISSING	*1*	*11*	*37*	*0*	*11*	*3*	*23*	*86*
G:LOOP	1	4	0	0	6	2	9	22
G:VDE	0	7	37	0	1	1	0	46
G:CALC	0	0	0	0	0	0	12	12
G:OUTPUT	–	–	0	–	4	0	2	6
SPURIOUS	*1*	*1*	*2*	*0*	*2*	*6*	*0*	*12*
G:LOOP	1	0	0	0	1	0	0	2
G:VDE	0	1	0	0	0	2	0	3
G:CALC	0	0	2	0	0	4	0	6
G:OUTPUT	–	–	0	–	1	0	0	1
TOTAL	*2*	*36*	*99*	*11*	*31*	*11*	*41*	*231*
G:LOOP	2	4	3	1	7	3	10	30
G:VDE	0	32	94	1	1	4	7	139
G:CALC	0	0	2	9	0	4	22	37
G:OUTPUT	–	–	0	–	23	0	2	25

tion and an incorrect one are shown. A correct implementation of P:ADD-43200-SECONDS requires that it be done after G:STANDARDIZE has been achieved, using the correct value of the constant. A correct implementation of P:ADD-12-HOURS requires that it be done before G:STANDARDIZE is achieved and that it check the possible case in which starting hour equals ending hour and a wrap-around should still be done (e.g., start is 4:32:04 and end is 4:26:35).

From Figure 10, we see that just a few more students chose to realize G:WRAP-AROUND (of G:CALC) using P:ADD-43200-SECONDS (16 students) than chose P:ADD-12-HOURS (11 students). However, while the former students almost invariably realized their plan successfully, the latter students almost invariably failed! The most common error made by students implementing P:ADD-12-HOURS was forgetting to consider the case in which starting hours and ending hours are equal.

Figure 10.   Portion of the GAP tree for G:CALC.

```
                              G:CALC
                                |
        -------------------------------------------------------
        |                                                     |
     P:S-W-D                                               P:W-S-D
        |                                                     |
 ---------------------------------           ---------------------------------
 |              |             |               |              |             |
G:STANDARDIZE G:WRAP-AROUND G:DIFFERENCE    G:STANDARDIZE G:WRAP-AROUND G:DIFFERENCE
 |              |             |               |              |             |
...       P:ADD-43200-SECONDS ...           ...       P:ADD-12-HOURS      ...
```

P:ADD-43200-SECONDS PLAN:		P:ADD-12-HOURS PLAN:	
=========================		=========================	
total times plan used:	16	total times plan used:	11
plan realized correctly:	15	plan realized correctly:	1
plan realized incorrectly:	1	plan realized incorrectly:	10

Figure 11.   Correct and incorrect code for two calculation plans.

Correct and Incorrect Code for P:ADD-43200-SECONDS

```
CORRECT:    01 Start_Time := 3600*Start_Hours + 60*Start_Minutes + Start_Seconds;
            02 End_Time := 3600*End_Hours + 60*End_Minutes + End_Seconds;
            03 if Start_Time >= End_Time then End_Time := End_Time + 43200;
            04 Elapsed_Time := End_Time - Start_Time;

INCORRECT:  05 Start_Time := 3600*Start_Hours + 60*Start_Minutes + Start_Seconds;
            06 End_Time := 3600*End_Hours + 60*End_Minutes + End_Seconds;
            07 if Start_Time >= End_Time then End_Time := End_Time + 4320;
            08 Elapsed_Time := End_Time - Start_Time;
```

Bug in Incorrect Version: Incorrect value of constant.

Correct and Incorrect Code for P:ADD-12-HOURS

```
CORRECT:    09 if ((Start_Hours > End_Hours) or
            10   ((Start_Hours = End_Hours) and (Start_Minutes > End_Minutes)) or
            11   ((Start_Hours = End_Hours) and (Start_Minutes = End_Minutes)
            12                         and (Start_Seconds >= End_Seconds)))
            13   then End_Hours := End_Hours + 12;
            14 Start_Time := 3600*Start_Hours + 60*Start_Minutes + Start_Seconds;
            15 End_Time := 3600*End_Hours + 60*End_Minutes + End_Seconds;
            16 Elapsed_Time := End_Time - Start_Time;

INCORRECT:  17 if Start_Hours >= End_Hours then End_Hours := End_Hours + 12;
            18 Start_Time := 3600*Start_Hours + 60*Start_Minutes + Start_Seconds;
            19 End_Time := 3600*End_Hours + 60*End_Minutes + End_Seconds;
            20 Elapsed_Time := End_Time - Start_Time;
```

Bug in Incorrect Version: No test for equal start and end hour wraparounds.

Achieving G:CALC: Interpretation

Why is P:ADD-12-HOURS buggier on the average than P:ADD-43200-SECONDS? From looking at the sample code in Figure 11, one is struck by the difference in complexity of the two plans for detecting the wrap-around condition. Viewing each of the two plans as organizing the same two subgoals, G:DETECTION and G:COMPENSATE, we can further localize the misconceptions of the student to the problem of achieving G:DETECTION. Three common buggy implementations of P:ADD-12-HOURS, which illustrate how G:DETECTION is not satisfactorily achieved, are shown in Figure 12.

The misconceptions of the novice programmer seem to arise in constructing a plan that successfully achieves G:DETECTION. In the first two incorrect implementations in Figure 12, it appears that the student did not consider all of the relevant cases and hence was unable to form all of the appropriate subgoals necessary to ultimately construct the appropriate plan. In the third incorrect implementation, however, it appears that the student was aware of the relevant cases in which minutes and seconds should be checked as well as hours, but was unable to form a plan correctly, which integrated solutions to each of the appropriate subgoals.

Therefore, we can say that in some sense P:ADD-12-HOURS is a "harder," and therefore buggier, plan. Summarizing the two possible explanations for the students' poorer performance on P:ADD-12-HOURS, we find: (a) judging from the absence of equal-hour tests in the code, most students did not consider the equal-hour case and (b) even if they did intend to handle the equal-hour case, the logic was much more complicated than in the other plan.

Achieving G:VDE: Description

Consider the code fragments in Figure 13, which were observed in some of the first syntactically correct programs produced by novices to guard against bad data in the reformatting problem. They show the two plans, P:IF-VALID and P:IF-INVALID, which are alternative ways of achieving G:VALID-DATA-ENTRY'S G:GUARD. The difference between the plans is that the former tests a data item to make sure that it is valid, whereas the latter tests to see if the data item is invalid. In the case of the problem type variable, this means that P:IF-VALID is used to see if the value of the problem type is a, b, or c; P:IF-INVALID is used to see if the value is not a, b, or c.

We see from Figure 14 that almost five times as many students chose to use P:IF-INVALID as selected P:IF-VALID. However, although all of the students who choose P:IF-VALID were able to implement the conditional correctly, the students who chose P:IF-INVALID did not fare so well. In fact, almost half of these students were unable to realize the plan correctly. The most common error made by the students implementing P:IF-INVALID was using the Boolean operator OR instead of AND between the terms in the condition.

Figure 12.   Buggy attempts at achieving G:DETECTION.

Incorrect Implemetation 1
```
01 if Start_Hours >= End_Hours then End_Hours := End_Hours + 12;
```

Incorrect Implementation 2
```
01 if (Start_Hours = 12) and (End_Hours = 1) then End_Hours := 13;
```

Incorrect Implementation 3
```
01 if (Start_Hours > End_Hours) or
02    (Start_Minutes > End_Minutes) or
03    (Start_Seconds > End_Seconds) then End_Hours := End_Hours + 12;
```

Figure 13.   Correct and incorrect code for two G:VDE plans.

Correct and Incorrect Code for P:IF-VALID *Guard Condition Plan*

```
CORRECT:   01 if (Problem_Type = 'a') or (Problem_Type = 'b') or (Problem_Type = 'c')
           02         then ...

INCORRECT: 03 if (Problem_Type = 'a') and (Problem_Type = 'b') and (Problem_Type = 'c')
           04         then ...
```

Bug in Incorrect Version: Boolean Operator AND instead of OR.

Correct and Incorrect Code for IF-INVALID *Guard Condition Plan*

```
CORRECT:   05 if (Problem_Type <> 'a') and (Problem_Type <> 'b') and (Problem_Type <> 'c')
           06         then ...

INCORRECT: 07 if (Problem_Type <> 'a') or (Problem_Type <> 'b') or (Problem_Type <> 'c')
           08         then ...
```

Bug in Incorrect Version: Boolean Operator OR instead of AND.

Achieving G:VDE: Interpretation

This result is quite interesting because it suggests that some students may possess a buggy version of DeMorgan's Rule. DeMorgan's Rule relates a conjunction of terms (A AND B) to a disjunction of terms (A OR B) via the Boolean equations:

(NOT (A OR B)) = ((NOT A) AND (NOT B))
(NOT (A AND B)) = ((NOT A) OR (NOT B))

In particular, it appears that some of the students who attempted P:IF-INVALID may have possessed a buggy version of DeMorgan's Rule in which:

(NOT (A OR B)) = ((NOT A) OR (NOT B)) ;Buggy

In this buggy version, the misconception would be that NOT distributes over OR; thus, to negate a Boolean expression one need only negate each term of

Figure 14. Two G:VDE guard condition plans: frequency of successful and unsuccessful program classifications.

Name	Times Used	Correct	Incorrect
Valid Condition Check P:IF-VALID	8	8 (100%)	0 (0%)
Invalid Condition Check P:IF-INVALID	38	22 (58%)	16 (42%)

that expression. Of course, if the assignment had required the students to negate a conjunction of terms, one might expect they would have had a similar problem (i.e., distributing NOT over AND). Distributing one operator over another may be a concept the students inappropriately transferred from their knowledge of algebra. This type of underlying misconception (i.e., wrong belief transferred from inappropriate domain) is quite common. Bonar and Soloway (1985) report that English is a common source domain, and Sleeman, Putnam, Baxter, and Kuspa (1985) describe the class of human reasoning powers which may get attributed to computers.

Alternatively, the students may be misapplying a more abstract P:CHECK-FOR-BAD-STUFF plan, which is of the form: **IF badthing1 OR badthing2 OR badthing3 ... THEN ....** Note that if the student instantiated this abstract plan with **badthings** being identified with terms like (**Problem_Type < >** 'a'), then the buggy P:IF-INVALID programming plan of Figure 14 results. The problem with this instantiation is that (**Problem_Type < >** 'a') is not a **badthing** all by itself. Instead, it is just a piece of a badthing — a complete bad thing would require that none of the three allowed values had occurred (e.g., (**Problem_Type =** 'd')). Notice, however, that in the case of P:IF-VALID, the term (**Problem_Type =** 'a') is a complete goodthing.

6. IDENTIFYING A CLASS OF HARD PLANS

In this section, we describe one class of buggy programs revealed by our analysis technique. This class of programs is particularly interesting because a significant number of novice programmers write programs of this type, and they appear to be buggier than other types. An example can provide an introduction to this class of programs and bugs.

Consider the simplified problem specification (derived from an actual programming assignment given to students) and program fragments in Figure 15. An effective program for this problem requires that three goals be achieved in the code: (a) G:INPUT — input the marital status and income, (b) G:GUARD — guard against invalid data, and (c) G:RETRY — if invalid data are detected, then prompt the user for new input. In the correct program fragment, these three goals are realized independently. G:INPUT, G:GUARD, and G:RETRY were achieved for the marital status data, and they were again achieved for the income data. However, in the buggy fragment, we see that

Figure 15.   Contrasting fragments with and without a bug. Prompts have been removed to highlight content lines.

```
PROBLEM: Write a program to read in a person's marital status
('m' = married, or 's' = single) and income. Guard against "typos"
by verifying that the input data is valid, and if it is not give
the person a second chance to enter the data. (Assume the second
time, the data will always be typed in correctly.)
```

Correct Fragment: Unmerged Goals
```
01 ...
02 readln(status);                         <---------------INPUT STATUS
03 if (status <> 'm') and (status <> 's)    <---------------GUARD STATUS
04   then realn(status);                    <---------------RETRY STATUS
05
06 readln(income);                          <---------------INPUT INCOME
07 if (income < 0)                          <---------------GUARD INCOME
08   then readln(income);                   <---------------RETRY INCOME
09 ...
```

Buggy Fragment: Merged Goals
```
01 ...
02 readln(status,income);                   <---------------INPUT STATUS&INCOME
03 if (income < 0) or (status <> 's') or (status <> 'm') <---GUARD STATUS&INCOME
04                                             (OR for AND bug)
05   then readln(status,income);            <-----------------RETRY STATUS&INCOME
06 ...
```

Corrected Fragment: Merged Goals
```
01 ...
02 readln(status,income);                   <---------------INPUT STATUS&INCOME
03 if(income < 0) or ((status <> 's') and (status <> 'm')) <-GUARD STATUS&INCOME
04   then readln(status,income)             <-----------------RETRY STATUS&INCOME
05 ...
```

---

these goals were merged: Both variables were input, guarded, and retried in the same piece of code. When we say "goals were merged," we mean that a single plan to achieve these two goals in an integrated manner was used. The merged plan may have been produced by taking two plans that would achieve the goals independently and combining them in some nontrivial manner (i.e., sequencing the plans one after the other is trivial), or it may have been produced in some other manner such that it bears little resemblance to any of the independent plans for achieving the goals. To achieve goals correctly in this merged manner often takes a bit of doing. As illustrated in the third code fragment in Figure 15, the Boolean condition in the IF statement must be structured in a complicated manner. Notice too that nowhere in the problem specification was there an explicit instruction to structure the problem one way or the other. It was up to the programmer to choose how to implement the goals in the code.

After analyzing hundreds of buggy programs, we are in a position to make the following observations: (a) significant numbers of students write programs in which goals are merged in their code; (b) students who write code in which goals are merged write programs that exhibit merge-related bugs, in addition to those in nonmerged programs, and the merged code is initially buggier than the unmerged. The example in Figure 15 is but one example; in what follows, we analyze in greater detail the difficulties involved in writing code with merged goals. In particular, we identify two specific types of bugs that result when goals are merged in code.

The organization of this section is as follows. First, we describe the data from which the foregoing observations were made. We also provide an overview of our goal and plan analysis technique applied to this problem. Next, we provide examples of two types of bugs that occur in merged code. This qualitative exposition is followed by a more quantitative exposition that discusses how frequently merging occurred and how often the merged plans were correct for a particular programming assignment. Finally, we offer some speculation as to the source of merged code and discuss some implications of these observations.

6.1. The Tax Problem

The assignment shown in Figure 16 was given to a group of about 200 college students enrolled in an introductory Pascal programming course. The following examples and statistics were all obtained from a detailed analysis of the first syntactically correct program of 57 of these students.

The assignment asks the students to write a program that calculates the amount of tax and net salary for a particular income and marital status. The assignment was the first in which the students in the course were asked to use Pascal procedures. Two procedures (one for the married tax formula and one for the singles tax formula) were to be used. The main body of the program was to manage getting the data, calling the appropriate subroutine, and displaying the answer. In addition, the program's main body was to contain a loop so that multiple records of information could be processed interactively in a single run. Besides the text of the assignment, many specifications dealing with programs in general were stressed during the course. In particular, students knew that whenever they read data in a program, they must guard against typographical errors that the user might make.

In the problem assignment in Figure 16, we can identify five main goals to be achieved:

1. G:CALC: This is G:CALCULATION, which corresponds to the intention of computing the tax and net income for both singles and married couples, based on the appropriate formula for each group (Lines 1–4, 8–10, 22–24).
2. G:LOOP: This goal corresponds to the intention of processing multiple records (Lines 6, 10–19).

Figure 16. The tax problem assignment.

```
01    Assume that a tax table specifies that married people pay 30% of their
02    combined salary for the first $10,000 and 32% for any amount over that.
03    However, a single person pays 30% on the first $8,000 and 32% for any
04    amount over that. Write a program that inputs records that have an 'M'
05    or an 'S' and a yearly salary figure ('M' stands for married, and 'S'
06    stands for single). The program should report for each record the
07    following: (1) type of input (M or S) (2) amount of salary (3) amount of
08    tax (4) net salary after tax. Use one PROCEDURE to calculate the taxes
09    for a married couple and another PROCEDURE to calculate the taxes for a
10    single person. Test your program with the following data:
11
12        M 12364.84
13        S 12364.84
14        S 12364.32
15        M  8941.12
16        M 27683.41
17        M 96218.19
18        S 84321.92
19        S 68440.07
20
21    The main routine of your program should simply call the procedures and
22    do the printing. All other computation should be in the procedures.
23    Remember, this problem is meant to exercise PROCEDURES -- so you MUST
24    use them in your program!!
```

3. G:VDE: This is G:VALID-DATA-ENTRY, which corresponds to reading in data to the program and making sure that the data are valid. If the data are not valid, then the user should be given a chance to retype it (Lines 4–6, 10–19).

4. G:DISPATCH: This goal corresponds to the intention of calling the appropriate tax formula subroutine at the appropriate time (i.e., dispatching on the value of the marital status variable) (Lines 8–10, 21).

5. G:OUTPUT: This goal corresponds to the intention of writing out the results of the calculation as well as the input values on which the calculation was based (Lines 6–8).

Each of these goals can be accomplished by using one of several programming plans that serve to organize subgoals of these main goals in terms of standard programming constructs. The subgoals in turn can be accomplished by using other programming plans. We represent the space of possible correct solutions for the tax problem with a GAP tree (see Section 2). Figure 17 shows a portion of the GAP tree for the tax problem. Each of the top-level goals in the simplified GAP tree for the tax problem has two plans, which represent two alternative ways of achieving this goal in a sample solution. Figure 18 and Figure 19 are sample programs that illustrate each of these alternate plans for the top-level goals. The solution in Figure 18 uses the upper plans shown in the GAP tree, and the solution in Figure 19 uses the lower plans. The differences between these plans are as follows:

Figure 17. Simplified goal and plan tree (GAP tree) for the tax problem.

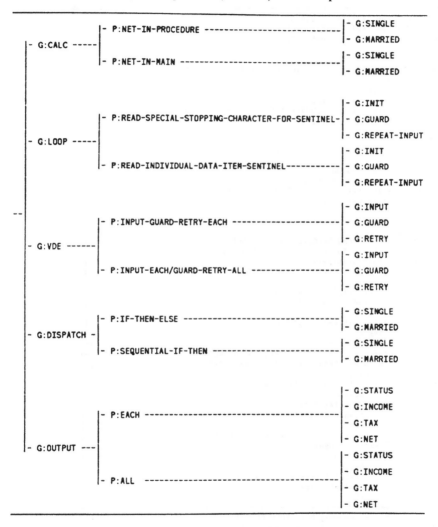

Figure 18.   A solution to the tax problem.

```
01     Program Tax(input,output);
02     Var Sentinel, Status : Char;
03         Income, Tax, Net : Real;
04
05   +-----------[ P:NET-IN-PROCEDURE ]--------------------+
06   | Procedure Married(Income:Real; VAR Tax, Net:Real)   |
07   | Begin                                               |
08   | if Income < 10000                                   |
09   |    then  Tax := Income * 0.30                       |
10   |    else  Tax := 10000 * 0.30 + (Income - 10000) * 0.32;|
11   | Net := Income - Tax;                                |
12   | End;                                                |
13   |                                                     |-- G:CALC
14   | Procedure Single(Income:Real; VAR Tax, Net:Real)    |
15   | Begin                                               |
16   | if Income < 8000                                    |
17   |    then  Tax := Income * 0.30                       |
18   |    else  Tax := 8000 * 0.30 + (Income - 8000) * 0.32;|
19   | Net := Income - Tax;                                |
20   | End;                                                |
21   +-----------------------------------------------------+
22     Begin
23   +--------[ P:READ-SPECIAL-STOPPING-CHARATER-FOR-SENTINEL ]---------+
24   |       writeln('To enter a record type "y". To exit type "n".'); |
25   |       readln(sentinel);                                         |
26   |       while (sentinel <> 'y') and (sentinel <> 'n) do           |
27   |          begin                                                  |-- G:LOOP
28   |          writeln('Please type a "y" or "n".');                  |
29   |          readln(sentinel)                                       |
30   |          end;                                                   |
31   |       while sentinel = 'y' do                                   |
32   |         begin                                                   |
33   +-----------------------------------------------------------------+
34   |       +----------------[ P:INPUT-GUARD-RETRY-EACH ]------------------+
35   |       |writeln('Enter marital status: ("m" married, "s" single).');|
36   |       |readln(status);                                             |
37   |       |while (status <> 'm') and (status <> 's') do                |
38   |       |   begin                                                    |
39   |       |   writeln('Please type a "m" or "s".');                    |
40   |       |   readln(status)                                           |
41   |       |   end;                                                     |
42   |       |writeln('Enter Income: (e.g., 17500.00).');                 |-- G:VDE
43   |       |readln(income);                                            |
44   |       |while income < 0 do                                        |
45   |       |   begin                                                    |
46   |       |   writeln('Please type a positive income.');               |
47   |       |   readln(income);                                         |
48   |       |   end                                                      |
49   |       +------------------------------------------------------------+
50   |       +------------[ P:IF-THEN-ELSE ]--------------+
51   |       |if status = 'm' then married(income,tax,net)|-- G:DISPATCH
52   |       |                 else single(income,tax,net);|
53   |       +--------------------------------------------+
54   |       +----------[ P:EACH ]----------------+
55   |       |writeln('Marital status:',status);  |
56   |       |writeln('Income:         ',income:0:2);|-- G:OUTPUT
57   |       |writeln('Tax:            ',tax:0:2); |
58   |       |writeln('Net Income:     ',net:0:2); |
59   |       +-----------------------------------+
```

388

```
60  +------[ P:READ-SPECIAL-STOPPING-CHARATER-FOR-SENTINEL ]----------+
61  |      writeln('To enter a record type "y". To exit type "n".');  |
62  |        readln(sentinel);                                        |
63  |        while (sentinel <> 'y') and (sentinel <> 'n) do          |
64  |           begin                                                 |- G:LOOP
65  |              writeln('Please type a "y" or "n".');              |
66  |              readln(sentinel)                                   |
67  |           end;                                                  |
68  |      end;                                                       |
69  +----------------------------------------------------------------+
70  End.
```

G:CALC plans: P:NET-IN-PROCEDURE (Figure 18, Lines 5–21) differs from P:NET-IN-MAIN (Figure 19, Lines 5–19, 46–48) in, as the names suggest, where the calculation of the net income appears in the program. Because the calculation is identical in both the married and single tax formula, it can be factored out and put into the main body of the program just before the output.

G:LOOP plans: P:READ-SPECIAL-STOPPING-CHARACTER-FOR-SENTINEL (Figure 18, lines 23–33, 60–69) differs from P:READ-INDIVIDUAL-DATA-ITEM-SENTINEL (Figure 19, lines 23–29, 52–57) in the variable that is used to control looping. In P:READ-SPECIAL-STOPPING-CHARACTER-FOR-SENTINEL, a separate sentinel variable is used, and in P:READ-INDIVIDUAL-DATA-ITEM-SENTINEL, the status variable takes on this additional function.

G:VDE plans: P:INPUT-GUARD-RETRY-EACH (Figure 18, Lines 34–49) differs from P:INPUT-EACH/GUARD-RETRY-ALL (Figure 19, Lines 30–39) in the order in which the three subgoals G:INPUT, G:GUARD, and G:RETRY are achieved for the two input variables, status and income, and whether or not they are combined. In P:INPUT-GUARD-RETRY-EACH, first all the subgoals are achieved for the status variable, and then they are all achieved for the income variable. However, in P:INPUT-EACH/GUARD-RETRY-ALL, first the status is input, then the income is input, and finally the guard and retry are handled together.

G:DISPATCH plans: P:IF-THEN-ELSE (Figure 18, Lines 50–53) differs from P:SEQUENTIAL-IF-THEN (Figure 19, Lines 40–45) in, as the names suggest, what programming construct(s) are used to achieve the dispatch. P:IF-THEN-ELSE takes advantage of the fact that there are only two possible values of the status variable, and so an IF-THEN-ELSE construct can be used. P:SEQUENTIAL-IF-THEN must make the other condition guard explicit.

G:OUTPUT plans: P:EACH (Figure 18, Lines 54–59) differs from P:ALL (Figure 19, Lines 49–51) in whether a **WRITELN** statement is used

Figure 19.   An alternate solution to the tax problem.

```
01    Program Tax(input,output);
02    Var Status : Char;
03        Income, Tax, Net : Real;
04
05    +------------[ P:NET-IN-MAIN ]---------------------------+
06    | Procedure Married(Income:Real; VAR Tax: Real)          |
07    | Begin                                                  |
08    | if Income < 10000                                      |
09    |     then  Tax := Income * 0.30                          |
10    |     else  Tax := 10000 * 0.30 + (Income - 10000) * 0.32;|
11    | End;                                                   |
12    |                                                  |-- G:CALC
13    | Procedure Single(Income:Real; VAR Tax: Real)           |
14    | Begin                                                  |
15    | if Income < 8000                                       |
16    |     then  Tax := Income * 0.30                          |
17    |     else  Tax := 8000 * 0.30 + (Income - 8000) * 0.32;  |
18    | End;                                                   |
19    +-------------------------------------------------------+
20
21
22     Begin
23    +---[ P:READ-INDIVIDUAL-DATA-ITEM-SENTINEL ]------+
24    | writeln('Enter marital status ("m" or "s").');  |
25    | writeln('To exit the program type "x".');       |
26    | readln(status);                           |-- G:LOOP
27    | while status <> 'x' do                          |
28    |    begin                                        |
29    +------------------------------------------------+
30    |    +--------[ P:INPUT-EACH/GUARD-RETRY-ALL ]-------------+
31    |    |writeln('Enter Income: (e.g., 17500.00).');         |
32    |    |readln(income);                                     |
33    |    |while ((status <> 's') and (status <> 'm')) or       |
34    |    |       (income < 0) do                              |
35    |    |    begin                                  |-- G:VDE
36    |    |    writeln('Try: status (s or m), income ( > 0).');|
37    |    |    readln(status,income);                          |
38    |    |    end                                            |
39    |    +---------------------------------------------------+
40    |    +-[ P:SEQUENTIAL-IF-THEN ]-----+
41    |    |if status = 'm'               |
42    |    |   then married(income,tax);  |-- G:DISPATCH
43    |    |if status = 's'               |
44    |    |   then single(income,tax);   |
45    |    +-----------------------------+
46    |    +-[ P:NET-IN-MAIN ]--+
47    |    |net := income - tax;|-- G:CALC          G:OUTPUT
48    |    +-------------------+                        |
49    |    +-[ P:ALL ]-------------------------------------------+
50    |    |writeln('For',status,income:0:2,' Result',tax:0:2,net:0:2);|
51    |    +---------------------------------------------------+
52    +----[ P:READ-INDIVIDUAL-DATA-ITEM-SENTINEL ]----------+
53    |    writeln('Enter marital status ("m" or "s").');  |
54    |    writeln('To exit the program type "x".');    |-- G:LOOP
55    |    readln(status);                             |
56    |    end;                                        |
57    +---------------------------------------------------+
58    End.
```

for each output variable separately, or whether all variables are output in a single **WRITELN** statement.

For a fuller discussion of the GAP tree for this problem, see Spohrer et al. (1985).

In the next section, we focus on two examples of merging that occur in solutions to the tax problem. The examples should be compared to the sample solution shown in Figure 18 of this section, which is unmerged. In particular, note that in the solution in Figure 18 G:VDE is completely achieved before G:DISPATCH. Similarly, G:DISPATCH is completely achieved before G:OUTPUT. The sequencing of the three plans to achieve three separate goals reflects unmerged goals, in contrast to the merged goals to be described.

Although the examples we present are particularly clear examples of merging, it is not always clear when two goals are actually merged. Not only is there a continuum based on degree of merging, from sequentially achieved goals (unmerged) to intricately entangled plans which achieve multiple goals (merged), but there is also another dimension to the problem of deciding when merging has occurred. In particular, we are really concerned with whether the merging process was being used by the programmer, and not just that a merged plan was realized in a particular piece of code. One can easily imagine that by the third or fourth time a merged plan is used, the process has been compiled into a standard plan; therefore, we would not expect as many or even the same sort of bugs as when it was created and used for the first time.

The examples of merging in the next section were also carefully chosen because of the bugs they exhibit. Although the example bugs appear to be clearly related to the merging process, at other times the bugs in merged code seem quite incidental. Seemingly incidental bugs, however, may have resulted from an additional cognitive load present during the merging process. In keeping with the exploratory nature of our current research into the merging process, we are interested in these seemingly incidental bugs as well as the more strongly related bugs. Using our GAP tree vocabulary, we now describe two types of bugs that occur when students have particular merged goals and plans in their programs.

6.2. Merging Can Lead to Goal Drop-Out

Description

Compare the manner in which G:LOOP is achieved in the two solutions shown in Figure 18 and Figure 19. In Figure 19, there is no separate sentinel variable used to control the loop. Instead, the status variable performs this function. About half of the novice programs analyzed used the merged plan P:READ-INDIVIDUAL-DATA-ITEM-SENTINEL to achieve G:LOOP, while simultaneously achieving a portion of G:VDE for the status variable.

Figure 20 shows a plan that merges the loop and the status valid-data-entry to an even greater extent. In the figure, we have used the names of goals in place of actual code to help focus attention on only the merged code. Also, when we need to refer to one of the subgoals, we precede the subgoal name with the names of goals above it in the GAP tree separated by slashes. Note that G:VDE/G:GUARD for the status variable has been integrated with G:LOOP/G:GUARD (Line 4). With these two guard goals integrated, the only trace of the valid-data-entry goal for the status variable inside the loop comes at the end of the loop body (Lines 9–10), where G:LOOP/G:REPEAT-INPUT is achieved.

Unfortunately, there is a problem with this merged code. Note that the body of the loop is only executed when the value of the status variable is one of the two valid values 's' or 'm.' What happens if the user makes a typo when trying to enter a status value? If this occurred, then not only would the loop be exited, but so would the program. The program is not robust enough to recover from status typos. This violates an implicit requirement: The students had been instructed in class that all programs should give the user a chance to correct any item typed incorrectly. The goal of including this retry feature (G:RETRY) can thus be considered an implicit requirement for this program, even though it was not explicitly mentioned in the assignment. Somehow in this merged code, G:RETRY for the status variable was "lost." We term this particular type of bug, which can occur in the code for merged goals, *goal drop-out.*

Interpretation

In attempting to explain this bug, we must first consider the following three scenerios:

1. *Unrelated:* The student would have made the bug under any circumstances. Even if the student had written an unmerged version of the program, he or she would have left out the retry; thus, merging was not the problem.
2. *Unintentional:* The student unintentionally made the bug as a side effect of attempting to achieve multiple goals with a single integrated plan. If the student had written an unmerged version of the program, he or she would not have made the bug; thus, merging was the problem.
3. *Intentional:* The student was aware of the bug, but decided it was more important to produce the merged code than restructure the solution to eliminate the problem. This assumes that the student was aware that he or she had not accomplished G:RETRY and knew it was a bug; however, he or she felt using merging somehow compensated for this problem (e.g., merged code is often more concise).

Of the three types of explanation, we are only interested in those of the second type in which novice programmers unintentionally make the bug as a nat-

Figure 20.   Merging the status guard and the loop guard.

```
01  ...
02  writeln('Enter marital status: ("m" = married, or "s" = single).')
03  readln(status);
04  while (status = 'm') or (status = 's') do
05      begin
06      G:VDE/G:INCOME
07      G:DISPATCH
08      G:OUTPUT
09      writeln('To continue enter marital status: "m" or "s".');
10      readln(status)
11      end;
12  ...
```

ural side effect of their inexperience with merging programming plans to achieve multiple goals in an integrated fashion. Two example explanations for the goal drop-out bug are described. The first example explains the problem in terms of a contextual memory retrieval effect; the second example explains the problem in terms of a more general processing strategy.

One plausible account of why G:RETRY is present in the unmerged case but lost in the merged case is based on the influence of varied context. In the unmerged case, as G:GUARD is being achieved within the context of G:VALID-DATA-ENTRY, the question "What do I do if the guard's conditions on the data are not met?" has the answer "Try to recover by achieving G:RETRY." However, the answer changes in the merged case as G:GUARD is being achieved within the context of G:LOOP. Now, the answer to the question "What do I do if the guard's conditions on the data are not met?" is "Exit the loop." In effect, the issue of error recovery is missed because of the inappropriate answer provided by the loop context.

A plausible alternative account is based on the manner in which many novice programmers achieve the goals in a program one after the other, without ever taking a global view of the program to see how the entire set of goals interacts. The novice's thinking, in other words, may be too local and too sequential. Merging is a departure from this one-goal-at-a-time strategy; it involves looking at two or more goals at once and finding a single plan to achieve them all. After implementing a merged plan, the novice may return to the one-goal-at-a-time processing strategy for the remaining goals. Bugs may result if merging the goals makes it impossible to achieve the remaining goals through separate, sequential plans.

In the program in Figure 20, one can imagine a novice first achieving G:INPUT of G:VALID-DATA-ENTRY in accordance with the one-goal-at-a-time strategy. However, when novices notice the similarity between G:VDE/G:GUARD and G:LOOP/G:GUARD, they decide to merge them, departing from their normal strategy. After the merge, novices resume the one-goal-at-a-time strategy for the goals that will be placed inside the loop, but in this case, the process of merging has resulted in resuming the one-goal-at-a-time strategy on the wrong goal. We return to the one-goal-at-a-time strategy in our discussion of the next merge-related bug.

6.3. Merging Can Lead to Goal Fragmentation

Description

In addition to the loop, the status guard was sometimes merged with the dispatch. About one quarter of the programs analyzed attempted to integrate G:DISPATCH and G:VDE/G:GUARD for the status variable. The code resulting from this merge is shown in Figure 21. There are several differences between this code and the unmerged code shown in Figure 18. First of all, note that the status guard no longer comes directly after the status input, but now is part of the dispatch. The dispatch now has explicit conditions for both values that status can take on ('s' and 'm'). In addition, the dispatch has an error message integrated into it in case the value of status is invalid. Note also that the code for achieving G:OUTPUT has been integrated into the dispatch. This was necessary in order to avoid the bug shown in Figure 22. Note that in Figure 22, when the value of status is invalid, not only will the error message be printed, but in addition, the output will still be done even though the procedures that calculate the tax formula have not been called. This will result in the output of invalid values of tax and net income.

In the unmerged case (see Figure 18), by the time G:OUTPUT is executed, G:CALC will always have been achieved because G:DISPATCH has only two options: It must call the married or single subroutine. However, in the merged case (see Figure 21), G:DISPATCH has a third option: It can signal an error condition, in which case no calculation is performed. If G:OUTPUT comes after G:DISPATCH (see Figure 22), the possibility exists that an output will be attempted when no calculation has been done. We refer to this problem, which can result from merging, as *goal fragmentation*. In these situations, G:OUTPUT has become disassociated from G:CALC and has taken on a "life of its own," ignoring constraints which should keep them sequenced within the same scope.

Interpretation

Like the goal drop-out case discussed earlier, the problem here seems to be that the novice programmer: (a) departs from the one-goal-at-a-time strategy long enough to implement a merged plan and (b) then returns to the one-goal-at-a-time-strategy without realizing that, as a result of the merge, the remaining goals can no longer be implemented one at a time. In particular, after merging G:GUARD for status with G:DISPATCH, one cannot resume the one-goal-at-a-time strategy with G:OUTPUT because the resulting code would permit output to be attempted without necessarily having performed a calculation first (i.e., when the value of status is bad).

Figure 21. Merging the status guard and the dispatch guard.

```
01 ...
02 G:LOOP/G:INIT
03 G:LOOP/G:GUARD
04    writeln('Enter marital status: ("m" = married, or "s" = single).')
05    readln(Status);
06    G:VDE/G:INCOME
07    if Status = 'm'
08      then begin
09           Married(Income,Tax,Net);
10           writeln('For input:',Status,Income:0:2);  <----- G:OUTPUT
11           writeln('Tax:',Tax:0:2,' Net:',Net:0:2);
12           end
13      else if Status = 's'
14           then begin
15                Single(Income,Tax,Net);
16                writeln('For input:',Status,Income:0:2);  <- G:OUTPUT
17                writeln('Tax:',Tax:0:2,' Net:',Net:0:2);
18                end
19           else writeln('BAD STATUS INPUT');
20    G:LOOP/G:REPEAT-INPUT
21 ...
```

Figure 22. Merging resulting in goal fragmentation bug.

```
01 ...
02 G:LOOP/G:INIT
03 G:LOOP/G:GUARD
04    writeln('Enter marital status: ("m" = married, or "s" = single).')
05    readln(Status);
06    G:VDE/G:INCOME
07    if Status = 'm' then Married(Income,Tax,Net)
08       else if Status = 's' then Single(Income,Tax,Net)
09            else writeln('BAD STATUS INPUT');
10    writeln('For input:',Status,Income:0:2);  <----- G:OUTPUT
11    writeln('Tax:',Tax:0:2,' Net:',Net:0:2);
12    G:LOOP/G:REPEAT-INPUT
13 ...
```

Another possible interpretation of this bug is that the student attempted a further optimization of the merged G:DISPATCH and G:VDE/G:STATUS. The student may have decided to optimize the merged plan further by merging G:OUTPUT/G:MARRIED and G:OUTPUT/G:SINGLE, which would involve factoring the outputs out of the dispatch and combining them into a single output after the dispatch. However, the precondition for this type of factor-out-and-merge-after optimization is that the same goal must be achieved last in each branch of the guard construct. This precondition is nearly satisfied, but the final branch outputs just an error message and not the results of the calculation. It is worth noting that this precondition would have been satisfied if not for the original G:DISPATCH, G:VDE/G:STATUS merge. Thus, this bug may be viewed as two negatively interacting mergings.

6.4. Bug Counts for Top-Level Goals

Description

Our discussion of merging in novice programs has been largely descriptive in nature. In this section, we begin a more quantitative analysis of the data. Specifically, we examine how frequently merging occurred for the tax problem, and how frequently it was successfully accomplished.

As described in Section 6.1, the tax problem has five top-level goals: G:CALC, G:LOOP, G:VDE, G:DISPATCH, and G:OUTPUT. Of the 57 programs analyzed, only 5 programs contained no merging at all. For these programs, each of the five goals was achieved with distinct plans, as in the example program in Figure 18. Of the 57 programs, 52 (91%) exhibited some merging of top-level goals (this is significant at $p < .001$ by sign test, and the 99% confidence band for the observed value of the proportion ranges between .7 and .975). On the average, three out of five top-level goals were merged per program. The most popular two goals to merge were G:DISPATCH and G:VDE, with 60% of all novice programs combining them in some way (usually merging G:VDE/G:STATUS/G:GUARD with G:DISPATCH). The second most commonly merged goals were G:LOOP and G:VDE, with 51% of all novice programs using some merged plan (i.e., P:READ-INDIVIDUAL-DATA-ITEM-SENTINEL) to achieve parts of these two goals in a single integrated manner. The bottom line is that using merged plans was a very attractive strategy for the novice programmers who attempted the tax problem.

The data in Figure 23 represent the analysis of the first syntactically correct version for the 57 student programs attempting the tax problem. In the figure, we show the number of times a goal was merged (or unmerged). For example, G:DISPATCH was merged with other goals 39 times, unmerged 15 times, and left out entirely just 3 times (out of a possible 57). Notice first that with one exception the number of times each goal was merged is greater than the number of times the goal was unmerged (i.e., G:LOOP was merged in 36 programs and was not merged in 7 programs). It is interesting that the one exception was G:CALC, which is the one part of the program that the students were explicitly instructed to place in subroutines. Second, notice that the students who wrote code with merged goals did so incorrectly more often than did those students who wrote code with unmerged goals (only 11% correct for merged compared to 45% correct for unmerged).

It is worth pointing out that one would expect the percentage of correct merged plans to be less than the percentage of correct unmerged plans, but the extent of the actual observed difference (11% vs. 45%) is larger than one would expect with a naive model of merging. For instance, assume the probability of correctly achieving unmerged goals is .45. The probability of two randomly selected goals being correct (assuming independence) is therefore about

Figure 23. Frequencies of merged and unmerged goals and how often they were correctly or incorrectly implemented based on an analysis of 57 novice programmers' first syntactically correct program for the tax problem.

GOAL	MERGED			UNMERGED		
	COUNT	#CORRECT	(%CORRECT)	COUNT	#CORRECT	(%CORRECT)
G:CALC	15	0	(0%)	41	15	(37%)
G:LOOP	36	1	(3%)	7	0	(0%)
G:VDE	51	3	(6%)	6	1	(17%)
G:DISPATCH	39	11	(28%)	15	14	(93%)
G:OUTPUT	32	4	(13%)	23	11	(48%)
TOTAL	173	19	(11%)	92	41	(45%)

.20 ($.45 \times .45 = .2025$). Thus, with this simple model, we would expect about 20% of the merged goals to be correct. However, we observe only 11% of the merged cases to be correct, which is about half as many correct as calculated with the simple model. Independent of the answer to the question of whether merged goals are buggier than unmerged goals, however, the main influence that the consideration of this question has had is to focus our attention on the difference between bugs occurring in merged code and those occurring in unmerged code. As the examples in the previous section attest, the fact that certain types of merging have characteristic bugs provides additional structure for hypothesizing the misconceptions and cognitive constraints on processing, which may have given rise to the bugs.

Interpretation

The analysis presented here supports the two conjectures made at the start of this section: Students tend to write code with merged goals (which in turn implies that they merge the programming plans that realize those goals), and those who use merged goals tend to write buggier code than those who do not use merged goals. A followup question to these results is: Why do novices merge goals? Consider the following suggestion: In the real world, the strategy of goal/plan merging is undoubtedly quite useful because, among other things, merging can lead to resource conservation. For example, we would think a person a bit odd who made a separate trip to the kitchen for each utensil while setting the dining room table. As recent data illustrate, novices use knowledge and processes from their nonprogramming experience in learning to program (Bonar & Soloway, 1983, 1985). Unfortunately, employing the strategy of goal/plan merging in programming requires considerable skill. We saw in the previous examples that merging code correctly requires a significant degree of competency. Moreover, even in nonprogramming, real-world situations, one must carry out goal/plan merging with some degree of care. Thus, the interpretation that novices are simply importing a nonprogramming processing strategy to programming provides a reasonable basis for understanding the degree to which novices do seem to generate code with merged goals and plans.

7. CONCLUDING REMARKS

At first glance, the huge amount of variation that exists in novice programs may appear chaotic and random. However, we have argued that by using a GAP tree representation, we can provide considerable structure to these data. We can then more effectively employ the data as a window into the misconceptions that underlie the bugs (Brown & Burton, 1978). A bug categorization scheme based on a problem-dependent GAP tree facilitates several types of analysis that could not be performed with existing problem-independent bug categorization schemes. The advantages of the problem-dependent scheme stem from the fact that GAP trees make explicit the goal and plan knowledge for a problem at many different levels of detail.

Unfortunately, developing GAP trees is still an art. Further research is required before we can automatically construct GAP trees and automate the analyses that the GAP tree enables. Another step in this research effort is to develop a taxonomy of the interpretations (plausible accounts) that describes why the bugs may have arisen. A taxonomy of this type would extend our descriptive theory and move us closer to our long-term research goal: a process theory of novice programming.

Acknowledgments.   We would like to thank the Summer Bug Busters, whose tireless efforts analyzing the novice programs were instrumental in developing the ideas expressed here: Michael Lipman, Warren Sack, and Scott Freiman. We are also indebted to Lewis Johnson, whose work pointed the way for much of the current bug categorization scheme. Other members of the Cognition and Programming Project have provided helpful discussion and comments: Beth Adelson, Stan Letovsky, and David Littman. Thanks to Saj-nicole Joni and Colleen Seifert for comments on drafts of this paper. We would also like to thank the reviewers of this paper for valuable suggestions, including alternative explanations for one of the bugs.

Support.   This work was sponsored in part by the National Science Foundation, under NSF Grant DCR-8302382 and NSF Grant DPE-8470014.

REFERENCES

Adelson, B. (1981). Problem solving and the development of abstract categories in programming languages. *Memory & Cognition, 9,* 422–433.

Bartlett, F. C. (1932). *Remembering.* Cambridge, England: Cambridge University Press.

Bonar, J., & Soloway, E. (1983). *Uncovering principles of novice programming.* Proceedings of SIGPLAN-SIGACT Tenth Annual Symposium on Principles of Programming Languages, Austin, TX.

Bonar, J., & Soloway, E. (1985). Preprogramming knowledge: A major source of misconceptions in novice programmers. *Human-Computer Interaction, 1,* 133–161.

Bower, G. H., Black, J. B., & Turner, T. (1979). Scripts in memory for text. *Cognitive Psychology, 11,* 177–220.

Brown, J. S., & Burton, R. R. (1978). Diagnostic models for procedural bugs in basic mathematical skills. *Cognitive Science, 2,* 155–192.

Brown, J. S., & VanLehn, K. (1980). Repair theory: A generative theory of bugs in procedural skills. *Cognitive Science, 4,* 379–426.

Card, S. K., Moran, T. P., & Newell, A. (1983). *The psychology of human-computer interactions.* Hillsdale, NJ: Lawrence Erlbaum Associates, Inc.

Gould, J. D. (1975). Some psychological evidence on how people debug computer programs. *International Journal of Man-Machine Studies, 7,* 151–182.

Graesser, A. C. (1981). *Prose comprehension beyond the word.* New York: Springer-Verlag.

Johnson, L., & Soloway, E. (1983). *PROUST: Knowledge-based program understanding* (Tech. Rep. No. 285). New Haven, CT: Yale University, Department of Computer Science.

Johnson, L., Soloway, E., Cutler, B., & Draper, S. (1983, October). *BUG CATALOGUE: I* (Tech. Rep. No. 286). New Haven, CT: Yale University, Department of Computer Science.

Ostrand, T., & Weyuker, E. (1982). *Collecting and categorizing software error data in an industrial environment* (Tech. Rep. No. 47). New York University, Department of Computer Science.

Schank, R. C., & Abelson, R. (1977). *Scripts, plans, goals and understanding.* Hillsdale, NJ: Lawrence Erlbaum Associates, Inc.

Shneiderman, B. (1976). Exploratory experiments in programmer behavior. *International Journal of Computer and Information Sciences, 5,* 123–145.

Sleeman, D., Putnam, R. T., Baxter, J. A., & Kuspa, L. K. (1985). *Pascal and high-school students: A study of misconception.* Unpublishd manuscript, Stanford University, School of Education, Stanford, CA.

Soloway, E., & Ehrlich, K. (1984). Empirical studies of programming knowledge. *IEEE Transactions on Software Engineering, 5,* 595–609.

Soloway, E., Ehrlich, K., Bonar, J., & Greenspan, J. (1982). What do novices know about programming? In B. Shneiderman & A. Badre (Eds.), *Directions in human-computer interaction* (pp. 87–122). Norwood, NJ: Ablex.

Spohrer, J., Pope, E., Lipman, M., Sack, W., Freiman, S., Littman, D., Johnson, L., & Soloway, E. (1985). *BUG CATALOGUE: II, III, IV* (Tech. Rep. No. 386). New Haven, CT: Yale University, Department of Computer Science.

19
NOVICE MISTAKES:
ARE THE FOLK WISDOMS CORRECT?

JAMES C. SPOHRER
ELLIOT SOLOWAY
University of Michigan

MOTIVATION AND GOALS

Researchers have recently been trying to gain an understanding of the kinds of mistakes novice programmers are likely to make [2, 4, 7, 11, 15, 19]. One of the main motivations for these efforts is to improve the quality of programming education through a better understanding of what goes wrong. In this article we focus on two common perceptions — what we will call folk wisdoms — about bugs:

- Just a few types of bugs can account for a majority of the mistakes in students' programs.
- Most bugs can be attributed to student misconceptions about language constructs.

Our empirical study leads us to argue that (1) yes, a few bug types account for a large percentage of program bugs, and (2) no, misconceptions about language constructs do not seem to be as widespread or as troublesome as is generally believed. Rather, many bugs arise as a result of *plan composition problems* — difficulties in putting the "pieces" of a program together (see sidebar) — and not as result of *construct-based problems,* which are misconceptions about language constructs. We also discuss the educational implications of our findings.

A reasonable pedagogical philosophy is *The more we know about what students know, the better we can teach them.* Yet in the past, what educators knew about novice programmers was largely "folklore": anecdotal evidence from their own and their colleagues' experiences. Our efforts have been directed toward obtaining more quantifiable data that will allow us to evaluate these perceptions empirically. Although our prescriptions for educators are as yet untested, we nevertheless feel that by replacing folklore with empirical findings we have a better chance than ever before of positively affecting the quality of programming education.

DATA COLLECTION

The descriptions of bugs that we report are based on actual student-generated programs. We augmented the operating system of the VAX 750 the students were using and, with their permission, obtained a copy of each syntactically correct program they submitted for compilation. We call such data *on-line protocols.* The data were collected during the spring 1984 semester at Yale University in an introductory Pascal programming course specifically designed for nonscience, humanities-oriented students. During this course, students were assigned 10 programming problems. Three problems were selected for further study:

- *the electric bill problem,* requiring the first use of nested IF-THEN-ELSE constructs
- *the reformatting problem,* requiring the first use of a loop;
- *the tax problem,* requiring the first use of procedures.

Because we were primarily interested in nonsyntactic errors, we selected a total of 158 "syntactically correct" programs for detailed analysis. The first syntactically correct program that a subject generated was chosen because the first version typically contains more bugts than later, partially debugged versions. Spohrer et al. [20] presents a complete description of the data.

ANALYSIS OF THE DATA

Table I summarizes some of the results of our analysis of the first syntactically correct programs for these three problems. An important distinction to be aware of in counting bugs is the type-token distinction. A *but token* is an instance of a bug in some program, and a *bug type* is a name for a group of identical bug tokens. There were about three example bug tokens, on average, for each bug type.

Identifying the bugs in novice programs can be quite tricky. Because there are many different ways to solve the same problem, there is no one correct program to which all the novice programs can be compared. To overcome this difficulty, we identified bugs by means of a *goal/plan analysis* of the programs (see box at end of chapter) . Goals are what must be accomplished to solve a problem, and plans correspond to stereotypical sections of code that can be used to achieve the goals. Bugs can then be identified as

TABLE I. Statistical Overview of the Results Obtained
for the Three Programming Problems

Type of statistic	Problem		
	Electric bill	Reformatting	Tax
Number of subjects analyzed	55	46	57
Assignment number (in sequence)	2	3	8
Lines of Pascal per program (average)	28	73	69
Total of observed bugs (tokens)	85	140	59
Number of unique bugs (types)	28	46	27

The assignment number (row 2) indicates the point at which the problems occurred in the curriculum. A token is an instance of a bug; identical tokens constitute a bug type.

differences between the correct plans and the buggy implementations actually used by the novices [7, 19]. In essence, a library of goals and plans for a problem becomes the yardstick against which novice programs are measured. The bug counts presents in the next sections are based on this type of goal/plan analysis of novice programs.

All Bugs Are Not Created Equal

Anyone who has taught programming and seen a large number of buggy programs has probably made an observation along th elines of what we call fold wisdom #1: *All bugs are not created equal. Some bugs occur over and over again in novices' programs, while others occur only rarely.* In order to test this observation, we kept track of the frequency of each bug in our analysis. In an even distribution, 10 percent of the bug types would accout for 10 percent of the bug tokens. However, as Table 19.2 shows, just 10 percent of the bug types account for between 32 percent and 46 percent of the bug tokens. Thus, a few high-frequency bug types account for the bulk of observed tokens. On average for the three problems, one-fifth (20 percent) of the bug types account for over half (55 percent) of the bug tokens. These data support, and quantify, the intuition that a few bug types account for a lot of the mistakes made by students learning a program.

Beyond Misconceptions about Constructs

Typically, the organization of introductory programming courses is centered about the successive presentation of various language constructs (e.g., first teach about assignment, then about conditionals, etc.). This construct-

TABLE II. Percents of Tokens Accounted
for by Specific Percents of Types

Percent of types	Percent of tokens accounted for (by problem)		
	Electric bill	Reformatting	Tax
10	44	46	32
20	55	64	46
25	62	69	56
50	80	84	77

centered focus is reinforced by the structure of most introductory program-ming textbooks. Although programming courses and textbooks do typically treat more than just the constructs, we have distilled a position from these observations that we term the *construct-based* view of programming, in contrast to our *goal/plan-based* view. From the construct-based view, we derive our second folk wisdom: *Most bugs arise because novices do not fully understand the semantics of particular programming language con-structs.* We found that some misconceptions about constructs do exist among novice programmers. For instance, Bayman and Mayer [3] show that novices possess a wide range of misconceptions about individual statements or constructs from the programming language they had learned. However, their study was designed to test novices' ability to interpret single statements after taking a three-session self-instruction course. Our data, which were collected in a more natural setting during a semester-long introductory programming course, provide a more complete picture of the types of bugs novices make in actually writing programs.

In order to empirically evaluate the validity of folk wisdom #2, we tried to identify the underlying source of each bug: what the student was (or was not) thinking about at the time. We call explanations of the origins of bugs *plausible accounts*. Developing and evaluating plausible accounts are not easy to do. We have drawn on the work of others [11, 15] who interviewed students, as well as our own studies [4, 7] in developing and evaluating the plausible accounts presented here. Thus, although the plausible accounts presented must be subjected to further scientific inquiry, they were by no means created from whole cloth; they have considerable grounding in psychological reality.

We will first examine plausible accounts for three bugs in detail, and then complete the evaluation of folk wisdom #2 through an analysis of 101 bugs. The initial bugs are highlighted for two reasons:

- they are high-frequency bugs made by over 25 percent of the novices;

- they show a range of plausible accounts for bugs, from a set that is clearly *not* construct based, to a set that clearly *is* construct based.

In addition, the first two bugs illustrate some nonconstruct-based problems of the type we call *plan composition problems*. These bugs illustrate that novices have difficulties putting groups of plans or parts of plans together correctly.

Bugs That Are Clearly Not *Construct Based.*   In Figure 1 (p. 628) we present a high-frequency nonconstruct-based bug from the tax problem data. The bug illustrates what can go wrong when a group of plans has to be put together. In order to better understand this plan composition bug, we briefly describe the relevant plans and plan composition methods used by the novices.

To solve the tax problem, novices must combine plans that achieve the following three goals: G:GUARD, G:DISPATCH, and G:OUTPUT (see the sidebar on page 625 for an explanation of notation and terminology). G:GUARD is the valid data guard goal for the marital status variable. Marital status can only take on two values: 's' for single or 'm' for married. The purpose of the guard is to alert the user if the input is neither of these two valid values. The plan for the second goal, G:DISPATCH, calls the appropriate tax computation procedure based on the marital status. The third goal, G:OUTPUT, must be achieved so that the results of the tax calculation can be printed out.

The two basic composition methods shown in Figure 1 are *abutment* and *merging*. When plans are abutted, they occur in sequence — one after the other. In this case, the order of the goals is first G:GUARD (lines 2–6), followed by G:DISPATCH (lines 9–11), and finally G:OUTPUT (lines 14–16). Given this order, the value of marital status will always be valid before the dispatch and output plans are executed. The merged case is more complex: The guard and the dispatch have been worked together so they share lines of code (see lines 2, 11, and 20), and the output code appears twice — interleaved after the procedure calls (lines 6–8 and 15–17).

A typical guard and dispatch merging bug is shown in the final code fragment in Figure 1. The basic problem is that the output (lines 9–11) is executed even if the marital status datum is bad and the tax has not been calculated. Although two of the possible execution paths (the ones through single and married procedure calls) cause the tax to be computed, the third and final execution path (printing an error message) does not cause the tax to be computed. The program will behave correctly as long as the status data are valid, but in the exceptional case when the data are invalid the program will output incorrect results. To remedy this problem, the output plan must be duplicated and interleaved so that the output appears directly after the procedure calls.

```
01 +---------------------------------------------------------------+
02 |WHILE ((Marital_Status <> 's') AND (Marital_Status <> 'm'))|
03 |   DO   BEGIN                                                  |
04 |          WRITELN('Type "m" or "s"');                          |-- G:GUARD
05 |          READLN(Marital_Status);                              |
06 |          END;                                                 |
07 +---------------------------------------------------------------+
08 +----------------------------+
09 |IF (Marital_Status = 'm')   |
10 |   THEN Married(Income,Tax) |-- G:DISPATCH
11 |   ELSE Single(Income,Tax); |
12 +----------------------------+
13 +--------------------------------+
14 |WRITELN('Status =', Marital_Status);|
15 |WRITELN('Income =', Income:0:2);    |-- G:OUTPUT
16 |WRITELN('Tax    =', Tax:0:2);       |
17 +--------------------------------+
```

(a) **Correct Abutment** Abutment is a plan composition method that allows different goals to be addressed sequentially.

```
01 +-------------------------------------------------------------------+
02 |IF (Marital_Status = 'm')                                          |-- G:GUARD &
03 |   THEN BEGIN                                                       |   G:DISPATCH
04 |        Married(Income,Tax);                                        |
05 |        +------------------------------------+                      |
06 |        |WRITELN('Status =', Marital_Status);|                      |
07 |        |WRITELN('Income =', Income:0:2);    |-- G:OUTPUT           |
08 |        |WRITELN('Tax    =', Tax:0:2);       |                      |
09 |        +------------------------------------+                      |
10 |        END                                                         |
11 |   ELSE IF (Marital_Status = 's')                                   |
12 |           THEN BEGIN                                               |
13 |                Single(Income,Tax);                                 |
14 |                +------------------------------------+              |
15 |                |WRITELN('Status =', Marital_Status);|              |
16 |                |WRITELN('Income =', Income:0:2);    |-- G:OUTPUT   |
17 |                |WRITELN('Tax    =', Tax:0:2);       |              |
18 |                +------------------------------------+              |
19 |                END                                                 |
20 |           ELSE WRITELN(Bad Input: Try Again.');                    |
21 +-------------------------------------------------------------------+
```

(b) **Correct Merging** Merging is a plan composition method that achieves different goals using a single plan.

```
01 +------------------------------------------------+
02 |IF (Marital_Status = 'm')                       |-- G:GUARD &
03 |   THEN Married(Income,Tax)                      |   G:DISPATCH
04 |   ELSE IF (Marital_Status = 's')               |
05 |           THEN Single(Income,Tax)              |
06 |           ELSE WRITELN(Bad Input: Try Again'); |
07 +------------------------------------------------+
08 +----------------------------------+
09 |WRITELN('Status =', Marital_Status);|
10 |WRITELN('Income =', Income:0:2);    |-- G:OUTPUT
11 |WRITELN('Tax    =', Tax:0:2);       |
12 +----------------------------------+
```

(c) **Incorrect Merging** In this buggy code segment, G:OUTPUT is misplaced; as a result, the output is executed even when the marital status datum is bad.

FIGURE 1   Putting Together Plans that Achieve G:GUARD, G:DISPATCH, and G:OUTPUT

406

It seems unlikely that this bug resulted from a misconception about a language construct. For instance, the bug did not arise because novices misunderstood the semantics of the IF-THEN-ELSE construct — the novices were using the construct in a quite sophisticated manner to achieve two goals (guard and dispatch) in an integrated fashion. Instead, there are a variety of reasons that can explain why novices may not have considered the potential negative interaction of abutting the output plan after merging the guard and dispatch. The following plausible accounts suggest possible misconceptions that novices may have had:

- *Summarization problem.* Some novices may have merged the guard and the dispatch plans, and then, for ease in future reasoning, summarized the resulting plan in terms of its main goal. Most novices would view the dispatch for the calculation as the main goal and the guard for the error message as a secondary goal that could be ignored.
- *Optimization problem.* Some novices may have originally considered duplicating the output plan for each of the two branches of the dispatch plan. However, upon noticing that only one output would be necessary if the output came after the dispatch (an optimization), they may have incorrectly concluded that the optimization would work on the merged guard and dispatch plan as well.
- *Previous-experience problem.* In earlier problems, the output plan had often been abutted after the calculation plan. In looking for the calculation plan in this case, novices may have viewed the merged guard and dispatch plan as achieving the calculation, and therefore abutted the output plan to the end.

These plausible accounts are not mutually exclusive. They should be viewed as contributing factors that may or may not have been present. However, the main point is that this bug cannot be blamed on misconceptions about a construct's semantics.

Bugs that May Possibly Be Construct Based.   While satisfactory non-construct-based plausible accounts exist for the bug described in this section, whenever there was a shadow of doubt (i.e., a construct-based plausible account that might apply in some cases), we classified the bug in the "maybe" category.

Figure 2 shows an OR-for-AND bug that occurred in novices' solutions to the reformatting problem. The Boolean connective used in the guard (lines 4 and 5) should be AND rather than OR. The code in Figure 2 was intended to achieve the G:VALID-DATA-ENTRY goal for the variable Problem Type, which can take on only one of three legal values: a, b, c. As the code

```
G:VDE/G:TYPE/G:GUARD:: MALFORMED G:COND (OR For AND)
01    WRITELN('Enter problem type');
02    READLN(Problem_Type);
03    +--------------------------------+
04    | IF ((Problem_Type) <> 'a') OR  |
05    |      (Problem_Type) <> 'b') OR  |
06    |      (Problem_Type) <> 'c'))    |
07    +--------------------------------+
08       THEN BEGIN
09             WRITELN('Type "a", "b", or "c"');
10             READLN(Problem_Type);
11             END;
```

FIGURE 2   An OR-for-AND Bug

is currently written, the Boolean condition (lines 4–6) will always be true, so the retry (lines 9–10) will always be performed.

Although the OR-for-AND bug seems to indicate that novices did not understand the semantics of OR, one piece of evidence seems to contradict this conclusion. Most novices used the OR Boolean connective correctly in another part of the program that detected whether a number was outside a particular range (i.e., P:INTERVAL-EXCLUSION plan: (X < SMALL-EST) OR (X > LARGEST)). The following plausible accounts suggest some possible misconceptions:

- *Specialization problem.* Some novices may possess an abstract guard plan of the form: If BadThing 1 OR BadThing2 OR BadThing3 . . . THEN retry. Novices correctly instantiated this plan for ordinal comparisons to get the P:INTERVAL-EXCLUSION plan. However, they incorrectly instantiated this plan for set exclusion comparisons because they thought Problem Type < > 'a' was a *whole* BadThing, when in fact it is only *part* of a BadThing. Problem Type = 'd' would be a whole BadThing. Note that Problem Type = 'a' is a whole GoodThing, so maybe the novices incorrectly reasoned that the negation of a whole GoodThing is a whole BadThing.

- *Natural-language problem.* Some novices may generate conditionals by first stating them in English and then using whatever Boolean connective worked for English. For example, a novice might think, "The retry should be done when Problem Type is not a, b, or c." Because OR is appropriate in this English statement of the task, the novice may have reasoned it would be appropriate in the Pascal program. Unfortunately, the NOT changes the OR to an AND in accordance with DeMorgan's Rule (i.e., (NOT (A OR B)) = (NOT A) AND (NOT B)).

- *Previous-experience problem.* Some novices may always use the connective OR in guard plans. These novices may possess an abstract guard plan of the form: IF Term1 OR Term2 OR Term3 . . . THEN retry. If some novices had only seen guard plans that used OR, then this might be the case. This possibility amounts to a default connective for putting the pieces (subgoals for each term) of a conditional together.

This example illustrates why the folk wisdom about novices' problems with constructs is so popular: Because people see bugs in terms of what it takes to fix them, they may assume that novices do not understand the semantics of the constructs required in repairs. For example, upon seeing the OR-for-AND bug, the tendency is to focus on the repair (replacing OR with AND), and therefore to assume that the novice needs to have the distinction between these two Boolean connectives clarified. Our approach to bug analysis stresses the importance of the goal and plan structure of the program as the starting point for understanding novices' misconceptions. When the focus shifts from repairs to how plans are formed and used, mistakes that at first appear to be definitely construct based may begin to suggest other explanations. In this case, misconceptions about the applicability of general plans and how to instantiate them may be at work, rather than any misunderstanding of the semantics of Boolean connectives. Nevertheless, there is a shadow of doubt, so we leave open the possibility that such bugs may be construct based.

Bugs that Are Definitely Construct Based. In the case of the high-frequency bug shown in Figure 3, novices apparently failed to understand that whitespace in the input data is a character that can be read, not just a separator that is automatically ignored. One could convincingly argue that this bug is in fact caused by a misunderstanding of how the READLN statement works in the context of characters. Possibly, some novices think that READLN ignores all whitespace when it is parsing an input line and assigning values to a sequence of variables because that is how READLN works on a sequence of numeric inputs. For this reason, we have classified this bug as definitely resulting from a misunderstanding of the semantics of the READLN language construct.

Results for All Bugs. Table III presents a breakdown of the 101 bugs into our three categories. The table shows that more than half (52 percent) of all bugs analyzed had plausible accounts that were definitely not construct based. Less than 10 percent of the bugs had plausible accounts

```
G:VDE[P:I-A/G-A/R-A]/G:TYPE&G:ACCURACY :: MALFORMED INPUT
01  WRITELN('Enter Id, Type, Start (h m s), End (h m s),Accuracy');
02  +--------------------------------------------------+
03  |READLN(Id,                                        |
04  |         Problem_Type,                            |
05  |         Start_Hour, Start_Minute, Start_Second,  |
06  |         End_Hour, End_Minute, End_Second,        |
07  |         Accuracy);                               |
08  +--------------------------------------------------+
```

(a)

```
09  WRITELN('Enter Id, Type, Start (h m s), End (h m s),Accuracy');
10  +--------------------------------------------------+
11  |READLN(Id,                                        |
12  |         Whitespace1, Problem_Type,               |
13  |         Start_Hour, Start_Minute, Start_Second,  |
14  |         End_Hour, End_Minute, End_Second,        |
15  |         Whitespace2, Accuracy);                  |
16  +--------------------------------------------------+
```

(b)

In code segment (a), a novice has used a space as a separator instead of as a character in line x. The error is corrected in code segment (b).

FIGURE 3   A Common Construct-Based Bug

TABLE III.   A Breakdown of the Number and Percentage of Different Kinds of Bugs according to Whether or Not They Can Be Attributed to a Construct Misunderstanding

Problem	No	Maybe	Yes
Electric bill ($N = 28$)	19 (68%)	9 (32%)	0 (0%)
Reformatting ($N = 46$)	20 (43%)	21 (46%)	5 (11%)
Tax ($N = 27$)	13 (48%)	10 (37%)	4 (15%)
Overall ($N = 101$)	52 (52%)	40 (39%)	9 (9%)

that were definitely construct based. So in the clear-cut cases, we see that most bugs are not construct based (significant at $p < 0.001$ by sign test). Even making the most conservative assumption possible (i.e., that all MAYBE are YES), less than half (48 percent) of the bugs have construct-based plausible accounts (NO and combined MAYBE-YES are not significantly different; $X^2 = 0.089$, $p > 0.20$). From this analysis of all the bugs in the three programming problems, we conclude that there is no empirical support for folk wisdom #2.

Overview of Underlying Problems.   We are still very much in the process of refining and developing our taxonomy of problems. Although our categories are not mutually exclusive or exhaustive, we felt it would be useful for educators to have at least the beginnings of such a taxonomy. See [18] for example bugs and plausible accounts illustrating all of these problems.

1. *Construct-based problems.* These are problems that make it difficult for novices to learn the correct semantics of language constructs.
   a. *Natural-language problem.* Many programming-language constructs are named after related natural-language words, and some novices become confused about the semantics of the constructs (see [4]).
   b. *Human interpreter problem.* Novices know how they intend a construct to be interpreted, and so they tend to assume that the computer will be able to arrive at a similar interpretation (see [15]).
   c. *Inconsistency problem.* Because novices understand how a construct works in one situation, they may assume that the construct will work in the same manner in another, slightly different situation (e.g., the READLN bug above).
2. *Plan composition problems.* These are problems that make it difficult for novices to put plans together correctly.
   a. *Summarization problem.* Novices may summarize complex combinations of plans in terms of some primary function, overlooking the implications of secondary functions on later plan compositions.
   b. *Optimization problem.* Novices may be so eager to optimize their plans that they do not adequately check if the optimization can really be carried out.
   c. *Previous-experience problem.* Novices constantly develop, recycle, and tailor plans on the basis of previous experience. Often, inappropriate aspects of previously used plans intrude on or *pollute* a related plan that is being used in a new situation (this problem is also known as the *plan pollution problem*).
   d. *Specialization problem.* Novices develop abstract plans that must be customized for a particular new situation. Sometimes, a particular abstract plan is inappropriate or not instantiated correctly.
   e. *natural-language problem.* Novices may possess natural-language plans or construct new plans based on a natural-language statement of a task. Mapping from natural language to a programming language tends to produce bugs.

f. *Interpretation problem.* Novices rely in part on their existing knowledge of goals and plans in interpreting assignments. Implicit specifications are left out or filled in only when plans for achieving them are easy to retrieve.

g. *Boundary problem.* Novices have difficulties deciding on appropriate boundary points in specializing a plan.

h. *Unexpected cases problem.* Novices occasionally write programs that work correctly for certain common cases, but not for all cases (e.g., uncommon, unlikely, or boundary cases).

i. *Cognitive load problem.* Novices may not detect losses of information from working memory [2]. Small but important parts of plans may be dropped out, or plan interactions may be overlooked.

Future research is aimed at verifying the plausible accounts we have hypothesized, finding alternative plausible accounts, and developing a student model of program generation.

CONCLUDING REMARKS

As we observed in the introduction, a not unreasonable assumption is that instruction can be improved when educators gain a better understanding of what students do and do not know. From our analysis we conclude that computer science instructors should strive to familiarize themselves with specific high-frequency bugs, and to learn as much as possible about the origins of all bugs. Both high- and low-frequency bugs seem likely to occur when students are unable to coordinate and integrate the goals and plans that underlie program code. Although additional studies must be carried out to test the stability of our results, our data nonetheless begin to pinpoint specific areas in which students have difficulty learning to program.

Given that educators are alerted to the bugs and their sources, what pedagogical strategy might be appropriate for dealing with the problems? We suggest the following:

1. Educators may be able to improve their students' performance by alerting them to the existence of specific high-frequency bugs, and by addressing the misconceptions underlying those bugs.

2. Educators may be able to improve their students' performance by teaching them strategies for putting the pieces of program code together, and by helping them learn the syntactic and semantic constructs of the language.

From our experience with introductory textbooks on programming, we conclude that students are not given sufficient instruction in how to "put the pieces together." Focusing explicitly on specific strategies for carrying out the coordination and integration of the goals and plans that underlie program code may help to reverse this trend. For example, students should be made aware of such concepts as goals and plans, and such composition strategies as abutment and merging [16]. We are suggesting that students be given a whole new explicit vocabulary for learning how to construct programs. From our empirical studies with expert programmers [17, 1], we have learned that experts have and use such concepts, although only on an implicit level. The claim that experts have and use all sorts of "tacit" knowledge implicitly [6] is not a new one, nor is it limited to programming: Researchers in fields such as physics [8] and mathematics [10] have observed this phenomenon. Students typically must acquire this tacit knowledge by induction from their teachers and their textbooks. A prima facie not unreasonable suggestion is that students should be taught these concepts explicitly [12]. Although this claim awaits empirical evaluation, at least we now have some concrete ideas of *what* needs to be taught — the next step is deciding *how* to teach it.

ACKNOWLEDGMENTS

This work was sponsored in part by the National Science Foundation, under NSF Grant DPE-8470014, and by the Army Research Institute, under contract MD903-85-K-0188.

This chapter has been reprinted by permission of the Association for Computing Machinery.

GOAL/PLAN ANALYSIS OF BUGGY PROGRAMS

What other perspectives are there for analyzing a program, other than a construct-based approach that breaks a program down into specific syntactic constructs of the programming language? In contrast to the construct-based, surface structure approach to program analysis, we have been developing a descriptive theory of buggy novice programs that is based on the cognitively plausible, deep structure knowledge that programmers have: goals and plans. A number of empirical studies have been carried out indicating that programmers perceive groups of code that work together (plans) for achieving particular desired results (goals) [9, 14, 17]. For example, subjects would not perceive the following two lines of code merely as two assignment statements (surface structure), but would see a counterplan and a running total plan (deep structure) indicative of a loop and initializations as well.

```
COUNT  := COUNT + 1;
TOTAL  := TOTAL + RAIN;
```

surface
```
assignment statement
assignment statement
```

deep
```
counter update
running total update
```

Being able to reason about goals and plans instead of just about individual language constructs is a powerful advantage during program understanding and generation. One part of a program can provide expectations that constrain the interpretation of other parts of the program. These same knowledge structures permit whole sections of code to be accessed and reasoned about at once. An ability to decompose problems, behaviors, or designed artifacts in terms of deep-structure knowledge (such as goals and plans), rather than just in terms of a surface-structure analysis, is a standard approach in cognitive psychology and artificial-intelligence research (e.g. [5, 13]).

Two important points about goals and plans are

1. a goal decomposes into subgoals, and plans organize the subgoals of a goal;
2. there are usually many different plans for achieving the same goal.

For example, consider the goal G:VALID-DATA-ENTRY, or G-VDE for short (the prefix "G:" is used to identify goals; the prefix "P:" to identify plans). This goal corresponds to getting valid input data into a program. Below are two different plans for achieving this goal for two input variables: **Marital Status**, which can only take on the two values 's' for single or 'm' for married, and Income, which must be a nonnegative number.

```
P:INPUT-GUARD-RETRY-EACH
01 READLN(Status);                              <-- G:INPUT
02 WHILE ((Status <> 's') AND (Status <> 'm'))  <-- G:GUARD
03    DO READLN(Status);                         <-- G:RETRY
04 READLN(Income);                              <-- G:INPUT
05 WHILE (Income < 0)                            <-- G:GUARD
06    DO READLN(Income);                         <-- G:RETRY


P:INPUT-ALL/GUARD-ALL/RETRY-ALL
01 READLN(Status, Income);                       <-- G:INPUT
02 WHILE (((Status <> 's') AND (Status <> 'm'))  <-- G:GUARD
03         OR (Income < 0))
04    DO READLN(Status, Income);                  <-- G:RETRY
```

G:VDE decomposes into three subgoals: G:INPUT, G:GUARD, and G:RETRY. The P:INPUT-GUARD-RETRY-EACH plan achieves all three subgoals for Status before achieving the subgoals for Income. The P:INPUT-ALL/GUARD-ALL/RETRY-ALL plan achieves the three subgoals for both of the input variables in a more integated fashion. All the goals and plans used by novices to solve a programming problem can be summarized in a Goal And Plan tree, or GAP tree, for the problem [19]. A small portion of a GAP tree for G:VDE is

```
                                              |-- G:INPUT ...
                                              |
                  |-- P:INPUT-GUARD-RETRY-EACH --------|-- G:GUARD ...
                  |                           |
                  |                           |-- G:RETRY ...
    G:VDE --|                                 |
                  |                           |-- G:INPUT ...
                  |                           |
                  |-- P:INPUT-ALL/GUARD-ALL/RETRY-ALL --|-- G:GUARD ...
                                              |
                                              |-- G:RETRY ...
```

To illustrate our bug analysis technique, consider the following piece of buggy code:

```
01 READLN(Status, Income);                <-- G:INPUT
02 WHILE (((Status <> 's') AND (Status <> 'm'))  <-- G:GUARD
03          AND (Income < 0))
04    DO READLN(Status, Income);           <-- G:RETRY
```

First we select the plan that best matches the code: in this case, P:INPUT-ALL/GUARD-ALL/RETRY-ALL. Note that the alternative plan for G:VDE, P:INPUT-GUARD-RETRY-EACH, does not match the code as well. Next we note plan differences between the observed plan and the correct plan; in this case, the AND in line 3 should be an OR. Once a program has been analyzed in terms of its goal and plan structure, we can identify bugs as deviations from the correct plan and categorize them in terms of the goal and plan context in which the bug arose [20], as shown below:

```
G:VDE[P:INPUT-ALL/GUARD-ALL/RETRY-ALL]  ::
MALFORMED G:GUARD (AND for OR)
```

This bug name indicates that P:INPUT-ALL/GUARD-ALL/RETRY-ALL was used to achieve G:VDE and that the G:GUARD subgoal was malformed because AND was used instead of OR. In short, a goal/plan analysis can be used to identify and categorize bugs based on the cognitively plausible, deep-structure knowledge underlying programming.

REFERENCES

1. Adelson, B., and Soloway, E. The role of domain experience in software design. *IEEE Trans. Softw. Eng. 11,* 11 (1985), 1351–1360.
2. Anderson, J.R., and Jeffries, R. Novice LISP errors: Undetected losses of information from working memory. *Hum.-Comput. Interaction 1,* 2 (1985), 107–131.
3. Bayman, P., and Mayer, R.E. A diagnosis of beginning programmers' misconceptions of Basic programming statements. *Commun. ACM 26,* 9 (Sept. 1983), 677–679.
4. Bonar, J., and Soloway, E. Preprogramming knowledge: A major source of misconceptions in novice programmers. *Hum.-Comput. Interaction 1,* 2 (1985), 133–161.
5. Card, S.K., Moran, T.P., and Newell, A. *The Psychology of Human-Computer Interaction.* Lawrence Erlbaum Associates, Hillsdale, N.J., 1983.
6. Collins, A. Explicating the tacit knowledge in teaching and learning. BBN Tech. Rep. 3889, Cambridge, Mass., 1978.
7. Johnson, L., and Soloway, E. PROUST: Knowledge-based program understanding. *IEEE Trans. Softw. Eng. 11,* 3 (1985), 267–275.
8. Larkin, J., McDermott, J, Simon, D., and Simon, H. Expert and novice performance in solving physics problems. *Science 208* (1980), 140–156.
9. McKeithen, K.B., Reitman, J.S., Rueter, H.H., and Hirtle, S.C. Knowledge organization and skill differences in computer programmers. *Cognitive Psychol. 13* (1981), 307–325.
10. Michener, E.R. Understanding understanding mathematics. *Cognitive Sci. 2* (1978), 283–327.
11. Pea, R.D. Language-independent conceptual "bugs" in novice programming. *J. Educ. Comput. Res.* To be published.
12. Resnick, L. Mathematics and science learning: A new conception. *Science 220* (1983), 477–478.
13. Schank, R.C., and Abelson, R. *Scripts, Plans, Goals and Understanding.* Lawrence Erlbaum Associates, Hillsdale, N.J., 1977.
14. Shneiderman, B. Exploratory experiments in programmer behavior. *Int. J. Comput. Inf. Sci. 5,* 2 (1976), 123–143.
15. Sleeman, D., Putnam, R.T., Baxter, J.A., and Kuspa, L.K. Pascal and high-school students: A study of misconceptions. *J. Educ. Comput. Res.* To be published.
16. Soloway, E. Why kids should learn to program. *Harvard Educ. Rev.* To be published.
17. Soloway, E., and Ehrlich, K. Empirical studies of programming knowledge. *IEEE Trans. Softw. Eng. 5* (1984), 595–609.
18. Spohrer, J.C., and Soloway, E. Analyzing the high frequency bugs in novice programs. In *Workshop on Empirical Studies of Programmers,* Soloway and Iyengar, Eds. Ablex, Norwood, N.J., To be published.
19. Spohrer, J.C., Soloway, E., and Pope, E. A goal/plan analysis of buggy Pascal programs. *Hu.-Comput. Interaction 1,* 2 (1985), 163–207.
20. Spohrer, J.C., Pope, E., Lipman, M., Sack, W., Freiman, S., Littman, D., Johnson, L., and Soloway, E. BUG CATALOGUE: II, III, IV. Tech. Rep. 386, Dept. of Computer Science, Yale Univ., New Haven, Conn., May 1985.

SECTION V:
DESIGNING PROGRAMMING
ENVIRONMENTS

How can programming environments be designed to make learning to program easier and more bug-free? The four papers in this section provide several suggestions:

1. graphical programming languages to make control flow explicit
2. no "hidden" actions or states; high visibility
3. simplicity of notional machine underlying languages
4. "training-wheels" should gradually fall away
5. short, simple, consistent naming conventions
6. graphical animations of program status during execution
7. multiple browseable representations of program state
8. adopt spatial metaphor and naive realism as design principles
9. interactive environment, tuned toward common applications
10. embedded instruction in applications

Each paper presents details of how these principles have been used in the development or refinement of new novice programming environments.

The Cunniff, Taylor and Black paper describes how FPL, a graphical programming language, effectively helps students avoid making certain bugs. By comparing the bugs students made using FPL versus Pascal, the researchers found a reduction in the number of missing syntax bugs as well as misplaced plan component bugs. In both cases, the reduction is attributed to the visual nature of FPL allowing students to more easily see how the code is grouped and ordered.

In the Eisenstadt and Brayshaw paper an integrated textbook, video, and software environment for novice and expert Prolog programmers is described. A key aspect of their environment is the notion of making available alternative graphical representations of program structure and execution history to the programmer. These new tools for viewing and manipulating otherwise "hidden" program state can be invaluable aids to novices attempting to build concrete models of Prolog. This paper also points out the need for textbooks and other instructional aids which are designed with a particular advanced programming environment clearly in mind.

Du Boulay, O'Shea, and Monk advocate the *visibility and simplicity principles*. The simplicity principle states that the idealized model of the computer ("notional machine") implied by the language constructs should be kept as simple as possible. The visibility principle states that novices should have methods for viewing selected parts and processes of the notional machine in action. Three languages (SOLO, an assembly language, and ELOGO) are examined in light of these principles.

The paper by diSessa and Abelson presents an exciting vision of what programming in the future may be like. BOXER is a reconstructible computational medium that is designed not so much for expert programmers to use in building efficient and reliable software, but for novices to use to help them easily get many small computational chores out of the way. Boxer adheres to two key design principles: *spatial metaphor and naive realism principles*. The spatial metaphor encourages people to interpret the computational medium in terms of everyday commonsense spatial relations — objects can be in places, they can be moved around, one object can be inside another object, etc. Naive realism is an extension of the idea of "what you see is what you get", and is related to the visibility principle discussed in the papers of the previous section. BOXER is being used to develop interactive textbooks that will allow the readers/users to make notes in the margins, run experiments, and write small programs to try out and explore certain ideas on their own, all in a very supportive, friendly computational environment.

One thing is certain — we've come a long way since the days of punch cards, and there is no turning back. The concept of programming is a rich concept, and appears to have a very bright, albeit potentially unrecognizable, future.

20

DOES PROGRAMMING LANGUAGE AFFECT THE TYPE OF CONCEPTUAL BUGS IN BEGINNERS' PROGRAMS? A COMPARISON OF FPL AND PASCAL

NANCY CUNNIFF
ROBERT P. TAYLOR
JOHN B. BLACK

**Department of Communication, Computing and Technology in Education
Center for Intelligent Tools in Education
Teachers College, Columbia University**

The effect of the graphical programming language FPL (First Programming Language) on the occurrence of conceptual bugs in programs written by novices was studied. The type and location for each bug, and the frequency for each type were all recorded following procedures developed in an earlier Yale University study of novice Pascal programming. The findings were compared with those of the earlier study, and suggest that FPL may help beginning programmers avoid some common conceptual errors in their programming.

INTRODUCTION

Understanding how people learn to program and how to make that learning process more efficient is important, particularly as the need for expert programmers continues to exceed the number available. At Teachers College, our interest in all this has led to the development of a new language, FPL (First Programming Language) to teach programming to adult beginners (see Taylor, 1982). FPL is a graphically represented programming language that offers students a vehicle for learning that is qualitatively different from that offered by Pascal, BASIC, FORTRAN, Logo or other textually based programming languages.

Several years of experience with students learning to program via FPL has suggested that this language might be particularly well suited to helping novices learn programming. Consequently, we became increasingly interested in formally determining whether FPL was really superior to other languages for teaching beginners to program, and began looking for appropriate research avenues that could help us find out. One such avenue was suggested by work at Yale University.

That work, by Elliot Soloway and his colleagues, has begun to provide a basis for understanding programming by examining the programs of students to see where, when and how often they commit errors while learning to program in Pascal (Johnson, Soloway, Cutler & Draper, 1983; Soloway, Ehrlich and Black, 1983; Spohrer, Soloway and Pope, 1985). We decided that it might be illuminating to conduct studies using the same programming problems that Soloway used, but have students solve them in FPL rather than in Pascal.[1]

In this paper we report an analysis of the conceptual bugs in FPL programs written by novice programmers. We present the findings of our study and compare these with the earlier studies at Yale. We discuss the findings in light of the design features of FPL, and we conclude with some judgments about the strengths of FPL as a first language for learning programming.

FIRST PROGRAMMING LANGUAGE

FPL was developed by Robert Taylor at Columbia University's Teachers College. It is the major instructional language used in the Computing and Education program at Teachers College. Students typically enter this program with little or no background in programming. FPL was developed in response to the needs of such beginners for a programming language that would help them understand the processes involved in computing while giving them a language which allowed them to write complex programs (Russman and Taylor, 1975).

FPL is a "thorough introduction to the basic logic structures involved in all programming" (Taylor, 1982, p. vi). It provides the necessary structures for writing complex computer programs. The unique quality of FPL in the world of computer languages, however, is that it is a graphic language; that is, FPL is built around a set of icons each of which stands for a specific programming instruction. These icons are graphical representations of programming concepts. There are eleven FPL icons; each represents a specific programming action. Eight of the icons include text, the variables and constants of the program. The icons replace the "reserved words," or instructions of text-based programming languages and thereby embody flow of control and logic. Figure 1 illustrates the FPL icons and their corresponding Pascal translations.

---

[1]We are grateful to Elliot Soloway for providing the programming problems and copies of his research reports for our use.

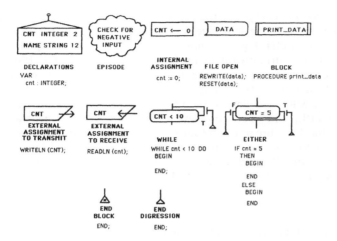

FIGURE 1   FPL Icons with Pascal translations.

The FPL icons alone, without text, provide information about the action and flow of a program; the text provides specific values for manipulation. Alone, neither is sufficient for interpreting the program successfully. For example, the FPL icon for an "External Assignment to Transmit" conveys meaning to the user about an action. It does not convey complete meaning about a specific programming assignment without some textual information. When text is added, a complete interpretation is possible. See figure 2 for an example.

The major difference between FPL and other programming languages is its graphic approach. Computer programs written in classical programming languages must be read in a linear, prose-like fashion even when the movement of the program is nonlinear. Because of its unique spatial layout of connected symbols, FPL allows a reader to traverse a program in a way that allows for visual branching as well as branching in the thought process, creating a computer program that can be "read" in a map-like fashion. The student can follow the program flow and can easily determine the order of the assignments.

Students studying FPL are encouraged to plan their programs on paper before working at the computer, sketching rough drafts using EPISODES

FIGURE 2   FPL external assignments.

(see Taylor, 1985). Such "paper and pencil" planning is an important aspect of FPL, and in fact, the language was originally designed for just this purpose (Taylor, 1982). Figure 3 shows a portion of a student's plan.

Versions of FPL currently run on the DEC20, the VAX and the IBM-PC. These implementations present the user with an interactive graphical interface which represents each type of programming icon as the user indicates what will occur next in the program flow. The student enters a program in FPL, and upon completion, the FPL software generates a drawing of the FPL program and an executable Pascal translation. The drawing is analogous to a listing of a program in traditional languages. Figure 4 gives an FPL and a Pascal solution to a simple programming problem. (See Taylor, 1985 and Taylor, 1982 for more detailed descriptions of FPL.)

CONCEPTUAL BUGS IN PROGRAMMING: SOLOWAY'S PASCAL RESEARCH

To understand why programmers make conceptual errors, it is necessary to know where and how often those errors occur. Isolated instances of a bug may point to one programmer's misunderstanding of a structure or process, but repeated occurrences of the same type of error indicate a concept which ought to be closely examined. Some studies recently conducted by Elliot Soloway and his colleagues at Yale University focused on such matters, examining Pascal solutions to a selected set of problems written by novice

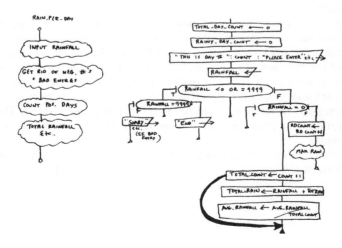

FIGURE 3   A student's sketch.

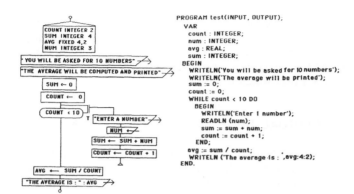

FIGURE 4   Sample FPL program with Pascal translation.

programmers. One aspect of this research counted and categorized conceptual (that is, non-syntactic) bugs (Johnson, Soloway, Cutler & Draper, 1983).

A bug classification scheme based on "the differences between the plans that the programmers intended to use, or should have used, and the actual code" (Johnson et al. 1983, p. 2) was proposed which identified four types of programming bugs:

— MISSING (required but omitted)
— SPURIOUS (not needed)
— MISPLACED (necessary but in wrong place)
— MALFORMED (incorrect, but in the right place)

Bugs of the above types were located, and then further categorized according to the type of programming plan component that was affected. Eight plan components were identified:

— INPUT (READ and READLN statements)
— OUTPUT (WRITE and WRITELN statements)
— INITIALIZATION (assignment statements giving variables initial values)
— UPDATE (assignment statements changing variables' values)
— GUARDS (IF tests, and WHILE and FOR termination tests)
— SYNTACTIC CONNECTIVES (BEGIN, END, ELSE)
— COMPLEX PLANS (plans which contain more than one component)
— DECLARATIONS (variables)

In this study, 204 students in an Introductory Pascal course at Yale University contributed Pascal solutions to a set of selected programs, and these student programs were analyzed for bugs using the protocol described above. Although the categorization of the bugs was but one aspect of this study, it was this aspect which first caught our attention.

CONCEPTUAL BUGS IN FPL PROGRAMMING

Our experience with FPL suggested that one of its strengths for beginning programmers lies in helping them avoid some common programming pitfalls. Since the Yale studies identified some of these pitfalls, application of that approach to FPL seemed to provide a way to examine which of these pitfalls FPL alleviates and which it does not.

Method

Subjects.   Programs were collected from six students enrolled in a programming course at Teachers College. These were graduate students who had all recently completed an introductory course in programming for non-computer science majors. The introductory course used FPL as the main teaching language, but all students had also done some programming in Pascal.

Procedure.   The students were given a set of nine programming problems and asked to keep an on-line journal of their programming sessions and to provide a copy of the FPL program and execution of the compiled program. For this study, we analyzed the first completed version of one of the problems, the Noah Problem (see Table 1) submitted by each student. Each program was analyzed for conceptual bugs using the categorization and classification scheme described by Johnson, Soloway, Cutler and Draper (1983).

Because this analysis is based on the students' first compiled solution, all of the bugs discussed are conceptual bugs.[2] Although syntax bugs may be of interest in understanding the behavior of beginners, we did not consider them in this study. However, there are some syntax-related logic bugs (such as placement of BEGIN-END in Pascal) which will be discussed.

---

[2]It should be noted that, in comparison with Pascal, every completed FPL program is free of syntax errors. Consequently, the programs analyzed in this study are truly the students' initial computer based attempts at solutions.

	INPUT	OUTPUT	INIT	UPDATE	GUARD	SYNTAX	COMPLEX PLAN	DECLAR- ATIONS
MISSING		1			18		2	
MISPLACED								
SPURIOUS	1		1	1				
MALFORMED		1				1	5	4

TABLE 2:   Bug frequencies in FPL programs

Results.   Six completed programs were received and analyzed. Figure 5 gives an annotated version of one student's program. Table 2 summarizes the number of bugs found in these programs, classified according to type.

Our analysis of these programs revealed a total of 35 bugs with an average of 5.8 bugs per program. Some programs had as many as ten bugs while others had as few as four. The most common bug was a MISSING GUARD, that is, a failure to check for valid or existing data (e.g., failing to determine whether the value of a counter was greater than 0 before using that counter as a divisor). This bug accounted for eighteen, or 51% of the bugs. It occurred more than once in every program. If the student failed to check for the existence of any valid data before computing the average rainfall (DIVIDE BY 0 GUARD MISSING), this resulted in two other guards also missing (AVERAGE NULL SET GUARD MISSING and MAXIMUM NULL SET GUARD MISSING). Consequently all programs but one exhibited all three of these bugs. This bug was also the category which accounted for 57% of the bugs in the analysis of the Pascal version of this problem (Johnson et al. 1983, p. 7).

The Noah Problem

Noah needs to keep track of the rainfall in the New York area to determine when to launch his ark. Write a program which he can use to do this. Your program should read the rainfall for each day, stopping when Noah types "9999," which is not a data value, but a sentinel indicating the end of input. If the user types in a negative value the program should reject it, since negative rainfall is not possible. Your program should print out the number of valid days typed in, the number of rainy days, the average rainfall per day over the period, and the maximum amount of rain that fell on any one day.

The second most frequent bug involved complex plans, either MISSING or MALFORMED. These accounted for seven (20%) of the bugs. This bug was most often caused by a failure to use the sentinel value as the loop controller, as was specified in the problem. A sentinel is a value used to

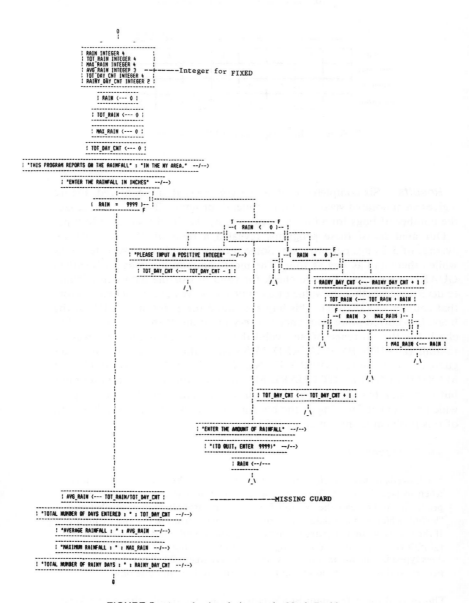

FIGURE 5 A student's solution to the Noah Problem.

indicate when the program should stop asking for input. In the Noah problem, the value '9999' is the sentinel; that is, the user should enter that value when he/she no longer wishes to enter rainfall for computation. Although in several cases this did not actually cause the program to fail, it is considered to be a bug because the student did not fulfill the problem requirements.

Another bug that occurred more than once was MALFORMED DEC-LARATION, which was caused by declaring AVERAGE as an integer rather than a fixed (real) number. Since the remaining bugs were single occurrences, they seem to be individual conceptual problems rather than consistent errors related to either the problem or the programming language.

Along with a count of the bugs that did occur, it is important to notice what bugs did not occur in the FPL programs. There were no examples of bugs related to syntax, although such bugs accounted for 6% of the Pascal bugs (Johnson et al., 1983, p. 7). These are not errors caught by the compiler, but rather refer to bugs which are related to such syntactic structures as the placement of BEGINs and ENDs.

In their analysis, Johnson et al. found that 14% of the Pascal bugs were related to initializations and updates. Most of these (97%) were MISSING, MALFORMED, or MISPLACED. In the FPL programs, there were only two bugs related to initialization and updating; all of these were SPURI-OUS assignments.

Interpretation and Discussion

The major source of bugs found in these programs, MISSING GUARD, was identical for both the FPL programs (51%) and their Pascal counter-parts in the original Yale study (57%). Considering that most of these bugs occurred at identical points in the two sets of programs (before calculation of the average and printing of the results), it seems reasonable to conclude that the students were unaware of the need for a guard against missing data. This is a conceptual misunderstanding that is not related to the language of implementation. It is not clear whether a language could be designed to eliminate this bug for beginners, but clearly FPL and Pascal do not.

The absence of any syntax-related bugs in the FPL programs is notable. All of the syntax related bugs found in the Yale study involved the use of BEGIN and END. In Pascal, a segment of code connected with a WHILE and the two segments connected within an IF-THEN-ELSE, is known as a compound statement if bracketed by BEGIN/END, and a simple statement otherwise. In FPL, these segments are visually isolated and are always known as DIGRESSIONS regardless of their complexity.

Since Pascal gives the student the option to use BEGIN/END or not, even with simple statements, the programmer must make a decision regarding the use of these delimiters. In FPL, all digressions are automatically assigned a "begin" and are required to have a specified end, which is referred to as an END DIGRESSION (see Figure 1). Consequently, the student is forced to identify the programming actions which take place within every digression, even if such a digression is "empty." It seems that this design feature prevents the syntax-related conceptual bugs often found in Pascal programs.

Other bugs not evident in the FPL programs analyzed were MISPLACED or MISSING INITIALIZATIONS and UPDATES. We hypothesize that this is due to the spatial arrangement of an FPL program. In an FPL program, all assignments which are embedded within a loop are physically positioned on a separate "trunk," indicating a digression from the main program line. This spatial arrangement allows the user to think more clearly about the placement of such assignments. This is especially helpful in the performance of updating and incrementing counters and running totals. The user is able to "see" where the looping begins and ends, resulting in a more clear-cut definition of the correct location for updating. This aspect of FPL may be the most helpful to beginning students in light of the importance of understanding and correctly using running total and counter variables (Ehrlich and Soloway, 1982).

CONCLUSION

It would be impossible to make any definitive judgments on whether FPL or Pascal is a more appropriate language for beginning programmers based on the small number of programs analyzed for this study. However the differences that apparently exist suggest that there may be some important advantages to the use of FPL. The avoidance of the common syntax-related bugs involving BEGINs and ENDs is not only desirable, it is helpful to the development of good programming habits. Since these bugs can be especially difficult for beginners to track down, eliminating any unnecessary spawning ground for them is desirable. The presence of multiple repetition options in Pascal may account for some of the difficulties novices encounter. FPL's WHILE construct gives programmers all of the required structures for repetition without creating confusion caused by having to choose among a set of seemingly identical options.

The fact that none of the errors in the FPL programs fell in the MISPLACED category indicates clearly that FPL's spatial nature affects students' understanding of the flow of a program. The graphical nature of FPL seems helpful to learners in determining placement of code details. In particular, the clear way FPL displays repetition helps beginners make correct decisions about where to place assignments. Because this bug-avoidance situation is directly linked to the graphical design of FPL, it would be impossible for Pascal to be modified to assist learners in this way.

This study suggests that a graphical programming language like FPL can aid beginners by eliminating some common bugs. These suggestive results merit more careful analysis and will be addressed in future studies with larger populations. We plan to look further at the use of repetition in eliminating the highly frequent MISSING GUARD bug.

ACKNOWLEDGMENT

This chapter has been reprinted by permission of the Association for Computing Machinery.

REFERENCES

Ehrlich, K. & Soloway, E. (1982). *An empirical investigation of the tacit plan knowledge in programming.* Technical report 236, Department of Computer Science, Yale University.

Johnson, W. L., Soloway, E., Cutler, B. & Draper, S. (1983). *Bug Catalogue I.* Technical Report 286, Department of Computer Science, Yale University.

Russman, G. M. & Taylor, R. P. (1975). A compiler-free approach to developing fundamental programming skills. In O. Lecarme & R. Lewis (Eds.), *Computers in education* (pp. 63–67).

Soloway, E., Ehrlich, K. & Black, J. B. (1983). Beyond numbers: Don't ask "How many"... ask "Why." *Proceedings of CHI'83,* 240–246.

Spohrer, J. C., Soloway, E. & Pope, E. (1985). Where the bugs are. *Proceedings of CHI'85,* 47–53.

Taylor, R. P. (1982). *Programming primer.* Reading, MA: Addison-Wesley.

Taylor, R. P. (1985). FPL: Graphical representation of classical programming. (In submission). Department of Computer Science, Yale University.

21
THE BLACK BOX INSIDE THE GLASS BOX: PRESENTING COMPUTING CONCEPTS TO NOVICES

BENEDICT DU BOULAY
Department of Computing Science, University of Aberdeen, Scotland

TIM O'SHEA
Institute of Educational Technology, The Open University, Englad

JOHN MONK
Faculty of Technology, The Open University, England

Simplicity and visibility are two important characteristics of programming languages for novices. Novices start programming with very little idea of the properties of the notional machine implied by the language they are learning. To help them learn these properties, the notional machine should be simple. That is, it should consist of a small number of parts that interact in ways that can be easily understood, possibly by analogy to other mechanisms with which the novice is more familiar. A notional machine is the idealized model of the computer implied by the constructs of the programming language. Visibility is concerned with methods for viewing selected parts and processes of this notional machine in action. We introduce the term "commentary" which is the system's dynamic characterization of the notional machine, expressed in either text or pictures on the user's terminal. We examine the simplicity and visibility of three systems, each designed to provide programming experience to different populations of novices.

INTRODUCTION

One of the difficulties of teaching a novice how to program is to describe, at the right level of detail, the machine he is learning to control. Novices are usually ignorant about what the machine can be instructed to do and about how it manages to do it. Basing one's teaching on the idea of a notional machine is an effective strategy for tackling this difficulty. The notional machine is an idealized, conceptual computer whose properties are implied by the constructs in the programming language employed. That is, the properties of the notional machine are language, rather than hardware,

431

dependent. For example, a novice learning BASIC will be learning how to work a BASIC machine; and this is quite different from a LISP machine (say), both in terms of the mechanisms he must learn to understand and the class of problems that can be solved easily with those mechanisms. For a strategy based on a notional machine to be effective, the notional machine must conform to two important principles. First, the notional machine employed should be conceptually simple, and second, methods should be provided for the novice to observe certain of its workings in action.

For example, Mayer (1979) represents the workings of a BASIC machine in terms of a small set of "transactions", where a transaction consists of an "operation", an "object" and a "location". Each BASIC instruction is described in terms of one or more of these transactions. The objects and locations are the components of the notional machine, and the operations are the ways in which these components can be used. Transactions are neither a description of the hardware on which the BASIC is implemented, nor a formal definition of the semantics of the programming language. Rather, they characterize what BASIC instructions do in terms of a simplified, functional model of a computer. A transaction, and hence the underlying notional machine, can be explained using analogies and concrete apparatus.

The transactions characterize a mechanism that has sufficient structure to explain the sequence of events while a BASIC program is running, but is simple enough to be grasped by a novice and avoids over-technical descriptions that would be confusing and irrelevant. Mayer's transactions are "black boxes" whose own internal workings do not need to be explained. Now the idea of a transaction is not limited to movements of data, say, in response to an instruction. It can also be used to describe the notional machine at other levels including the movement of a complete program from backing store to the workspace.

Functional simplicty can be achieved by limiting the set of transactions and by ensuring that each instruction does not need too many transactions to describe its action. This aspect of the simplicity of the notional machine must be distinguished from two other aspects of simplicity in a first programming language, namely *logical* simplicity and *syntactic* simplicity. Logical simplicity implies that problems of interest to the novice can be tackled by simple programs, i.e. the tools are suited to the job. Syntactic simplicity is achieved by ensuring that the rules for writing instructions are uniform, with few special cases to remember, and have well chosen names.

Functional simplicity of notional machine is not enough on its own to guarantee learnability or ease of use since the majority of the machine's actions will usually be hidden, and will have to be inferred by the novice unless special steps are taken. This problem can be acute. For instance the manuals accompanying certain makes of pocket calculator make no attempt to explain the reason why given sequences of button presses carry out the given computations. The user must follow the manual's instructions blindly because it is difficult for him to imagine what kind of underlying machine could be inside that demands these particular sequences of presses. During the course of a calculation, he has to guess the current state of the device using his recollection of what buttons he has pressed since the device's previous recognizable state (e.g. all registers cleared) because the device gives little or no external indications of its internal state.

Computers larger than calculators usually provide the user with more information about their internal states, but even so people still get confused about which environment they are in. Florentin & Smith (1978) give examples of the sorts of clue that experienced programmers use to infer the state of the machine they are using, and they comment on the unintelligibility of some novices' communications with a computer where they had lost track of what state it was in. Now languages for novices can be implemented in such a way that some form of *commentary* is available. This commentary is the "glass box" through which the novice can see the "black boxes" working. It functions rather like the cut-away models of machines to be found in technical museums, and indicates the more important events going on inside. What counts as important depends on both the programming language and on the task in which the novice is engaged. If the novice is transferring a program from his workspace to backing store (say) he ought to be able to see a diagram showing the movement of the program as a unit. Whereas if he is tracing the execution of a BASIC program, step by step, he may wish to see a more detailed representation of the current transaction. In neither case, however, does he need to be aware of such fine hardware distinctions as that between the arithmetic unit and the central processor.

Adherence to this approach requires that programming should be learned initially on an interactive system, since batch entry and turn-around delays only increase the remoteness of the notional machine. It also means that the implementation of the programming language and the preparation of teaching materials must be developed as a whole, so that each refers to the machine in the same terms. The commentary, whether pictorial or written, should be at a level of detail appropriate to the novice's task and to his level of understanding of the underlying concepts. Its terminology and diagrams should be properly matched to the other explanations that are provided, for example, in teaching materials. Error messages are a crucial part of the commentary and they form an important window into the machine. So care is needed to ensure that they describe errors in terms of the components of the notional machine known to the novice. Thus if it is decided that the novice need not be aware of a stack, say, then stack overflow error messages should be reworded in terms of some other notion he has been told about, such as some less precise notion of "store size".

A conceptually simple notional machine does not necessarily imply either a low level language (such as a simulated assembler) or a weak high level language (such as BASIC). There is no reason why a high level language such as PROLOG, with its pattern-matching and backtracking facilities, could not be implemented to present the novice with a simple and visible notional machine. PROLOG (Pereira, Pereira & Warren, 1979) is a declarative language in which programs are written as a series of sentences that specify goals and sub-goals, rather than as an algorithm. The order in which the sub-goals are attempted is largely left up to the system to decide. Pattern-matching is used to select the next sub-goal to be attempted. One of the "transactions" of PROLOG would be concerned with the pattern-matching mechanism, and this would be treated as a given and not explained in terms of some more primitive machinery. Increasing the visibility of PROLOG would involve some method of dynamically displaying the stack of sub-goals and the process of scanning through the sentences of the program searching for one which matches the pattern of a sub-goal. One question that needs further investigation is whether this type of language has advantages for novices. For example, Miller (1975) found that novices were more at home with "qualificational" rather than "conditional" languages. They preferred instructions of the sort "put all red things in box 1" to the conditional form, "if thing is red then put it in box 1". That is a statement of the goal rather than an algorithm for achieving it. This preference probably derives from the way instructions are usually given in English, for instance in workshop manuals, and underlines the fact that instructing a computer is an "unnatural" activity and not at all like instructing a person. But caution must be exercised in attempts to make programming languages that look like English, lest the novice be fooled into believing that he is communicating with a machine with human capabilities and knowledge (Plum, 1977). The argument for PROLOG is not that it is like English syntactically — it is very different — but that the specification of plans in terms of goals rather than in terms of an algorithm has precedents in English.

We have found that some highly experienced programmers find special languages for novices quite distasteful, and regard pedagogically simple explanations as not telling the "truth". We believe that this arises from their attempts to use such languages in ways that they were not designed for, and from their concern for elegance and generality rather than human factors. For example, the simple line editors of LOGO and BASIC are fine for novices, working at teletypes, because their action is easy to understand, but very frustrating for those who have mastered more powerful facilities. In just the same way we might expect to find that racing drivers are impatient with slow, family saloon cars, though the latter are much better than racing-cars for the learner driver. Experienced programmers forget just how many of the implicit conventions about programming they have absorbed in their exposure to a variety of programming languages. For example, the work of Mayer (1976), Miller (1974) and Sime, Arblaster & Green (1977*a*) has demonstrated how much novices need to learn about flow of control specified by conditionals.

There is a certain amount of empirical evidence to support the intuitively plausible case for simplicity and visibility in a first language, though one difficulty about testing programming ability has been both the small samples used and the large variation in subjects' ability. Mayer (1975) has conducted a series of experiments which show that novices, given a description or a model of their first language's notional machine, learned programming more effectively than those without these aids. The benefit was greater when the problems subsequently given to the novices were unlike the training tasks and demanded more understanding of programming. However, presenting the model only at the post-testing stage did not help the students to answer these questions. So the students had to have their initial exposure to programming using the aids. Both Miller (1974) and Sime *et al.* (1977*a*), who wanted to test novices' ability to write and debug certain kinds of program, were able to dispense with a long, prior training session by describing and providing a concrete model of the notional machine employed.

One of the advantages of simulated assembly languages as first languages is that they are easy to explain in terms of a simple model of the computer. Their disadvantage is that they are hard for novices to apply to any but the simplest (mathematical) problems. As far as we are aware, only one experiment has compared the ease with which a high and a low level language is learned by novices. The experiment was conducted using high school children, aged between 12 and 15 years, and compared their progress while learning LOGO then SIMPER, SIMPER then LOGO and LOGO together with SIMPER (Weyer & Cannara, 1975). SIMPER is a simulated decimal assembly language. Rather surprisingly, pupils progressed best who learned both languages together. Although there was a certain amount of confusion between the languages, each illuminated aspects of the other and this advantage outweighed the effects of interference between the conventions of the two languages.

TOWARDS SIMPLICITY

One path towards simplicity is by limiting the repertoire of both input and output to the notional machine. The former is achieved by having a small language with few constructs and the latter by restricting the machine's possible actions. This will almost certainly reduce the generality of the language but, if the domain of action is well-chosen, will provide a congenial environment in which to learn programming, especially if the range of machine action is clear to the novice. One example of this approach is provided by that subset of LOGO concerned with controlling a "Turtle". A Turtle is a small vehicle with an attached pen that leaves a trail on the floor as it moves in response to instructions to go forward, go backward or turn. By sequencing drawing instructions appropriately, the novice can make the Turtle draw pleasing patterns. Sometimes a Turtle simulated on a display screen is used to provide faster and more accurately drawn pictures than can be produced by the mechanical Turtle. With a repertoire of about 10 instructions and through the use of procedure/sub-procedure calls, it is possible to initiate a rich and interesting, but clearly delimited, set of machine actions, namely line drawings.

However, both simplicity and visibility of the notional machine can be spoiled by poor language design or implementation. Underlying functional simplicity can be masked by surface syntactic features which can give rise to ambiguities and can blur important distinctions. For example in BASIC the same symbol "$=$" is used to do a variety of different jobs, including assignment and testing for equality, so that the meaning of the symbol is heavily context dependent, thus offending against Weinberg's (1971) design criterion of "uniformity". Gannon & Horning (1975) found that students confused the assignment operation "$:=$" with the test for equality "$=$" in a comparison of two languages that differed in the way that assignment was denoted, as well as in other features. Gannon and Horning argued that some quite different symbol should be used, such as ← used in APL. Weinberg (1971) gives examples of lack of uniformity such as the restrictions in FORTRAN on the form of index arithmetic expressions. Such special cases increase the amount that has to be learnt by the novice by complicating the properties of the notional machine. In many implementations of LOGO the distinction between invoking a procedure and passing its name as an argument is glossed and the choice made by the interpreter is context dependent, thus rendering the language more complex than it need be. This problem can be solved in LOGO by demanding a more uniform parsing scheme, but it makes the language syntactically less like English. This in itself is no bad thing since it emphasizes the difference between a dialogue with a LOGO machine and a dialogue with a human.

Sometimes a superficial simplicity is achieved at the expense of expressive power by limiting the repertoire of inputs to the machine in an unhelpful way. Thus the naming restrictions and lack of control constructs in BASIC seem to give the novice less to learn, but quickly trap him in programs that are hard to read and understand. Although LOGO has its defects, its procedural nature and unrestricted naming allow interesting results to be obtained quickly by novices writing simple programs. Such logical simplicity is achieved by matching the language to problems of interest to the novice. What are suitable, simple problems in the given domain should be solvable by simple programs, so there can be no universal best first language. For example, SOLO with its data-base and pattern-matching is much more suitable than BASIC, say, for students of cognitive psychology because simple inferencing can be modelled easily without the overheads of string manipulation or equivalent necessary BASIC mechanism. Of course, writing programs to do number crunching in SOLO would be horrendous. Some attempts have been made to extend BASIC so that it can do simple text-processing (e.g. Brown, 1972; Raskin, 1974) in order to teach arts students programming. The domain seems more suitable than one in which problems about averages or tax computations might have to be set.

TOWARDS VISIBILITY

Various attempts have been made to make aspects of a notional machine more accessible to the novice. A Slot Box (Hillis, 1975) can be used to illustrate flow of control through a program using the movements of a Turtle. The slot box is an input device consisting of a row of slots, representing a simple linear address structure, into which are placed tokens representing instructions to move the Turtle. The tokens are about the size and shape of credit cards and, as well as having an instruction name printed cn them, have a computer-readable code designating that instruction. A program consists of an arrangement of these cards in the sequence of slots in the box. This program can be run and flow of control is indicated by the successive illumination of the bulbs beside the slots and is further external-ized in the sequence of Turtle movements. Program editing is achieved simply by rearranging the tokens in the slots. A Turtle, consisting of a light spot on a display screen, is now implemented as part of an introductory course in Pascal (Bowles, 1979).

Another fruitful line of attack is by implementing a language in such a way that either pictorial or written traces can be displayed that comment on the actions taken by the notional machine during a program run. This requires the facility for single-stepping a program, so that the effect of each instruction can be examined.

Two kinds of information are useful to the programmer, sequential and circumstantial (Green & Arblaster, 1980). The former is concerned with the sequence of events as they occur in the program, while the latter is concerned with the particular circumstances which lead the program to be in a given state. More work has been done to provide automatic access to sequential information than to circumstantial information. For example, BIP is an impressive system developed at Stanford (Barr, Beard &

Atkinson, 1976) that displays the effects of a BASIC program entered by the student. Sequential flow of control is illustrated by a pointer following the instructions as they are executed, and assignment is specifically commented upon on the display screen so that the student can see the current values of variables. Similar systems have been developed for FORTRAN (Shapiro & Witmer, 1974), for an operating system (Tracz, 1974) and for an assembly language (Schweppe, 1973), though BIP functions as programming teacher as well as a simulator for a BASIC machine.

BIP's multiplicity of roles, e.g. as a tutor, a BASIC interpreter, an editor and a commentator on BASIC programs, can lead to difficulties for the novice who must keep in mind with which of these notional machines he is dealing. It is commonly found (see, for example, Huckle, 1980; Florentin & Smith, 1978) that novices get confused when the computer changes state in this way. The novice finds it difficult both to discriminate between the various states of the machine and to remember the particular language conventions associated with each state. One way of reducing the latter difficulty is to give the programming language, the command language and the editing language the same syntax. This will not help the novice distinguish which environment he is in, but it will reduce the load of language learning to a single set of conventions. ELOGO (see below) goes some way in this direction by constraining the novice to carry out what would otherwise be command language instructions, such as program storage and retrieval, from within ELOGO using the same syntax as the rest of the language.

Novices make inferences about the notional machine from the names of the instructions, so it is important to choose names that have the appropriate connotation. Kennedy (1975) gives an example where novices, learning to use a computerized hospital filing system, confused the everyday meaning of some of the command names with the specialized meaning implemented in the system. This led them to use the filing system incorrectly. The users' understanding of the functional components of the filing system did not match reality. Some words, commonly used for instruction names such as LOAD and STORE, have much more specific connotations for experienced programmers than for novices. LOAD and STORE are usually used to label two actions where each is the inverse of the other. LOAD is used to mean move some object into a place where it can be worked on (e.g. a file into a workspace or a number into an accumulator) whereas STORE means the reverse movement. Both LOAD and STORE usually involve copying data destructively into the target location, *and* leaving behind a copy at the source location. These specialized meanings have only a very loose connection with the everyday use of these two words, and need special explanation if introduced as part of a first language.

THREE EXAMPLES

In this section we describe three languages developed specifically for novices. In each case the language was implemented under different constraints and for a different population of novices. SOLO is an interactive data-base language used by Open University students learning cognitive psychology and artificial intelligence. Our second example concerns a microprocessor based assembly language used in another Open University course for managers in industry. Our third example is ELOGO, an Edinburgh dialect of LOGO, designed as a language for school pupils, aged about 12 years, to explore mathematics.

SOLO

Students of Cognitive Psychology at the Open University learn SOLO, a language for manipulating a relational data-base (Eisenstadt, 1978). Here the "black boxes" are such mechanisms as inserting a symbolic description into the data-base, or pattern-matching against descriptions already in the data-base. In terms of the amount of machine code they involve, the instructions for carrying out these actions are more complex than BASIC instructions but their effects and properties are no harder to grasp. They function as primitive, undecomposable parts of the SOLO notional machine in just the same way as Mayer's transactions do for the BASIC machine. Eisenstadt (1979) found that Open University students were able to learn SOLO quite effectively, despite the fact that they had no previous programming experience and were working mainly on their own at remote terminals where help was not usually available.

Functional simplicity was achieved in SOLO by restricting the scope of the data-base searching mechanism and by "locking up" certain language features until the novice had progressed beyond a given point. Syntactic simplicity was increased by arranging that when a student typed the "IF" part of a conditional he was automatically prompted for both the "THEN" and the "ELSE" part. Sime, Arblaster & Green (1977b) showed that this was a successful method of reducing errors in conditionals. Some automatic spelling correction is carried out on the user's input.

Only a certain amount could be done to ensure the visibility of the language, because most of the users would be working at teletypes rather than at display screens, and teletypes are limited in the extent to which they can reproduce diagrams. However, data-base items to be displayed are presented at the terminal in a form that both suggests the meaning of the item and is in agreement with the teaching material, as follows:

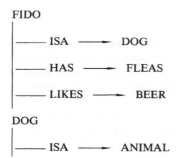

SELF SIMULATION ON A MICROPROCESSOR

The general principles of simplicity and visibility can be applied to much simpler programming systems. Recently the Open University produced a course for managers in industry that aims to familiarize them with some aspects of microprocessors (Open University, 1979). Part of the course provides "hands-on" experience of a small microcomputer. It was designed to give people some feel for what tasks a microcomputer can do and how it can be made to do them. The clients for this course are not expected to have any prior experience and the course is designed to help them appreciate the problems faced by their own development teams, and give them some understanding of their jargon. Cost played a part in determining the facilities of the microcomputer, which is sent through the post. The practical work is just one part of a course detailing the effects of the introduction of microprocessors in industry.

The small size of the system based on an Intel 8049, precludes a comprehensive introduction to programming, but this is not needed by the customers of the course. The system provides only 10 instructions: LOAD, STORE, ADD, DECREMENT, JUMP, JUMP IF ZERO, INPUT, OUTPUT, CALL, EXCLUSIVE OR. Each instruction has its own button bearing an abbreviated form of the instruction name. Most of the store is taken up by an interpreter for these instructions, which are a subset of the microprocessor's own instruction set. Thus the main task of the device is to simulate a simplified version of itself. Only a small amount of space is left for user's programs and consists of 63 locations for programs and eight registers for data. This architecture forces a strong data/program distinction, though this is not necessarily a disadvantage in this context.

Instructions may be entered in one of three modes, binary, denary or mnemonic. There are buttons with mnemonics for each instruction that allow them to be keyed in easily (see the buttons on the bottom right-hand side of Fig. 1). A light indicates which mode is currently being used. The contents of a location can be observed as either binary or denary codes.

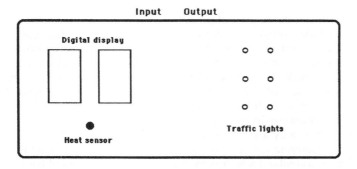

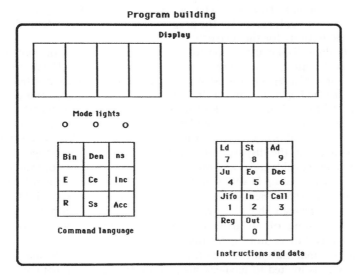

FIGURE 1   Microcomputer layout.

The other buttons, on the bottom left, form the "command language" and enable instruction entry, examination of program locations and registers, and running or single stepping programs. These are the instructions for dealing with a program (e.g. editing it) as opposed to the instructions that comprise a program. This distinction has proved hard for novices (see, for example, Weyer & Cannara, 1975) and the separation of the two sets of buttons was designed to underline the difference.

The system contains a number of pre-defined subroutines that can be called by a user's program and whose instructions can be examined by him, though the code for the interpreter itself is inaccessible to the user. These subroutines are used as a "kit of parts" in a variety of applications and illustrate the idea of modularity of programs. The applications described in the manual include a program to display temperature as a two digit number read from a temperature sensitive input device, and a program to control six coloured light bulbs in a way similar to traffic lights. The timing subroutine can be made to work over periods of minutes and this underlines the fact that a microprocessor, obeying thousands of instructions per second, can be made to react over a much longer timescale.

An attempt is made to distinguish between those input and output devices that can be accessed by a user's program and those whose job is solely to allow him to communicate his program to the machine and examine or debug it. This is a similar distinction to that between the command language and the programming language. The two kinds of devices are physically separated in the layout, except for the program readable sense switch, which is among the buttons for the instructions.

The eight-digit display can be set to show either the address or contents of a program location, or the contents of the program counter. The multiple use of the same display leads to ambiguity since the novice cannot tell by looking at it whether it is showing the contents of the program counter or some other address. A similar lack of information was described earlier in the case of a pocket calculator. It could be solved by increasing the cost and complexity of the device and providing further display lights. The small number of digits in the display restricts the scope of error messages and other comments considerably, and most of them are just strings of symbols that have to be looked up in a table in order to decipher them. One solution to this would be to have the comments generated by having the words of the message cycle through the display, rather like messages on advertising hoardings consisting of an array of light bulbs. This solution would, however, demand more store space than was available.

The teaching materials introduce the notion of the "state" of the machine and the novice is invited to navigate around a state-transition network by pressing keys and comparing the observed behaviour of the machine with the descriptions on the nodes of the network. The transitions in the diagram correspond roughly with Mayer's (1979) transactions.

The notional machine is functionally simple, but this simplicity is achieved at the expense of having a complicated program interpreting the user's key presses. Attempts are made at visibility, e.g. the mode lights, the examinable code of the standard subroutines and the single stepping facility. Visibility could be improved by adding more "command language" buttons, e.g. to display the contents of the program counter, and by improving the error messages.

Despite the restrictions, the user can be introduced to a large range of computing ideas including: planning, coding, running and debugging programs, flow of control, subroutines, stack, conditional jumps, input and output of information, internal representation of data, addresses and contents. An important notion which is not covered is naming of both data and programs.

ELOGO

ELOGO is a procedural, interactive language with facilities for drawing using a turtle and for symbol manipulation using integers, words and lists as data-types (McArthur, 1974). The language is used to help children and adults develop their mathematical thinking by writing programs and by running pre-defined programs with interesting (usually pictorial) mathematical effects (du Boulay, 1980; Howe, O'Shea & Plane, 1980).

Special attention was paid to the problems faced by novices, including both their difficulties with typing and their unfamiliarity with the purposes and powers of a programming language. The initial introduction to programming is via a button-box and turtle, where each button stands for an instruction, see Fig. 2. The design of the buttons themselves gives clues to the language syntax. FORWARD and LEFT can be followed by one of the five number buttons, and DEFINE can be followed by one of the blank buttons.

The labels on the buttons correspond to what the novice must type when he progresses to using a teletype. The blank buttons can be labelled by the novice and can be used to run or store a procedure of his own definition. A user-defined procedure can call other user-defined procedures or can call itself recursively. The simple notional machine implied by the button box

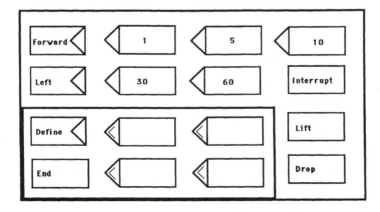

FIGURE 2 Button box.

and Turtle system is used as a foundation to build the user's understanding of the more complex, complete ELOGO system implemented on a mainframe computer. Our experience has been that this introduction allays the fears that many novices have about computers in general and also their worries about not being able to type. The button box succeeds in introducing, in a straightforward and non-threatening way, many important computing concepts including: commands, arguments, stored procedure, subprocedure call and recursion.

Once the novice has mastered the button box system he moves on to use the full ELOGO system. This contains many more facilities, some of which he probably will not need and will not be told about, such as an inferencing mechanism used to teach Artificial Intelligence (Bundy, 1978). Each novice is introduced to only those parts of the language that he needs to solve his programming problems.

In ELOGO the main task for the novice is the interactive definition, testing and debugging of procedures. The novice decomposes a complex programming task into simpler sub-tasks. This decomposition is mirrored in the structure of the procedure/sub-procedure calls of his program. Sub-tasks may need further decomposition and so sub-procedures may need to call sub-sub-procedures, and so on. A procedure, once defined, can be debugged, filed and run as an individual unit, so the sub-procedures of a program can be thoroughly tested before testing a procedure which calls them (although, chronologically, the super-procedure may have been defined prior to the sub-procedures).

Drawing a picture with the Turtle quite naturally decomposes into the sub-tasks of drawing the different parts of the picture, and each part can be drawn by its own, named procedure. In this context the novice can see the sense of the modular programming methodology, outlined above, and can attempt to apply it later on when dealing with, for example, more complex list-processing problems which involve decomposition into functions as well as procedures.

Efforts were made to keep the notional machine functionally simple. For example, the basic programming unit is the procedure, and the filing system was arranged so that individual procedures could be easily stored, loaded and borrowed from other users. A simple line editor is used (like that for BASIC) and this has proved adequate for novices working at teletypes.

Visibility was sought by ensuring that most of the important hidden actions, such as storing a procedure, were concluded with a written comment from the system. The teaching materials, a primer (du Boulay & O'Shea, 1976), were developed along with the language implementation. This meant that the comments from the system, such as error messages, could be worded using the same analogies as those used in the primer. Attention was paid to the debugging facilities which allow various forms of procedure tracing and single-stepping through a procedure.

CONCLUSION

Novices should be introduced to programming through languages that embody simple notional machines with the facilities for making certain of the actions of the notional machine open to view. This will almost certainly mean that much of the code in the language implementation will be used to make life easy for the novice, rather than to run his programs. This loss of efficiency is a worthwhile price to pay in order to make programming more pleasantly accessible to a wide cross-section of people.

ACKNOWLEDGMENTS

We thank Thomas Green, David Hall, Jim Howe, Fran Plane, Peter Ross and Hugh Smith for helpful comments on a draft of this paper. Benedict du Boulay acknowledges the support of a Social Science Research Council grant while at the Department of Artificial Intelligence, University of Edinburgh.

This chapter has been reprinted by permission of Academic Press, Inc.

REFERENCES

Barr, A., Beard, M. & Atkinson, R.C. (1976). The computer as tutorial laboratory: the Stanford BIP Project. *International Journal of Man-Machine Studies,* **8,** 567-596.

Bowles, K. L. (1979). *Microcomputer Problem Solving Using Pascal.* New York: Springer-Verlag.

Brown, P. J. (1972). SCAN: A simple conversational programming language for text analysis. *Computers and the Humanities,* **6,** 223-227.

Bundy, A. (Ed.) (1978).*Artificial Intelligence: An Introductory Course.* Edinburgh: Edinburgh University Press.

du Boulay, J. B. H. & O'Shea, T. (1976). How to work the LOGO machine: a primer for ELOGO. *D.A.I. Occasional Paper No. 4,* Department of Artificial Intelligence, University of Edinburgh.

du Boulay, J. B. H. (1980). Teaching teachers mathematics through programming. *International Journal of Mathematics Education in Science and Technology,* **11,** (3) 347-360.

Eisenstadt, M. (1978). *Cognitive Psychology: Artificial Intelligence Project.* Milton Keynes: Open University Press.

Eisenstadt, M. (1979). A friendly software environment for psychology students. *A.I.S.B. Quarterly,* **34.**

Florentin, J. J. & Smith B. C. (1978). Guessing the current state of the computer. *Proceedings of the Workshop on Computing Skills and Adaptive Systems,* Liverpool.

Gannon, J. J. & Horning, J. D. (1975). Language design for programming reliability. *IEEE Transactions on Software Engineering,* **SE-1,** (2) 179-191.

Green, T. R. G. & Arblaster, A. T. (1980). *As You'd Like It: Contributions to Easier Computing.* MRC Social and Applied Psychology Unit, Sheffield, Memo No. 373.

Hillis, D. (1975). *Slot Machine: Hardware Manual.* Massachusetts Institute of Technology. Cambridge, Massachusetts: LOGO Working Paper No. 39.

Howe, J. A. M., O'Shea, T. & Plane, F. (1980). Teaching mathematics through LOGO programming: an evaluation study. In (Lewis, R. & Tagg, E. D., Eds.) *Computer Assisted*

Learning: Scope, Progress and Limits. Amsterdam: North-Holland.

Huckle, B. A. (1980). Designing a command language for inexperienced computer users. In (Buck, D., Ed.) *Command Language Directions.* Amsterdam: North-Holland.

Kennedy, T. C. S. (1975). Some behavioural factors affecting the training of naive users of an interactive computer system. *International Journal of Man-Machine Studies,* **7,** 817–834.

Mayer, R. E. (1975). Some conditions of meaningful learning for computer programming: advance organizers and subject control of frame order. *Journal of Educational Psychology,* **68,** (2) 143–150.

Mayer, R. E. (1976). Comprehension as affected by structure of problem representation. *Memory and Cognition,* **43,** 249–255.

Mayer, R. E. (1979). A psychology of learning BASIC. *Communications of the ACM,* **22,** (11) 589–593.

McArthur, C. D. (1974). EMAS LOGO: user's guide and reference manual. *DAI Occasional Paper No. 1.* Department of Artificial Intelligence, University of Edinburgh.

Miller, L. A. (1974). Programming by non-programmers. *International Journal of Man-Machine Studies,* **6,** 237–260.

Miller, L. A. (1975). Naive programmer problems with specification of flow of control. *Proceedings of National Computer Conference, AFIPS,* 44.

Open University (1979). *Microprocessors And Product Development, A Course For Industry.* Milton Keynes: Open University Press.

Pereira, L. M., Pereira, C. N. & Warren, D. H. D. (1979). User's guide to DECsystem-10 PROLOG. *D.A.I. Occasional Paper No. 15.* Department of Artificial Intelligence, University of Edinburgh.

Plum, T. (1977). Fooling the user of a programming language. *Software Practice and Experience,* **7,** 215–221.

Raskin, J. (1974). FLOW: a teaching language for computer programming in the humanities. *Computers and the Humanities,* **8,** 231–237.

Schweppe, E. J. (1973). Dynamic instructional models of computer organisation and programming languages. *SIGCSE Bulletin,* **5,** (1) 26–31.

Shapiro, S. C. & Witmer, D. P. (1974). Interactive visual simulation for beginning programming students. *SIGCSE Bulletin,* **6,** (1) 11–14.

Sime, M. E., Arblaster, A. T. & Green, T. R. G. (1977a). Structuring the programmer's task. *Journal of Occupational Psychology,* **50,** 205–216.

Sime, M. E., Arblaster, A. T. & Green, T. R. G. (1977b). Reducing programming errors in nested conditionals by prescribing a writing procedure. *International Journal of Man-Machine Studies,* **9,** 119–126.

Tracz, W. (1974). The use of ATOPSS for presenting elementary operating system concepts. *SIGCSE Bulletin,* **6,** (1) 74–78.

Weinberg, G. M. (1971). *The Psychology Of Computer Programming.* New York: Van Nostrand Reinhold.

Weyer, S. A. & Cannara, A. B. (1975). Children learning computer programming: experiments with languages curricula and programming devices. *Technical Report No. 250,* Institute for Mathematical Studies in the Social Sciences, Stanford University, California.

22

An integrated textbook, video, and software environment for novice and expert Prolog programmers[1]

Marc Eisenstadt and Mike Brayshaw

Human Cognition Research Laboratory
The Open University
Milton Keynes MK7 6AA, UK

Abstract: The paper describes a Prolog execution model which serves as the uniform basis for textbook material, video-based teaching material, and an advanced graphical user interface for Prolog programmers. The model, based upon an augmented AND/OR tree representation of Prolog programs, uses an enriched 'status box' in place of the traditional AND/OR tree node to show precise details of clause head/body processing and to deal correctly with the 'cut'. The purpose of our integrated environment is to address two hitherto unreconciled goals: (i) to provide a clear and consistent model of Prolog program execution for novices that can be used for teaching, exercises, and self-paced study, and (ii) to provide an advanced graphical interface for logic programming that is usable by Prolog experts in real world application domains and that requires no conceptual change from (i). The end result comprises (a) a textbook/workbook combination which enables students to work through 'paper-and-pencil' execution snapshots; (b) video animation sequences showing detailed run-throughs of moderately complex Prolog programs; and (c) a working graphical tracer/debugger currently running on Apollo workstations.

Topic Areas: Teaching Logic Programming, Human-Machine Interface, Curriculum Issues.

1 Introduction

1.1 Motivation

Existing Prolog textbooks (e.g. Clocksin & Mellish, 1984; Bratko, 1986; Sterling & Shapiro, 1986) provide adequate descriptions of the language, yet novices still 'come unstuck' when having to write or debug Prolog programs that exhibit anything other than the most trivial forms of backtracking and unification (Coombs & Stell, 1985; Taylor, 1987). It could be that the language is just inherently 'tricky', and requires lots of practice. Alternatively, it might be the case that novices are never provided with (or at least never acquire) a clear execution model, and this leads them astray. The analysis of Bundy et. al. (1986) suggested that texts such as Clocksin & Mellish (1st edition, 1981) contained several different and potentially conflicting 'stories' of Prolog execution, and that this was a source of possible confusion. To their credit, Clocksin & Mellish provided a much more coherent story of Prolog execution in the second edition of their book (1984). Nevertheless, there is a rather wide gulf between what is presented in any existing text and what is observed when a real Prolog program 'acts funny' (Taylor, 1987).

The importance of clear models of the underlying machine has been highlighted elsewhere (e.g. Du Boulay, O'Shea & Monk, 1981;Halasz and Moran,1982). Here we present a notional machine that is based directly on a meta-level interpreter, thereby allowing us to follow execution steps in very precise detail. The advantages that this conceptual model gives us are twofold:

[1]To appear in *Proceedings of the 2nd International Conference of the Prolog Education Group (PEG-87)*, Exeter, UK, 8th-10th July, 1987. This work was supported by UK SERC/Alvey Research grants GR/C/69344 & GR/E/2333, plus a grant from the SERC Information Technology Training Initiative. The graphical tracer is being developed as part of Alvey IKBS Project number 161, conducted jointly with Expert Systems International. We would particularly like to acknowledge the following for their valuable assistance: Malcolm Dixon, Hank Kahney, Frank Kriwaczek, and Peter Ross for co-authoring/revising the course notes; David Thomas, Chris Hogger, and numerous other members of the UK Logic Programming community for their original efforts in helping to launch the Prolog course; Glan Thomas and Mike Peat for producing the videos; Malcolm Story and Adam Gawronski for implementing the OU Prolog interpreter.

(i) Far from inundating the novice with 'too much truth', we feel on the contrary that describing the machine at such a level makes the basic concepts of the language unambiguous, more readily accessible, easier to understand, and hence less error-prone.

(ii) We can present a story directly based upon the machine rather than introducing extra artificial layers of description and metaphor (e.g. Carroll and Thomas,1982).

Our focus has been on producing an account of the language which is rich enough to satisfy the needs of experts but has the descriptive power and clarity for teaching difficult concepts to a novice programmmer. Our work has developed from two ends simultaneously. That is, we were developing video-based teaching material for novice Prolog programmers at the same time as we were implementing graphics facilities for helping experts observe a 2- or 3-thousand node search space. Only by forcing these two paths to converge could we cater for the 'upwardly mobile student' who learned about Prolog in the early phases and then went on to become a serious Prolog user.

1.2 Pedagogically-motivated tracers

Amongst the numerous tracing and debugging packages built for Prolog and other languages, several have been motivated explicitly by pedagogical considerations. Here we mention only the four most relevant. For a detailed overview of other work the reader is referred to the excellent summary found in Rajan (1986).

Mellish has developed an animated AND/OR tree trace which displays the run-time behaviour of small Prolog programs on VT100-style terminals connected to a machine running the Sussex University/System Designers Ltd. POPLOG environment (Hardy, 1984). This tracer was developed as part of an effort to provide a consistent 'execution story' for the student learning Prolog, and indeed the second edition of Clocksin & Mellish (1984) conforms with the style and content of the animated tracer. Two important problems with Mellish's facility are (a) variables are destructively replaced by their instantiations on the screen in 'real' (or slightly slowed down) time, so it can be hard to 'go back' and see what actually happened; (b) only toy programs can be viewed. The principle of showing an animated AND/OR tree is nevertheless fundamentally important.

Rajan's (1986) single-stepper works its way through Prolog code by highlighting relevant portions in the database at the appropriate moments, and by instantiating clause bodies in their entirety 'in place' in the code being traced. By showing unification in painstaking detail, a very clear account of execution can be presented to novices. However, Rajan's single-stepper doesn't fully show variable renaming, and can only deal with relatively small execution spaces. Although both the renaming and search space problems were not relevant for the class of beginners Rajan was addressing, they are problems which need to be resolved for longer-term users.

Brown and Sedgewick(1984) in their BALSA environment have sought to use animated displays as a way of demonstrating algorithms and teaching basic computing concepts. Although they include the important notion of a 'replay' facility in their program, the system is an algorithm viewer, rather than a true trace facility (i.e. ordinary users cannot type in original code and see a graphical trace of it).

DEWLAP is a Prolog debugger by Dewar and Cleary (1986) that graphically shows the state of the program execution by using a fisheye zoom to show detailed information about the item of current focus and gradually less about those that are further away and of less interest. The system shows individual clause head unification and allows the user to specify special ways to view individual data objects. The trace display rapidly gets very complicated even on small examples and the nature of the zooming they use means that is not possible easily to compare parts of the tree that are a large distance apart. Although Dewar and Cleary acknowledge the desirability of seeing the program's behaviour in terms of an AND/OR tree, they compromise in the DEWLAP diagram with a resulting loss of clarity.

1.3 A way forward

We have been most influenced by the work of Rajan (1986) and Bundy et. al. (1986). We share with Rajan the desire to 'tell the truth' about Prolog execution in gory detail, and to show unification details in terms which map directly onto the user's source code. We differ from Rajan in preferring to show large execution spaces graphically rather than textually. The work of Bundy et. al. has cogently highlighted the virtues of sticking firmly with an AND/OR tree execution model in preference to other possible models, including OR trees and 'Byrd Box' models (Byrd, 1980). Our work differs from that of Bundy et. al. in three important respects: (i) in our 'close up' view we display much more detail about clause head matching and unification, but without sacrificing the basic clarity of an AND/OR tree representation; (ii) our 'long-distance' view is consistent with our 'close up' story, and is not only suitable for machine implementation, but is also capable of displaying the execution of enormous Prolog programs; (iii) we don't require separate 'resolution tables' or 'database' displays, although we naturally assume that in a modern Prolog environment the user can trivially display a window showing relevant source code.

Our work started with the following two premises: (i) it is essential both for teaching and debugging purposes to show the full execution space of large Prolog programs; (ii) it is essential to base both teaching material and a working trace package on an execution model which discriminates between clause head matching and clause body execution.

We have stuck with these two premises partly because of the challenge of resolving their underlying contradiction: premise (i) involves a global view of things, while premise (ii) involves a very close up view. Our aim has been to reconcile these differences without losing the advantages provided by either. We feel strongly that different levels of detail (i.e. different grain-size of analysis) involve different conceptual views of what is happening, and therefore a simple 'aerial view/close-up zoom' facility does *not* provide a magical solution. It is nevertheless possible to accommodate both premises, despite the commonly-held misconception that both are 'too hard' are 'too messy' to achieve. The key insights which enable this accommodation, and which drive the whole of the work described in this paper, are the following:

- It is possible to display an execution space involving thousands of nodes on today's graphics workstations.

- When a Prolog programmer is debugging a program which he or she has personally been developing over a period of weeks or months, an overall graphical view of the execution space of that program is highly meaningful to that programmer, because it conveys its own gestalt.

- The concept of a 'node' in a traditional AND/OR tree is needlessly impoverished. With just a few enhancements, and for a very small computational overhead, a simple node can become a 'status box' which concisely encapsulates a goal's history, including detailed clause head matching information.

- The traditional AND/OR tree does not reveal the difference between one clause containing a disjunction and two separate clauses. More specifically, the distinction between clause head and clause body is not shown in AND/OR trees, despite the overwhelming importance of the head/body distinction to the debugging of Prolog programs. A minor notational variant enables us to overcome this problem.

The layout of the paper is as follows: section 2 describes the basic representation and discusses various examples; section 3 outlines the teaching material; section 4 overviews the graphical debugger; section 5 contains conclusions and a discussion of the future directions of the work.

2 A model of Prolog execution

The sub-sections which follow introduce an idealised model of the Prolog machine which we dub the Transparent Prolog Machine, introduced originally in Eisenstadt & Brayshaw (1986).

2.1 The Procedure Status Box

The cornerstone of our convention, illustrated in figure 1, is the *procedure status box*. This box replaces the simple and/or tree 'node' in our display of the execution space. The upper part indicates the *goal status*, and informs us whether the goal is currently being processed (a '?'), whether it has succeeded (a tick), whether it has failed (a cross), or whether it initially succeeded and then failed upon backtracking (tick/cross combination). The lower half is a *clause counter*. The clause counter tells us which of several clauses for a given relation in the database is currently being processed. Circular nodes are used instead of procedure status boxes to depict system primitives, and may contain any of the following four symbols: question mark, tick, cross, tick/cross combination (corresponding to their meanings as above).

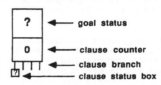

Figure 1. The procedure status box

The small branches dangling down underneath the box in figure 1 correspond exactly to the individual clauses in the database, and are therefore called *clause branches*. The leftmost clause branch corresponds to the first clause, and the next one corresponds to the second clause, etc. When there are more than five clause branches, a special 'collapsing' convention is adopted. The square boxes at the end of clause branches are *clause status boxes*. Such boxes use the same question-mark, tick, cross, and tick/cross combination to depict the status of individual clauses. If a given clause head does not unify, then a short horizontal *dead-end bar* is added instead of a clause status box. Clause branches correspond to 'or' choices, but are drawn differently from their traditional counterparts in order to make the processing of individual clauses obvious at a glance.

Consider the following four-clause database:

```
drinks(tom, wine).
drinks(john, beer).
drinks(sue, wine).
drinks(X, water). % everyone (everything) drinks water
```

Figures 2a and 2b show the states of affairs at the beginning and end of processing the query
?- drinks(sue, wine).

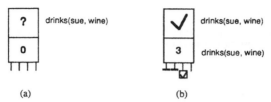

(a)   (b)

Figure 2. Processing the query ?- drinks(sue, wine). (a) shows the status box at the beginning of the query, and (b) shows the outcome.

2.2 Unification and renaming

To illustrate unification, the relations and arguments next to the top half of each procedure status box depict the state of play when the goal was invoked, whereas the relations and arguments next to the bottom half of each procedure status box depict the matching clause head found in the data base. User-chosen variable names are subscripted automatically to indicate renamed variables. The subscript counter is incremented for each new nonground clause invoked as a (sub)goal. The diagrams use a sideways '=' with arrowheads to show unification. Up arrows indicate output variables; down arrows indicate input variables. Given the four clauses for **drinks/2** used earlier, Figure 3 shows the status box representation of the following three interactions:

a)   ?- **drinks(john, X)**.
     X = beer

b)   ?- **drinks(foo, water)**.
     yes

c)   ?- **drinks(foo, X)**.
     X = water

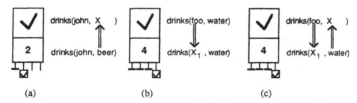

(a)   (b)   (c)

Figure 3. Unification details, showing input and output variables for three different goals.

Right-angled arrows indicate a variable 'passed across' or shared with a sister goal. Headless arrows can be used for teaching purposes to indicate directly-matching terms, particularly in cases where the match is subtle. Often there is a direct visual correspondence between a variable and the arrow showing its instantiation in the diagram. Whenever the correspondence is 'indirect', i.e. the instantiation has come 'from elsewhere', we place a small lozenge beneath the variable to show its instantiation at the moment of the execution 'snapshot'. An example of this is provided in section 2.3.

2.3 AORTA Diagrams

The full space of goals traversed during execution is described in terms of an AND/OR Tree, Augmented (hence AORTA) by the above status boxes and unification details. Consider the following program:

```
g :- d1(X), d2(X).
g :- d3(X), d4(X).

d1(a).    d2(d).    d3(f).    d4(i).
d1(b).    d2(e).    d3(g).    d4(j).
d1(c).              d3(h).    d4(h).
```

Figure 4 shows the AORTA diagram depicting the *full search space* for the query ?- **g**. The clause head labels, **C1** and **C2**, are here only displayed for convenience. The display developed for teaching purposes would only show that part of the search space which is actually traversed during execution. In our graphical tracer implementation, we distinguish between the execution space which has been traversed thus far, and the execution space which we can guarantee (via behind-the-scenes analysis) will *eventually* be traversed. We call this latter space of nodes the 'pre-ordained execution space'.

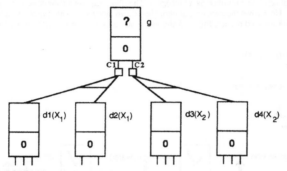

Figure 4. A sample AORTA Diagram, showing the full search space for **g**.

In order to describe clearly the actions of the Prolog interpreter, we employ a family metaphor to describe the relationships among the goals in the tree. Thus we speak of primary goals as 'mother' goals, and their subgoals as 'daughter' goals. In figure 4, for example, **d1** and **d2** are sister goals with **g** as their mother. To indicate that two subgoals are fully-fledged sisters notice that they are linked together by a 'conjunction bar'. **d3** and **d4** are also sisters with **g** as their mother, but have a different lineage from **d1** and **d2** because they are part of a different clause. Metaphorically we can account for this by attributing different fathers to **d1-d2** as compared with **d3-d4**. These fathers are illustrated by the clause branches **C1** and **C2** in the diagram. Thus, **C2** is a *step-father* of **d2**, and **d2** and **d3** are *step-sisters*. To reflect the chronology of execution, we also note that **d1** is an *older sister* of **d2** (because goal **d1** was 'born' first). Analogously, we refer to **C2** as a *future stepfather* of **d2**.

The family metaphor makes descriptions of backtracking and the cut straightforward. When the interpreter backtracks, the 'backtracking point' (i.e. the place to resume processing) is easily identified in an AORTA diagram. To do this, it is only necessary to first identify the immediately older sister of the just-failed goal. If that older sister is a primitive (a circular node), it itself is the backtracking point. Otherwise, the backtracking point is that older sister's 'youngest surviving heir', i.e. the rightmost, most deeply-nested *clause* status box with a tick in it. When a cut is encountered, three things happen:

1)   older sister goals and their descendants are frozen
2)   future step-fathers are eliminated
3)   the goal succeeds

'Freezing' is described as the process of enshrouding AORTA diagram boxes in a 'frozen cloud' which makes them inaccessible to backtracking during the current invocation. To illustrate this notation in action, consider the following program, which is contrived to illustrated a large number of our conventions in a small space:

```
party(X):- happy(X), birthday(X).
party(X):- friends(X,Y), sad(Y).   % have a party to cheer up a  sad friend

happy(X):-hot, humid, not raining,  !, swimming(X).
happy(X):-cloudy,  watching_tv(X).
happy(X):-cloudy,  having_fun(X).

cloudy.
hot.
humid.   %today's weather

having_fun(tom).
having_fun(sam).

swimming(john).

watching_tv(john).

sad(bill).
sad(sam).

birthday(tom).
birthday(sam).

friends(tom,john).
friends(tom,sam).
```

Figures 5 and 6 represent respectively an intermediate and final AORTA 'snapshot' of the query ?- party(Name).

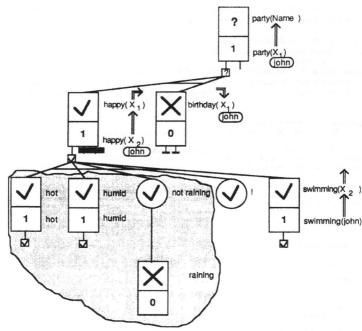

Figure 5 Intermediate AORTA snapshot after the query ?- party(Name). **birthday/1** has just failed.

Let's consider the details which lead up to figure 5. For the top goal **party**, clause one is attempted, which leads to the first clause of **happy** being tried. This in turn leads to **hot** and **humid** succeeding. Notice that the clause counter indicates that both succeed on clause one, and moreover they must both be facts, otherwise we would have seen their subgoals, and they can have had only one clause each because their procedure status boxes show only a single clause branch underneath. Next, **not raining** is attempted, and succeeds because **raining** fails. There is no definition of **raining** in the database, hence no clause counter or clause branches (which indeed would cause a run-time error in many implementations of Prolog). Next, **not** and 'cut' succeed. The result of executing the cut is to freeze any of the cut's older sisters and their descendants (e.g. any subgoals like **raining**), indicated by the *frozen cloud* about them, and to eliminate any other possible future step-fathers, hence the 'strike-out' bar over the second and third clause branches of **happy**. Next, **swimming** succeeds, causing **happy** to succeed and **birthday(john)** to be attempted. **birthday(john)** fails to unify on either of its two clauses, producing the 'dead-end-bars' beneath the clause branches and a 'cross' in the top part of its procedure status box. This is the precise moment at which the snapshot in figure 5 is taken. Now let's look at the remaining steps leading up to the final execution snapshot depicted in figure 6.

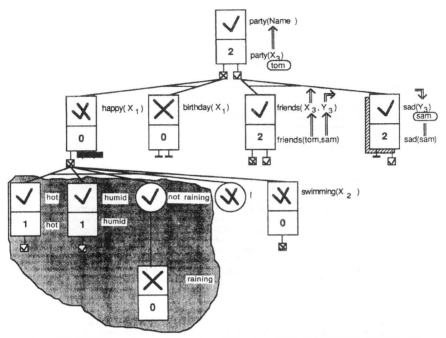

Figure 6 Final AORTA snapshot after the query ?- party(Name). party/1 has just succeeded with **Name** = tom.

At the instant that **birthday** fails, the 'backtracking point' (the 'youngest surviving heir' of the older sister of the just-failed goal) is the *clause* status box corresponding to clause 1 of **swimming** in figure 6. The technique for backtracking is to identify the backtracking point, then turn that tick into a tick/cross combination, and 'carry on'. Since there are no other clauses for **swimming**, it fails at this point (hence the tick/cross combination in its *procedure* status box), and likewise for the cut. There are no other accessible backtracking points (the 'darkening' of the frozen cloud indicates that an attempt was made to backtrack into it), so clause one of **happy** receives a tick/cross combination to show that it initially won only to fail on backtracking. Clause branches two and three of happy have been eliminated by the cut, (for this invocation only, of course), so the *procedure* status box for happy becomes a tick/cross combination as well. The *clause* status box for clause 1 of **party** therefore receives a cross (failure), and clause two of party is now attempted. The **friends** goal succeeds initially on clause one i.e. **friends(tom,john)**, but sad(john) fails. After backtracking (which leaves a tick/cross in the *clause* status box for clause 1 of **friends**), now **friends** succeeds on clause two with **friends(tom,sam)**. This leads to a new invocation of the **sad** goal. To indicate that there has been a previous invocation at the same relative point in the search space, a shaded *ghost status box* is drawn. The goal **sad** now succeeds on clause two, as does **party**. Notice in figure 1 that X_3 (and hence **Name**) is instantiated to **tom**, Y_3 is instantiated to sam and that this instantiation is passed to the goal sad. The goal **sad**(Y_3), with Y_3 instantiated to

sam, matches directly against the fact **sad(sam)** in the database.

The above notational conventions provide a thorough description of Prolog execution. This in turn provides a coherent description for teaching about Prolog as well as a vehicle for implementing practical tracing and debugging facilities for experienced Prolog users. An overview of our Prolog curriculum and a description of our implemented tracing/debugging facilities are presented in the upcoming sections.

3. A textbook, video, and workbook curriculum

The AORTA diagram representation was developed to fulfill a dual need, as stated in section 1. In this section, we want to focus on the way the notation is integrated into our teaching material. Incidentally, in case you have been thinking to yourself, 'Learning Prolog was easy, but this notation is really tricky,' we have at least anecdotal evidence that our students and the users of our graphical tracer feel this way for the first day, and then spontaneously use AORTA diagrams in their own 'scribblings' to help them understand what is really going on.

3.1 Curriculum motivation

We have developed a Prolog course (Eisenstadt et. al., in press) as part of an Alvey/SERC initiative. This initiative identified a need among computing professionals to learn about Prolog in a distance-teaching setting (i.e. in their own environment). We felt that since the 'essentials' of Prolog were adequately covered in Bratko's *Prolog Programming for Artificial Intelligence* (Bratko, 1986), the most appropriate thing to do would be to build upon it by providing detailed diagrammatic 'execution snapshots', re-working some of the more difficult examples, and adding our own emphasis on program design and sophisticated Prolog techniques. We thus concentrated our efforts on clarifying the inner workings of the interpreter, and helping students evolve an execution model which would lead to a clearer (and hopefully less bug-riddled) understanding of Prolog execution. The AORTA notation we had been developing for our advanced graphical debugger appeared to fit the bill, particularly since 'conceptual clarity' was already a high priority objective for that research project.

To encourage wide acceptability of the course, the teaching material works with all the most popular implementations of Prolog, including Quintus Prolog, C-Prolog, LPA MacPROLOG, Arity Prolog, Prolog-2, and even (up to the point where we discuss meta-interpreters and infix notation) Turbo Prolog. For those students who haven't yet decided which commercial Prolog to buy, we include a sample 'core' (Edinburgh syntax) Prolog interpreter on a 5.25" IBM-PC compatible floppy disk so that they can get started immediately. The interpreter is minimal, in that it has no editing environment, but it will run all the examples in the course. We also include full source code listings of all the examples used in the course, both in hard copy and on the course disk.

3.2 Course objectives

Students completing our 80-hour study package are expected to achieve the following objectives:

- Use any of a range of hardware/software configurations to enter, run, and debug sophisticated Prolog programs.
- Explain the practical significance of logic programming terminology (e.g. 'functor', 'unification', 'backtracking').
- Implement a program to determine whether a person is eligible to receive free prescriptions.
- Implement a travel planning program which can propose times, flights, and routes for an airline trip from city A to city B via intermediate cities.
- Improve existing planning programs so that they avoid 'endless loops'
- Implement an expert system shell which can answer 'why' and 'how' queries about its own

reasoning process.

These objectives are addressed through a graded series of presentations and exercises contained in the material outlined in the next sections.

3.3 Course contents

The course comprises a set of course notes, a workbook, a set book, a 120-minute video cassette, and a floppy disk. The main study material is 160 pages in length, and is subdivided as follows (only the top-level headings are shown, along with comments about the underlying pedagogical principles):

Part I: Essential Prolog

1 Prolog in twenty minutes

> The basics of Prolog are easy, so students are launched into examples based on airline flight reservations straight away.

2 Program development

> Here we introduce the concept of a conservative 'design/edit/invoke Prolog/load/pose queries' cycle

3 Behind the scenes

> The declarative and procedural views of Prolog are presented, and a model of Prolog execution, based on AORTA diagrams, is introduced. Exercises include such things as identifying backtracking points by locating nodes in an AORTA diagram, and working through a series of unification problems.

4 Building problem solving programs from scratch

> We provide a handle for getting into a good mental style for solving problems in Prolog. A suggested technique involves a series of steps including: identify problem area; consider an elementary concrete case; sketch objects and relations; invent functors and arguments; encode the sketch in terms of functors/arguments; invent problem query; decompose problem into easy and hard variants; add facts or rules to cope with easy variants; add rules to cope with main subproblem; generalise query to take more variables; test program; use richer structures; etc.

5 Understanding recursion

> The concept of 'procedure invocation' is explored in detail, and a series of AORTA snapshots is used to explain recursion. Video 1 follows this up in an animated sequence.

Part II: The Power of Prolog Representation

6 Representation style and deductive reasoning

> We discuss problems of choosing 'good' functors and arguments, and links to logical deduction.

7 Elementary list manipulation

> Basic list processing, **member/2**, and lots of unification exercises are presented.

8 Using structures

> We describe more stylistic issues such as data abstraction and 'good representation' involving structures.

9 A closer look at unification

> Some subtle cases of unification are described in detail. Bratko's 'Monkey and Banana' problem is illustrated step-by-step to show a particularly tricky case of shared variables becoming instantiated in a counter-intuitive way. Lots of AORTA snapshots are used here.

10 Special list processing techniques

> We show how to use an 'accumulator' argument to perform cycle detection, and how to use 'successive instantiation' (building up a list structure in the clause head) to return results. Video 2 amplifies these points with extensive AORTA diagram animations. Students are asked to augment Bratko's travel-planning program so that it deals correctly with cycle detection.

11 Generators and failure-driven loops

> A specific set of programming cliches is introduced and explicated.

12 Reshaping the search space: the cut, not/1, and once/1

We use AORTA diagrams and the family metaphor to show precisely what happens when a cut is encountered, and how this can be used to implement (a form of) negation. Exercises require students to draw 'frozen clouds' and to 'chop off' clause branches on AORTA diagrams to see precisely the effect and scope of the cut. Video 3 uses more AORTA animations to reinforce these concepts.

Part III: An Expert System Shell

13 Choosing a representation and building a basic shell

A 'rational reconstruction' of Bratko's expert system shell is presented, starting from a minimal meta-level interpreter. The accompanying Video 4 shows an expert travel planning program (developed by Expert Systems International for Thomas Cook) in action, and relates it to the shell and travel planning programs used in the course.

14 'How' explanations and truth values

The primitive shell is augmented to deal with 'how' explanations and explicitly-stored negative facts.

15 Other enhancements: query-the-user and 'why'

The shell is spruced up to deal with interactions with the user and a sensible 'why' explanation facility.

The above notes are accompanied by a workbook of exercise material, 48 pages in length. The workbook includes a 'how to get started' guide, which summarizes this differences among the 10 most popular implementations of Prolog. There are lots of 'unfilled' AORTA diagrams for the students to fill in as part of their worked exercises. The accompanying video material (120 minutes) relies extensively on AORTA diagram notation, and presents numerous animated sequences. A separate 16-page set of video notes is used to help the students to work through some of the exemplary problems contained in several stop/start video sequences.

4 The Graphical Tracer Implementation

It is one thing to have a 'paper and pencil' execution model, but quite another to have a consistent implementation of it running on a computer. Normally, there are very different constraints influencing what is appropriate to present in text, on video, and in a working computer-based trace package. Our feeling was that we should present a consistent story line across different media as far as was humanly possible. This section describes the graphical tracer as currently implemented.

4.1 The Long Distance View (LDV)

A practical tracer poses an interesting set of constraints for the Prolog environment designer. The search tree for serious Prolog programs can be enormous, and may thwart the designer who has a nice 'toy' paper and pencil execution model. Our aim has been to make our AORTA diagram the heart of a practical Prolog tracing package aimed at experienced Prolog users. The key lies in the use of a large graphics display and a compressed long-distance view of the AORTA diagram which can be zoomed in upon to provide the kind of detail described above.

The long distance view (LDV) shows the *execution space* of the program (as opposed to the full *search space*). This is done by means of a schematized AND/OR tree in which individual nodes summarize the outcome of a call to a particular procedure. Something must always be sacrificed for the benefit of full global perspective, so we eliminate the clause counter and detailed clause head information (clause branches and clause status boxes) of the AORTA diagrams. This leaves us with a nearly-traditional AND/OR tree, but with enriched 'nodes' in the form of collapsed status boxes. To provide the most meaningful display of information in the smallest space, we rely on colour in our colour-workstation implementation. Thus ticks are green, indicating success, crosses are red, indicating failure, tick/cross combinations are pink ('nearly red'). In the collapsed status box, it is sufficient to display just the colour, e.g. a very small fully-shaded green box instead of a box with a hard-to-see green tick in it. We simulate this in our black and white display using the correspondence shown in figure 7.

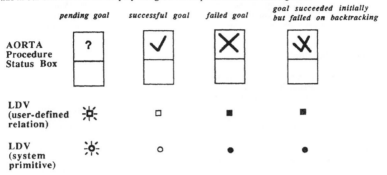

Figure 7 Correspondence between full status boxes and collapsed status boxes, used to simulate colour. Filled in white = green (success); black shading = red (failure); grey shading = pink (success followed by failure on backtracking).

Given the program for **party** in section 2.3, the LDV is shown in figure 8.

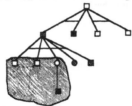

Figure 8 Long Distance View showing the execution of the query ?- **party(Name)**.

The concise manner of the LDV representation facilitates the analysis of very large Prolog programs. At the current resolution of our Apollo workstation displays, we can fit an execution space of 2,500 nodes on a single screen, with the individual status shadings/colours still discriminable. Even if the execution space is too large to be meaningfully displayed within a single graphics pane, the user is able to scroll around the pane, selecting the area of the tree which he or she wishes to look at. A facility will be provided that allows users continually to monitor which part of the tree they are currently looking at.

Associated with such a view are strong notions of gestalt throughout the tree. Similar relations with similar arguments and calling patterns will produce similar shapes of execution space throughout the entire LDV. Likewise certain lumps of code will have characteristic tree 'shapes' associated with them. Put yourself in the position of a programmer who has been developing the associated code over a period of days, and has become accustomed to the repetition of certain familiar shapes. We believe that ascribing functionality to large branches of the tree will be straightforward, and thus, locating 'items of interest' in the tree is surprisingly easy. Such items of interest can, of course, be inspected more closely, even while preserving a considerable degree of surrounding context. In section 4.2 we describe our 'selective highlighting' facility which enables the programmer rapidly to locate nodes in the tree which satisfy some particular constraint or behavioural description.

In the future it is intended that the user may be able to specify various graphical shorthand notations in order to simplify the display. Currently we cater for concepts based on the notion of the *shallow cliche*, e.g. simple tail recursion, as in the classic **member/2**. We hope in the future to be able to provide the user with the facility to abstract arbitrary amounts of code via 'graphical portray' declarations made alongside source code.

4.2 Selective Highlighting

When debugging a program a frequent observation we have made is that it would be nice if we could ask questions like 'where did variable **X** get instantiated to such-and-such' or 'where in the program does foo get called by **bar**' and our debugger would immediately tell us. To accommodate this wish we provide a Selective Highlighting option in the LDV display. This option allows you to specify a given relation or argument(s), or combination of relation and arguments for highlighting. This may be further constrained by specifying a similar combination for a parent goal that both child and parent have to satisfy. As a further constraint you can specify a legal Prolog goal that must also be satisfied for the highlight condition to hold. When you specify such a combination, this results in those nodes in the tree that satisfy the conditions being highlighted. For example, suppose we have a bug in a production rule interpreter. The symptoms are that a rule, **rule12**, that we expected to be used is inexplicably overlooked by some goal, say **select_rule**, but only when the calling goal **rule_cycle** has an arbitrary 'debug flag' set. To debug this we need to be able to find out exactly what is going on when this happens. Using the selective highlight facility we can ask to see every time the goal **select_rule** is called with the list of rules **Rule_set** as its argument, by the mother goal **rule_cycle**, with one of its arguments set to be the flag **trace**; however since we're only interested in the times this occurs when the rule **rule12** is in the rule set we can specify the further constraint **member(rule12,Rule_set)**. The result of such an action is to cause the specified items to be highlighted *wherever* this combination occurs in the LDV. The facility allows for rapid location and tracing of given relations or variables. It also allows the user to effectively spy a variable or a particular variable instantiation and observe its behaviour retrospectively in the trace. Using different shapes for highlighting (or colours in our coloured display implementation) several things can be highlighted at once, making it possible, for example, to consider occasions when **rule_cycle** got called without its trace flag set but with **rule12** still in the rule set.

4.3 Replay

The nature of backtracking means that certain aspects of program execution, e.g. new calls to previously failed goals, can best be explain dynamically. We deal with this problem by providing a replay facility whereby the user can see the dynamic execution of the program through the LDV execution space or AORTA diagrams, clearly indicating failure and subsequent backtracking, re-attempting of goals, subsequent failure, resatisfaction or retries. The replay facility thus allows the user to view the execution space at any given time, or at any particular goal invocation. The user can control the speed of the replay with slow motion and single step options being available.

Our replay capability is possible only because we store an exhaustive history of the program's execution. Our experience is that being able to home in quickly on buggy code is sufficiently rewarding to justify the storage overheads of history preservation. Endless loops must, of course, be trapped for example by a depth bound interpreter using stack monitoring (à la Shapiro,1982).

The replay facility allows the user to step through a piece of execution history and reason out what actually happened. This is true especially when the user wants to figure out a complex case of backtracking and wishes to find out where final or interim instantiations came about. The user can tell the program to stop at a particular point, which may either be pre-specified or else indicated via a mouse click 'live' during replay. The utility thus allows the user to effectively freeze the program at any step of its execution and use any of the other existing tools on the program at that point, or to step backwards or forwards one more 'frame', or to carry on with the execution.

The user can also watch the program re-run as many times as necessary, but because we display the execution space continually the user can watch backtracking and its scope 'live' as it happens. In the event of extensive backtracking which eventually succeeds we can imagine seeing large areas of successful nodes (green or white) turn to failure (red or black) until finally the process stops and the successful nodes starts to regain their lost territory. The whole process can be stopped and frozen at an instant to allow for closer inspection by a mouse click. What is also important here is for the *gestalt* to be right, i.e. for the display not only to be informative, but also to feel like an accurate version of the underlying Prolog machine.

In the preceding section we introduced the notion of a *ghost status box*, where the ghost indicated that a previous or future invocation of a goal in the same place in the execution space has/will take place. It is possible to turn the time clock back to that point where the ghost goal was about to be attempted by simply clicking on the shaded part of its status box. In this way information about backtracking through conjuncts (e.g. in a permutation algorithm where you have a generator and test relations as sister goals) may be readily gained.

4.4 Zooming

Zooming links the LDV and AORTA representations by allowing the user to switch between the two, enabling the user to zoom in on the execution/unification history of the clause from the LDV. In this way the complementary nature of the two views is emphasised. The LDV allows the user to view the program from a clear perspective, uncluttered by unwanted information, and explore its behaviour in an orderly, informed manner. Switching from the LDV of a particular node to the AORTA view thus increases the amount and type of information available to the user. Not only is this AORTA view useful for teaching novices, but it also (in conjunction with the LDV and zooming) allows the expert rapid and easy access to a large amount of unification history and surrounding information.

The 'close-up' view shows not only the 'focussed upon goal', but also that goal's mother, step-fathers, sisters, and children. It thus provides both clarity of detail and some surrounding context within which to perform debugging. We call this our 'three ply close up view', because three generations of goals are visible at once. The replay facilities described in section 4.3 are also available in the close up view, which means that the precise details of the unification history can be observed if necessary.

Since zooming and highlighting requests always begin with the LDV, all the perspective information associated with the LDV is available at the point of choice, allowing the user clearly to understand the context of the code which is being observed 'close up', thus removing the 'forest-vs-trees' problem associated with conventional 'spy' packages. In such packages, once a 'spied' goal is reached it may no longer be clear how you arrived there, how the instantiations of the variables have been derived, what state the program is in, what side-effects have taken place, whether the program has only reached this point on backtracking, and (if a 'redo' is involved) the nature, cause, and scope of the backtracking involved. By the combination of the LDV, AORTA, zooming, selective highlighting and replay facilities, the user may more readily understand the state of the program, and thus arrive rapidly at the source of problematic bugs.

4.5 A worked example of the graphical tracer

The following program is a buggy quicksort:

```
qsort([],[]).                              %the sort of an empty list is an empty list
qsort([X|Xs],Result):-                     %sort list with head X, tail Xs, to give Result
      split(Xs,X,Lo,Hi),                   %split Xs around X intoLower and Higher
      qsort(Lo,Sorted_Lo),                 %recursively sort Lo list into Sorted_Lo
      qsort(Hi,Sorted_Hi),                 %recursively sort Hi list into Sorted_Hi
      append(Sorted_Lo,[X|Sorted_Hi],Result). %glue together in Result

split([X|Xs],Crit,[X|Lo],Hi):-             %X is head of Lo list if
      X < Crit,                            %X is lower than the split criterion
      split(Xs,Crit,Lo,Hi).                %recursively split rest of list
split([X|Xs],Crit,Lo,[X|Hi]):-             %X is head of Hi list if
      X > Crit,                            %X is greater than split criterion
      split(Xs,Crit,Lo,Hi).                %recursively split rest of list

append([X|Xs],Y,[X|Zs]):-                  %place head on front of output list
      append(Xs,Y,Zs).                     %process rest of Xs recursively
append([],Ys,Ys).                          %stopping condition,leave Ys alone
```

If we pose the query ?- **qsort([2,1,3],P).** to the Prolog top-level, then the query will fail. Invoking the graphical tracer, the user is presented with the LDV shown in figure 9.

Figure 9 LDV for the query **qsort([2,1,3],P).**

From the above diagram we can immediately see that the top goal **qsort** only attempted one sub-goal. This must have been its first, **split**. Now as **split** only calls itself or the primitives > and <, they are clearly the rest of the tree that we're seeing, thus it must be one of them that's causing the error. To confirm this we can highlight all occurrences of the goal **split** called by the goal **split** itself, i.e. all the recursive invocations of **split**. This is illustrated in figure 10.

Figure 10. Selective highlighting of all occurrences of the goal **split** called by the goal **split** (i.e. just the recursive calls). The arrow (which is not part of the LDV) shows the node on which we're about to zoom.

From figure 10 there are a large number of things that we can observe about the program. We can see that there were two recursive calls of **split**. Notice also that we can see a characteristic shape for the **split** goal: it calls a primitive in one or the other of its clauses, and if that is successful calls itself, leaving a characteristic shape that we could spot in a much larger trace if we knew **split** was to be called. The initially successful primitive goals are plain by their shading in the diagram, i.e. they must have failed on backtracking. In such circumstances we can always also identify the source of such backtracking: it must be the youngest sister of the goals that are grey-shaded, or the youngest subgoal of that goal following on down the tree. Thus from the LDV alone we can spot that it must be the youngest **split** goal that failed and caused the backtracking that led to the failure of the **qsort** goal. To confirm this and to shed more light on the actual cause of the failure we can zoom in on the node. Since the suspect doesn't have any children, we might as well zoom on the parent node to obtain more contextual information. This is the node to which the cursor arrow is pointing in figure 10. Our selective highlighting facility allows us to 'freeze' the action at the moment just *before* the first failure of **split**. The result of zooming is shown in figure 11. The 'faded out' lines depict the execution space which will be traversed later.

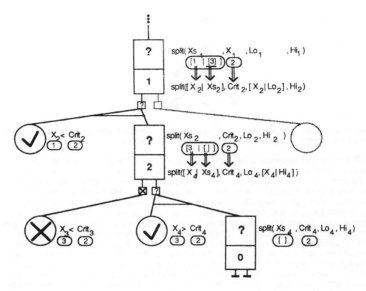

Figure 11 AORTA produced by a zoom on the node pointed to by the arrow in figure 10. This node is the **split** node in the middle of the diagram.

The AORTA diagram reveals that the youngest **split** node, the one which we suspected from the LDV, failed to unify on either of its two clauses. Thus we can see that the null case of **split** is not catered for, leading to the failure of the goal and the subsequent failure of the primary goal **qsort([2,1,3],P).** The AORTA zoom thus confirms our suspicions from the LDV that the final **split** goal was the cause of the failure, and further rapidly indicated the reason for this failure.

In our current implementation, only relation names are shown next to the procedure status boxes, with argument and unification details available as 'popup' options. More detailed examples, including traces and replays involving an expert system and a small compiler (involving much larger execution spaces), are described in Eisenstadt & Brayshaw (1986).

5 Conclusions

Our aim has been to reconcile a global view of Prolog program execution with the 'truth' about unification and clause selection. Moreover, we have wanted to satisfy both the needs of novices learning Prolog and the needs of expert Prolog users writing and debugging very large programs. These intentions have, in turn, led us along a pathway of 'creative tension' to satisfy somewhat contradictory constraints. The key ingredients of our approach have been (i) appreciation of the power of gestalt patterns, (ii) recognition of the need (and the ability) to display thousands of nodes at a time, (iii) enhancement of traditional AND/OR tree branches with individual clause details, (iv) enhancement of and/or tree nodes with goal 'status boxes' and (v) ability to vary the type of detail being investigated with the particular grain size, rather than using a physical 'zoom'.

The result of our effort has been a complete 'cradle-to-grave' environment in the form of text, video, and a computer-implemented trace package. The integrated environment conveys a consistent 'party line' in a manner that makes execution intuitively clear and at the same time provides real hands-on debugging power for experienced users. We eagerly await empirical studies of this integrated environment to analyse its real effectiveness.

6 References.

Bratko I., *Prolog Programming for Artificial Intelligence*. Reading, MA: Addison-Wesley, 1986.

Brown M.H., and Sedgewick R. Progress Report: Brown University Instructional Computing Laboratory, *ACM SIGCSE Bulletin 16, 1,(February 1984)*

Bundy, A., Pain, H., Brna, P., and Lynch, L. A proposed Prolog story. DAI Research Paper 283, Department of Artificial Intelligence, University of Edinburgh, 1986.

Byrd, L. Understanding the control flow of Prolog programs. In S-Å Tarnlund (Ed.), *Proceedings of the 1980 Logic Programming Workshop*, pp. 127-138, 1980.

Carroll J.M. & Thomas J.C. Metaphor and the Cognitive Representation of Computing Systems, *IEEE Transactions on systems, man, and cybernetics*, SMC-12(2), 1982.

Clocksin W.F., and Mellish C.S. *Programming in Prolog (First Edition)*, New York: Springer-Verlag 1981.

Clocksin W.F., and Mellish C.S. *Programming in Prolog (Second Edition)*, New York: Springer-Verlag 1984.

Coombs M.J., and Stell, J.G. A model for debugging Prolog by symbolic execution: the separation of specification and procedure. Research Report MMIGR137, Department of Computer Science, University of Strathclyde, 1985.

Dewar A.D., and Cleary J.G. Graphical display of complex information within a Prolog debugger, *Int. J. Man-Machine studies* (1986), **25** 503-521.

DuBoulay, J.B.H., O'Shea, T., and Monk, J. The black box inside the glass box: presenting computing concepts to novices. *International Journal of Man Machine Studies*, 14 (3), 237-249, 1981.

Eisenstadt, M., and Brayshaw, M. The Transparent Prolog Machine (TPM): an execution model and graphical debugger for logic programming. *Journal of Logic Programming*, in press. Also available as Technical Report no. 21, Human Cognition Research Laboratory, The Open University, Milton Keynes, 1986.

Eisenstadt, M., Dixon, M., Kahney, H., and Kriwaczek, F. *Intensive Prolog*. Milton Keynes, U.K.: Open University Press (in press).

Halasz F., and Moran T.P.. Analogy Considered Harmful, in *Proceedings of Human factors in Computing Systems*, Gaithersburg, Maryland, March 15-17th., 1982.

Hardy S. A new software environment for list-processing and logic programming, in T. O'Shea, and M. Eisenstadt (Eds.), *Artificial Intelligence: Tools, Techniques, and Applications*. New York: Harper & Row, 1984.

Rajan T.. APT: A Principled Design for an Animated View of Program Execution for Novice Programmers, Technical Report No. 19, Human Cognition Research Laboratory, Open

University, Milton Keynes, December, 1986.

Shapiro E.Y. *Algorithmic Program Debugging*. Cambridge, MA: MIT Press, 1982.

Sterling L. and Shapiro E.Y. *The Art of Prolog: Advanced Programming Tecniques,* Cambridge, MA: MIT Press, 1986.

Taylor J.,Programming in Prolog: An in-depth study of problems for beginners learning to program in Prolog. PhD. Thesis, Cognitive Studies Programme, University of Sussex, 1987.

23

BOXER: A RECONSTRUCTIBLE COMPUTATIONAL MEDIUM

ANDREA A. DISESSA
University of California, Berkeley

HAROLD ABELSON
Massachusetts Institute of Technology

Writing is an everyday activity for most people in our society — whether it be in the form of a list, a letter, or a scribbled note in the margin of a book — even though few possess expert writing skills. Within a generation, programming will also be a part of the everyday lives of many people who do not have expert programming skills. Naturally, popular programming languages will differ from current general-purpose computer languages, which are designed primarily for programming professionals. Indeed, the very idea of what it means to "program" will change as we come to recognize that, as with writing, the significance of programming derives not only from the carefully crafted works of a few professionals, but also from the casual jottings of "ordinary" people.

This article presents a view of what programming could be like as a common everyday activity for most people. The central image is that of controlling a reconstructible medium, much like written language, but with dramatically extended interactive capabilities. We begin with some general observations about programming in this context and continue with a description of Boxer, a reconstructible medium that we are designing for particular applications in education.

RECONSTRUCTIBLE MEDIA

Computers are commonly used for text processing, although most text written using computers is still intended to be ultimately printed on paper. As more and more people have access to computers, it becomes increasingly worthwhile to exploit the possibilities of the computer screen itself as an expressive medium. It is easy to imagine interactive books with elaborately structured text, moving illustrations, built-in simulations, and special-purpose dynamic tools whose interactive capabilities go far beyond canned presentations. For instance, a science textbook on optics could include text with multiple organizations and multiple means of access; moving illustrations of the wave properties of light; simulations that perform ray tracing through lenses and mirrors; databases of optical properties of various substances; and graphing and analysis tools for processing experimental data gathered through photo-electric sensors.

A computer-based medium for constructing such a book may seem like a great advance over present-day printed media. Yet, if viewed only as a way to produce fancy books, it lacks an essential quality necessary for a truly popular medium: the possibility for personal construction by users at all levels of competence. The optics book represents the "grand image" of the medium, such as one would see in commercially produced textbooks or in a finished novel. A popular medium of expression, however, must also be usable in ways that might suit the personal needs of children, teachers, or other noncomputer specialists.

In particular, a popular computational medium must be easy to program. In the hypothetical optics book, for example, all elements of the book, beyond simply entering the text, would be created through some sort of programming. We would like everyone to have access to the same kinds of tools used for constructing the book. The medium should also serve beginners and casual users, even if they never reach the stage of producing an exemplar of the grand image.

One major benefit of programmability is that even professionally produced items become changeable, adaptable, fragmentable, and quotable in ways that present software is not. Not only would professionals be able to construct grand images, but others would be able to *reconstruct* personalized versions of these same images. Giving all users access to the behind-the-scenes organization of an interactive book means that new ideas — the dynamic equivalent of famous quotations — can enter the culture with the medium.

Beyond interactive books, a reconstructible medium should allow people to build personalized computational tools and easily modify tools they have gotten from others. This concept is in strong contrast to the current situation in applications software — professionals are designing tools only for large populations with a common need. Since only experts can craft such systems or tune them to particular purposes, designers must predict every possible variation that users might need, and supply often ad hoc methods of selecting among options. With a reconstructible medium, there is no need to play guessing games to this extent, and changes to any application tool can be made uniformly — through programming.

PROGRAMMING LANGUAGES REVISITED

Most research into the design of programming languages has been in the tradition of programming as a way for experts to get computers to perform complex tasks efficiently and reliably. Programming as a means of controlling an interactive medium sets very different needs and constraints on languages. Here are some traditional desiderata for programming languages that ultimately are not of major importance in creating a popular medium:

- Formal simplicity—a computer scientist's or a mathematician's measures of simplicity are simply not at issue. A better criterion is accessibility to a seven-year-old child.
- Efficiency—there are so many other important attributes of a language for controlling an interactive medium that efficiency must take a backseat. If present-generation machines are now powerful enough, we can wait for the next.
- Verifiability—rigor is not a primary requirement of an expressive medium. Much more important is the ability to accommodate a wide variety of expressive styles.
- Uniformity—the demands of multifunctionality are great, and it is likely that some degree of uniformity will have to be sacrificed.

More telling is what emerges as important to a broadly based computational medium:

- Understandability—this is a primary and unavoidable goal if nonexperts are to successfully use this new medium.
- Tuned toward common, directly useful functionalities—if the medium is to be useful and widely used, it will have to seem more "familiar"; for example, basing data structures on text and pictures rather than on abstract, though perhaps more general objects such as arrays or lists.
- Tuned toward small tasks—the ability to implement simple ideas easily is much more important in this context than the ability to do complex tasks efficiently.
- Interaction—user interfaces are often considered to be separable from programming language semantics and almost an afterthought in language design. Worse, most present languages assume only character-stream input and output. A useful medium must be much more flexibly interactive.

BOXER

Much of Boxer's character is determined by two key principles—the *spatial metaphor* and *naive realism.*

People have a great deal of commonsense knowledge about space that can be used to make computers more comprehensible. The spatial metaphor encourages people to interpret the organization of the computational system in terms of spatial relationships.[1] Using a Boxer system is like moving around in a large two-dimensional space. All computational objects are represented in terms of boxes, which are regions on the screen that contain text, graphics, or other boxes. Boxes within boxes represent hierarchical structures. For example, (1), a variable is a box containing the variable's value; for a compound data structure (such as a record with named fields) the variable contains other variables; (2) a program is a box containing the program text; internal subprocedures and variables (as in block-structured programs) are represented as subboxes. When you enter a box (by moving the cursor into it), you gain access to its contents. Thus, any box can be a special-purpose environment with its own data and behavior (programs).

Naive realism is an extension of the "what you see is what you have" idea that has become commonplace in the design of text editors and spreadsheets, but not for programming languages. The point is that users should be able to pretend that what they see on the screen is their computational world in its entirety. For example, (1) any text that appears on the screen—whether typed by the system, entered by the user, or constructed by a program—can be moved, copied, modified, or (if it is program text) evaluated; (2) you can change the value of a variable simply by altering the contents of the variable box on the screen. If a program modifies the value of a variable, the contents of the box will be automatically updated on the screen. In general, there is no need to query the system to display its state, nor any need to invoke a state-change operation to affect the system indirectly.

Following are some highlights of Boxer's most important features. Our aim is to suggest how users can move smoothly from simple text and data manipulation, through modifying and producing personal computational tools, to dealing with larger systems such as interactive books. Of key interest is the way in which the basic box structure is elaborated to support many important functions of a reconstructible medium. (Additional examples and discussions of the theoretical and empirical motivations for specific choices in Boxer's design can be found in [3] and [4].)

---

[1]Boxer's use of the spatial metaphor was encouraged by work on spatial data management systems at the MIT Department of Architecture [2].

Boxer currently exists as a prototype, including all of the features described below, implemented on Symbolics and Texas Instruments Lisp machines. We are about to start implementation on a more modest machine so that we can begin testing the system extensively in a variety of settings.

Boxes and Text

The text shown in Figure 1 is part of a tutorial on Boxer, organized using boxes. Note particularly the way in which, by shrinking and expanding boxes, detail can be hidden or shown for brief inspection. By expanding a box to full screen, the user effectively enters a subenvironment (box). Figure 1 shows how essentially all of the mechanics of making, inspecting, and modifying boxes can be learned and used without knowing anything at all about programming.

At first glance, boxes may seem to be nothing more than a variant on the windows used in many display-oriented systems. Windows, however, have no computational semantics except as places to display interaction with a program or application — a window's position on the screen and its relation to other windows do not generally reflect any information about the objects in the computational system. Boxes, in contrast, *are* the system's computational objects, and box containment reflects meanings such as

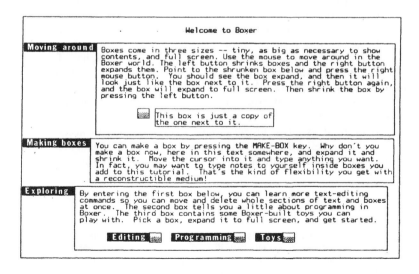

A mouse is used as a pointing device to move around the system and to shrink and expand boxes.

FIGURE 1   A "Page" from a Boxer Tutorial.

subprocedures as parts of procedures and records as parts of databases. The part-whole relation implied by box containment is fully operational, and the box structure can be traversed, inspected, and changed by programs as well as manually. Boxer's spatial metaphor is a recognition that spatial relations are extraordinarily expressive and should not be wasted by being used only for transient needs (where there is space to pop up a window) or by divorcing spatial relations from fundamental semantics. Similarly, the concept of naive realism dictates that one should see computational objects, not just interfaces to them.

Simple Programming

Figure 2 shows some simple Boxer programs that draw designs using the turtle graphics commands introduced in the educational computer language Logo.[2] It is important to observe how text, programs, and graphics have been intermixed to produce a tutorial about drawing using arcs; note in particular that the bottom line of the figure is a menu of commands for the user to try. This menu was created simply by typing the commands in place and leaving them on the screen to be run or modified — the principle of naive realism dictates that anything that appears on the screen should be manipulable in this way. Here, as indicated by the mouse cursor, the user has selected to run the command SUN with an input of 0.7. The graphics output appears in a graphics box. Graphics boxes can also be named, copied, and moved using Boxer's editor interface.

Two of the procedure boxes in Figure 2, ARCLEFT and SUN, have been expanded to illustrate the form of Boxer procedures. Note that SUN contains an internal procedure RAY; box containment is being used here to implement block structuring of procedures. In general, the scoping rules of Boxer — definitions are accessible inside a box, but not outside of it — allow for boxes to be used as environments that users enter to gain access to procedures and data defined inside. Assimilating the computational idea of scoping into the intuitive notion of "inside" is central to the spatial metaphor.

---

[2]Boxer is in many ways an extension of Logo. Simple Boxer procedures — especially those for graphics — resemble Logo procedures. Our work in Boxer has been motivated largely by a desire to extend Logo-style activities to a much broader range of possibilities. Although Logo took very seriously the benefits of making programming a popular activity, it did not begin with the image of a medium encompassing written language, hierarchical structures, databases, and interactive graphical tools. (See [6] for an overview of Logo, and [1] for a development of geometry based on turtle graphics.)

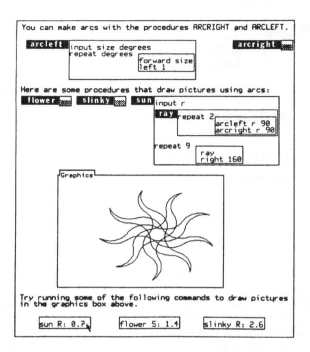

FIGURE 2   Turtle Graphics in Boxer.

A Simple Database Tool

The box named **PHONE-BOOK,** shown in Figure 3, is a simple utility for storing and retrieving phone numbers. When a user types a name in the box marked **NAME** and presses the **FUNCTION-1 KEY,** the corresponding phone number will appear in the box marked **NUMBER. PHONE-BOOK** contains a database called **LIST,** which is a box containing other boxes with a standard format: subboxes **NAME, ADDRESS,** and **PHONE.** The boxes in the database, as well as the **NAME** and **NUMBER** boxes, are *data boxes.* Marking a box as data indicates that, when the box is used by a program, the contents are to be interpreted as literal text rather than as a program to

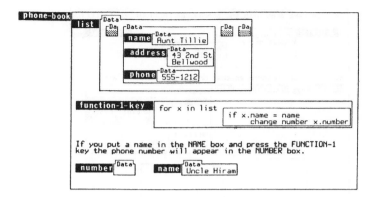

FIGURE 3   The PHONE-BOOK Box.

This box is a utility for finding phone numbers. Its local database is a box called LIST that contains subboxes with a standard format. The procedure named FUNCTION-1-KEY will be run whenever the FUNCTION-1 key is pressed.

be executed. (This is similar to the use of QUOTE in Lisp.) Named data boxes are variables.

The FUNCTION-1 -KEY is a procedure that looks up the designated name and supplies the corresponding phone number.[3] Boxer contains pattern-matching capabilities that make the lookup operation trivial, but we have written the procedure here in a way that illustrates some more basic Boxer capabilities: A FOR loop steps through the LIST, searching for a box whose NAME field matches the designated NAME. When the box is found, the NUMBER box is changed to the corresponding PHONE field. (There are obvious improvements to be made here, such as stopping the iteration when a match is found, and using an ordered database, but we have chosen to show only the very simplest procedure.) Note the use of the dot syntax < box-name > . < subbox-name > for specifying named subboxes of a box.

Boxer's naive realism automatically supplies an input/output mechanism for the procedure. The boxes NAME and NUMBER are ordinary variables. Typing something in the NAME box automatically sets the variable NAME that is referenced by the procedure. Similarly, when the procedure changes the variable NUMBER, the new contents will automatically appear on the screen in the NUMBER box.

In a user's overall Boxer environment, PHONE-BOOK is a special-purpose subenvironment. Boxer's scoping rules dictate that the binding of

---

[3]The use of -KEY as a suffix automatically binds the operation to the specified key. Any key can be bound in this way.

the function key to the lookup procedure will be active only when the user enters the **PHONE-BOOK** box. Other boxes in the system are free to bind this function key (or any other key) for their own purposes.

Extending the Database Tool

It is easy to make personalized extensions to the **PHONE-BOOK** as illustrated in Figure 4. The point of the phone-book example is not that everyone should write a phone-number-fetching procedure from scratch; rather, we want to illustrate how Boxer enables people to build or modify their own little tools of whatever idiosyncratic sort. Boxer is an environment designed for invention and functionality in little pieces, where understanding the system better in any particular context results in more power generally. For example, learning how to change the value of a variable is far more than a trick for the **PHONE-BOOK** program; it is an essential feature that allows users to modify any piece of Boxer.

Objects and Message Passing

The graphics box in Figure 5a is the home of two graphical objects (known in Boxer as *sprites)* named Minnie and Mickey. Also shown is the **STAR** procedure, which takes two parameters, **SIZE** and **ANGLE**, and draws a symmetric shape by repeating 360/ANGLE times the following sequence: Call the procedure **STEP** with an input of **SIZE**, and then the procedure **RIGHT** with an input of **ANGLE**. In the figure, Minnie and Mickey have

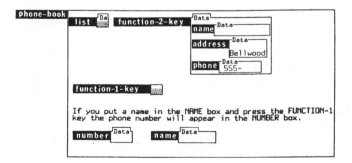

When the FUNCTION-2 key is pressed, Boxer will insert at the cursor a template for a record with address and phone fields partially filled in that can be added to the LIST. In order to make this extension, the user needed only to type the template and label it with the name FUNCTION-2-KEY. (The template shown here is especially useful if you happen to know many people who live in Bellwood whose phone numbers begin with 555.)

FIGURE 4   Extension to the PHONE-BOOK.

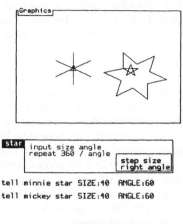

<pre>
┌Graphics┐
</pre>

<pre>
star input size angle
      repeat 360 / angle
                         step size
                         right angle
</pre>

```
tell minnie star SIZE:40 ANGLE:60
tell mickey star SIZE:40 ANGLE:60
```

This graphics box contains two sprites—Minnie (the small triangle) and Mickey (the small five-pointed star). Each sprite has been told to run the procedure called STAR. The designs drawn are different, because each sprite has its own definition of the STEP procedure when executing STAR.

FIGURE 5a   A Graphics Box.

each been told to perform **STAR** with a **SIZE** of 40 and an **ANGLE** of 60. Observe that the two sprites draw different designs. This is because, as we shall see below, Minnie and Mickey use different **STEP** procedures when executing **STAR**.

Turtle graphics, and the sprite extensions that appear in some versions of Logo, are known to be congenial forms of interaction for simple graphics programming. But the fact that the state of these graphical objects cannot be seen and directly manipulated violates the naive realism principle. Boxer is therefore arranged so that a graphics box is only an alternate form for an ordinary box structure that includes sprites as subboxes. Attributes of sprites—their position, heading, speed (if in motion), and shape (expressed as the procedure that draws the shape) are visible and manipulable as ordinary variables. Changes to these variables, whether by direct editing or under program control, automatically affect the graphical representation.

Figure 5b shows the nongraphical (data) version of the same graphics box with its resident sprites Minnie and Mickey. Minnie and Mickey each have their own version of the procedure STEP, which they use when they perform **STAR**. Naturally, additional local procedures or variables can be added at any time simply by entering the sprite box and typing the definition in place.

Packaging local data and procedures together and organizing computations by sending messages to these packages via TELL are paradigms of *object-oriented programming,* popularized by the language Smalltalk [5]. Boxer's spatial metaphor assimilates such packaging to box containment, thereby making the object structure visible and concrete. Object-oriented programming in Boxer is not limited to sprites and graphics. Any box can be told remotely to execute any command that might ordinarily be locally executed from within that box.

Point-and-Poke Interaction

Figure 5b also reveals that Minnie contains a procedure named M-CLICK. A sprite's M-CLICK procedure is automatically executed whenever the middle mouse button is clicked over the sprite in graphics presentation. In this case, pointing at Minnie with the mouse and clicking the button will make her go forward.

A simple game that could be constructed by a child using a few lines of code and the above interactive capabilities is shown in Figure 6. The graphics box contains five sprites: a planet, a rocket, two arrows, and a BOOST! icon. Because sprites have touch-sensing capabilities, it is easy to include obstacles, such as the planet, that the rocket must avoid in order not to crash.

Ports and Sharing

Boxer's spatial metaphor should prove to be an important factor in helping people deal with computational structures. It does, however, impose a significant constraint on the structures that can be represented — box containment is a strictly hierarchical relation. Using containment only, shared data structures could not be represented, nor could two widely

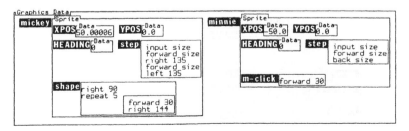

Here is the graphics box of Figure 5a, shown in data form so that all of its computational structure is visible, changeable, and extendable in ordinary Boxer textual format. The XPOS, YPOS, and HEADING variables show the position and head-

ing of each sprite. In addition, Mickey has a SHAPE procedure that makes him appear as a five-pointed star; Minnie has no SHAPE procedure and hence appears in the default shape, a triangle.

FIGURE 5b   The Data Form of a Graphics Box.

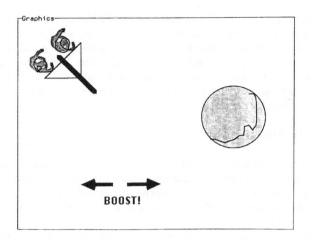

A graphics box with five sprites includes a control panel for piloting a rocket. A click on the BOOST! sprite gives the rocket a little thrust; a click on the arrows rotates the rocket to the right or left.

FIGURE 6   Interaction with Sprites.

separated boxes be viewed at the same time without moving one of them and thus changing the state of the system.

In order to overcome this limitation, Boxer includes a structure called a *port,* which is simply a view of a box at some other place in the system. A port behaves in most respects identically to the box it views — any change in one will automatically cause the same change in the other. Figure 7 shows

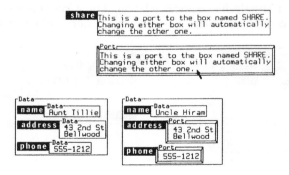

The second box is a port to (the alternate view of) the box named SHARE above it. Text typed into the port at the arrow cursor has also automatically appeared in the SHARE box.

The two lower boxes illustrate how ports can be used to implement shared data: Any change to the ADDRESS or PHONE fields in either box will also appear in the other box.

FIGURE 7   Examples of Port Structure in Boxer.

a typical application of ports. Ports can also be used to provide cross-referencing in interactive books or databases, to obtain multiple views of computational objects (e.g., to view a sprite in its graphics and data form at the same time), to share combinations of local data and procedure among objects, and to implement various nonstandard scoping disciplines for procedures.

THE GRAND IMAGE

As a final example, Figure 8, page 868, shows a page from the interactive book on optics proposed earlier. It should be clear how such a book can be constructed in Boxer as a natural evolution of text editing combined with writing simple procedures. It should also be apparent that, once produced, such a book can be readily modified and *reconstructed* by its users — both in small ways, as by adding marginal notes, and more extensively, as by modifying the simulations and tools included in the book.

It is exciting to contemplate the possibilities of interactive books,

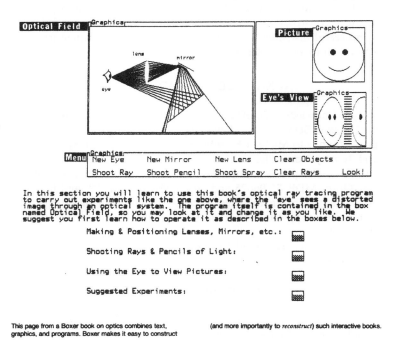

This page from a Boxer book on optics combines text, graphics, and programs. Boxer makes it easy to construct (and more importantly to *reconstruct*) such interactive books.

FIGURE 8   A Sample Page from an Interactive Book.

published on high-density media, such as compact disks that would appear to users as parts of their personally changeable Boxer systems. We would also love to extend Boxer to incorporate sound and high-quality moving pictures in graphics boxes. This is, however, the grand image of the medium, and most users' time will be spent in far more modest pursuits than constructing such books. The important point is that we can imagine a progression from the equivalent of scribbling in this new medium, as children scribble with pencil and paper, to the profound "scribblings" of experts—a path in which each new stage of understanding and competence is rewarded with new opportunities for personal expression.

CONCLUSION

Boxer challenges, in a small way, the current view of programming languages. More significantly, it challenges the current view of what programming might be like, and for whom and for what purposes programming languages should be created. We have argued that some computer languages should be designed for laypeople, and have presented an image of how computation could be used as the basis for a popular, expressive, and reconstructible medium. Computers will become substantially more powerful instruments of educational and social change to the extent that such an image can be realized.

ACKNOWLEDGMENTS

We gratefully acknowledge the efforts of all those members of the Boxer Groups at MIT and Berkeley who have helped to make Boxer (almost) a reality. Special thanks to Michael Eisenberg. Gregor Kiczales, Leigh Klotz, Ed Lay, and Jeremy Roschelle.

Research for this chapter was supported by the National Science Foundation under Grant MDR-85-96025 and Grant MDR-86-42177, and by the Defence Advanced Research Projects Agency of the Department of Defense, and monitored by the Office of Naval Research under Contract N00014-83-K-0125.

This chapter has been reprinted by permission of the Association for Computing Machinery.

REFERENCES

1. Abelson, H., and diSessa, A.A. *Turtle Geometry: The Computer as a Medium for Exploring Mathematics.* MIT Press, Cambridge, Mass., 1981.
2. Bolt, R.A. Spatial data-management. Rep., Dept. of Architecture. MIT, Cambridge, Mass., 1979.

3. diSessa, A.A. A principled design for an integrated computational environment. *Hum.-Comput. Interaction 1,* 1 (1985), 1–47.
4. diSessa, A.A. Notes on the future of programming: Breaking the utility barrier. In *User-Centered Systems Design,* D. Norman and S. Draper, Eds. Lawrence Erlbaum, Hillsdale, N.J., 1986.
5. Goldberg, A., and Robson, D. *Smalltalk-80: The Language and Its Implementation.* Addison-Wesley, Reading, Mass., 1983.
6. Papert, S. *Mindstorms: Computers, Children and Powerful Ideas.* Basic Books, New York, 1980.

CREDITS

Chapter 8 "The Concept of Variable in Programming: Its Meaning and Use in Problem-Solving by Novice Programmers" by Renan Samurçay, 1985, *Education Studies in Mathematics, 16*(2), pp. 143–161. Copyright 1985 by D. Reidel Publishing Co. Reprinted by permission of Kluwer Academic Publishers.

Chapter 9 "Do We Really Have Conditional Statements in Our Brains?" by Jean-Michel Hoc, 1984, *Readings on Cognitive Economics—Mind and Computers,* pp. 92–101. Copyright 1984 by Springer-Verlag Publishing Co. Reprinted by permission.

Chapter 10 "Cognitive Strategies and Looping Constructs: An Empirical Study" by Elliot Soloway, Jeffrey Bonar, and Kate Ehrlich, 1983, from *Communications of the ACM, 26*(11), pp. 853–860. Copyright 1983 by the Association for Computing Machinery. Reprinted by permission.

Chapter 11 "What Do Novice Programmers Know About Recursion?" by Hank Kahney, 1982, *An In-Depth Study of the Cognitive Behaviour of Novice Programmers,* Human Computer Research Laboratory, Technical Report No. 5, pp. 4-1-4-31. Copyright 1982 by Hank Kahney. Reprinted by permission.

Chapter 12 "Learning Flow of Control: Recursive and Iterative Procedures" by Claudius M. Kessler and John R. Anderson, 1986, *Human-Computer Interaction, 2,* pp. 135–166. Copyright 1986 by Lawrence Erlbaum Associates, Inc. Reprinted by permission.

Chapter 13 "Conditions of Learning in Novice Programmers" by D.N. Perkins, Chris Hancock, Renee Hobbs, Kay Martin, and Rebessa Simmons, 1986, *Journal of Educational Computing Research, 2*(1), pp. 37–55. Copyright 1986 by Baywood Publishing Company. Reprinted by permission.

Chapter 14 "Some Difficulties of Learning to Program" by Benedict du Boulay, 1986, *Journal of Educational Computing Research, 2*(1), pp. 57–73. Copyright 1986 by Baywood Publishing Company. Reprinted by permission.

Chapter 15 "A Summary of Misconceptions of High School Basic Programmers" by Ralph T. Putnam, D. Sleeman, Juliet A. Baxter, and Laiani K. Kuspa, 1986, *Journal of Educational Computing Research, 2*(4), pp. 459–472. Copyright 1986 by Baywood Publishing Company. Reprinted by permission.

Chapter 16 "Children's Mental Models of Recursive Logo Problems" by D. Midian Kurland and Roy D. Pea, 1985, *Journal of Educational Computing Research, 1*(2), pp. 235–243. Copyright 1985 by Baywood Publishing Company. Reprinted by permission.

Chapter 17 "Preprogramming Knowledge: A Major Source of Misconceptions in Novice Programmers" by Jeffrey Bonar and Elliot Soloway, 1985, *Human-Computer Interaction, 1*(2), pp. 133–161. Copyright 1985 by Lawrence Erlbaum Associates, Inc. Reprinted by permission.

AUTHOR INDEX

SUBJECT INDEX

For Product Safety Concerns and Information please contact our EU
representative GPSR@taylorandfrancis.com Taylor & Francis Verlag GmbH,
Kaufingerstraße 24, 80331 München, Germany

Printed and bound by CPI Group (UK) Ltd, Croydon, CR0 4YY
01/05/2025
01858337-0002